INDUSTRIAL POLICIES
AFTER 2000

RECENT ECONOMIC THOUGHT SERIES

Editors:

Warren J. Samuels
Michigan State University
East Lansing, Michigan, USA

William Darity, Jr.
University of North Carolina
Chapel Hill, North Carolina, USA

Other books in the series:

INDUSTRIAL POLICIES AFTER 2000

edited by

Wolfram Elsner
University of Bremen

John Groenewegen
Erasmus University Rotterdam

Kluwer Academic Publishers
Boston/Dordrecht/London

Distributors for North, Central and South America:
Kluwer Academic Publishers
101 Philip Drive
Assinippi Park
Norwell, Massachusetts 02061 USA
Telephone (781) 871-6600
Fax (781) 871-6528
E-Mail <kluwer@wkap.com>

Distributors for all other countries:
Kluwer Academic Publishers Group
Distribution Centre
Post Office Box 322
3300 AH Dordrecht, THE NETHERLANDS
Telephone 31 78 6392 392
Fax 31 78 6546 474
E-Mail <orderdept@wkap.nl>

 Electronic Services <http://www.wkap.nl>

Library of Congress Cataloging-in-Publication Data

Industrial policies after 2000 / edited by Wolfram Elsner, John Groenewegen.
    p. cm. -- (Recent economic thought)
  Includes bibliographical references and index.
  ISBN 0-7923-7750-8
   1. Industrial policy. 2. Economic policy. 3. Economic forecasting.
 I. Elsner, Wolfram. II. Groenewegen, John, 1949- III. Series

  HD3611 .I376 2000
  338.9--dc21   99-059016

Printed on acid-free paper.

Printed in the United States of America

Contents

vi

ACKNOWLEDGEMENTS

This publication was initiated by Warren Samuels a long time ago. The idea to create a volume on industrial policy at times when deregulation, privatization and small government dominated the debate was a challenge to us. We aimed at bringing together contributors from both different countries (i.e. different institutional contexts) and from different theoretical perspectives. Managing and editing a process of such diversity is normally very time consuming. We are grateful to thank Warren, the contributors and the publisher very much for their patience.

A special word of thanks goes to Wilma Speijer, Rotterdam, for her dedication in preparing a camera-ready copy of the original manuscript of this book, and to Andrea Gross and Stefan Meyer, Bremen, for their management support of the editing process.

Wolfram Elsner, University of Bremen, Germany
John Groenewegen, Erasmus University Rotterdam, the Netherlands

1 INTRODUCTION: INDUSTRIAL POLICY; ISSUES,THEORIES AND INSTRUMENTS

John Groenewegen

The Issues

Industry policy is about government intervention in markets. Because markets fail in terms of an efficient adaptation to changes of comparative advantages, government can stimulate firms to undertake investment decisions in another direction, do more of the same, or to implement plans at a higher speed. Government can replace, guide or facilitate firms' decision-making. In market economies firms are the actors primarily responsible for making the right investment or disinvestment decisions, but there can be situations in which firms are not able or willing to take decisions that are considered efficient from a social point of view. When, for instance, the comparative advantage of an industry is due to relatively low labour costs and because of an increase in wages and taxes this advantage disappears, firms have to disinvest in labour intensive activities and move into other areas with more capital or knowledge intensive products and services. If firms are reluctant, or incapable in taking adequate action, government through industrial policies can stimulate firms to move into a publicly more preferred direction.

Issues of (dis)investments concern the structure of the economy: the composition of economic activities spread over different sectors and regions of the economy (in contrast, the conjuncture of the economy concerns the level and not the composition of activities). When government purposefully intervenes with the objective to influence the structural development of the economy, then government is said to make an industrial policy. The structure of the economy can be defined in terms of sectors (government subsidizes the steel sector), regions (government reduces industrial activities in the northern regions), size of firms (government promotes large firms or small and medium sized enterprises) and finally an industrial structure can be described in terms of networks or clusters of economic activities (government stimulates for instance subcontracting networks in telecommunication).

Institutional Embeddedness and Path Dependence

Industrial policies have differed from country to country and have changed character over time. Industrial policy in the United States has been very different from the Japanese approach and industrial policy in France in the 1990s is very different from that in the 1970s. This is due to the "embeddedness" of national policies on the one hand and to changing internal and external factors on the other. Japanese policy is embedded in a fundamentally different institutional structure than the American one; for instance, the values and norms of group orientedness result in another role of government in the economy in general and in another responsibility for industrial developments in particular. With respect to changing internal and external factors, Europe in the 1990s offers good examples of the constraints caused by national industrial policies for the European integration for national industrial policies (role of the European Central Bank, harmonization of merger regulations, social regulation, and the like).

Both the influence of the embeddedness and the impact of changing parameters on national policies can be illustrated with a brief overview of the industrial policies of two countries, where government has an outspoken reputation of being interventionist: France and Japan.

In the 1960s in France the economic system was known as a system of indicative planning: national objectives were formulated in a national plan. Special planning institutions were created to guide the planning process, the formulation of the objectives and the implementation of the plan. At macrolevel there was not much difference with other European market economies, but at meso level of industries and regions as well as at microlevel with nationalizations and "national champions" there certainly was. Rooted in a long tradition of state intervention going back to minister Colbert under Louis XIV, French government had the ambition to guide the structural development of the economy in specific directions. This process is controlled by a small elite of civil servants, politicians and managers, who are trained at special schools ("Grandes Ecoles") and who are member of closed elitist circles. French industrial policy is embedded in a specific interventionist history during which a well equipped bureaucracy was established, that was held responsible by society for an efficient adaptation of the industrial structure. Behavior of politicians, bureaucrats and managers became routinized in history and their habits of thought and action determine largely their policies and strategies under specific circumstances.

Under specific internal and external conditions an economic system like the French one can be successful in terms of industrial adaptations. Analysis of the so-called "Large National Programs" (transport, nuclear energy, space, telecommunication, computers, semi-conductors) show the conditions under which a strong interventionist industrial policy can be effective or can easily fail. Control of the demand in the market by government turns out to be a crucial condition for successful industrial policy, while centralization of research into public institutes, control over financial instruments and centralization of production in "national champions" were also crucial in most French cases. The control of the economy demands an ambitious and capable group, of which the members easily communicate and who share common values and norms. The conditions for effective industrial policies cannot be created overnight, but are rooted in a long history during which politicans, bureaucracy and management have "learnt" their roles.

When external conditions change, e.g. the opening of markets, globalization of firms, change of international trade regulations, and the like, then the possibilites to fulfil the conditions mentioned above disappear and industrial policy should be adapted to the new circumstances. This was clearly the case in France in 1983 with the fundamental change of economic policy under President Mitterrand and the process of privatization and deregulation that followed. However, it would be a mistake to conclude that changing external conditions like the widely discussed globalization result in a unification of national systems and policies (Groenewegen, 1997). Careful analysis of the introduction of elements from other more market oriented systems into the French one, shows that behavior of French firms and government is definitely adapting to new world standards, but in its own way ("changement à la française"). As will become clear from several contributions in this volume this not only holds for France, but for every economic system: the embeddedness of the economy in the historically developed culture and socio-political relations sets the boundaries for change and more or less determines the "path of development". This can also be illustrated with the recent developments in Japan and the Asian crisis.

In describing the changes in Japanese industrial policies often a distinction is made between the more guiding—and sometimes even directing—role of the Ministry of Industry and International Trade (MITI) before and after the mid-sixties. In the beginning of 1960s the MITI controlled the parameters of the firms: import of technology, export of goods, credit allocation, cartels, etc. External and internal changes in the mid-1960s forced the MITI to adopt a more indirect approach. Externally the conditions set by the OECD, IMF and GATT influenced the range of policy measures and internally it was the growing independence of the firms due to higher profits that limited the effectiveness of the industrial policies. In general policies proved to be effective in the introduction and stagnation stages of the product life cycle and ineffective in the expansion stage. The situation changed again after the first oil crisis: a more powerful MITI was able to adopt new more intervening measures, but after the Plaza agreement in 1985 and definitively after the Asian crisis in 1997, external forces limited the effectiveness of industrial policies drastically. In the history after the effectiveness of industrial policies drastically. In the history after World War II the Japanese government, buraucrats and managers "learnt" how to play the game. In a path dependent development the institutional structure was able to adapt efficiently until the middle of the 1990s. With the crisis becoming really visible in 1997 it became also clear that the existing institutional structure does not fit anymore into the new external and internal circumstances.

The cases of France and Japan show the importance of "embeddedness", the path dependency in the evolution of industrial policies and the changing effectiveness due to changing internal and external conditions.

Towards Uniform Policies?

Many analysts nowadays conclude that because the European Union forces national economies to adopt an uniform macro policy, because of the collapse of the former centrally planned economies, and because of the Asian crisis, there is only one system to survive: the Anglo-American market economy in which there is no room for industrial policies. In this volume is shown that national systems certainly do change and that the globalization of the economy is a real phenomenon forcing national firms to be prepared for a fierce competition. Cost reductions are necessary and the possibilities to hide behind artificial protection barriers are limited more and more. Globalization forces firms and governments to rationalize production and distribution of private as well as public goods. It is true: capital and production facilities move around the globe much easier than before, but recognition of that development does not automatically imply a converging development into the direction of one uniform global system, nor does it imply the elimination of a role of government with respect to industrial development. Several chapters in this volume discuss the forces of change and show the need to adapt industrial policies. The contributions also show the embeddedness of economic systems with the consequent changes in policies to fit into the specific situation of a specific time and place. Several chapters also indicate the growing importance of institutions at regional level and the growing medium sized enterprises (SMEs) to enter new directions of development.

Theoretical Perspectives

From the description above follows that the issue of industrial policy is first of all a dynamic one: it refers to the adaptation of structures to changes in the environment. Through their investments firms are the principal actors in that process, but—as pointed out in quite a few chapters in this volume—firms are not passive actors only adapting to changes in their environment. On the contrary: firms are constantly trying to improve their position through active strategic management aiming at changing the environment in their own advantage. This is a matter of efficiency on the one hand and of power, control and manipulation on the other.

The issue of changing industrial structures as described above raises at least two questions: first are firms able and capable to make the right decisions in order to organize an efficient adaptation and second: what individual firms consider efficient, is that also a desirable outcome from a public welfare point of view?

Below we discuss theoretical perspectives relevant for issues of industrial policy. The neoclassical and the institutional approach can be presented as opposites resulting in contrasting conclusions about market efficiency and government policies.

Neoclassical Approach

Whether firms and markets need correction by a public actor has been a controversial issue for many years. Basically two positions can be distinguished: when the prices are right and competition is fair then the market with private actors takes care of the efficient adaptation of the industrial structure. This could be called the "Market Approach". However, others share the opinion that even when prices are right, actors lack sufficient information to anticipate structural changes to come. Moreover, competition can be fair but for whom?

Let us have a closer look at the two positions in order to get a clearer picture of the underlying theoretical assumptions.

Prices ought to reflect scarcities: when oil becomes more scarce the price should rise, consumers demand less oil and more coal, wind, solar, or nuclear energy. Producers and consumers adapt their behavior based on prices which reflect scarcities. A new equilibrium results. This is fine in a static world, but the moment dynamics, process and investments are brought into the picture problems arise in terms of the information prices reflect about the future. Firms making investment decisions for, let's say, the coming five, or ten years, need to know about relative scarcities (and prices and profits) in the future. However, prices reflect scarcities here and now. Only in the very abstract world of "a full set of contingent claim markets" of the Arrow and Debreu type, the future is turned into the present through prices alone. In real life markets are very limitly capable to look into the future simply because actors are confronted with chronic information problems.

Economic theories are not really able to deal with this fundamental issue of coordination of investment in such a way that equilibria result in the future. Economic theory has done rather well in accurately modelled worlds of static environments and mechanistic actors. Based on those ideas of markets, government is advised to get the prices right to develop an effective competition policy and conjunctural policy. Then the black box of the market will steer decisions into the right direction of a new equilibrium. No room available for industrial structural policy.

Another important stream of thought in economics, which has many commonalities with neoclassical economics, is the so-called New Institutional Economics (NIE). The insights of NIE in general, and of Transaction Cost Economics in particular, is important for the evaluation of governance structures created by the private actors themselves. Contrary to neoclassical economics the forms of private ordering should not be considered as market imperfections to be forbidden by competition law, but as efficient devices that lower transactions costs. Based on an assumed underlying selection mechanism as a result of which the most efficient governance structures survive, new institutionalism favors a minimal role for government. Again: no room available for industrial policy.

Traditional economic theory has problems the moment real uncertainty and strategic actors enter the stage. Uncertainty has been very difficult to integrate into the substantive rationality of the neoclassical individual. "Parametric uncertainty", i.e. calculable risk, was not that big a problem to integrate into the constraints or utility functions, but for "strategic uncertainty" following from the behavior of other actors in the market, the neoclassical theory has not found a satisfying solution yet. Is game theory the answer? In this volume several contributions apply game theory in order to get an idea of behavior of private actors so the complementary role of government becomes clear.

Game Theory

In order to get an understanding of the contribution of game theory to the theoretical foundation of industrial policies, a distinction can be made between the so-called "rationalistic game theory" and the "evolutionary game theory" (Groenewegen and Vromen, 1999). In the first type agents are hyperrational and able to anticipate behavior of others. In the second version of game theory, behavior of individuals is preprogrammed and evolution is driven by impersonal factors. In both cases there is no room for real strategic behavior to be understood as proactive, creative and uncertain. Vromen (1995) explains that a hyperrational or preprogrammed individual alone cannot do the trick: only when individuals are positioned in specific structures the outcome of their behavior can be predicted. In game theory the rules of the game play that role: the individual with specific rules of behavior is positioned in a specific situation and in that way game theory can show outcomes. Presented in this way there is no fundamental difference between the modeling in game theory and modeling in neoclassical economics.

However, Elsner in this volume attempts to develop game theory further into the direction of institutional theory. In that way he is able to ground policy recommendations on a game theoretic analysis. Stimulation of cooperation, increasing the number of participants, facilitating learning, are examples of his policy recommendations based on a game theoretic approach.

Institutional Economics

The opposite of neoclassical economics is institutional economics, not to be confused with the NIE.

Hodgson (1998) explains that the institutional approach does not aim at building a general, all-embracing theory, but that institutionalists analyze concrete phenomena using general as well as specific theories and specific tools. The embeddedness of an economic issue like the structural adaptation of an industry in the economy, is the starting point of analysis. What is the specific institutional context of values, norms, rules and organizations? What is the nature of that institutional context rooted in a specific history. What are the habits of the actors, what are their cognitive structures with which they perceive the world around them? The actor in institutional theory is not preprogrammed nor hyperrational, but molded by his or her environment and in trying to realize specific private objectives, actors mould the environment. So no actor is given, no environment is given.

Institutionalism applies general theories about human behavior, institutions and economic systems and from there it makes use of more specific theories in order to understand the specificities of the issue at hand. In analyzing concrete economic phenomena in that way, institutionalism operates at different levels, which ought to be carefully linked. Institutional analysis aims at identifying the complex interdependencies which prevail at specific level and aims at identifying positive and negative feedbacks in the system in order to get an idea of the dynamics of the issue at hand. A stabilizing factor which brings continuity into behavior and brings path dependency into the dynamics of systems, is the habits of economic actors. Habits are reinforced by institutions like norms and rules and make developments understandable and sometimes predictable. Crucial, however, is the lack of the pretention to develop a general universal theory aiming at predictions. The institutionalists' aim is first to understand and from there probably an explanation is possible, and in extreme cases of internal and external stability, prediction is within reach. In analyzing the research of institutionalists one learns that the general concepts of demand, supply, elasticity, marginal utility, and the like, get real meaning only when these general concepts are filled with concrete specific material of time and place. A general theory of, for instance, inflation offers so to speak the "skeleton", the meat is put on the bones by specific theories and by doing so the resulting "body" gets a specific shape, color, etc. Then it becomes clear that bodies differ and that their history and specific path of development needs to be analyzed in order to understand the nature of the body at hand. In getting hold of the evolution of concrete phenomena, institutionalists are prepared to open the box of the different, interdependent forces that play a role. Although efficiency also is a major explanatory variable in institutionalism, it is certainly not the only one. Culture, power, psychology are potentially equally important; the concrete specific conditions at hand determine which approach is a good starting point. That can be economic efficiency, but political power or sociological group orientedness are equally relevant candidates. From there the research continues in an interdisciplinary way. Dealing with different levels of analysis and moving from the general to the specific and backwards, the institutional research moves from mono-disciplinary to interdisciplinary and backwards. A good starting point for institutionalists often is a statistical correlation; then specific theories are applied to find causalities and in the end processes of cumulative causation might be discovered. A good example of such research is Hayden and Bolduc in this volume.

Institutional economics adds an important perspective: creation of governance structures is not only motivated because of efficiency, but also aims at the control of competitors; mergers and acquisitions, or alliances as means to gain a powerful position so others can be forced into certain, not necessarily efficient, directions.

Institutional analysis arrives at very different conclusions with respect to government policy: the minimal government is often shown to be victim of strategies of private and semi-public actors and the selection in the markets turns out to be a selection in favor of a very small and well defined powerful group. The market as a neutral selection mechanism turns out to be a filter of which the outcome depends on a series of specific conditions: not only the market structure (competition policy), but also the socio-political structure plays a crucial role (relations between ministries and firms, banks and politics, labor unions and big business, etc.) The results of the activities of the different actors

in the market place should be evaluated from a societal point of view :
the "lower" rationality of the private actors has to be compared with the
"higher" rationality of the community.

Pluralism, Interdisciplinary Analysis

Haring discussed neoclassical and institutional economics as the two
opposites, the question arises how these approaches and the more
intermediate theories like game theory and NIE, can be applied to issues
of industrial policy. Figure 1.1 is helpful to discuss this question.
The societal embeddedness level refers to institutions like norms,
tradition, etc. These have an enormous impact on economic behavior,
change very slowly over long periods of time and are more subject to
evolutionary processes than calculative action of individuals. The
second level contains institutions like legal rules: institutions that
belong to politics and bureaucracy. The economics of property rights
is located at this level. The third level is the domain of transaction costs
analysis: private ordering resulting in markets, hybrids, firms and public
agencies is explained on calculative grounds. Neoclassical economics
and agency theory is located at level 4 of rational agents selecting ex
ante the optimal combination based on a marginal analysis.
    That institutions matter is nowadays generally recognized in
economics, but the way institutions are taken on board in the analysis
differs substantially among the different schools of thought. At one
extreme we find the analysis where no reference at all is made to
institutions. Agents operate in a social vacuum of production and utility
functions. At the other extreme the feedbacks between all layers are
analyzed over time so processes of cumulative causation, in which also
habits and norms change, become visible. The question for research in a
domain like industrial policy is the selection of the right level of
analysis and how to proceed. The different theories located at the
different levels in Figure 1.1 are not a priori right or wrong; the
question is which one is relevant for what kind of research. For issues of
industrial policy the theories that allow for dynamics are often more
relevant than the static theories, which can only be used for drawing a
static picture of the situation. So the issue at hand determines what

Figure 1.1 Economics of institutions

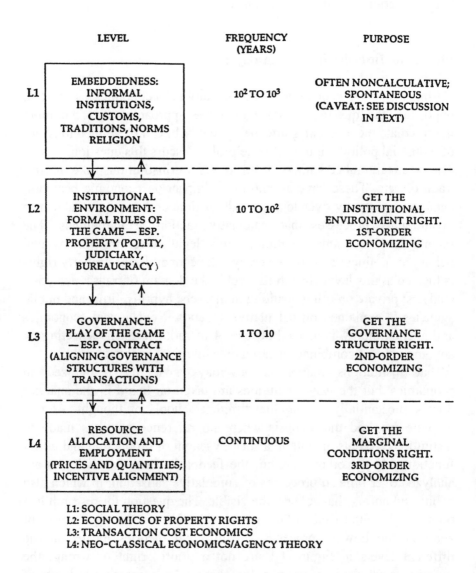

LEVEL		FREQUENCY (YEARS)	PURPOSE
L1	EMBEDDEDNESS: INFORMAL INSTITUTIONS, CUSTOMS, TRADITIONS, NORMS RELIGION	10^2 TO 10^3	OFTEN NONCALCULATIVE; SPONTANEOUS (CAVEAT: SEE DISCUSSION IN TEXT)
L2	INSTITUTIONAL ENVIRONMENT: FORMAL RULES OF THE GAME — ESP. PROPERTY (POLITY, JUDICIARY, BUREAUCRACY)	10 TO 10^2	GET THE INSTITUTIONAL ENVIRONMENT RIGHT. 1ST-ORDER ECONOMIZING
L3	GOVERNANCE: PLAY OF THE GAME — ESP. CONTRACT (ALIGNING GOVERNANCE STRUCTURES WITH TRANSACTIONS)	1 TO 10	GET THE GOVERNANCE STRUCTURE RIGHT. 2ND-ORDER ECONOMIZING
L4	RESOURCE ALLOCATION AND EMPLOYMENT (PRICES AND QUANTITIES; INCENTIVE ALIGNMENT)	CONTINUOUS	GET THE MARGINAL CONDITIONS RIGHT. 3RD-ORDER ECONOMIZING

L1: SOCIAL THEORY
L2: ECONOMICS OF PROPERTY RIGHTS
L3: TRANSACTION COST ECONOMICS
L4: NEO-CLASSICAL ECONOMICS/AGENCY THEORY

Source: Williamson, 1998.

theory is relevant. Also conditions play a role; when theory assumes competition to work as an anonymous selection mechanism and the prevailing conditions show a cartel type of control, then that theory is not relevant. In other words: not only the questions asked (the issues), but also the conditions make a theory more or less relevant. In this volume this problematic link between theory, conditions and relevancy is often addressed. Interesting complementarities of institutional and, for instance, game-theoretic arguing are presented.

The Contributions

The first contributions in this volume discuss the theoretical foundations of industrial policies. *Malcolm Sawyer* addresses fundamental   questions of the interrelatedness between markets, competition, and the nature of state activities. Different forms of industrial policy are discussed based on different views of competition and the state. Sawyer presents Austrian, neoclassical and institutional approaches and discusses the competences of states and the warranted attitudes of political elites linked to different types of industrial policies. Also the differences between static and dynamic characteristics of products are put into perspective resulting in different processes of learning and productivity. From there the domain of competition as a process is entered with Myrdal's cumulative causation and Schumpeters claim that neoclassical economics and perfect competition was concerned with "how capitalism administers existing structures", but that the relevant problem is "how it creates and destroys them". With respect to the nature of the state, Sawyer develops the distinction between the regulatory and developmental state and demonstrates how state entrepreneurship should be based on strategic positioning.

Jonathan Michie departs his analysis from the statement that according to many, globalization makes national industrial policy worthless. After having discussed the position of new growth theory that trade policy may be an important form of industrial policy, Michie demonstrates the limitations of the theoretical framework of the new growth theory, specifically that it ignores the demand side. Supply and demand side need to be integrated in theory as well as policy, an issue also central in the contribution of Pascal Petit and Mark Setterfield. Crucial then is innovation which is fostered by networks of firms and other economic actors. Policies can facilitate effective collaboration among suppliers, customers, and institutions of education, training and science and technology. Referring to Friedrich List, who developed these issues in the nineteenth century, Michie shows how crucial the development of endogenous capabilities is in order to enlarge the range of expertise in firms and regions.

Pascal Petit and Mark Setterfield discuss the relationship between macro policies (MP) and industrial policies (IP). How come that IP for long time have been considered "junior partners" in that relationship and served only as minor complements to macro policies? This has to do with the origin of IP in Anglo-Saxon cultures: the natural market order can only fail in exceptional cases and then IP is needed. It has also to do with the relative success of MP which can be understood in terms of what Petit and Setterfield call the "coordination nexus". According to the tradition of the French Regulation School the authors define the coordination nexus as the information and knowledge infrastructure which strongly influences the mind set of the agents, their expectations and behavior. The central message of their contribution is that policy makers should have a clear idea of the coordination nexus in order to develop effective policy instruments. The authors claim to elucidate key elements of the coordination nexus at specific historical junctures. More specifically: macro policies used to be effective in the past because of a specific infrastructure of information and knowledge and because that structure changed fundamentally in the "post Fordist" period another type of policy is needed for 2000 and beyond. The authors present the so-called "Comprehensive Industrial Policies" (CIP) as the new alternative. CIP include all those policies capable of influencing, in a consistent and coordinated way, both the structure of production and of demand formation in order to improve the performance of the economy over a mediate or long term horizon. Such a policy can be conducted centrally but also locally, and may concern industries a s well as households. The authors explain that the current conditions warrant CIP, of which the type of interventions are designed by Petit and Setterfield for the areas of local districts, national infrastructures, monitoring of international markets and the domain of science and ecology.

After the chapters that deal with the theoretical foundations, this volume contains contributions that focus on the firm and the relationship between government and firms. First *Wolfram Elsner* develops a theory of cooperative industrial policy. Using game theoretical insights he concludes that actors have problems to start cooperation, but once the process has begun it can—under specified conditions—evolve into a closer and tighter form of cooperation. With positive incentives actors can be stimulated by government to start, or stabilize and accelerate cooperation and by multiplying the areas of cooperation, by increasing the number of participants and by guaranteeing the continuity of the cooperation, government can positively influence the evolution of the cooperation over time. These theoretical insights and recommendations for industrial policy are illustrated with policies at regional level in Germany.

Michael Dietrich and John E. Burns discuss the complex interaction between organizational lock-in, technological lock-in, and industrial policy. The first refers to actions and decisions of individuals (or groups) with sufficient power to control and dominate organization-specific strategy. Institutional inertia is viewed as the central problem for industrial policy; it implies that industrial policy should go beyond the technological conception and include institutional factors. Dietrich and Burns position a dynamic industrial policy center stage: the policy should be about facilitating organizational and industrial change. The emergence of new developmental trajectories is central and awareness of the different lock-ins and their principal stakeholders is a precondition for guiding industrial change. Industrial policy makers ought to be aware of the specificities of the different actors and organizations and their strategic framework, as well as the wider institutional factors. Financial incentives are often necessary but certainly not sufficient: industrial change demands breakthroughs and for facilitating such fundamental changes, deep knowledge of the mechanisms creating path dependencies and lock-ins is crucial. Financial incentives as such would be unlikely to dislodge the dominant strategic paths. The message from the case study Dietrich and Burns have undertaken, is that industrial policy measures must be very sensitive to the complex institutional dimensions of organizational life. Especially attention for the institutional embeddedness (level 1 in Figure 1.1) is warranted. The institutional analysis in the case study shows that such a more holistic understanding of the interaction of organizational and technological lock-ins under different institutional settings does not provide general theories for industrial policies. The general ideas are illustrated with an interesting case study showing the role of accountants, their mental maps and the resulting finance-orientated strategies of UK firms.

Rainer Markl and Werner Meissner discuss the tensions between competition policies and industrial policies; often antitrust policy prevails but in many other cases powerful anticompetitive structures are not touched by the anti-monopoly authorities. This can be understood if the analysis crosses borders and the international market is the focal point. Then the promotion of mergers and interfirm cooperations can serve as an instrument of strategic trade policy helping to shift oligopoly rents from foreign to domestic firms. The question then raised concerns the objective to develop an international competition law that explicitly covers anticompetitive actions of governments, or will it be sufficient to harmonize the antitrust laws of trading nations? The focus of the analysis of Markl and Meissner is on R & D subsidies as a strategic trade policy. Subsidizing the R&D efforts of private firms turns out to be a rather inappropriate measure to shift rents in favor of domestic firms. There is no need to control these subsidies, but to permit them because of the positive externalities. With respect to the national policy towards mergers and acquisitions and the interfirm cooperation, Markl and Meissner conclude that these can be properly dealt with by national authorities provided that coverage and enforcement of national law will be improved. So their analysis supports the policy towards a harmonization of national laws.

The issue of anti-trust is also related to the recent waves of mergers and acquisitions. In this volume that strategy of firms is discussed in relation to industrial policies by *Hans Schenk*. In the 1990s many large firms have changed organizational structures due to the unprecedented peaks in merger and acquisitions. Schenk discusses the effects of those mergers in terms of productive and dynamic efficiencies. Although traditional economic theory assumes firms to undertake activities like

M&A because they are driven by the urge to become more competitive than their rivals, Schenk demonstrates how questionable such an assumption is. He discusses the so-called "purely strategic mergers", defined as those mergers which firms feel compelled to undertake despite of an expected return of zero or worse. These mergers are motivated by the prospect of strategic comfort rather than wealth creation, or the appropriation of monopoly rents. Since purely strategic mergers can only persist when market power is obstructing an efficient operation of market mechanisms, and current merger control policies are apparently unable to prevent this, it follows that policy adaptations are necessary. Recommendations with respect to competition policies refer to the demand of what Schenk calls a "full efficiency test". The burden of proof that the merger or acquisition is efficient should be on the shoulders of the acquiring firm. This is attractive for the realization of a lean and mean merger control. With repect to industrial policies Schenk concludes that government should favor de-mergers and management buy-outs, and should develop programs to facilitate SMEs at regional level, of which his proposal of local stock markets on the internet is fitting the next century.

In the contributions so far government is often presented as the coordinator, facilitator and stimulator. However, government is also vulnerable and easily a vitim of private enterprise that captures policy. The contribution of *F. Gregory Hayden and Steven R. Bolduc* is a perfect example of an institutionalist analysis showing how powerful firms determine contracts with government. The relationship between governmental institutions and powerful private actors is governed in complex interorganizational forms "(....) whose content, interpretation, and final function are determined by the actions taken in dynamic transorganizational networks". The costs of coordination in those networks through contracts are explicitly quantified by means of a detailed analysis of the pattern of relationships. The analysis aims at understanding causes and effects in a system and how different actors influence the process, what their objectives, beliefs, power base and instruments are. A well structured and detailed analysis of the case of the Central Interstate Low Level Radio Waste Compact (CIC) shows the interaction between individuals, organizations and structures at different levels of the system. It is surprising to read how the cost-plus formula was constructed over time and complicated through the influence of different interest groups. Result: costs of the project have become exorbitant and cost overruns became normal practice. The institutional tool of the Social Fabric Matrix (SFM) proves very useful in analyzing the relationships in the network that produces the high costs and in showing the negative feedbacks that bring system to stability as well as the positive feedbacks that produce growth or decay. The analysis of the CIC clearly shows the circular, cumulative causation. "When a system begins to deteriorate, the forces that are creating the deterioration continue to recirculate and accumulate greater and greater capacity for destruction. This happens because systems provide feedback among the component parts such that any impact on a system which is inconsistent with the welfare of the system becomes magnified through the feedback process". Clearly shown is the necessity to have a good understanding of the social beliefs, the rules and habits of the actors involved in order to grasp who determines "efficiency" in what terms. Hayden and Bolduc present a perfect example of solid institutional analysis: the contract turns out to be the result of battles and conflicts and power relations.

The last chapters of this volume focus on regions and small and medium sized enterprises (SMEs).

In several chapters in this volume attention is focused on SMEs and the role of the regions. Industrial policy is in the discussion often related to the issue of unemployment: investment, disinvestment, industrial clusters, technology diffusion, all have consequences for the net growth of employment. Particularly, the debate centers around the relationship between firm size and the net creation of jobs: how can government in industrial policy take the role of SMEs into account aiming at employment creation? It should be recognized that the empirical findings on the relationships are often lacking a theoretical foundation. *Paul Schreyer* fills this gap. After briefly discussing the static picture of the relationship between SMEs and employment, he focuses on the dynamics. What are the net employment changes in relation to the size of employment in small and large establishments? With respect to the methodological question two views are presented. One is based on the existence of an equilibrium path that firms are assumed to follow. The pattern of employment then shows fluctuations around a trend. The other—more promising—view is based on the Austrian perspective on markets and entrepreneurship: center-stage is the degree of "turbulence" across countries, industries and over time. Crucial is the degree of entrepreneurship: the search for new processes, niches in markets, differentiation of products, new organizational structures, etc. Using a simulation model Schreyer translates the findings into a number of policy recommendations. Central is a policy that facilitates the functioning of the market process; firms should be facilitated in their search processes, as well as in their possibilities to enter and exit (see level 2 in Figure 1.1). Establishing the appropriate rules and institutions is of major importance, but also could government influence the social acceptance and desirability of entrepreneurship, which makes it more attractive to become one (see level 1 in Figure 1.1).

Patrizio Bianchi discusses the role of SMEs, the territorial agglomerations, the process of inter-firm specialization, and how networks and clusters can foster firms capabilities. The tendency towards further concentration ought to be controlled by a severe competition policy on the one hand and stimulation of SMEs on the other. Bianchi lists the measures taken by the European Union and discusses furthermore the role of SMEs in developing and transition economies. With respect to the latter socio-economic stability is of utmost importance and to that end entrepreneurship and growing employment in smaller firms operating in networks have an important role to play.

In the chapter on "Regional Paths of Institutional Anchoring in the Global Economy", *Arnoud Lagendijk* applies the institutional perspective to describing and analyzing the empowering of regions. National competitiveness largely depends on the position of regions in the networked economy. With the process of globalization and the creation of international filières, the strategy at the regional level should be a positioning of the region in those international linkages based on specific regional capacities. This type of industrial policy should be implemented at different levels of the system from international linkages, national regulations, regional structures to individual firms. Because regions differ, policies should also differ: this is illustrated with two case studies of regions with a rich industrial past, but in need to create new institutional capacities. The institutional capacity of regions largely determines the possibilities of developing an entrepreneurial economy in which the innovative capacity is the source of an ongoing process of adaptation. Institutional capacity is generated within the context of regional governance structures, including public and semi-public institutions as well as business associations, chambers of commerce, educational institutions, technology centers, financial institutions, and the like. Regions as strategic places of coordination, which should be monitored and guided by some form of democratic control. The view on regions as integrated communities where *voice* rules, is criticized from a political economy point of view: large firms exploit their power and regions that are peripheral are easily used by the more powerful private agents.

Friedhelm Hellmer et al. question the emergence of a new type of "post Fordist" industrial policy. Analyzing the so-called "normal regions" (regions with an average structure and not typically high tech or stagnating sectors), do not show drastic changes in their supply networks. On the contrary: based on case studies, Hellmer et al. conclude that the customer-supplier relationships are not characterized by drastic changes in terms of the setting up of supply networks. They found that the supplier relationships are basically market-oriented, i.e. purchases are made where technical competence is available and prices are best. Physical proximity is not that important as most of the writings on industrial network suggest. Hellmer et al. furthermore discuss the industrial policies in eastern Germany after the unification; the role of the "Treuhandanstalt", responsible for the transition process, is analyzed. Also here the conclusion is that industrial policies were largely of a traditional subsidizing kind; old conceptual schemes and instruments were only marginally improved. The message is that the "normal" regions are clear examples of path dependant developments without breaks, or "fundamental discontinuities".

In the concluding chapter *Wolfram Elsner* puts the different contributions into perspective and draws conclusions about the institutional dimensions, strategies and measures of future industrial policies.

References

Groenewegen, J. 1997. "Institutions of Capitalism: American, European, and Japanese Systems Compared". *Journal of Economic Issues*, June, 333—347.

Groenewegen, J. and J. Vromen 1999. *Institutions and the Evolution of Capitalism; Implications of Institutional Economics,* Aldershot: Edward Elgar.

Hodgson, G.M. 1998. "The Approach of Institutional Economics". *Journal of Economic Literature*, Vol. XXXVI, March, 166—192.

Vromen, J. 1995. *Economic Evolution: an Inquiry into the Foundations of New Institutional Economics*, London: Routledge.

Williamson, O.E. 1998. "Transaction Cost Economics: How it Works; Where it is Headed". *De Economist* 146, 23—58.

2 THE THEORETICAL ANALYSIS OF INDUSTRIAL POLICY

Malcolm Sawyer

Introduction

The central purpose of this chapter is to explore some of the theoretical issues involved in the analysis of industrial policy. In doing so, we start from the proposition that there is not (and probably never can be) a single coherent theory of industrial policy, but rather different theoretical perspectives on and aspects of industrial policy. It is a rather obvious (if not always acknowledged) point to say that the analysis of industrial policy and strategy has to deal with three interrelated elements, namely the analysis of the operation of a market economy which includes the nature of markets and of competition as well as of networks and industrial and spatial clusters, the nature of the State activity, and the role of specific policy instruments. The focus of this chapter is on the first two of those, and limitations of space preclude discussion of specific industrial policies. We also offer some remarks on the constraints imposed by globalization on the pursuit of industrial policy.

Since there are differing analyses of the operation of markets and competition and differing views on the nature of State activity, the way is opened for many different theoretical perspectives on industrial economies and on a global scale; hence its characterization as "global policy". Indeed, even what may be regarded as industrial policy differs according to the particular analysis of the market and of the State adopted. Some would regard industrial policy as akin to that covering monopoly, merger and restrictive practices (and perhaps regulation of utilities). Others would interpret industrial policy (and often use the term industrial strategy rather than industrial policy) much more broadly to include policies on credit (e.g. selective credit, use of interest rates), on training and skill formation through to forms of indicative planning: in effect any policy instrument which is used to influence industrial performance and development.[1] It can be expected that what is perceived as industrial policy at any time and place will be much influenced by the prevailing economic orthodoxy as well as the more general perceptions of the roles of the market and of the State.

This chapter takes the view that different forms of industrial policy can only be understood by reference to different views of competition and of the State.[2] There is some general association between the views which a person adopts on the nature of markets and competition with the views which that person has on the role of the State (e.g. there is a tendency for a neo-classical view of markets and competition to be combined with a regulatory State, as discussed below), but there is not usually any logical link.

Much of the Anglo-Saxon analysis of industrial policy is predicated on an essentially neo-classical view of competition which views a large number of firms in and free entry into an industry as desirable. Actual industrial policy in the Anglo-Saxon countries diverges in many respects from the promotion of atomistic competition and free entry but we would argue that the neo-classical perception of competition has a profound influence on industrial policy (and even more on the justifications for that policy). In some contrast, the East Asian industrial policy draws on the notion of excessive competition, "a term used by Korean (and Japanese) policy makers to describe the well-known propensity of industries with large sunk costs to engage in price wars.

As a result serious attempts were made to restrict entry and regulate capacity expansion in such industries" (Chang, 1994, p. 111).

We do not provide a precise definition of industrial policy in this chapter, and indeed, as already remarked, we would argue that what is meant by industrial policy varies considerably. But the approach here is an encompassing one: that is we consider approaches which would use a broad definition of industrial policy as well as those who use a relatively narrow one, and in particular we use the term industrial policy to encompass, for example, monopoly and merger policy as well as a more broadly based industrial strategy.

The potential for industrial policy (almost however that is defined) depends on a wide range of factors. But we would signal three sets of factors as being particularly relevant. The first concerns the competencies, in a broad sense, of the State. The relevant competencies range from ability to gather and process relevant information and to ensure effective decision making through to the integrity and honesty of the decision making process. There has been a tendency to discuss industrial policy without any detailed regard to the competencies of the State, either assuming an omnipotent State or an incompetent one.

The second relates to the prevailing attitudes, particularly amongst the political elite, towards the relative roles of the State and the market, and the nature of the relationship between them (e.g. supportive or antagonistic). Chang (1994, p. 119) has pointed to the similarities between industrial policy in Korea and that in a number of other countries but asks "why does industrial policy work so well in Korea and not in many other countries?" His answer relates to the Korean government's ability to limit the damage arising from rent-seeking activities (to gain the subsidies and assistance from government which are generated by a developmental strategy).

The third concerns the stage of economic development. It may be observed that the scope for an active industrial policy is more extensive in economies in the early stages of industrialization, and more significantly in the early stages of the evolution of what may be termed markets (though see discussion below on the meaning of markets). The role of the State in the early stages of industrialization has been various, ranging from the provision of infrastructure, undertaking land reform, legislation to provide for contracts and the operation of markets, and the provision of finance.

Within industrial economics in the Anglo-Saxon world, the analysis of industrial policy was dominated up to at least the early 1970s by the essentially neo-classical approach embedded in the structure-conduct-performance paradigm. This paradigm has the two crucial factors of providing a static equilibrium analysis and of tending to regard perfect competition as having some desirable properties (in terms of static allocative efficiency).[3] The theory of State activity which this entails is related to notions of market failure, namely that the operation of markets may not reach optimal outcomes (which may be perfect competition or it may be some intermediate position which combines some of the benefits of perfect competition with some from monopoly), and the State, acting in some perception of the public interest, can and/or will correct those market failures.[4] This analysis has not been accepted uncritically, and much attention has been given to government failure in comparison with market failure, and the well-known argument that in order to correct a market failure requires knowledge of the nature of the failure, the technical ability of the government to correct the failure as well as the incentives for the government to do so.

The chapter now proceeds by discussion of the nature and role of markets, of networks, of products and of competition. It offers some remarks on the State and then its relationship with the market before moving to discuss some of the impact of globalization on industrial policy before finally discussing overall implications and conclusions.

Markets

The economies of the industrialized world would generally be described as market economies, in which competition and rivalry amongst enterprises play significant roles. Industrial policy clearly involves interventions by government in the operation of markets and the process of competition but could also be seen to include the legal framework within which firms operate. The potential for and desirability of government intervention must depend on how markets and competition actually operate. At least as significant for theorising on industrial policy are the perceptions of how markets and competition operate, or more formally on the analysis of markets and competition. In this section we make some remarks on the conceptualization of markets and on the role of prices and in the following section discuss the analysis of competition.

The significance of "the market" in market economies depends on how "the market" is defined. We have discussed elsewhere (Sawyer, 1992a) the difficulties of defining "the market" and of distinguishing between market and non-market activities. By the problem of defining "the market" we do not mean the problems associated with defining the boundaries of a particular market, say, that for wheat (though that does present problems) but rather the problems of delimiting the "market system" from the rest of the economic system. "The market" would usually be taken as referring to transactions between independent agents (firms, households etc.) and to the unconscious coordination of economic activity between them exclusively through prices. It would then be quickly recognized that much economic activity takes place within organizations (enterprises, households, charities etc.) and cannot readily be described as market activities in the sense referred to in the previous sentence. Coase (1937) and the latter transaction costs approach (e.g. Williamson, 1986) has emphasized the firm as conscious coordination and the market as unconscious coordination, and also that the boundaries between firm and market are influenced by the relative transaction costs involved.

What happens inside the organization will be heavily influenced by what is happening in the market outside of the firm. But the reverse is also true, what happens in the market is strongly influenced by what is happening outside of the market within the organization. Indeed, there is a sense in which the organization should be given priority over the market in that the market can only operate (by the exchange of goods and services) if those goods and services have been produced within organizations. This can be expressed as saying that markets can provide the forum for exchange but cannot produce the goods and services (Fourie, 1989).

In a similar vein, exchange between individuals can take many forms ranging from the buying and selling one through to gift relationships, and this raises the question as to which exchanges should be deemed market activities and which not. The neo-classical (and other) analyzes would focus on those which involve direct "spot" exchange of goods and services for money (though the general equilibrium analysis is an analysis of "reals" in which money does not play any key role and can be viewed as "a veil"). In other words, "the market" is analysed without any regard to direct interdependencies between firms, and coordination between firms exclusively through prices.

The market as analysed in neo-classical economics involves the features of prices given as far as the individual agent is concerned (parametric prices), anonymity (in the sense that from whom a person buys something is irrelevant to the purchaser), and homogeneous products. These features combine to provide an analysis of a spot market with no continuing relationship between buyer and seller. For our discussion there are two significant aspects of this analysis. First, there is the lack of any direct interdependence and of any direct interaction between the participants in the market, and this is so whether or not the analysis is extended to cover futures markets. Second, the mechanism of coordination is through price which brings demand and supply into balance at the equilibrium. It is also the case that here the only role of price is perceived to be that of the coordination of economic activity (whereas price may play a variety of other roles, e.g. used by firms to limit entry into their industry, influence the distribution of income). It is important to note here that when price "solves" the coordination problem, there is no role for government or indeed any other agency (such as the enterprise or industrial associations) in respect of coordination. But, as is well-known, this "solution" of the coordination problem relies not only on equilibrium but also on perfect information.

It is increasingly recognized that whilst parametric prices have been the cornerstone of most economic analysis of markets and competition, they form an extreme case.[5] The new Keynesian approach to macro-economics[6] has emphasized the ways in which prices are formed and how prices need not adjust in the face of excess supply (applied to the labour market in the form of efficiency wages, and to the financial market in the form of credit rationing : see, for example, Stiglitz and Weiss, 1981, Stiglitz, 1994 chapters 3 and 4, Lindbeck and Snower, 1988). Further, the relationships between enterprises and between enterprises and consumers are often long-term ones, involving understandings and agreements between enterprises. The thrust of much recent literature is that these relationships have a rationale other than collusion to raise prices. Further, it can be recognized that "prices are a simplifying mechanism, consequently they are unsuccessful at capturing the intricacies of idiosyncratic, complex and dynamic exchange" (Powell, 1990).

It can also readily be acknowledged that, in practice, market economies involve a range of interdependencies and interactions between firms, including a variety of forms of cooperation as well as competition. Whilst much cooperation may be between vertically related (i.e. supplier-purchaser), there are many instances of horizontal cooperation (e.g. joint ventures). The neoclassical response to cooperation amongst firms has been to detect collusion and attempts to create cartels and monopoly power, and to recommend legislation (a form of industrial policy) to strike down collusive arrangements and restrictive practices. Without assuming that actions which take place must have some purpose, ways in which cooperation between firms can be mutually (and socially) beneficial can be readily found.

There are in effect two rather different and competing perspectives on the nature of market economies involved here. The first one is the familiar presumption that making the actual economy resemble the perfectly competitive market economy is required. This entails the removal as far as possible of "inflexibilities" and "imperfections" (to use frequently used terms) from the market economy, where those "inflexibilities" and "imperfections" are often seen as arising from government actions. In the context of the labour market (which falls outside the scope of this chapter), this approach leads to the reduction or removal of trade union rights (to, for example, recognition) and the creation of the so-called flexible labour market.

The second perspective is a recognition that since many of the "inflexibilities" have a purpose, their removal will have some adverse consequences. Hirschman (1970) drew attention to the distinction between "voice" and "exit" effects, where "exit" is associated with the competitive market and "voice" with situations in which problems and solutions can be articulated and discussed. In this context, "voice" can be broadly interpreted as there are a range of non-verbal as well as verbal means of communication. In effect, the "exit" option is a blunt instrument to record dissatisfaction whereas the "voice" option can articulate the reasons for dissatisfaction and propose solutions for its rectification.

It is also noticeable that the third part of the title of Hirschman (1970) was loyalty. It is clear that a low degree of loyalty and trust is destructive of cooperation and long term relationships, and hence the lack of loyalty undermines the benefits which could flow from cooperation. Further, the spot market mentality is not conducive to the development of loyalty and trust, or indeed of cooperation and long-term relationships, and indeed the spot market is more likely to generate "short-termism". Long-term recurrence of interaction is one of the conditions for cooperation. Of particular significance for economic growth is the view that some of these "inflexibilities" promote long-term relationships and some degree of stability which themselves are conducive to the provision of training and skill formation, and of research and development, and more generally underpins learning processes. As Shapiro (1991) argues, following a line of argument from Schumpeter "a pure market economy cannot be as dynamic as the capitalist economy because market relations and incentives are not sufficient for innovation". The "capitalist economy" differs from the "pure market economy" in that the former includes monopoly and oligopoly, cooperation as well as competition and a system of networks whereas the latter corresponds to the neo-classical analysis of the market outlined above.

Networks and Clusters

The observations that there are a variety of types of relationship between firms and that production involves a degree of vertical disintegration and hence vertical links between firms can lead into a perspective which focuses on networks. "The key feature of networks ... is the way cooperation and trust are formed and sustained within networks. In contrast to either hierarchy (notably within firms) or market, networks coordinate through less formal, more egalitarian and cooperative means" (Thompson, 1991). Lorenz (1989), for example, focuses on "continuing and recurrent relations between French firms and their subcontractors. These are relations involving mutual dependency, where each firm's actions influence the other".

Networks operate with varying degrees of formality, and the industrial associations, chambers of commerce etc. can be viewed as the more formal end of the spectrum. There are generally externalities involved in the operation of a network, which is reflected in the observation that "cooperation and trust are formed and sustained amongst the network of firms despite the strong competition existing between them. They forgo short-run profit maximization for the longer-term benefits of mutual cooperation" (Thompson, 1991, discussing the work of Lorenz, 1989).

When networks involve relatively small firms in a geographical concentrated area, they can be seen to form "industrial districts" where the cooperation amongst the firms contributes to their competitive strength. Authors such as Best (1990) chapter 7 for the so-called Third Italy Lorenz (1990) for the engineering industry around Lyons in France and Piore and Sabel (1984, pp. 286—295) for the United States have analysed such networks and industrial districts.

The significance of networks and clusters for our discussion of industrial policy is two fold. First, it points to the variety of relationships between firms and the possible benefits which can arise from a system of cooperation and long term relationships. This presents a challenge to the restrictive practices legislation which seeks to limit cooperation (at least horizontally amongst firms producing similar products).

Second, industrial districts or clusters can be a source of economic strength, but may require support from industrial policy, for example to permit agreements amongst companies, or to foster joint endeavours over, say, training or marketing. But "a variety of partly private, partly public institutions ... are crucial to the idea of an industrial district" (Best, 1990), and hence the promotion of industrial districts would involve the encouragement of the private institutions and the building of the public ones.

Products

The way in which goods and services are conceptualized can have an influence on the analysis of industrial policy. In particular, regarding products as having essentially the same properties is likely to lead to an undifferentiated industrial policy concerned with issues of monopoly, whereas a focus on the difference between products generates a differentiated policy.

Most conventional analysis involves the essential "sameness" of products and of industries: products are "goods" in that they provide utility for consumers but there are costs of production of those goods, albeit under different cost conditions. But there is no fundamental distinction between products: as some have expressed the point, there is no essential difference between a potato chip and a computer chip. Differences in cost conditions between countries permits beneficial trade between countries, and the view that economies should specialise on the products for which they have a comparative advantage. The essential "sameness" of products also leads to a concern as to whether the products are priced at the most appropriate level and thereby whether the overall composition of outputs is the best one, and how sub-optimal compositions can be improved upon. The concern over prices and over the composition of output is more formally expressed in terms of the Pareto optimality of perfect competition and the welfare losses associated with monopoly.

Comparative advantage, at least in its original formulation, is a static nature-oriented concept. Factor endowments from nature determine what each country is relatively proficient at producing. The nature-oriented aspect is modified when the capital stock (physical and human) is brought in since over time the capital stock can be enhanced or diminished. The notion of competitive advantage, in some contrast with the notion of comparative advantage, has strong overtones that the relative standing of a country or of an industry can be changed. It implies a more dynamic perspective, and one that through relevant investment decisions (in physical capital, research and development, skill formation and work organization etc.) is malleable. An economy is then able to build up advantages in specific sectors (with the Japanese experience outstanding in this respect), but those advantages which can be threatened by developments in other countries.

It could be said that products differ in their static and dynamic characteristics, but it is the latter which are the more significant for the formulation of industrial policy. The static characteristic of relevance is the cost conditions under which the product is made, namely whether there are increasing or decreasing returns to scale (relative to the market size). The dynamic characteristics are an amalgam of related features on both the demand and supply side. The growth of external demand for a product is a relevant consideration. Balance of payments constraints imply that it is difficult for a country to have a persistently growing trade deficit (relative to GDP) for that would imply growing borrowing requirements, foreign debt and interest repayments. The strong version of this constraint yields the following equality (often referred to as Thirlwall's law) of the growth of the domestic GDP with the growth of world GDP times income elasticity of demand for exports of the domestic economy divided by the income elasticity of demand for imports. The structure of the demand for the production of an economy (as summarized by the income elasticity of demand), which depends on nature of the products produced and their quality and reputation etc. becomes significant for the growth potential of the economy.

The dynamic cost characteristics relate first to the degree to which the production of the product is subject to productivity growth and to learning effects (broadly conceived). A second aspect is the degree to which the nature of the product is evolving through technical change, and that the development of the next generation of related and other products depends on the successful production of this generation of the product.

What is the significance of these remarks for industrial policy? It can first be noted that decisions made on investment, research and development etc. are inevitably made under conditions of considerable uncertainty, where uncertainty is used in the sense of Knight (1921) as distinguished from risk where agents do not know the precise outcome which will result from an action but do know the probability distribution of outcomes. Authors such as Keynes, (1936), Shackle (1961) and Davidson (1990) have stressed the effects which uncertainty have on investment, and more generally on the operations of the macroeconomy. In the context of uncertainty perhaps the one thing that is certain is that mistakes will be made.[7] The "market" (that is firms operating on an independent and uncoordinated basis) may tend to underinvest in the more dynamic sectors (as compared with an economy involving interdependencies and relationships between firms). This may reflect a degree of short-termism, whereby more weight is placed on short-term returns than on (discounted) long-term returns (Hutton, 1996).

Further, the development of a new sector requires the inputs of a range of firms making appropriate capacity creating decisions and those firms have to be able to draw on workers with the relevant skills and expertise. Individual firms will be reluctant to engage in expansion in a new sector by itself as its success requires the expansion of other firms, which is an illustration of network externalities to which reference was made above. Industrial policy then has a role to provide a degree of coordination between firms and others. This point is well summarized by Chang and Rowthorn (1996) who argue that "the coexistence of widespread interdependencies and private control of the means of production means that success in a major economic transformation requires concerted efforts coordinate by the state" (p. 40).

Competition

Markets usually involve some form of competition and rivalry, though the nature and degree of competition varies (both in practice and in our perceptions). There is some tendency to suggest that "marketization" involves a greater "dose" of competition. Although there is this intimate link between markets and competition[8], it may be useful to discuss them separately. But attitudes towards the operation of markets (however that may be defined) are strongly influenced by perceptions of the ways in which competition operates, and specifically whether competition is on balance beneficial.

Within economic analysis, the term competition has been used in many ways but two broad usages stand out. First, within the neo-classical framework, competition has become identified with atomistic or perfect competition. On this basis, as exemplified in the structure-conduct-performance approach, an industry is said to be more or less competitive depending on whether it has more or less enterprises[9] or whether the profit margin is low or high. Within that framework, competition is viewed in a static sense and more competition is viewed as better than less competition. The working out of perfect competition generates equilibrium outcomes in which factor rewards tend to be equalized across industries and regions (and the equilibrium is deemed to involve the maximization of economic welfare on the basis of the Pareto criteria, that is to be a Pareto optimal position).

The particular significance of perfect competition is not so much whether it does or does not reflect the real world (for few would argue that it is a realistic portrayal of most industries) but rather in the way in which it sets up a benchmark against which industries and firms are judged. Market "imperfections" with the associated overtones can be any features which would be absent from perfect competition. Thus, long-term relationships between firms, prices which do not adjust in the face of excess demand etc. and bargaining between workers and employers would be viewed as "imperfections", whereas these features may have some positive role to play under real world conditions which include direct interdependencies, recurrent interactions, imperfect information, uncertainty, dynamic effects and learning. But because this approach focuses on the dichotomy between competition and monopoly, the absence of competition is monopoly, whereas on another dichotomy the absence of competition is cooperation.

The Austrian conception of competition differs in many respects from the neo-classical conception, and emphasises the role of the entrepreneur, and competition as a discovery process. There is a strong belief amongst economists of the Austrian school that competition in markets leads to beneficial outcomes (though the static analysis of perfect competition is rejected), and that in capitalist market economies there are few, if any, barriers to the operation of competition which do not arise from the operation of government.

The idea of contestable markets (e.g. Baumol et al. 1982) focuses on the role of barriers to entry and exit. It postulates that in the absence of such barriers (and notably the absence of exit barriers created by sunk costs), that is the case of a perfectly contestable market, the performance of firms in that market has some optimal properties. The relevance of this is that competition is identified with structural characteristics, namely the absence or presence of barriers to entry and exit, and this is reflected in the conflation of industry and market. Further, the recommended government policy is to avoid regulations which create barriers to entry and exit, and more generally to facilitate entry and exit.

The second broad usage is where competition is taken to mean rivalry in the pursuit of profits, market shares etc., and to involve a dynamic process. In this context, more competition means more rivalry, which could involve a greater commitment to seek to out-do one's rivals, and probably more importantly the ability of firms to compete with each other increases. It would seem to be the view of authors such as Auerbach (1988), Clifton (1977), when they point to the fall of transport and communication costs etc. which enhances competition with a greater (than previous) tendency for the equalization of the rate of profit. The terms rivalry and competing have a dynamic "ring" to them: at a minimum competing is a process which goes on through time. Two important (though generally related) aspects of economic competition in this sense of rivalry are the extent to which enterprises compete through the creation of new assets (whether of physical capital equipment, research and development etc.) and the creation of winners and losers. Marx was one of the first economists to envisage competition as a dynamic process in which there are winners and losers and where there are forces of centralization and concentration.

There are a number of other analyses which share the basic idea that since competition involves winners and losers, profits and losses, it will generate disparities and inequalities, and that profits enable investment which leads to expansion and further profits. Kaldor (e.g. 1972) focused on the role of static and dynamic economies of scale especially in the manufacturing sector so that larger and faster growing firms faced lower and declining costs (compared with the smaller and slower growing firms). Myrdal (e.g. 1957) has discussed on a broader canvass the economic as well as the socio-political forces generating cumulative causation. Cowling (e.g. 1987) has focused on the centralising forces arising under competition for which he coined the phrase "centrapetalism". There are also a range of "first mover" advantages (some of which have just been mentioned) which can be seen in a similar light. At the international level, it suggests that there will be at best weak tendencies for the operation of market forces to enable poorer countries to catch-up with the wealthier ones. As Önis (1991) notes "all successful cases of "late industrialization" have been associated with a significant degree of state intervention".

These notions on the competitive process generate many implications for industrial policy, and we touch on a few here. At the level of competition and monopoly policy, it points to the emergence of monopoly from competition (Marx, 1976) and the growth and change of the character of firms (Berle and Means, 1932), and hence the difficulties of restoring and maintaining atomistic competition. Further, a position of market dominance arises from some superiority over others (in the narrow sense that one firm has won and others have lost). Thus seeking to establish competition (in the sense of a large number of firms) is likely to be frustrated by those very forces, and this has been apparent in the recent experience of privatization and "liberalization" (i.e. the destruction of social institutions) in the UK where there has generally been an initial increase in the number of firms, followed by mergers and consolidations. The process of competition involves winners and losers, and atomistic competition dissolves into oligopoly and monopoly. It would also mean that the theory on which the pro-competition policy is based (perfect competition) is found wanting since it contains no suggestion that atomistic competition will be unstable.

Further, the winners in the competitive struggle have some advantages over the losers in terms of technical efficiency, innovative capabilities etc., and the use of anti-monopoly policy against the "winners" appears as punishing the successful (Marris, 1972). The "winners" may have also employed what some would label "anti-competitive" behavior, but in a competitive struggle enterprises will use whatever weapons are available to them.

At the national level, any concern over the inequalities and disparities generated point in the direction of some forms of regional policy to stimulate economic activity in the relatively depressed regions (where region here should be taken to include relatively small areas such as say an inner city).

The market mechanism is often presented as a democratic institution in which people vote with their dollars for the goods and services which they prefer, and can combine goods and services in whichever proportions they wish (subject to relative prices and their budget constraint) in contrast to the political process where policies are bundled together in a party manifesto and the choice is only between broad policy groupings (apart from any issues of elected parties carrying out the manifesto). Whatever the merits of that argument, it does not confront the question of who are the key decision makers within a market economy. This has at least two aspects. First, it may well be the case that consumers can choose which car to buy from a range, but it is the producers who have initially determined the range to be put on offer. The structure of production in a country clearly depends on the decisions made by producers. Galbraith (1967) described this as the revised sequence whereby producer preferences dominate consumer preferences (in contrast to the accepted sequence based on consumer sovereignty).

Second, within each enterprise, there is generally a clearly defined group of managers who are the effective decision makers over a wide range of issues including employment practices and product development. These two aspects interact to lead to the view that the general path of industrial development is set by a relative small group of people. The decision to close down a factory is taken by a few people though it has a major impact on the employees and suppliers, with knock-on effects on local demand and employment prospects.

Cowling and Sugden (1994) summarise these arguments in the following way. "We suggest that the present reality of the free market economy is that it is dominated by giant economic organizations with a transnational base: the transnational corporations. . As a consequence of this dominance, we shall argue that markets are controlled and manipulated by a powerful subset of the population—the few who control the transnationals. This élite influences situations and events for its own benefits and hence observed outcomes will be optimal for some but not for society as a whole. As a consequence a free market economy is a socially inefficient economy" (p. 22), where free here can be interpreted as free of social institutions and controls.

There is a strong tendency amongst economists to view more competition (usually in terms of number of firms involved) as better than less competition, and that the process of competition moves towards some (often desirable) equilibrium. This is strongly embedded within the neo-classical analysis of perfect competition and monopoly, and largely spills over into the structure-conduct-performance paradigm (though there has long been a recognition in the discussion on research and development that both perfect competition and monopoly are unconducive to technological change). As illustrated by much empirical work on research and development, there may be some "optimal" number of firms (the precise number varying by industry) for reasons of economies of scale. The "optimal" degree of competition is institutionally conditioned, and the welfare effects of competition are in some doubt. This general idea, which also leads to the notion of wasteful competition (i.e. too many firms operating on too small a scale and often duplicating research) which has been influential in industrial policy in a number of Pacific Rim countries (especially Korea and Japan). This raises issues for traditional monopoly policy. There is the question of whether (in the presence of some "optimal" number of firms) there are forces which lead to the emergence of the "right" number of firms.

Although perfect competition is stated to have some desirable properties (though even that can be doubted in the presence of economies of scale and externalities) those properties are essentially static ones. The gains or losses from dynamic considerations such as technical change, innovation and investment are likely to be much larger. In a more general vein, Schumpeter (1950) argued that neoclassical economics and perfect competition was concerned with "how capitalism administers existing structures" but that "the relevant problem is how it creates and destroys them". Policies designed to correct "market imperfections" may bring small static gains but run the danger of generating much larger dynamic losses. Another question is whether we can make any explicit statement about who benefits from "dynamic" competition, as power (and hence the distribution of gains and losses) comes into consideration.

The Nature and Role of the State

This section offers some remarks on the nature and role of the State which are relevant to the issue of industrial policy. We would not pretend to offer anything like a general theory of State, even for industrialized countries. Even at a relatively concrete level, the nature and role of the State varies significantly across countries, and as a consequence their ability and potential for the pursuit of industrial policies (or strategies) varies considerable. Indeed, it could be said that there is an interdependence between the nature of the state in a specific country and the prevailing theories on state activity in that country. It is not coincidental that the prevailing theory of the State in Anglo-Saxon economics is that of the regulatory state (as discussed below) and that the prevailing theory (and ethos) limit the State to largely regulatory activities.

It is useful to distinguish (at the conceptual level) between a regulatory role for the state and a developmental one, and to talk of ideal types (in the Weberian sense of extreme forms with which actual forms may be compared) of the regulatory state and the developmental state. The terms are perhaps self explanatory. Whilst there is no unanimity over the precise nature of the regulatory and the developmental state (and particularly the latter has been subject of much discussion), the key aspects can be briefly indicated. The regulatory state would be one in which a major role of the State was the regulation of market activities, through a variety of mechanisms (for example, control over entry into an industry, over the quality of products, over employment conditions as well as anti-monopoly and the use of taxes and subsidies).

The concept of the developmental State has been particularly advanced in the analysis of the industrialization processes of Far Eastern countries, notably Japan, Korea, and Taiwan.[10] The key aspect of a developmental State is, not surprisingly, its concerns with economic development, usually with an emphasis on industrialization. It was widely perceived that the role of the State and industrial strategy has been crucial in the development process of many of Newly Industrialising Countries around the Pacific Rim as well as Japan, but recent economic crises in those countries have raised doubts. In particular, it has been argued that the "moral hazard" which encourages risky investment in the belief that the government will come to the rescue if there is failure and "cronyism" of the close links between business and the State, both of which can be associated with developmental industrial strategy have been significant factors behind the crises. In contrast, others including Chang, Park and Yoo (1998) "the current crisis in Korea is *not* the result of excessive government intervention that encouraged "moral hazard", as it is often believed. We show that the crisis resulted from uncoordinated and excessive investments by the private sector, financed by imprudent amounts of short-term foreign debt, which in turn had been made possible by rapid and ill-designed financial liberalization (especially capital account liberalization) and a serious weakening of industrial policy".

Leftwich (1995) lists six major components which he sees as defining the developmental state model. The first of these is "a determined developmental elite", where the core elite may be relatively small in number and "usually close to the executive head of government who was instrumental in establishing the developmental regime and its culture" (p. 405).

The second is "the relative autonomy of the developmental state" and its elites. In this context autonomy means "that the state has been able to achieve relative independence (or insulation) from the demanding clamour of special interests (whether class, regional or sectoral) and that it both can and does override these interests in the putative national interest" (p. 408).

The third is "a powerful, competent and insulated economic bureaucracy". The fourth is a "weak and subordinated civil society", where civil society is "the web of all privately-organized interests and groups, above the family level but below that of the state" (p. 415). Leftwich notes that the economic success of the developmental state often stimulates an active civil society, which may thereby undermine the developmental state.

The fifth is "the effective management of non-state economic interests". The final component relates to "a grim feature" of developmental states which "is the combination of their sometimes brutal suppression of civil rights, their apparently wide measure of legitimacy and their generally sustained performance in delivering developmental goods" (p. 418). The suppression of civil rights has clearly been a feature of many economies which have sustained rapid industrial change though such suppression has also been a feature of many more which have not experienced rapid economic growth. However, we would view the legitimacy of the State as particularly relevant in this context and the acceptance by the population of change and the associated re-distribution of income and opportunities, often imposed by the State.

The developmental State differs from a welfare State though there is the question of the degree to which a specific state could have attributes of both. The welfare State could be envisioned along three dimensions. One dimension would see the welfare state as akin to regulatory state which corrects market failure, and where market failures in the fields of education and health provision, and in the provision of insurance for unemployment, sickness and old age are particularly acute. A second (and not unrelated) dimension would stress the re-distributive aspects of the welfare state (which could treat the income distribution arising from market activities as "unfair" and in a sense a failure of the market[11]). A third would focus on the education and health aspects as involving a resource creation aspect, and hence be in line with a developmental role for the State.

In the regulatory approach, there is a strong sense of the State and the market being in opposition in that regulation is imposed to limit the actions of the market. In contrast, in the developmental approach there is (at least potentially) a complementarity between the actions of the State and those of the market.[12] The State is committed to a process of development (usually involving industrialization), and has a general strategy towards the promotion of development (for example, in the case of Japan a strategy in terms of the development of specific industries in a defined sequence and effected through MITI and the banking system). The involvement with the developmental process need not involve public ownership nor high levels of expenditure (though it can do so) but rather the State's role comes through a wide range of interventions, in, for example, controls over international trade and over the allocation of finance by the banking system.[13]

Three questions of particular interest arise here. First, how far is the developmental State democratic? It is difficult to perceive of a developmental role being undertaken by a State which lacked effective power, and this has led to the notion of the developmental State as being a strong State. But strength has different connotations: it may refer to a degree of authoritarianism, it may refer to a degree of autonomy for its actions or it may refer to general support for and acceptance of its actions. An important dimension of the State can be described as the perceived legitimacy of the State. By this we mean the degree of acceptance by the populace (or at least the political elites) that the State has the right to carry out a range of policies even where those policies conflict with their own (at least short-term) interests. A State lacking that type of legitimacy (which will be a matter of degree) can be described as a weak one : it may exhibit authoritarian features to a greater or lesser extent. Further, such a State is much more likely to have to offer deals, payments etc. to ensure some degree of compliance with its policies.

The second question relates to the role of labour. In most discussion of industrial policy, reference to the employees and to labour in general are noticeable by their absence. In the market failure literature, there is an assumed technical efficiency and the focus is on the conditions under which the product is sold (that is a question of market power) or on the externalities involved in production. However, a broad conception of industrial policy would be concerned with work organization through its effects on the level and growth of productivity, and the introduction of new processes and products. It would also be concerned with who are the effective decision-makers and the quality of their decision-making.

A number of authors (Gordon, 1996, Singh, 1996, Pfeffer, 1994) have talked in terms of two different roads which an economy can follow (though no doubt there are many in-between roads) which they label the "high road" and the "low road". The "low road" broadly corresponds to an economy based on competition, incentives and rivalry in which intensity of work and productive efficiency are enforced through unemployment and competition for work. It also involves a low wage strategy in that downward pressure unit labour cost feeds through to pressure on wages rather than on labour productivity, and also that companies compete more on the basis of price than on of quality. However, there is a sharp distinction between the (perhaps) prevailing (right of centre) orthodoxy on how competitive markets work and the view which is implicit in the writings of the above mentioned authors. For the orthodox, competition (especially in its perfectly competitive guise) promotes full employment, a degree of equality (at least the elimination of "unwarranted" inequalities) and provides incentives for growth.

In contrast, the "high road" seeks to build an economy in which there are high levels of investment and technological change (as the basis for high levels of productivity) in which there is substantial worker involvement.

Third, what is the relevance of the notion of the developmental state to already industrialized economies? It is recognized that the appropriate involvement of the State is a vital ingredient in the industrialization process: "the state has played a central part in the economic development in virtually all industrial societies, with the possible exception of early nineteenth century Britain (Marquand, 1988). But equally the State can act to hold back industrialization.[14] The developmental role of the State can be presented as preparing the ground for the emergence of fully fledged markets through, for example, the development of a legal framework, the building of the infrastructure, and overcoming the obstacles presented by a fledgling financial system.

It is often argued that resources devoted to industrial policies will be siphoned off into "rent-seeking activities": profits can be gained through winning subsidies from government, through the award of government contracts etc., which may be secured by bribery and near bribery. The profits to be gained from government support are considerable so that it is worthwhile for firms to expend resources to secure that support. But how far government subsidy is dissipated by "rent seeking" activities and how far those subsidies are channelled into asset creation appears to vary between countries, and may well depend on the nature of the relationship between the State and industry.

The use of protection of an industry (using infant industry arguments) may lead to the growth of that industry into adulthood (as, for example, in the outstanding cases of the car industries of Japan and Korea) or can lead to a cosy existence behind the tariff walls and pressures against any removal of the protection. There may be subtle differences in apparently similar policies which account for the different outcomes but we would argue that a particularly significant aspect is the nature of the State-industry relationships. A "soft state" (to use the terminology of Myrdal, 1968) may be unable to adequately implement its policies but is also concerned to buy support from significant groups in society, and to curry favor with particular interest groups by focusing subsidies on to a particular enterprise or industry   which wins favor with those associated with that enterprise as workers etc. It is well known that the benefits of such a policy are visible and concentrated whereas the costs are difficult to precisely identify and are spread out. A weak government would find it difficult to "pull the plug" on subsidies. In contrast, a strong government (a better phrase might be confident and accepted government) would be better able to resist the pressures to introduce and continue particular subsidies. Further, overlaying the differences in the "strength" of the government is the industrial policy paradigm within which the government and others work.

The State and the Market

The relationship between the State and the market is viewed here in two dimensions: first, whether there are activities which the State can do which the market cannot (and vice versa), and second, in what ways does the State enhance and in what ways inhibit the functioning of the market. A third dimension which is not discussed here is the ways in which the functioning of the market inhibits the operation of the State: for example, the perceived responses of financial markets to macroeconomic policies may serve to limit the willingness of the State to pursue expansionary fiscal policies. The difficulties of defining the market were remarked upon above. In this section when we use the expression market we simply mean the collective operation of business enterprises involved in production for sale.

What can the State do that markets cannot (and vice versa)? We would seek to avoid the suggestion that there is some kind of perfect market which could eventually be reached, and departures from which are the consequence of the government (whether through acts of commission or of omission). But it may be useful to indicate that there are actions etc. which governments can take which are difficult for the markets to do. This is rather broader than the market failure cum public good approach which has featured so strongly in the neo-classical approach. This broader agenda of government actions would include, first, offsetting the forces of cumulative causation. However, as Myrdal (1944) indicated, the forces of cumulative causation are not confined to the economic sphere, and indeed his mighty work on the position of the Negro in pre-war USA indicated many routes through which cumulative causation worked. There is a rather straight forward way in which it can work in the context of the State, namely that localities in which tax revenues are higher are able to undertake higher levels of expenditure on, e.g., education, health etc. which generates higher levels of income etc. in the future. It is clearly possible that a government can re-distribute tax revenue within its own jurisdiction, but there is clearly no inevitability about that.

Second, the State can collect and disseminate information (as in the context of indicative planning), adopt a strategic role and seek to build institutions. Chang and Rowthorn (1996) argue that "we are not here asserting that the state necessarily has a superior ability to identify a better future course for the national economy (although this may well be the case ...), but only that the provision of a "focal point" around which economic activities may be organized in times of major economic change can be extremely useful. Our case for state entrepreneurship, then, is mainly based on its *strategic position*—that the state, by definition, is the only agent which may (although it may not) represent the interest of the whole society—although it will be naïve to assume that all existing states have the organizational coherence, the political desire, or the power to exploit such a strategic position to national advantage" (pp. 36—37).

In relation to institutions, Amsden, Kochanowicz and Taylor (1994) argue that "when advocates of this "market fundamentalism" refer to "institutions" and the necessity of "institution building" in order to foster capitalism, they have in mind a strictly limited agenda: the specification of property rights, contract law enforcement, and the removal of impediments to private enterprise. The market mechanism in the East Asia case, by contrast, has been relied on instrumentally rather than as a matter of ideological conviction; institutions—including a bureaucratic, "developmental" state—assume a major role in allocating investment resources. Institution building in this context refers not just to the establishment of clear property rights and contract law but also to the creation of private and public organizations capable of carrying out the expansionary macroeconomic policies as well as investment, trade, competition, and technology policies, all operating under the umbrella of what has loosely come to be called industrial policy" (p. 4).

The third is the correction of externalities, provision of public goods etc. These have been the traditional fare of the economic analysis of government intervention to overcome perceived market failures. The analysis appears normative (as to what governments should do) though it is often given a positive interpretation (as an explanation of what governments actually do). It is well known that this analysis assumes that full information is available to the government and that government will act in some notion of the social interest. It is now often pointed out that governments have at best imperfect information, and may not be able to make and implement effective decisions. Further, the government may act more in the interests of the bureaucrats and politicians than in the more general social interest. In this regard, there are ever present problems of agency, that is in the case of the government (as agent) acting in the interests of the people.

Globalization

Globalization will clearly have some profound implications for the formulation and implementation of industrial policies, and at the limit may make active industrial policy impossible. The specific implications of globalization will vary between different types of industrial policy. Globalization has many dimensions including increasing international trade, rising importance of foreign direct investment as well as the emergence of a more integrated set of financial markets. Questions can be raised (e.g. by Hirst and Thompson, 1996; Kleinknecht and ter Wengel, 1998) over whether there has been an upward trend in international trade and foreign direct investment (FDI) over this century rather than a more recent trend which has brought trade and FDI back to the levels attained in the earlier part of the century. It can also be questioned whether what is being observed is more a growth of integration between national economies within regional blocs rather than globalization on a literal interpretation of that word. We limit any discussion of trends to the post-war period, recognising that this period has been one of the "opening up" of national economies following a much more protectionist era.

Globalization in the form of increased international trade does not raise many issues for industrial policy. Trade may bring competition for the domestic firms (though as Cowling 1982, has argued there are often links between domestic producers and foreign producers, and may, in the form of transnationals, be the same companies). The support for firms and industries on the basis of "infant industry" arguments may require some reduction in trade and the construction of trade barriers. But in other respects, the purpose of industrial policy is the strengthening of the productive base of a country, and that purpose may be strengthened rather than weakened in the context of international trade.

Globalization in the form of increasing foreign direct investment and the footloose nature of capital does raise much more significant issues for industrial policy. The mobility of capital enhances the power of capital relative to labour and to the state. In so far as the implementation of industrial policy requires that the state can exert leverage over private companies, globalization reduces the possibilities for industrial policy. This would be relevant for regulation type industrial policies as well as for policies to boost spending on investment and on research and development.

Much discussion of industrial policy implicitly relates to policy implemented at the level of the nation state, but two rather different issues arise. The first is whether the nation state can effectively implement industrial policy, and this is the focus of our discussion below. The second is whether the national level is the appropriate tier of government. There is no straight forward answer to that question as it may well depend on the size of the country concerned and the nature of the regional bloc within which the country is situated. That is the considerations for countries within the European Union, for those within NAFTA and those in other blocs may be rather different. It could further be argued that within the European Union, some aspects of industrial policy (e.g. merger policy) should be operated at the EU level, while other policies (such as the encouragement of SMEs and networks) should operate at the regional level.

The growth of foreign direct investment, and more the presence of large foreign owned firms in most industrialized countries clearly undermines any notions of "national champions" and the promotion of "our companies". The promotion of a particular sector of industry may in effect be the promotion of foreign owned companies. The term industrial policy suggests a focus on the industry rather than on the firm, but in reality much industrial policy is concerned with the operations of specific firms. Globalization (especially in the form of foreign direct investment) obviously loosens the links between a company and a specific country. The leverage by national governments over companies is diminished and incentives provided to a company (say in the form of investment grants, funding for research and development) can be readily siphoned abroad.

The implications for industrial policy which we would draw from this brief discussion are as follows. First, developmental industrial policies need to be designed and operated so as to maximise the benefits generated within the country concerned, and to limit the degree to which benefits are siphoned off by transnational corporations elsewhere.[15] Second, it suggests that industrial policy should not focus on support of transnational companies nor on seeking to attract foreign direct investment, but rather on the strengthening of firms which are not footloose, whether in the form of small and medium sized firms (SMEs) in the context of networks, of workers cooperative and mutual organization and of public sector firms. Third, it pushes industrial policy more towards the provision of infrastructure (broadly defined to include training and skills as well as transport systems) of a "public good" character rather than the provision of private benefits to individual firms.

Implications and Conclusions

The theoretical discussion of industrial policy can seek to set an agenda for possible policies, though as we have argued above different theoretical approaches will yield different policy conclusions. The application of industrial policy, particularly those of a more strategic nature, requires a state which has the necessary competencies and objectives to pursue such policies, where competencies would include not only the administrative capabilities but also political strength, which we would hope would be in a participative democratic sense.

There are numerous analyses of how market economies work, and even when a few broad approaches can be identified there are many variations within those broad approaches. Yet any theory of industrial policy has to be based on some analysis of the operation of market economies.

We would argue that three broad approaches to the operation of a market economy can be identified, from which there is a reasonable clear set of implications for industrial policy. The first would be the Austrian approach which portrays the market as bringing about the unconscious coordination of economic activity. Further, although there are no formal criteria, there are strong suggestions that the operations of markets unconstrained by government will bring overall benefits. Government intervention in the market economy is seen as generally harmful, and the policy implications are for the minimal level of government intervention of the so-called "night watchman" type of the provision of law and order and national defence.

The second is the neo-classical approach which portrays the possibility of an optimal outcome from perfect competition. Within that framework, deviations from perfect competition can be identified, with the presumption that the removal or reduction of those deviations would be beneficial: that is the general market failure approach. This approach is essentially an undifferentiated policy with regard to the nature of the product or the industry, and instead focuses on the "correction" of the market failures whether arising from monopoly or from externalities. This approach views the (competitive) market as the only relevant institution for economic coordination. While there may be recognition that there may be coordination failures, there is little exploration of the role of the state in improving coordination whether through its own direct actions or through institution building.[16]

The third approach blends a number of elements discussed above together. It recognises that there are forces of cumulative causation in operation, which tend to re-inforce disparities of economic performance, and hence that there is a role for the State in offsetting those disparities. It also recognises that some products are more important than others for the reasons discussed above, and hence would see the need for a differentiated industrial policy. Finally, there is the recognition that a market economy draws on a number of coordinating mechanisms with some of those mechanisms at the level of the firm, but others at an industry or economy level.

Although it is acknowledged that they form ideal types, it is useful to distinguish between the "regulatory state" and the "developmental state", even though any particular state incorporates elements of both types and indeed of other ones. Further, there are other aspects to the operation of the State, of which the "welfare state" and the "night watchman state" are two illustrations. The general idea of a "regulatory state" (and the common use of phrases such as the "nanny state") has been the dominant one in the discussion of industrial policy in the Anglo-Saxon world (as reflected in competition policy, correction of market failure and the regulation of privatized utilities). In contrast, it could be argued that the developmental role of the state has been much more apparent in a number of European countries and much more so in a range of East Asian ones. The developmental role for the state does not preclude a regulatory one, and indeed some of the "market failure" aspects of the regulatory state find echoes in the developmental role. A clear example of this is the argument that private enterprises will tend to underinvest in research and development (as compared with some socially desirable rate) for reasons of uncertainty, difficulties of securing finance and problems of appropriating the benefits of research and development. The involvement of the state in the promotion of research and development may be bolstered by such arguments, and would be consistent with the notion of a developmental state as well that of a regulatory state.

Notes

1. A policy instrument (e.g. interest rates) may influence industrial performance and development (in this example through influence on investment decisions), but the policy instrument may be used in pursuit of other objectives (in this example, now often that objective is the control of inflation). Whether a particular policy instrument is to be regarded as part of industrial policy would depend on the intention of the policy makers in the use of that instrument and the context in which it was used. In present circumstances in the UK, USA and many other countries, interest rate policy would not be part of industrial policy as interest rates are used in pursuit of restraint of inflation.

2. I have argued elsewhere (Sawyer, 1992b) that three broad approaches to industrial policy could be identified : the neo-classical/SCP, the Austrian, and an approach which I labelled industrial strategy. Each of those approaches, I argued, had its own view on the operation of markets, and the nature and role of the State, and more generally different views on the nature of economic analysis and on methodology.

3. This is subject to the caveat that the discussion on technical change and advertising within that paradigm did include the possibility that technical change and advertising would reach their peak under oligopoly (as compared with monopoly or perfect competition).

4. It can be noted that the market failure type analysis tends to slip from a normative analysis of what could be done to a positive analysis of what is done.

5. A related issue is the specification of the product: parametric prices only have a full meaning in the case where the product is well-defined for both sides of the market.

6. The new Keynesian approach to macroeconomics is rather misnamed for it has little to do with Keynesian and is essentially microeconomics, as the brief discussion in the text may indicate.

7. In conditions of uncertainty, it is difficult to ascertain ex post whether a mistake has indeed been made, for that would require comparisons of the results of the actual decision with those which would have resulted from hypothetical alternatives.

8. Note though that the Lange analysis of market socialism was markets (enterprises responding to price given by the Central Planning Board, with prices

adjusted in response to excess demand, and competition in any meaningful sense was absent. Indeed, this was a major element of the critique mounted by economists of the Austrian school, such as Mises and Hayek (see Lavoie, 1985).

9.   The number of enterprises would not be a complete measure as allowance has to be made for the inequality of enterprise size, and the development of concentration measures as (inverse) measures of competition have sought to address that problem.

10.   Chalmers Johnson (1982), Tabb (1995) (for Japan), Amsden (1989), Chang (1993, 1994) (for Korea) and Wade (1990) (for Taiwan) perceive crucial roles for the State in the industrialization processes.

11.   The framework of "market failure" does not permit consideration of income distribution issues. Hence we use the term failure of the market rather than market failure.

12.   The concept of the developmental State has evolved in the context of what were seen as market economies with mainly private ownership of industry. How far centrally planned economies such as the Soviet Union conformed to the notion of a developmental state is a matter of debate. China since the economic reforms of the late 1970s (and beyond) could be described as a market socialism with the State playing a strong developmental role. (Nolan, 1996)

13.   It is perhaps the low levels of public ownership and of public expenditure in a number of countries such as Japan which has lead some to argue that the development has been market-led rather than State-led.

14.   Nye (1997), for example, raises question of why France did not develop in the way in which the UK did in the 18th and 19th centuries, and the role of the State in that 'what remains to be fleshed out is why one state, Britain, was so successful in creating a stable and fiscally able central administration while the other, France, was not. I have elsewhere suggested that the British and French sovereigns should not be viewed as fundamentally different either in their attitudes toward the economy or the state' (p.136).

15.   This should not be interpreted as an argument against support for economic and industrial development in third world countries, but rather that a different set of policies is required for such development.

16.   There are exceptions to this could be seen as the coordination failure associated with the Keynesian literature, and the game theoretic analysis of . There

is discussion of some related aspects in the mainstream literature, and two come to mind. The first is the role of the government in the correction of coordination failure, associated with the new Keynesian literature. The second is the game theoretic analysis of interactions between economic agents which can illustrate the gains from cooperative over uncooperative behavior, and the emergence of norms of behavior.

References

Amsden, A. 1989. *Asia's Next Giant: South Korea and Late Industrialization*, New York and Oxford: Oxford University Press

Amsden, A., J. Kochanowicz and L. Taylor 1994. *The Market Meets its Match*, Cambridge, Mass: Harvard University Press.

Auerbach, P. 1988. *Competition: the Economics of Industrial Change*, Oxford: Blackwell.

Baumol,W., J. Panzar and R. Willig 1982. *Contestable Markets and the Theory of Industrial Structure*.

Berle, A.A. and G.C. Means 1932. *Modern Corporation and Private Property*, New York: Harcourt, Brace and World

Best, M.H. 1990. *The New Competition*, Cambridge, Mass.: Harvard University Press.

Chang, H-J 1993. "The Political Economy of Industrial Policy in Korea", *Cambridge Journal of Economics*, Vol. 17, 131—157.

——— 1994. *The Political Economy of Industrial Policy*, London: Macmillan.

Chang, H-J and R. Rowthorn 1995. "Role of the State in Economic Change: Entrepreneurship and Conflict Management". In H-J Chang and R. Rowthorn eds. *The Role of the State in Economic Change*, Oxford: Oxford University Press.

Chang, H-J, H-J Park and C.G. Yoo 1998. "Interpreting the Korean Crisis: Financial Liberalization, Industrial Policy, and Corporate Governance", *Cambridge Journal of Economics*, Vol. 22, forthcoming

Clifton, J. 1977. "Competition and the Evolution of the Capitalist Mode of Production", *Cambridge Journal of Economics*, Vol. 1.

Coase, R. 1937. "The Nature of the Firm", *Economica*, Vol. 4.

Cowling, K. 1987. "An Industrial Strategy for Britain", *International Review of Applied Economics*, Vol. 1.

Cowling, K. and R. Sugden 1994. *Beyond Capitalism*, London: Frances Pinter.

Davidson, P. 1990. *Collected Writings of Paul Davidson*, Vol. 1, London: Macmillan.

Fourie, F.C. 1989. "The Nature of Firms and Markets: Do Transactions Approaches Help?", *South African Journal of Economics*, Vol. 57.

Galbraith, J.K. 1967. *The New Industrial State*, London: Hamish Hamilton.

Gordon, D. 1996. *Fat and Mean*, New York: Martin Kessler Books.

Hirschman, A. 1970. *Exit, Voice and Loyalty*, Cambrdige, Mass: Harvard University Press.

Hirst, P. and G. Thompson 1996. *Globalization in Question: The International Economy and the Possibilities*, Cambridge: Polity Press.

Hutton, W. 1995. *The State We're In*, London: Jonathan Cape.

Johnson, C. 1982. *MITI and the Japanese Miracle: the Growth of Industrial Policy, 1925-1975*, Stanford: Stanford University Press.

Kaldor, N. 1972. "The Irrelevance of Equilibrium Economics", *Economic Journal*, Vol. 82.

Keynes, J.M. 1936. *The General Theory of Employment, Interest and Money*, London: Macmillan.

Kleinknecht, A. and J. ter Wengel 1998. "The Myth of Economic Globalization", *Cambridge Journal of Economics*, Vol. 22, 637—647

Knight, F. 1921. *Risk, Uncertainty and Profit*, Boston: Houghton Mifflin.

Lavoie, D. 1985. *Rivalry and Central Planning: the Socialist Calculation Debate Reconsidered*, Cambridge: Cambridge University Press.

Leftwich, A. 1995. "Bringing Politics Back In: Towards a Model of the Development State", *Journal of Development Studies*, Vol. 31, No. 3, 400—427.

Lindbeck, A. and D. Snower 1988. *The Insider Outsider Theory of Employment and Unemployment*, Cambridge Mass.: MIT Press.

Lorenz, E.H. 1989. "Neither Friends nor Strangers: Informal Networks of Subcontracting in French Industry". In D. Gambetta ed. *Trust: Making and Breaking of Cooperative Relations*, Oxford: Blackwell.

Marquand, D. 1988. *The Unprincipled Society*, London: Fontana.

Marris, R. 1972. "Why Economics Needs a Theory of the Firm", *Economic Journal*, Vol. 82.

Marx, K. 1976. *Capital Vol. 1*, Harmondsworth: Penguin.

Myrdal, G. 1944. *The American Dilemma: the Negro Problem and Modern Democracy*, New York: Harper & Row.

———— 1957. *Economic Theory and Underdeveloped Regions*, London: Duckworth.

———— 1968. *Asian Drama: An Inquiry into the Poverty of Nations*, New York: Twentieth Century Fund.

Nolan, P. 1993. *State and Market in the Chinese Economy*, London: Macmillan.

———— 1996. "Post-Stalinist System Reform in China and Russia : Contrast and Implications". In P. Arestis, G. Palma and M. Sawyer eds. *Markets, Unemployment and Economic Policy: Essays in Honour of Geoff Harcourt, Volume Two*, London: Routledge.

Nye, J.V.C. 1997. "Thinking About the State: Property Rights, Trade, and Changing Contractual Arrangements in a World with Coercion". In J.N. Drobak and J.V.C. Nye eds. *The Frontiers of the New Institutional Economics*, San Diego: Academic Press, 121—142.

Önis, Z. 1991. "The Logic of the Developmental State", *Comparative Politics*, October.

Pfeffer, J. 1994. *Competitive Advantage through People: Unleashing the Power of the Workforce*, Boston, Mass.: Harvard Business School Press.

Piore, M.J. and C.F. Sabel 1984. *The Second Industrial Divide*, New York: Basic Books.

Powell, W.W. 1990. "Neither Market nor Hierarchy: Network Forms of Organization", *Research in Organizational Behavior*, Vol. 12, 295—336.

Sawyer, M. 1992. "On the Theory of Industrial Policy and Strategy". In K. Cowling and R.Sugden eds. *Current Issues in Industrial Economic Strategy* Manchester: Manchester University Press.

———— 1992a. "The Nature and Role of the Market", *Social Concept*, Vol. 6, No. 2. (A slightly revized version appeared in C. Pitelis ed. *Transaction Costs, Markets and Hierarchies*, Oxford: Blackwell, 1993.)

Schumpeter, J.A. 1950. *Capitalism, Socialism and Demoncracy*, New York: Harper and Row.

Shackle, G. 1961. *Decision, Order and Time in Human Affairs*, Cambridge: Cambridge University Press.

Shapiro, N. 1991. "Firms, Markets and Innovation", *Journal of Post Keynesian Economics*, Vol. 14, No. 1, 49—60.

Singh, A. 1994. "Institutional Requirements for Full Employment in Advanced Economies", *International Labour Review*, Vol. 134, 471—495.

———— 1996. "Expanding Employment in the Global Economy", In P. Arestis, G. Palma and M. Sawyer eds. *Markets, Unemployment and Economic Policy: Essays in Honour of Geoff Harcourt, Volume Two*, London: Routledge.

Stiglitz, J. 1994. *Whither Socialism*, Cambridge, Mass. : MIT Press.

Stiglitz, J. and A. Weiss 1981. "Credit Rationing in Markets with Imperfect Information", *American Economic Review*, Vol. 71, 393—410.

Tabb, W.K. 1995. *The Postwar Japanese System*, New York and Oxford: Oxford University Press.

Thompson, G. 1991. "Networks: Introduction". In G. Thompson, J. Frances, R. Levacic and J. Mitchell, *Markets, Hierarchies and Networks*, London: SAGE.

Wade, R. 1990. *Governing the Market : Economic Theory and the Role of Government in East Asian Industrialization*, Princeton: Princeton University Press.

Williamson, O.E. 1986. *Economic Organization, Firms, Markets and Policy Control*, Brighton: Harvester Wheatsheaf.

3 THE IMPLICATIONS OF GLOBALIZATION FOR INDUSTRIAL, TRADE, AND INNOVATION POLICIES

Jonathan Michie

Introduction

The implications of globalization have been interpreted as implying that it is no longer necessary for individual countries to pursue national trade policies. Trade deficits, it is argued, can now be readily financed by global financial markets. And since trade imbalances are the result of individuals' decisions to save, such imbalances will in time be self correcting. Porter (1994) paraphrases the globalization thesis as follows:

> In a world of global competition, it is argued, location is no longer relevant. Geography and political boundaries have been transcended. The firm, in particular, can shed its locational identity or dependence entirely (p. 35).

There have already been a number of critiques of such arguments, as well as of the other variants of the globalization literature; in addition to this article by Porter, see, for example Michie (1996) and Michie and Grieve Smith (1995). The important point for the present discussion is that the form taken by the processes described by some as "globalization" has been determined by the politics of the 1980s and 1990s and the balance of class forces both within the advanced capitalist economies and on a global scale; hence its characterization as "global neoclassicism" (Schor, 1992, p. 4).

This has been accompanied by a positing of national economic policy objectives as being to seek stability where this is interpreted, perversely, as stability of policy instruments—interest rates, exchange rates, fiscal balances and so on—despite the fact that stability in these may provoke or exacerbate instability in real economic variables. It is rather these real economic variables, of growth, employment and the like, which should be stabilized through the active use of economic instruments including industrial, trade, and innovation policy.

Instead, economic policy is dominated by *laissez faire* economics, despite the failure of such policy analysis in the 1980s and 1990s to bring about the sort of economic growth and high employment witnessed through the 1950s and 1960s. The dominant feature of international trade theory is the assumed superiority of free trade and non-intervention. As has been argued elsewhere,[1] the neoclassical case for free trade is based on inappropriate assumptions; relax these assumptions and the case for non-intervention goes with them. This chapter therefore argues that to return to a situation of reasonable stability and balanced growth for individual countries, and for the world economy as a whole, increased management of the international trading and monetary systems will be required, along with new industrial policies domestically. The primary institutional vehicle for pursuing such industrial policies will remain national governments. But that does not mean that such policies should be pursued solely at the national level. On the contrary, it is vital that they be grounded at the local and regional level, and also where appropriate include an international dimension. Indeed, in many industries such as aerospace, industrial policy can only be sensibly pursued by national governments collaborating.

The chapter discusses the implications of these arguments as follows. In Section 1, the recognition by new growth theory that trade policy may be an important form of industrial policy is considered but, it is argued, the restrictive assumptions of the theory mean that such industrial policy considerations get cut off from what should be an accompanying macro-economic agenda—specifically, the latter gets assumed away in the assumed world of continuous full employment. The theoretical case for a *laissez faire* domestic policy is considered in Section 2, as is the case, in theory, for governments to intervene in fostering industrial development. Section 3 then considers what form such intervention should take in an era of rapid technological advance where innovation may benefit from diversity. Section 4 concludes.

1. The Theory and Practice of Trade Policy

The standard case for free trade is based on a number of assumptions and simplifications. First, much of the literature ignores the macro economic context. Secondly, each economy is assumed to be small and open and therefore unable to affect relative prices internationally. Thirdly, production is assumed to operate with constant or diminishing returns to scale. And fourthly, the economy is assumed to be always at full employment, by definition, and with no other distortions in the economic system. There have been various attempts to revise orthodox trade theory, with Mundell (1961) and others considering the macroeconomic context of tariff policy and exchange rate regimes; the ability to affect world prices being considered in the optimum tariff literature; and the role of increasing returns being incorporated within the so-called "new trade theory".

Imperfect competition and economies of scale have been introduced into international trade theory to explain the extensive and growing intra-industry trade between industrialized countries, with intra-industry trade flows being due to the existence of differentiated products produced under increasing returns. A diversity of tastes amongst consumers provides an incentive for product differentiation and the presence of economies of scale implies that each country will have to specialize in a limited number of products. The existence of increasing returns and imperfect competition indicates that price is above marginal cost, giving rise to the possibility of welfare-improving interventions. Thus, protectionism may offer a "second best" instrument for raising welfare. Within new trade theory the impact of tariffs depends on the specific market structure under consideration—perfect competition, monopoly, monopolistic competition or oligopoly. Within the perfect competition model increasing returns are assumed to be external to the firm. This Marshallian approach therefore creates the case for protecting or supporting those sectors that generate large positive externalities such as technological spillovers. With alternative market structures the case for protection is not simply one of externalities but also the potential to shift rent to domestic producers. Much recent work has focused on cases of oligopoly which are the most difficult to deal with given the diversity of possible features. Under oligopolistic conditions foreign firms are earning pure profits in the domestic market. Tariffs can be used as a method of rent shifting, both through their revenue-raising effect and by switching profits away from foreign to local firms.

However, new trade theory has remained firmly microeconomic in character with protection being considered as an extension of industrial policy; the macroeconomics of tariffs in a world of increasing returns has rarely been considered by mainstream economics. Even when increasing returns are incorporated, full employment is still assumed and the competitive process is still reduced to alternative specifications of market structure—monopolistic competition, oligopoly and so on. This is why new trade theory is unable to deal with protectionism other than as an industrial policy—evaluating the benefits of protecting "strategic" sectors or industries—and is incapable of considering trade policy as part of a macroeconomic or development strategy. The macroeconomic possibility of domestic demand and output increasing is ignored, as are the dynamic gains from such economic growth.

The point being argued here is not that protectionism—or indeed any sort of active trade policy—need necessarily be pursued. On the contrary, it is that the apparent support which new trade theory might be interpreted as giving to such policies, as appropriate industrial policy, is so limited in its theoretical framework as to be a quite inadequate way of viewing either industrial or, for that matter, trade policy. Specifically it ignores the demand side. And one of the points which this chapter seeks to make is that not only are industrial policies—what might be termed "supply side" policies, despite the mis-use of that term to describe the sort of Reaganite and Thatcherite agenda of the 1980s—desirable, but that it is vital that these be consistent with demand side policies. We have argued elsewhere (Michie and Pitelis, 1998) that demand and supply side analysis needs to be integrated in theoretical as well as policy work, given that the sort of recognition made by mainstream theorists of the realities of oligopolistic structures and so forth indicated above remains alongside assumptions of perfect competition in much of demand side theorizing. However, this dichotomy is not the subject of the present chapter; instead the following section moves on to consider the theory and practice of industrial policy itself.

2. The Theory and Practice of Industrial Policy

The globalization of markets and the accompanying intensification of international competition has been associated with extensive deregulation of economies as well as measures to reduce taxes and government expenditure. This "liberalization", taken together with the abandonment of public ownership in both the former socialist and mixed economies has created a widespread impression that the market system has triumphed and that state intervention in the economy has been shown to be impotent. On the other hand, the intensification of international competition has led to a growing preoccupation with the determinants of competitiveness. Interest is increasingly focused on issues relating to productivity and technical change. While some claim that the same forces make for static and dynamic efficiency so that all that is required is a continuation of the 1980s program of liberalization and deregulation, the market oriented reforms of the 1980s led in various ways to the neglect or undervaluation of assets and structures which are vital for long term development.

Neoclassical general equilibrium theory provided the basis for microeconomic policy during the post-war period at least up until the early 1980s. This theory which emphasized the optimality properties of free market outcomes also sanctioned a wide range of government interventions designed to deal with market failure. The latter could be due to the absence of a market, the presence of externalities, increasing returns to scale and high transactions or information costs all of which are ubiquitous features of real economic systems. From the late 1970s onwards, the view that government intervention could provide a means of overcoming market failure was increasingly questioned. For some (such as Hayek, 1944) intervention was to be discouraged because it interfered with individual liberty. For others, what was problematic was the welfare economist's assumption of an autonomous state acting in the public interest. Finally, there was the issue of the state's ability to achieve what it set out to do—Government failure, it was argued, was just as pervasive as market failure and no antidote to it. As Chang (1994) has noted, government failure arguments provided a valuable corrective to the naive belief that the benevolent state can solve all market failure problems. However, rather than explore the issue of how state failures can be remedied, many of those contributing to the government failure literature seem to have regarded it primarily as part of a case for non-intervention.

As well as these negative arguments against state intervention, positive arguments were put forward to support the pro-market case. One set of arguments based on the newly devised theory of contestable markets seemed to suggest that in sectors where entry was free and exit costless, potential competition could be as effective as actual competition in disciplining market power (Baumol, 1982). All the properties of perfect competition: cost minimization, zero economic profits and price equal to marginal cost would be reproduced in an industry with two or more firms. Even in natural monopoly, price would equal average costs and there would be cost minimization. This powerful new theory indicated that the scope for effective competition had previously been underestimated and that there were grounds for widespread deregulation in industries such as airlines and freight where the assumption of complete redeployability or absence of sunk costs (necessary for free entry and exit) was most likely to be met.

The theory of contestable markets suggested that a small number of firms in a market did not necessarily imply a need for government intervention to counteract the effects of market power. It soon became clear however that the key requirement of the theory, complete redeployability or absence of sunk costs, was not often met and that in its absence competitive results were unlikely to be achieved.

In evaluating proposed reforms, neoclassical economists use the benchmark of Pareto efficiency. Classical and neo-Schumpeterian economists, on the other hand, use that of economic progress. Assuming winners compensate losers, economic progress will lead to Pareto improvements though the new position need not be Pareto efficient.

Ideally, of course, we would like to exhaust the gains from bargaining and trade as well as maximizing economic progress. But as Schumpeter (1947) and more recently Metcalfe (1995) have warned, the two objectives may be fundamentally incompatible in which case it becomes necessary to have a view about which objective is dominant. Over the long run, it is clear that the gains from technical progress dwarf potential efficiency gains. In the short to medium term, the matter may be less clearcut. If time horizons are short, efficiency gains may dominate the gains from progress. This becomes problematic if the pursuit of short term efficiency gains reduces the potential of the economic system for future progress.

For governments to use industrial policy to promote long term economic progress rather than simply short term efficiency gains, one of the main aims, particularly within the context of increasing competitive pressures internationally, must be to create an innovative economy. There is evidence that networks and groups of firms can increase the scope for innovation.[2] However, they do not always do so; the problem may be due to coordination failure, or to inadequate capabilities in some part of the productive process. A good example of the latter comes from the highly successful Taiwanese electronics industry. In the main, the industry is made up of small and medium-sized enterprises which concentrate almost exclusively on the manufacturing function to the neglect of areas such as marketing and R&D which are necessary for the upgrading of their technological level. As a result, the role of the state has been extremely important in building competence in advanced electronics with leadership of the industry vested in public research organizations and public enterprise.[3]

While industry structure and related to that firm level competence are important for innovative performance, it is necessary to note that, in general, firms' ability to change strategic orientation is constrained by the nature of their existing capabilities. This tendency towards lock-in even in large firms with strong R&D bases suggests that there is considerable scope for intervention to promote technological and product diversification. An important task here is the early identification of technological opportunities and the creation of a framework in which these opportunities can be tested in practice. This may involve improving the incentives for firm diversification through advanced procurement policies. It may also involve such things as investments to create appropriate skill and research bases in advance of industry need. Creation and facilitation of networks of firms and networks involving both firms and other institutions may also be important.[4]

3. Innovation Policy

Friedrich List (1841) understood that the development of endogenous capabilities had to be considered within the context of what was already in his day seen as the growing internationalization of economic activities. This offered an opportunity for late-comer nations to acquire best-practice techniques, although there was no guarantee that all nations would benefit to the same extent. On the question of how a late-comer could attempt to upgrade in the context of an increasingly global economy, he suggesting four policy options:

- Investing in education to promote an adequately trained workforce.
- Creating a network of infrastructures to allow the dissemination of the most important economic resource, namely know-how.
- Creating economic ties among countries, such as customs unions; to strengthen their effectiveness, he also advocated the development of institutional systems of states.
- Last—and actually, least—protecting infant industries to allow them to develop the expertise needed to face international competition.

A century and a half after List, the concept of national systems of innovation is once again on the academic and policy-making agenda. The country case-studies published in Nelson (1993) and the thematic issues discussed in Lundvall (1992) are reminiscent of, respectively, parts one and two of List's main work. Taken together, the resulting body of literature today on National System of Innovation (NSI) identifies the following crucial aspects in defining the structure and explaining the behavior of nations:[5]

i) Education and training
Education and training are vital components of economic development. In spite of the international diffusion of education and of the increasing, although still limited, number of students enroled in foreign universities, education is still largely national in scope. Substantial differences can be found between countries in the proportion of the relevant age group actually participating in education, whether in primary, secondary or higher. Moreover, the distribution of students by disciplines also varies markedly across countries, as shown with reference to the East Asian countries by Mowery and Oxley (1995, Table 7).

ii) Science and technology capabilities
The level of resources devoted by each nation to formal R&D and other innovation-related activities (such as design, engineering, tooling-up, and so on) represents a basic characteristic of NSI. The bulk of the world's R&D activities is carried out in industrially advanced countries, while developing countries report a very small fraction of world R&D activities. Even within the relatively homogeneous group of OECD nations, there are significant differences in R&D intensity: a small club of countries, including the United States, Japan, Germany, Switzerland and Sweden, devote around three per cent of their GDP to formal R&D activities. Other countries report a much smaller R&D intensity, although they might be less disadvantaged in terms of other innovative inputs. Another difference relates to how R&D expenditure splits between the public and the business sectors; big government programs in space, defense and nuclear technologies often shape the entire structure of the Science and Technology (S&T) system of a nation.

iii) Industrial structure
Firms are the principle agents of technological innovation. The industrial structure of a nation heavily conditions the nature of its innovative activities. Large firms are more likely to undertake basic research programs and are also more likely to be able to afford long term investment in innovative activities whose pay-back may not only be spread years into the future but may also be extremely uncertain. The level of competition faced by companies in their domestic market also plays a crucial role in the R&D investment outcome.

iv) S&T strengths and weaknesses

Each country has its own strengths and weaknesses in different S&T fields. Some nations have specializations in leading-edge technologies, while others have strengths in areas which are likely to provide only diminishing returns in the future. Moreover, some countries tend to be highly specialized in a few niches of excellence, while others have their S&T resources distributed more uniformly across all fields. There are several determinants of national S&T specialization, including the size of a country, R&D intensity, market structure, and its position in the international division of labor. The resulting S&T specialization may influence a nation's future economic performance since countries with technological strengths in rising areas are likely to benefit from increasing returns which in turn will allow them to expand their technological and production capabilities.

v) Interactions within the innovation system

The propensity of the different institutions to coordinate their activities and to interact with other actors differ widely across countries. Governments do interact heavily with large domestic firms (the so-called "national champions"). Fransman (1995) describes the working of the Japanese Ministry for International Trade and Industry (MITI), one of the most cited successful institution for the promotion of innovation in industry. In other countries, small firms have been keen to share their expertise and cooperate in developing a common competitive strategy, as demonstrated by the Italian industrial districts.[6] Such interactions are often able to multiply the effects of innovation undertaken at the country level and increase its diffusion, or make innovation possible under conditions of strong uncertainty. Its absence can hamper substantially the economic effectiveness of resources devoted to S&T.

vi) Absorption from abroad

The operation of these various aspects of national systems of innovation need to be considered within the context of increasing international integration. In the postwar period, several countries have benefited from an international regime which has deliberately encouraged the international transmission of knowledge (Nelson and Wright, 1992). Some countries, especially in the Third World, have benefited from bilateral technology transfer. A general lesson drawn from recent research, however, confirms List's original insight that no technology transfer can be effective without an endogenous effort to acquire that knowledge; see Bell and Pavitt (1997), Freeman (1995), and Mowery and Oxley (1995).

4. Innovation, Competition, and Collaboration

There are large and significant differences in competitive strategy between innovating and non-innovating firms. One of the important ingredients for achieving competitive success appears to be to establish effective collaboration with others—customers, suppliers, higher education establishments and so on. Such collaboration allows firms to expand their range of expertise, develop specialist products, and achieve various other corporate objectives, and is one of the most important means of fostering innovation. Half of the innovating firms in a recent survey—by the UK Economic and Social Research Council's Centre for Business Research—had entered into collaborative partnerships, whereas only one in six of the non-innovating firms had entered into such arrangements (Cosh and Hughes, 1996, Figure 3.1).[7] Also, collaboration is particularly important for firms facing foreign competition; as the process of globalization continues apace such collaborative behavior may become more important as domestic firms face stiffer competition in both home and overseas markets.

The overall impact of increased innovation and collaboration is improvements in both output and employment growth rates—for individual businesses as well as for the economy as whole. In terms of employment, fast growth firms were almost twice as likely to have collaborated compared to firms with negative or no growth. Looking at the distribution of employment growth in firstly, innovating and non-innovating firms and secondly, collaborating and non-collaborating firms, we find innovating firms to be far less likely to have zero or negative employment growth than were non-innovating firms. Conversely, innovators were far more likely to have achieved fast growth in employment. A similar picture is found in the contrast between collaborators and non-collaborators—superior employment growth being shown by the collaborators. This superior performance of innovating firms and of collaborating firms is also apparent in terms of turnover growth and in terms of the growth of profit margins.

5. Conclusion

The fostering of collaborative structures may thus be an important element in creating a competitive and successful economy.[8] This opens up a very different policy agenda than that which was pursued in the UK during the Thatcher and Major Governments of the 1980s and 1990s. Instead of the "freeing up" of labor and product markets through policies of deregulation and casualization we need industrial, innovation, and macroeconomic policies which will develop new forms of corporate finance and create effective mechanisms of corporate governance; provide a modern productive infrastructure which private firms can utilize, in many cases in a cooperative fashion; ensure a macroeconomic regime conducive to the creation of new industrial capacity, including low interest rates and a competitive exchange rate; ensure the expansion of employment opportunities so that investment in education and training will translate into the increased output levels which in the long run will repay such investments; and promote productive cooperation and industrial innovation.

None of this is made any less relevant by the continued globalization of economic activities. If anything, the opposite is true. The more open trading and investment regime means that any loss of competitiveness risks a swifter and larger loss of market share, at home and abroad. The implications of globalization are therefore twofold. Firstly, the term "globalization" is often used both to describe the fact of increased openness—for example as measured by levels of trade—and also to describe the *form* that the world economy has adopted over the past decade or so. Globalization should not therefore be seen as some natural or technological phenomenon that cannot be challenged. It can take many forms and itself is the result of active policy intervention by multinational corporations, national governments and others. Industrial and trade policies can and should play a part in shaping more acceptable international economic arrangements. Secondly, given these arrangements—either the current ones or different—the importance of interventionist industrial and innovation policies to enhance economic performance and outcomes is as great, if not greater, than ever. This chapter has outlined the form that such intervention should take in an era of rapid technological advance where innovation may benefit from diversity.

Notes

1. See for example Kitson and Michie (1995) from which the following paragraphs draw.

2. See Buckley and Michie (1996) and some of the readings reproduced in that volume.

3. For further discussion, and references, see Michie and Prendergast (1997).

4. For further discussion—and evidence—of this see Kitson and Michie (1998) which also provides further references to the relevant literature.

5. For more detailed discussion of these points, and further references, see Archibugi and Michie (1997). The way in which the theory of NSI bares upon the new growth theory and the theory of strategic trade policy is discussed in Archibugi and Michie (1998).

6. See Antonelli and Marchionatti (1998).

7. For further evidence on these points, see Kitson and Michie (1998) which also provides additional information on the Centre for Business Research survey itself.

8. This is argued in Deakin and Michie (1997) which discusses a range of new empirical work.

References

Antonelli, C. and R. Marchionatti 1998. "Technological and Organizational Change in a Process of Industrial Rejuvenation: The Case of the Italian Cotton Textile Industry", *Cambridge Journal of*

Economics, Vol. 22, No. 1, January, 1—18.

Archibugi, D. and J. Michie 1997. "Technological Globalization and National Systems of Innovation: An Introduction". In D. Archibugi and J. Michie eds. *Technology, Globalization and Economic Performance*, Cambridge: Cambridge University Press.

————— 1998. "Trade, Growth, and Technical Change: What are the Issues?" In D. Archibugi and J. Michie eds. *Trade, Growth and Technical Change*, Cambridge: Cambridge University Press.

Baumol, W.J. 1982. "Contestable Markets: An Uprising in the Theory of Economic Structure", *American Economic Review*, 72: 1—15.

Bell, M. and K. Pavitt 1997. "Technological Accumulation and Industrial Growth: Contrasts between Developed and Developing Countries". In D. Archibugi and J. Michie eds. *Technology, Globalization and Economic Performance*, Cambridge: Cambridge University Press.

Buckley, P. and J. Michie 1996. "Introduction and Overview". In P. Buckley and J. Michie eds. *Firms, Organizations and Contracts: A Reader in Industrial Organization*, Oxford: Oxford University Press, 1—20.

Chang, H.-J. 1994. *The Political Economy of Industrial Policy*, Basingstoke: Macmillan.

Cosh, A. and A. Hughes 1996. *The Changing State of British Enterprise*, Cambridge: ESRC Centre for Business Research.

Deakin, S. and J. Michie 1997. "The Theory and Practice of Contracting". In S. Deakin and J. Michie eds. *Globalization and Economic Performance*, Cambridge: Cambridge University Press.

Freeman, C. 1995. "The 'National System of Innovation' in Historical Perspective", *Cambridge Journal of Economics*, Vol. 19, No. 1 (February), 5—24; reprinted in D. Archibugi and J. Michie eds. *Technology, Globalization and Economic Performance*, Cambridge: Cambridge University Press.

Hayek, F. A. 1944. *The Road to Serfdom*, London: George Routledge & Sons Ltd.

Kitson, M. and J. Michie 1995. "Conflict and Cooperation: The Political Economy of Trade and Trade Policy", *Review of International Political Economy* Vol. 2, No. 4 (Autumn), 632—657.

Kitson, M. and J. Michie 1998. "Markets, Competition, and Innovation". In J. Michie and J. Grieve Smith eds. *Globalization, Growth, and Governance*, Oxford: Oxford University Press.

List, F. 1841. *The National System of Political Economy*, English Translation London, Longmans & Co., 1885.

Lundvall, B.-Å. ed. 1992. *National Systems of Innovation*, London: Pinter Publishers.

Metcalfe, J. S. 1995. "Technology Systems and Technology Policy in an Evolutionary Framework", *Cambridge Journal of Economics*, Volume 19, No. 1 (February), 25—46; reprinted in D. Archibugi and J. Michie eds. *Technology, Globalization and Economic Performance*, Cambridge: Cambridge University Press.

Michie, J. 1996. "Creative Destruction or Regressive Stagnation?", *International Review of Applied Economics*, Volume 10, No. 1 (January), 121—126.

Michie, J. and J. Grieve Smith eds. 1995. *Managing the Global Economy*, Oxford: Oxford University Press.

Michie, J. and C. Pitelis 1998. "Demand and Supply-Side Approaches to Economic Policy". In J. Michie and A. Reati eds. *Employment, Technology, and Economic Needs—Theory, Evidence, and Public Policy*, Cheltenham: Edward Elgar.

Michie, J. and R. Prendergast 1997. "Innovation and Competitive Advantage". In J. Howells and J. Michie eds. *Technology, Innovation and Competitiveness*, Cheltenham: Edward Elgar.

Mowery, D. C. and J. E. Oxley 1995. "Inward Technology Transfer and Competitiveness: The Role of National Innovation Systems", *Cambridge Journal of Economics*, Volume 19, No. 1 (February), 67—94; reprinted in D. Archibugi and J. Michie eds. *Technology, Globalization and Economic Performance*, Cambridge: Cambridge University Press.

Mundell, R.A. 1961. "Flexible Exchange Rates and Employment Policy", *Canadian Journal of Economics*, Vol. 27, 509—17.

Nelson, R. 1993. *National Innovation Systems*, New York: Oxford University Press.

Nelson, R. and G. Wright 1992. "The Rise and Fall of American Technological Leadership: The Postwar Era in Historical Perspective", *Journal of Economic Literature*, Vol. 30, December.

Porter, M.E. 1994. "The Role of Location in Competition", *Journal of the Economics of Business*, Vol. 1, No.1 (February), 35—39.

Schor, J. 1992. "Introduction". In T. Banuri and J. Schor eds. *Financial Openness and National Autonomy*, Oxford: Clarendon Press.

Schumpeter, J. A. 1947. *Capitalism, Socialism and Democracy*, 2nd ed., London: George Allen and Unwin.

4 COMPREHENSIVE INDUSTRIAL POLICIES AND THE CONTEMPORARY COORDINATION NEXUS

Pascal Petit and Mark Setterfield

1. Introduction

Industrial policy (IP) and macroeconomic policy (MP) are typically characterised as being dichotomous. The short-term, aggregate, demand side focus that is attributed to MP is contrasted with the more local, supply side and long-term focus of IP. Furthermore, IPs have long been considered "junior partners" in this relationship, serving as minor complements to MP. Indeed, even the worth of IPs restricted to the selective promotion of specific activities and support for R&D has been hotly contested. During the "Golden Age" of capitalism—an era of state interventionism and, in particular, MP activism—such policies were frequently accused of being ineffective at best and, at worst, prone to picking losers rather than winners.[1]

This prevailing wisdom merits challenging in two ways. First, it creates a false dichotomy and promotes an attenuated conception of IP, all of which begs the question as to how IP should be defined in the first place. As Amable and Petit (1997) remark, this problem is rooted in the "market-failure" origins of the notion of IP in Anglo-Saxon cultures, which is immediately suggestive of a limited (by some "natural market order"), corrective, supply-side role for IP, in contrast with the more developmental conception of IP (common in continental Europe) which conceives IP as being creative/transformative and as being concerned with both supply and demand conditions. Whilst many of the objectives of IP are, indeed, ultimately long term, successful IP must, nevertheless, be capable of responding rapidly—i.e., over much shorter time horizons —to new challenges. Furthermore, successful IPs need to monitor the functioning of product markets and demand formation processes and are thus inevitably concerned with demand as well as supply side issues.[2] Finally, when processes connected with industrial organization and innovation are linked to growth, then the potential effects of IP are clearly aggregate rather than just local.

This suggests that we can adopt a macroeconomic perspective on the role of IPs if we consider all those policies capable of influencing, in a consistent and coordinated way, both the structure of production and of demand formation in order to improve the global performance of an economy over a medium or long term horizon. Let us define as Comprehensive Industrial Policy (CIP) those policies that aspire to such generality and coherence. Note that CIP can be conducted centrally or locally, and may concern either a few key industries and/or groups of households, or apply across the board to them all. In this chapter, we will argue that current conditions warrant CIPs, i.e., that the contemporary context in which economic actions and transactions take place necessitates such interventions. Our development of this hypothesis makes extensive use of appreciative theorizing, owing to the lack of any significant and lasting attempt to implement a CIP in the developed economies during the last few decades.

Implicit in the definition of CIP above is the fact that CIP excludes as MP all those policy measures that are macroeconomic in essence, such as changes in interest rates.[3] This point serves as more than mere clarification. It suggests that MPs are essentially akin to mass produced goods, applying across the board to all activities simultaneously, whereas CIPs are differentiated products which have to be thought out specifically in accordance with the context in which they will be applied. We shall argue in section 2 that the central importance of this distinction is that the way in which one can fruitfully intervene in the decisions of economic agents varies with the general context of economic activity, in what we think of as a "post-Lucasian" approach to economic policy. Hence the Lucas (1976) critique was not altogether wrong to suggest that Keynesian economic policy did not take sufficient account of the expectations of agents and how these are affected by policy interventions. But it is wrong to assume that agents are fully rational and perfectly informed. Rather, economic agents draw on historically determined channels of information and knowledge when formulating their actions, and these change over time. By taking serious account of the state of the structures which influence the information and knowledge that agents possess (and hence their subsequent decisions and actions)—or what we define below as the *coordination nexus*—we show that it is possible to elucidate the changes that have taken place in the relative importance of IP and MP in contemporary capitalist economies since WWII.

Section 3 succeeds this argument by illustrating the constraints imposed on IPs during the 1950s and 60s by the then-prevailing coordination nexus. Section 4 describes the factors that have created new opportunities for CIP interventions in what is identified as the new growth regime of the 1980s and 90s. Section 5 then discusses the form that these interventions might take and finally, section 6 offers some tentative conclusions.

2. Why Different Forms of Economic Policy Intervention Suit Different Historical Eras

When Shonfield (1965) coined the phrase "modern capitalism" in the 1960s, the characteristic of the rapid post war growth experienced by some western countries that he particularly sought to stress was the role of the state in monitoring economic activity. This state intervention typically took the form of standard macroeconomic policies, even though the period began with the creation of many new institutions designed to frame the context in which economic agents were to interact, within both firms and markets.

But despite the ubiquitous use and widespread success of MPs during the Golden Age, the structure of capitalist economies is not uniform and nor is it static. Firms differ from one country to another with regard to the kind of internal information structures on the basis of which they operate (Aoki, 1988), while markets themselves are structured by the forms in which information flows and by the nature of intermediation (Kirman, 1998). The effectiveness and accuracy of any policies designed to monitor or regulate market outcomes are thus *a priori* constrained by the form of these information structures.

The ubiquity and success of Golden Age MPs, then, did not occur in a vacuum. Rather, it so happened that during the Golden Age, countries benefited from information structures that were functionally suited to standard Keynesian macroeconomic policies. The Lucas critique would doubtless contest this claim, arguing, on the contrary, that the problems experienced during the 1970s arose precisely because standard Keynesian policies were *ill*-fitted to their context, having failed to account for agents "rational expectations". This critique should be and has been taken seriously. It is impossible to influence the decisions of agents if Walrasian markets predominate and if agents are fully informed and rational. Such was the perspective of those who argued that Keynesian policies were ineffective. However, the issues appear in a different light if one discards this neo-Walrasian vision and allows for uncertainty, imperfect information and bounded rationality on the part of agents and policy makers. From this perspective, the appropriate conclusion arising from the Lucas critique is not that policies are irrelevant, but that one should have a clear understanding of the structures conditioning the information and knowledge on which the decisions of agents are based before designing any specific policy intervention. Hence the effectiveness of Keynesian or any other policy interventions will depend, in part, on the information and knowledge infrastructure which prevails at the time of their implementation. This infrastructure determines the extent to which individuals involved in the innately social activities of consumption and production understand how the economy works, and thus what type of actions they should plan and undertake, and what kind of results can be expected. Producers, for instance, must have some sense of how markets work when they embark on production and/or investment projects, while consumers need to know what they can expect to buy and at what price, what forms of credit are available, in what order to rank their consumption projects, and so forth. In real-world economies, then, a variety of quantitative and qualitative, price and non-price factors contribute to the information and knowledge infrastructure that informs, for example, the investment and employment decisions made by firms, or the consumption activities of households. Concrete examples of these "signposts" for behavior that were actually operative during the Fordist era include: the frame of reference provided by the technological frontier for firms in lagging countries engaging in investment; and the perception of a hierarchy of commodities determining consumption patterns at various different levels of household income.[4]

Ultimately, the crisis of Keynesian economics prompted by the rational expectations critique does force us to reconsider the formation of expectations by agents and their role in the economy. But Keynes himself, of course, was ahead of his time on this subject and in light of what has been said above regarding the Lucas critique, it would appear that the challenge that presents itself is that of further developing his vision in which there are limits to knowledge, and in which importance attaches (in the determination of social outcomes) to the ways in which knowledge is acquired, what is "known", and hence the expectations that individuals form. But how are the conceptions of reality that advise agents' decision making structured, and how do they evolve over time? There are clearly difficulties associated with distinguishing the issues at hand here from the more general issue of the historically and geographically specific institutional context within which the workings of an economy are rooted. Moreover, the nexus formed by agents' conceptions of reality is clearly complex, comprising many interdependent levels corresponding to the various contexts in and levels of aggregation at which decisions are made. But despite its complexity, the fact that individual agents can come to share common visions of how the economy works suggests that this nexus plays a crucial role in the coordination of economic agents' behavior.

The issues raised above have, of course, been addressed before at various different levels of abstraction and by different disciplines within the social sciences. The sociologist Anthony Giddens, for instance, makes an extensive examination (in his Structuration Theory) of agents' partial rationalizations of their environment, how these evolve and how they are operationalized. Economists, however, have traditionally focused rather narrowly on the role of prices in conveying information and coordinating behavior. From a strict neoclassical perspective, prices constitute the core information required for the operation of a market economy. But it has become obvious that the price system cannot work without there being specific mechanisms that convey information about prices to agents; the auctioneer cannot be justified as a convenient abstraction, but must instead be understood as a real mechanism that requires careful explanation (Kirman, 1998). Furthermore, the price mechanism is not sufficient for the successful functioning of a market economy. As stressed by Richardson (1995), markets cannot be analyzed without reference to the nature of hierarchical, non-market organizations such as firms, or the information content of non-price conventions such as consumer loyalty.

More generally, the workings of an economy rely on a wide ranging fabric of institutions and as intimated above, the way in which this fabric relates to our notion of an information and knowledge infrastructure presents itself as a central issue. In effect, institutions are, in and of themselves, information structures. They are commonly conceived as sets of rules which are repeatedly and more or less deliberatively followed by agents, whether they act as constraints or as coordinating principles that facilitate and enlarge the scope for action on the part of agents.[5] Institutions can differ, however, especially with regards to their duration and the strictness with which they specify behavior. They are instrumental to the establishment and workings of organizations, be it the organization of production (firms) or of social activities; organizations are, in effect, predicated upon the fabric of institutions. Public policy can, of course, impact institutions, although usually policies tend to change institutions only marginally (in contrast with the more radical adjustments that occur at special historical junctures, the prime example being during the aftermath of WWII).

Ultimately, then, our notion of an information and knowledge infrastructure—or what we shall refer to hereafter as a *coordination nexus*—is designed to capture the set of conceptions of reality derived from the information structures of the economy that contribute to the formulation and operationalization of economic decisions—always in accordance with the margins for manœuvre determined by prevailing institutions—at particular points in time and space. This coordination nexus is multi-faceted, comprising a fabric of interrelated conceptualizations that advise behavior in various different contexts and at various different levels of aggregation. It can be thought of as an interface between individuals and organizations on one hand, and institutions (broadly conceived) on the other, and should be understood as being much more sensitive to the contemporary historical, socio-economic context than are institutions themselves. Furthermore, it is precisely at this intermediary level that ordinary public policies can be implemented and made to take effect by the various bodies involved in policy making.

We cannot pretend to offer a very much clearer *a priori* account of the precise conceptions of reality in which the decisions of agents acting in a given institutional context are rooted. In what follows, however, our claim is that we can elucidate key elements of the coordination nexus at specific historical junctures, and that importance attaches to examining the changes that occur, from one historical period to another, in the overall structure of this nexus. To be more concrete, our contention is that the coordination nexus has changed along with the general economic environment over the last few decades, and that an important distinction exists between the coordination nexus that functioned during the Golden Age and that required during the contemporary "post Fordist" period. This is the basis on which we will attempt to show that the current, new growth regime is more open to—indeed, in need of— specific types of coordinated (but differentiated) IP interventions than the previous regime, during which standard MPs alone sufficed to meet the requirements of macroeconomic regulation.

When assessing the significance of this transformation, much depends on how one analyses the growth process in the context of which any particular coordination nexus operates. We adopt a macro-institutionalist perspective, according to which the growth regime during the Golden Age differs from that of the contemporary period.[6] An important task for any growth schema is to capture the dynamics and transmission mechanisms of which economic policy can take advantage. Kaldor's model of cumulative causation offers clear insights in this regard, as it stresses how productivity gains are transformed into prices, profits and wages, how the various components of demand are then formed and how demand, in turn, acts to stimulate further productivity gains.

This general growth schema enables us to develop a consistent exposition of the characteristics of the different growth regimes that have characterized recent capitalist history. As such, it can help us to understand why the regime change observed during the last few decades requires us to rethink the nature of and scope for CIPs, and hence the balance between CIP and MP. Essentially, our argument is as follows. Following WWII, innovation, diffusion, competition in markets and the expansion of demand all conformed to specific patterns, with MP effective in monitoring the pace at which national economies expanded. However, this growth regime did not survive beyond the early 1970s and during the last 25 years, substantial changes have occurred, ushering in a new growth regime. Central to these changes have been three types of structural change: internationalization, the introduction of a new technological system and a change in the way that production is organized. This new growth regime has, in turn, transformed the conditions under which policy interventions must operate, so much so that it now seems that a new balance between CIP and MP may be appropriate. Hence the growing openness of national economies to international conditions coupled with changes in technology and organization seems to have reduced the room for manoeuvre of standard national MP whilst simultaneously creating new opportunities and a new necessity for various kinds of policies aimed at coordinating and monitoring economic activity at the local, national and international levels.

A central hypothesis of this chapter is that changes in the economic and political environment invite us to reappraise the status of CIP and in particular, its potential usefulness as a policy tool directed towards essentially macroeconomic objectives. It is important to emphasise that our perspective is not advised by the recent debate on demand versus supply side policies, but might instead be thought of as being informed by the traditional post war debate concerning the various kinds of Keynesian policies. We treat the potential for effective demand failures and the concomitant need for policies directed towards the management of demand as an intrinsic feature of capitalism.

In the sections that follow, we develop the view that the context provided by the new growth regime, in contrast to the context created by technology, the organization of production, the functioning of markets and demand dynamics under the previous regime, has created a new range of possibilities and a new need for active CIP.

A dynamic schema for assessing the characteristics of different growth regimes

As intimated above, in order to represent the essential properties of the different growth regimes with which we are concerned, we begin with a basic world view that is informed by Kaldor's cumulative growth schema (see, for example, Kaldor, 1970, 1972, 1985). A central feature of this Kaldorian vision is that we must take serious account of both supply and demand conditions, *and* the conditions necessary for the reconciliation of supply and demand at acceptable rates of growth and levels of unemployment. In other words, we cannot afford to focus solely on the conditions of supply assuming that there is some mechanism that will automatically reconcile the structure and level of demand to these supply conditions.

Kaldor's growth schema can be characterized as follows. First, productivity growth responds positively to output growth because the latter permits the realization of dynamic increasing returns.[7] Dynamic increasing returns accrue through a variety of channels, and may be either internal or external to the individual firm. Some of these channels involve investment in fixed capital which embodies technological progress, whilst others are intangible, involving the accumulation of knowledge about the production process through learning processes.[8] Together, these relationships constitute what may be referred to as the Productivity Regime.

Second, the growth of demand responds positively to productivity growth, as well as to autonomous influences such as changes in policy instruments. Productivity growth may affect demand growth through one, or both, of two channels. The first is the enhanced price competitiveness of one economy relative to another that results if productivity gains which lower unit costs of production are passed on the in form of lower final selling prices in an effort to increase market share. The second channel involves a relative improvement in non-price competitiveness. Productivity gains may fuel qualitative changes in what is sold, including product innovation, improvements in product quality, increased provision of after sales service, and so forth. Although it is not always emphasized in Kaldorian analyzes,[9] it is important to note that there is also a structure to the demand side and that the dynamics of demand growth may involve changes in the *composition* of demand. This draws our attention to factors such as the structure of product markets and the distribution of income in the course of growth. Together, the relationships described here constitute what may be referred to as the Demand Regime.

Finally, a basic tenet of Kaldorian growth analysis is that output growth is demand-led. Bearing this in mind, it is clear that what emerges is a two-way or joint interaction of the Demand and Productivity Regimes described above, giving rise to self-reinforcing fast or slow demand, output and productivity growth outcomes in the form of virtuous or vicious circles, respectively. There is, of course, no necessity that the realized rate of growth that emerges from this schema will be that required to push an economy towards full employment or maintain the economy's progress along a full employment growth path. This creates an obvious macroeconomic rationale for policy intervention.

It should be emphasized that the cumulative growth schema described above does not operate in a timeless, mechanical fashion. Rather, the Demand and Productivity Regimes described above may take on different precise forms during different periods or episodes of growth, which may either enhance or hinder the workings of the causal relationships they embody, with straightforward effects on growth outcomes. At this point, then, our vision borrows from the *Regulation Theory* the notion that capitalist growth and development occurs in the context of relatively enduring institutions which codify and help to normalize the otherwise rivalrous and un-coordinated relationships between the principle actors in the economy (capital, labor and the state). As mentioned earlier, these institutions help to spontaneously coordinate the ways in which economic agents process information and make decisions.

Economic policy of all kinds—including CIP and MP—together with what was defined earlier as the coordination nexus are, of course, important constituents of this matrix of institutions. What emerges from all this, then, is an *extended* Kaldorian growth schema in which cumulative processes are understood as being typical of capitalistic growth, but in which these cumulative processes are conditioned by the *structural forms* (including economic policy and the coordination nexus) characteristic of the institutional matrix within which growth is occurring.[10]

3. Economic Policies and the Coordination Nexus During the Golden Age

The extended Kaldorian growth schema outlined above is consistent with the idea that there are structurally distinct episodes, phases or *regimes* of growth in capitalist economies. Using this growth schema, we now turn our attention to the post-war period, distinguishing between an old and a new growth regime in the period since WWII.

The dominant characteristics of the old or "Fordist" growth regime are summarized in Table 4.1. Some of the standard organizational traits of production processes and demand formation during the period have been highlighted in order to illustrate the constituents of its coordination nexus. We carry out the same exercise for the new growth regime in section 4, though rather more tentatively, as the characteristics of this new regime are far from being commonly acknowledged.[11]

We have already suggested that a coordination nexus is a complex matrix of conceptions of reality which draws on various forms of organizations and channels through which information and knowledge are accumulated and processed, under the broad influence of a national institutional fabric. For the purposes of the following analysis, we shall draw attention to only some of the key "sign posts" that help to constitute a coordination nexus, and that guide the decisions of agents either in organizing production or in choosing their consumption patterns. The three basic components of the coordination nexus that we wish to highlight in order to analyze the determinants of economic growth are:

Table 4.1 Characteristics of the old growth regime

	Structural characteristics	**Specific decision criteria**
1. PRODUCTIVITY REGIME *(conditions on the dynamics of supply)*	- Technology: mechanization of transfer and trans-formation, decicated assembly line - Organization: hierarchical, Separation of knowledge from shop floor	- Imitation of organizational and technological choices of more developed competitors - Technology transfers occur as part of a chatch-up process
2. DEMAND REGIME *(conditions on the dynamics of demand)* Household	 - Mass markets for durable goods, - Hierarchy of incomes activating, with delays but little differentiation, similar patterns of consumption - Key infrastructure: housing, transport, energy	 - Importance of prices - Imitation effects based on patterns already established by more affluent consumers
External	- Trade specialization, limited globalization	- Price competition desisive

1) those "sign posts" that influence the decisions of firms in their choice of the organization of production (as this concerns the quality of workers and/or the nature of equipment);
2) those bearing on households' decisions regarding their consumption patterns; and finally,
3) those that govern export markets.

These three components are of direct concern to standard economic policies seeking to influence the levels of investment, consumption or exports respectively, in order to either reflate or slow down the pace of economic growth.   As mentioned above, Table 4.1 presents the structural characteristics of the old growth regime, drawing attention to the "sign-posts" or guidelines orienting the decisions of both firms and consumers. It thus depicts the context in which economic policies operated during this era. Meanwhile, Figure 4.1 positions the three key coordination mechanisms influencing the choices of organization and investment by firms, the choices of goods by consumers and finally, the nature of exports with respect to their impact on the Kaldorian growth schema outlined earlier.

Why this environment favored MPs and limited the role of IPs

Our essential point is that activist MPs designed to stabilize demand around a full employment growth path were sufficient to ensure compatibility between the demand and productivity regimes—and hence the realization of a virtuous circle—during the Golden Age. The explicit interest of public policy in demand management contributed to the creation of a fast growth/FE demand regime in straightforward way. This demand regime was, in turn, conducive to investment in fixed capital (either directly through monetary policy, or indirectly through the accelerator effects of expanding output) in an environment in which the realization of returns to scale demanded standardized investment in fixed capital, pushing lagging economies towards the technological frontier. This catch-up process, which involves movement towards a known and clearly identifiable technological frontier, was central to the workings of the Golden Age productivity regime (as was first realized by Cornwall (1977) and later by Abramovitz (1986)) and hence to the

Figure 4.1 Cumulative growth and coordination nexus

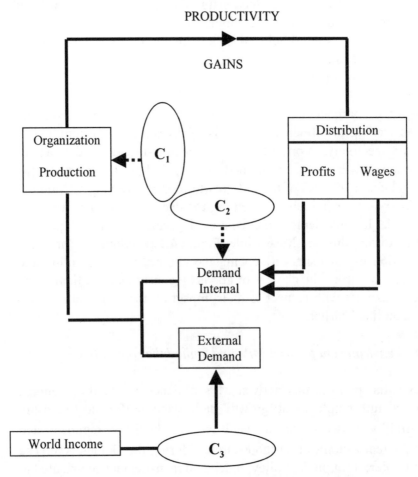

effectiveness of MPs, since the technology frontier gave a clear indication to all firms of the nature and type of investment necessary to realize technical progress, leaving only the aggregate volume of investment activity (which MP could successfully influence) unresolved. In sum, during the Golden Age, MP was successful in promoting exactly the level of investment activity—the nature/type of which was implicitly coordinated, independently of policy, by the information contained in the technology gap—necessary for a functional (high growth/FE) productivity regime.

A similar process of implicit coordination in consumption patterns meant that MP, combined with the demand side effects of investment, sufficed to ensure that the demand regime supported the productivity regime described above, simply by creating *enough* demand for potential output to become realized output. Hence the hierarchical patterns of consumption enshrined in the commodity hierarchy identified by Cornwall (1977) coordinated the nature and type of consumption demand, leaving only its volume unresolved. Households shared similar views about the "modern way of life", and for the vast majority, these views determined their consumption patterns. Only differences in income forestalled the convergence of each household towards the pattern of consumption mapped out by marginally more affluent consumers, as evidenced in the analysis of status seeking by the sociologist Vance Packard. Technological change and income growth during the Golden Age led to a more or less continuous upgrading of consumption baskets in a process of "keeping up with the Jones's" that nevertheless rendered the *structure* of consumer spending quite stable and hence predictable.[12]

The essential feature of the old growth regime, then, was that all agents knew *what* to do, even though they may not, at any given point in time, have had the means or incentives to engage in these activities to a *larger extent*. Policies thus needed to act only on the *levels* of activity, without having to frame and hence coordinate the *nature* or *type* of decisions that private agents were making. This channeling of agents' decisions was taken care of by the "sign posts" implicit in the technological frontier and the commodity hierarchy—although it was also influenced by the reorganization of institutions and public bodies that took place in the aftermath of WWII.

In this context, the role of IPs was very limited. In the first place, the structure of the public sector was very much a result of conflicts and debates during the 1930s and the immediate post war period. Thereafter, much of the debate about IPs was forced to take this structure as given, rather than being allowed to instigate a rethinking of the role and hence structure of the state. Moreover, the importance of and hence attitudes towards public enterprises differed greatly among countries for historical reasons, further complicating the debate. Only interventions responding to obvious market failure, such as the case of infant industries in promising new fields, were able to gain any legitimacy.

Furthermore, there was no particular *need* for IPs, as the "sign posts" implicit in a clearly perceptible technological frontier and commodity hierarchy contributed to the constitution of a coordination nexus within the old growth regime that was functional to fast growth and FE. As long as MPs were used to influence the *levels* of accumulation and consumption, the old growth regime met the requirements for macroeconomic regulation consistent with a virtuous circle without any further policy interventions.

4. Economic Policies and the Coordination Nexus in the New Growth Regime.

A generalized revival of interest in IPs

Given the association between the restricted, "market failure" vision of IP and the predominant culture within Anglo-Saxon economics mentioned earlier, it is perhaps ironic to find that there has been increased discussion of IP within the neoclassical mainstream in recent years. Although it may at first appear surprising, this apparent contradiction is easily explained. Mainstream interest in IP is chiefly associated with the flourishing literature on neoclassical endogenous growth (NEG) theory. Whereas the first generation of neoclassical growth theory (see, for example, Solow, 1956) emphasized the exogeneity of the growth rate in a model in which accumulation could only affect the *level* of per capita income, the essential characteristic of NEG theory is that it amends the Solovian production function so that accumulation—together with innovation—is now central to the determination of growth. Moreover, since neoclassical theory reduces the processes of accumulation and innovation to branches of the applied theory of resource allocation, anything which improves the allocation of resources and which, in the Solow model, would only impact the level of per capita income, can now be shown to affect the rate of growth (Fine, 1998). This includes, of course, IPs designed to solve intrinsically static market failures. Hence despite the restricted conception of IP common to mainstream economics, it is ultimately not surprising to find that even such renowned anti-interventionists as Lucas (1988) have drawn attention to the potential usefulness of IPs in the context of NEG models.

The NEG approach, then, has raised interest in IPs and has also begun to incorporate some features of the new growth regime, such as the importance for competitiveness of product variety and quality (see Grossman and Helpman, 1991; Ioannidis and Schreyer, 1997),[13] into its analysis. In this way, the development of NEG theory lends some support to the argument that we have entered a new era of growth, during which new kinds of policies akin to our notion of IPs (or even CIPs) may be required. Nevertheless, NEG theory retains a fundamentally limited vision of capitalist growth and development. First, it plays down (to the point of ignoring) the demand side, while it has a renewed crucial importance in the reshaping of the growth regime as it develops a new relationship with the dynamics of supply side. Say's law is well alive in NEG theory (Setterfield, 1999). Second, it has no systematic vision of the social and technical structural regimes that give rise to qualitatively and quantitatively different episodes of accumulation and growth in capitalist economies. Finally, its formal models fail to capture the inescapable complexity of the interventions they appear to sanction. This is probably why those associated with NEG theory and its collateral, "new" trade theory, frequently tend to renounce intervention altogether, despite what their models have to say about its ultimate desirability (see, for example, Krugman, 1987).[14] For these reasons, despite the recent rise to prominence of NEG theory in mainstream economics, we retain the extended Kaldorian conception of growth and development outlined earlier in order to effect our analysis of the nature of and scope for policy intervention in the new growth regime.

IPs in the new growth regime

The rationale for the development of new IPs—or, more specifically, CIPs—in the context of the new growth regime must be articulated at a variety of levels. The first and standard one is negative—the idea that MPs do not work any more, or at least that they have been subjected to new institutional constraints owing to the development of new international agreements and regional accords.[15] According to this view, standard policies are still part of the menu of policy interventions, but they are severely constrained, having become embedded within a new context determined not only by the integration of national economies in regional alliances and in international accords, but also by the new dynamics of innovation and the part played by information and knowledge in the working of contemporary economies. During the period of rapid growth in the 1950s and 60s in the now developed economies, states and governments were heavily involved in economic activities. As public sectors were enlarged and regulatory frameworks enriched, standard Keynesian macroeconomic policies, utilizing monetary and fiscal instruments, played a central role in the regulation of economic outcomes. The new context, which provides economic agents either more or less directly with an enhanced global reach, limits the power and scope of these policies, while favoring public sector deregulation and privatization. The sort of obstacles that constrain MP in the new growth regime include:

- international capital markets—which desire high interest rates and "sound" public finance
- greater openness and hence leakages due to enhanced propensities to import
- institutional constraints, for example, the EMU membership criteria.

These obstacles to national MPs have only served to reinforce pre-existing political preferences for non-interventionism.

Even under the conditions outlined above, it may be possible for MPs to re-emerge at a regional level (e.g. in the EU). However, neither the institutions nor political will necessary for this transition to occur are currently evident. In the first place, the funds available to regional bodies (such as the European Parliament) are small as compared with the size of the national budgets formerly devoted to MP interventions. Furthermore, these funds have traditionally been designated for forms of expenditure that we would consider to be constituent of CIPs rather than MPs.

However, regardless of the "negative" argument outlined above concerning the constraints on MP, CIP must become more prominent in the new growth regime owing to a change in the essential character of the productivity regime since the end of the Golden Age. This has altered the process by which dynamic increasing returns compatible with a virtuous circle of fast growth must now be realized. In short, productivity gains emanating from the catch-up based accumulation of fixed capital are now rather exhausted. As such, the old, simple, link running from MP to investment by sectors and to a productivity regime functional to fast growth has now been broken. The policy "support" required for a functional productivity regime is now more complex because the source of increasing returns has changed. It now involves (for most advanced countries) shifting the technological frontier rather than moving towards an externally determined frontier. This has enhanced the importance of establishing networks and realizing externalities in R&D relative to the process of investing in fixed capital which already embodies established states of technology closer to the technological frontier. It requires, to a new extent, collaboration among firms, be it on R&D projects or on plans to access and develop new markets, as well as new relationships between users and producers at all stages of production. (These and other pertinent features of the new growth regime are captured in Table 4.2).

The changes in the character of the growth regime described above imply that the coordination nexus which contributed to the regulation of the old growth regime is now likely obsolete. The "sign posts" generated by the technology gap and the commodity hierarchy are no longer relevant once the technological frontier itself has been approached and goods have become highly differentiated. Hence the emergence of a new growth regime requires a change in the coordination nexus. This is most clearly evident with regard to the monitoring of the productivity regime, wherein the "unexplained" productivity slowdown has highlighted the need for rethinking and reinvigorating the processes by which technical progress is achieved. Thus the support for a productivity regime conducive to a virtuous circle now requires support for networking, joint ventures in innovation, the internalization of local externalities and so forth. There is clearly a significant difference between this situation and the

Table 4.2 Characteristics of the new growth regime

	Structural characteristics	**Specific decision criteria**
1. PRODUCTIVITY REGIME (*conditions on the dynamics of supply*)	- Technology : ICTs , networks, no dedicated line, integrated automation - Organization: more autonomous, less hierarchic, less separation of knowledge inside firms - More segmentation of knowledge between firms - Importance of intangible Investments	- Technological choices according to contexts, reversibility valued - Accords, agreements, ooperation between firms - Development of user/ producer relationship at all stages - Technology transfers occur through service logistics, professional organizations, inter firm division of know how - No best practices, adjustment to context Major role of share holder governance in decision making
2. DEMAND REGIME (*conditions on the dynamics of demand*)		
Household	- Highly differentiated markets combined with low quality mass markets - Metropolization - Wealth effects linked to the development of financial portfolios - Key infrastructure : ICYs for large service networks change the nature of access to markets, financing consumption, getting information.	- Importance of differentiated products, quality, lasting relations, combined products. Diffusion of non price competitiveness criteria. - Know how required, new consumer groups - Importance of education and weak networks of personal relations (importance of local proximity) - New segmentation of social classes, according to education, localization, personal relationships - Influence of signals from the financial world
External	- Globalization of many markets, internationalization of all - Development of intra-industry trade and FDI	- Use of globally recognised trade marks and brand names

previous regime, in which boosting investment in fixed capital embodying known technical standards provided sufficient support for a virtuous circle.

It should be noted that, as indicated in Table 4.2, the need for a new coordination nexus and for CIPs do not stem only from changes in the nature of the productivity regime. Despite the supply-side orientation of the debate over the productivity paradox, it should be clear that changes in the demand regime have also contributed to the exhaustion of the Golden Age coordination nexus. The new importance of lasting and finely tuned user-producer relationships, together with the corresponding proliferation of differentiated products (and the resultant splitting of the mass markets into strata differentiated by income and education) has transformed the dynamics of consumption (see also Petit and Soete, 1997). This has eroded the efficacy of the coordination nexus in the Golden Age demand regime, which was largely based on a commodity hierarchy tied to an income hierarchy and an associated ranking of social classes. The problems of coordination facing the new growth regime thus concern both its demand and productivity regimes.

Obviously, then, the new growth regime has enhanced the importance of CIPs relative to that of MPs. Instead of acting purely on the *level* of activity in the productivity and demand regimes, policy is now required to monitor the *nature* or *type* of activity. The purpose of policy in the new regime is to clarify and legitimize signposts that will then guide individual decisions more or less automatically, and in ways that generate predictable advantages at the macro level. If they are successful in achieving this objective, of course, then CIPs will re-create conditions favorable to the regulation of the macroeconomy by means of traditional MPs. This does not mean that CIPs should necessarily be thought of as strictly transitional policies, however. Rather, the inherent dynamism of the coordination nexus suggests that the maintenance (including the periodic reconstruction) of adequate signposts designed to channel private accumulation and consumption behavior may have to remain an ongoing priority of policy.

The logic of the new growth regime thus demands that there be a new balance between CIPs and MPs. It is more necessary than ever, of course, that the productivity and demand regimes be made to work in tandem in order to generate fast growth and FE within the cumulative growth schema outlined earlier. But this synchronicity must now be achieved in new ways, since the key questions facing firms are now where to locate, which networks to join, what types of R&D to engage in etc., rather than simply how much fixed investment to undertake. Meanwhile, workers/consumers also face similarly new questions: where should they work; how should they combine work and leisure; how should they plan and organize their use of large network systems (such as education, health, banking, communication or transport)? In the remainder of this chapter, we attempt to discuss how CIPs can help to address these ubiquitous challenges.

5. Problems and Opportunities Confronting the Implementation of Contemporary CIPs

Essentially, the challenge that confronts contemporary CIPs is to create and legitimise signposts which coordinate private behavior in a manner that is consistent with fast growth and FE. As intimated above, if the new coordination nexus is a permanent one, then policy making will again benefit from the sort of momentum enjoyed by traditional MPs during the Golden Age. If, however, the coordination nexus continues to evolve, then CIPs will need to engage in continual monitoring of the nature of private behaviors and the extent to which they cohere. In the event, reality may even lie somewhere between these two extremes, characterized by a mixture of fields in which coordination continually needs to be restored and fields where changes need only be made once and for all.

In order to be successful in recreating an efficient coordination nexus, CIPs will need to operate at a variety of different levels of aggregation and in various different fields—and to some extent, this can be expected to pose problems for CIPs. To quote Storper (1996) who has a similar approach of the need for a new structure of coordination, "policy's task is to support the development of worlds of production" to which we would add the objective to coordinate the new worlds in the process of constituting a new growth regime. Policy makers are thus presented with a variety of opportunities to render a virtuous circle of fast growth and FE consistent with a number of other social objectives. The complexity of the coordination nexus that is necessary to revive growth can, in this way, be turned to the advantage of policy makers if its multifaceted nature can be successfully utilized to achieve a plurality of potentially complementary economic and social goals.

To better appreciate the challenges that lie ahead and in order to determine to what extent the precise content of CIPs can be expected to result from policy choices rather than from the "fundamentals" of the new growth regime (including characteristics of the new technological system, globalization, and the phase of tertiarization associated with the emergence of a so-called "knowledge economy"), it is important to consider precisely what kinds of signposts CIPs can successfully promote and to what purposes. In general, creating sign posts is equivalent to building a consensus on priorities and ensuring that information and knowledge on issues under view are widespread enough to facilitate some coalescence of private decisions (which are then rendered open to the more-or-less predictable influence of various stimulants, which can be of either a monetary (taxes, transfers, interest rates) or a non-monetary (advantages of nature, rents created by legal arrangements, positive externalities tied to some public investment) form. However, the answers to the questions posed above will necessarily differ according to the specific field considered—whether a signpost is intended to affect how agents invest, develop specific markets (either locally or abroad), consume, save, spend their leisure, or whatever. In what follows, we focus attention on four broad fields, attempting in each case to illustrate (without being exhaustive) how CIP interventions could and/or must be designed. The fields on which we focus are:

a) the development of local districts
b) the reorganization of national infrastructures
c) the monitoring of wholly internationalized markets
d) the promotion of international ethical goodwill issues.

a) Supporting local development

One of the main challenges that CIPs face is that they must inevitably work in an environment where local and international forces have already acquired a new importance *vis a vis* their national counterparts. It is obvious that the existence of global or multinational firms increasingly calls into question the meaning and relevance of many policies that have been traditionally implemented at the level of the nation state. In some cases, multinationals behave as better corporate "citizens" than do national firms—although in other cases it is apparent that they do not. It is difficult, if not impossible, however, for governments to create an analog to national boundaries that might serve as the basis for disciplining multinational capital. The current OECD guidelines with respect to FDI, for example, provide little more than a voluntary standard of good international behavior.

A major issue for the development of all policies (including CIPs) is, then, how they can be designed to cope with the "footlooseness" of large internationalized firms, which make an important contribution to the dynamics of domestic growth even if they are by no means the only constituent of these dynamics.

At the same time, CIPs face the challenge of confronting and (where possible) taking advantage of the new concerns and governance structures that have emerged at the local level. Changes in the productivity and demand regimes have opened new possibilities for policy interventions at the level of intra-national territories. This does not mean that all localities face equal opportunities for development, nor that this new economic geography will necessarily create more decentralization. (There is, on the contrary, a feeling that a process of further metropolization is under way.) Nevertheless, features of the new growth regime—such as cooperation, networking and producer/user relationships—have all contributed to the trend towards localization, despite the fact that new information and communication technologies have alleviated the need for geographical proximity.

Of particular importance in the local context is the infrastructure linked to the innovation system. It is this infrastructure that provides the major incentive for private investment in intangible resources, including human resources, and for private sector link-ups with public research institutes (which may result in the creation of specialized centers of excellence, training partnerships, technical information agencies, etc.). The actual location of a given firm's plant will thus depend heavily on local infrastructural factors—such as local skills, or physical infrastructure and access to knowledge, for example. At the same time, the firm itself will contribute to the long-term growth and availability of human resources, access to knowledge, local suppliers' know-how and producer networks. These often scarce and sometimes geographically "fixed" factors are vital to the cumulative, increasing returns based dynamics of long term growth and development in the new growth regime, and may ultimately lead to a local interactive learning cluster or to the establishment, in a particular product or market niche, of a so-called global "competence center".

In this way, geographically mobile multinational firms can be understood to both take advantage and contribute to the emergence of local infrastructural advantages. This exploitation of and contribution to local advantages by multinationals creates a number of important challenges for policy makers. Foremost among these is the fact that in the new growth regime, CIPs are confronted with the familiar choice between seeking to promote one or two large metropoles, or developing a plurality of more regional centers, the latter promising more balanced national development while at the same time confronting more limited prospects for generating positive externalities and international competitiveness. Because metropolization creates many negative environmental and civic externalities, CIPs should favor regional development and the signposts that they endeavour to create in order to channel the behavior of local decision makers and multinational firms might profitably be designed to reflect this objective. The first caveat in this recommendation, however, is that the suggested regional bias should not hamper the coherent development of metropoles. A second caveat is that CIPs be able to select and monitor the regional centers in which development takes place. This is important because the revival of local development policies might otherwise result in rivalries emerging between local centers with regard to the services they offer to incoming firms.[16] The result of this, as is evident from European experience, is likely to be the establishment of multiple new growth sites, science parks or technopoli, none of which reach the size necessary to foster the externalities and increasing returns growth features capable of sustaining a virtuous circle.

CIPs must, therefore, strike a balance between local forces, the pressure of international forces and the trend favoring the development of large metropoles in time of increased uncertainty. At the same time, by helping to restore an adequate coordination nexus that can be shared by local authorities and governance bodies and the strategy makers of large multinational firms alike, they can and should seek to direct the behavior of these agents in a manner consistent with broad based regional development.

One thing that is evident from the foregoing discussion is that although CIPs need to simultaneously operate at different levels of aggregation (the local, national and international), there remains, in our view, a crucial role for national policy making in their implementation. In part, this stems from the unique role that national policy makers can play in coordinating local, national and international forces and hence the unique contribution that they can make to the reconstruction of a coordination nexus functional to fast growth and FE outcomes. It must be clear to local, national and international policy makers what the priorities in local development are, what sources of funding will be available, where policies should seek to improve tangible and intangible networks, and so forth. The EU structural funds and associated eligibility conditions provide one example of such signalling. Nation states, as long as they retain the power to distribute funds, can and should act even more clearly and decisively. To some extent, creating coordination at these different levels of aggregation is rather like developing a normalization procedure, as is done in the world of production. The workings of this coordination process also imply some informed bargaining between local and national or international policy makers. Clear norms would make a substantial contribution at this contractual phase.

b) Modernization policies for national infrastructures

As intimated earlier, the structural changes brought about by the transition from the old to the new growth regime have increased the need and scope for national industrial and structural policies aimed at reorganized and improving nation wide infrastructures such as transport, communication, banking , distribution but also education and health. Both the economic efficiency and competitiveness of a territory depend greatly on the quality and scope of the territory's infrastructure. If this infrastructure is well matched with the geographical, historical and cultural background of its location, then positive external effects are more likely to emerge. This, in turn, contributes to the creation of competitive advantage. The key elements of a territory's infrastructure are the education and training of its labour force and large network services (such as transport, communications, distribution and finance) —both of which are essential for the functioning of markets and the operation of production processes. Nevertheless, the questions remain as to which specific combinations of these factors increase positive externalities and at what level (local, national or regional) they should be organized?

The most appropriate response to these questions depends, to a large extent, on the specific component of the infrastructure that is under consideration. In some cases, such as telecommunications, the deregulation and the regional if not global harmonization of service provision is well advanced. In other cases, such as education and training, regulation occurs at the national level with more or less autonomy at the local level. Ultimately, nation states have a complex role to play. With regard to logistics, which are basically organized under international regulations, they may help to develop schemes "downstream", facilitating specific uses of logistics aimed at particular groups of people or particular local regions. As for components of the infrastructure that are strongly influenced by local needs, national policy makers need to avoid promoting a too stringent specialization and create, instead, schemes that embody flexibility and allow for adjustment to local conditions—particularly in the cases of education, mobility and retraining. In all of these cases, the challenge with which policy makers are presented is that the sign posts of a successful coordination nexus need to be harmonized at a wider regional level and simultaneously fitted to meet local needs.

To achieve such matching requires a comprehensive customization of the services under view as well as some adequate interconnections of national networks .

c) Acting at the heart of international regimes

Given its multi-faceted, socio-economic nature, it is evident that CIPs can—indeed, we would argue, must—attend not only to the traditional conditions of economic development in specific territories, but seek also to address the general environment in which social and economic activities occur in their efforts to reconstruct and manipulate the coordination nexus. Two kinds of structural issues that concern local development and local life but which are clearly determined at a global level are of particular importance in this regard: classic environmental issues; and the issues raised by various rent-oriented product markets (a category of markets that we define more concretely below).

Some markets for natural resources are now organized at a world level. The independence of these markets from nation states is captured by the notion of the "international regime", which is immediately suggestive of the relative autonomy of the structures and organizations of these regimes from nation states. The most commonly cited example of an international regime is the oil industry. Nation states use their political power to establish oil rights and the prices of oil exploitation and distribution. The hierarchy of nation states, coupled with the more or less hegemonic power exercised by the United States during the twentieth century, has contributed to the unique development of this global market.

But apart from natural resources, other internationalized products —including finance and intellectual property—have led to the creation of large rents. In both financial and intellectual property markets, ownership rights and conventions are responsible for establishing the value of what is sold; each of these markets is properly classified as rent-oriented.

Financial markets provide another example of an international regime, although the role of the nation state in this regime differs markedly from its role in the oil industry, not least because much financial activity remains in a few historical markets. Nation states are the only actors likely to prevent the financial system from taking on too much risk and ultimately collapsing. Their involvement remains crucial, as is made apparent by their willingness to bail out bankruptcies, without which actions a profound lack of confidence would quickly bring to an end the expansion of the financial sector. The lasting importance of nation states in the governance structures of the banking system thus provides policy makers with some opportunity to adjust financial regulations to suit the operations of CIPs.

Intellectual property rights (IPR), which are crucial in determining competitiveness, condition the existence and duration of nearly all of the rents that accrue to innovation. They are thus pivotal to the dynamics of non-price competitiveness, which is, in turn, central to the new growth regime. The fact that the most successful firms of the last few decades (such as Microsoft) produce and sell intangibles vividly illustrates the strategic importance of IPR. The widespread and hierarchical international organization of production processes in key high technology industries (such as electronics or pharmaceuticals) is largely based on the nexus of national and international laws, private inter-firm agreements and public cooperation, which together constitute the regime of intellectual property rights. The ability to coordinate the design of CIPs with the regime of IPR is likely a key factor determining their effectiveness.

What both of these examples (financial markets and IPRs) illustrate is that private behaviors are already coordinated to some extent within international regimes, and that nation states play a role in the configuration of these regimes. Hence in seeking to reconstruct a coordination nexus functional to fast growth and FE outcomes, nation states must surely take into account the forms of coordination that already exist within international regimes. At the same time, however, the influence that nation states have over these regimes suggests that the design of CIPs need not and should not be subservient to the current structure of international regimes. Of course, the prospects for consistency between the objectives and workings of international regimes and CIPs will be enhanced from the very beginning if CIPs are implemented or at least coordinated at the level of international regions such as the European Union. However, the disconnected nature of international regimes, each of which is concerned with a different activity, limits the degree of coordination between regimes—a problem that would confront even a supra-national policy maker such as the EU. Meanwhile Europe, where the regional process is well engaged, has no common energy policy and is more a follower than a leader with regard to IPR or global financial issues. These problems obviously complicate the task of coordinating CIPs with international regimes, even when the former are organized at the level of the supra-national region. Nevertheless, there would seem to be reason to believe that the embracing of CIPs by international regions is likely to be a prerequisite for the former to be truly effective.

d) Intervening in basic issues of science and ecology

There are two important and interrelated fields in which CIPs designed to direct and coordinate private behavior could be applied as part of the already necessary policy interventions of nation states. One of these fields is science and technology, the other is the field of environmental problems. Once the complexity of science and technology is taken into account in all its dimensions, the advantages of international interaction, networking and the coordination of government sponsored basic and long term research (as is taking place in a *de facto* fashion in the private sector with respect to privately funded research), appear obvious. When the challenge of environmental problems is involved, the need for cooperation on matters of basic science becomes imperative. These structural issues create problems for policy makers, but at the same time create opportunities for the signposts that they seek to construct and legitimize to be rendered consistent with broader social objectives in the context of a fast growth/FE regime. Our contention is that, suitably conceived, CIPs may provide an appropriate vehicle for coordinating the policy interventions of nation states in the crucial and interdependent fields of basic science and environmental issues. In turn, these interventions may contribute to the coordination nexus that we have identified as a prerequisite for fast growth and FE, whilst at the same time broadening the impact of this coordination nexus to ensure that these growth outcomes are environmentally sustainable.

The advantages of international cooperation in science and technology are most obvious in the case of so-called "big science" research efforts, where no single country, nor even a triadic bloc, can provide the full variety of scientific disciplines, approaches and methodologies that are required to undertake such research, much less afford the rapidly increasing equipment and material costs associated with it. This global responsibility is even more striking once the global demand side and the truly global environmental problems with which the world is confronted are introduced into the analysis (not to mention the related problems of famine, disease, desertification, energy consumption, and so forth). Environmentally sustainable development requires a wide range of complementary policies, if only to support investment in the new environmentally-friendly technologies that such development requires.

No existing international institution can face the challenge of science, demand and environmental problems of the magnitude that we are alluding to. Most of these bodies have been created with a precise mandate and, paradoxically, both their room for manoeuvre and autonomy seem to have been eroded as the globalization process has gathered pace. Nation states can, however, coordinate their actions in such a way as to establish the institutional bodies necessary to address problems on this scale. But even as the multinational character of these problems and their solutions suggests an important role for new supra-national organizations, so, at the same time, the localized nature of many of the sources of, for example, pollution, together with differences in the institutions and solutions that have been developed in order to address problems of this nature, suggests that any successful policies will require extensive involvement on the part of international, national *and* local actors. Developing such cooperation and coordination is, of course, no easy task. However, the necessity for nation states to intervene does at least provide us with an opportunity to begin thinking about the contribution that CIPs might make to this intervention—thus creating the possibility for the operation of CIPs on a grand new scale. Entertaining this possibility seems only reasonable, given the nature of the coordination issues central to the big science and environmental issues identified above and their relationship to the prospects for successful (sustainable) development on the one hand, and the central concern of CIPs with the reconstruction of a coordination nexus adequate for supporting faster growth and improved employment outcomes on the other.

6. Conclusion

This chapter has argued that private behaviors in a market-based economy are coordinated by an information and knowledge infrastructure or coordination nexus, derived from the information structures (including markets, organizations such as firms, and the broader institutional context within which activity takes place) of the economy. Furthermore, it has been argued that since WWII, capitalist economies have undergone a transition from an old to a new growth regime, and that the coordination nexus implicit in the former—based in particular on the signposts provided to producers by the technological frontier, and to consumers by the commodity hierarchy—has now been exhausted. As such, whilst traditional macroeconomic policies acting on the *level* of investment and consumption behavior—the *nature* of which was already coordinated by the signposts mentioned above—sufficed to maintain fast growth and FE outcomes during the Golden Age, they no longer do. Instead, policy makers must seek a new balance between MPs and what we have defined as comprehensive industrial policies (CIPs) if a virtuous circle of growth is to be restored. This is because the exhaustion of the Golden Age coordination nexus in the context of the new growth regime means that policy makers must now pay explicit attention to creating signposts to channel or guide the very nature of private investment and consumption behaviors, rather than seeking only to act on the levels of these behaviors. It is possible that this need for CIP activism represents a transitional phase and that once an adequate coordination nexus is restored, policy making can and should revert to the manipulation of traditional MP tools. If, however, the coordination nexus continues to evolve, the need for CIP interventions is likely to be more enduring.

We have also argued that if they are to be successful in this endeavour, CIPs must seek to function at a variety of different levels of aggregation and in various different fields. Whilst this undoubtedly presents challenges to the successful design and implementation of CIPs, it also presents policy makers with a variety of opportunities to manipulate the precise form of the coordination nexus in order to render a virtuous circle of fast growth and FE consistent with more broadly based social objectives. Whether or not all of this can be achieved in practice does, of course, remain to be seen. Of one thing, however, there can surely be no doubt: the stage is now set, in both the national and international arenas, for new debates about the possibilities for CIPs which address the coordination of activities at the international, national and local levels in such a way as to render tangible growth and employment benefits in a manner consistent with a variety of other socio-economic policy objectives.

Notes

1. This is borne out by, for example, the post-war history of IP in France.

2. The notion that MP is concerned wholly with short-term, demand side issues is, of course, equally inappropriate. Even short-term, policy-induced changes in demand can affect the supply side and shape the long term path of an economy. See, for example, Setterfield (1999).

3. Admittedly, this distinction between CIP and MP remains imperfect, as illustrated by the borderline policy of subsidies across the board to all activities.

4. These examples are discussed in more detail in section 3 below.

5. See Hodgson (1988, 1998) for a fuller discussion of the different conceptions of the notion of institutions.

6. The *Regulation Theory* develops such a perspective by providing an extensive assessment of the institutional forms on which each growth regime is based (see Petit, 1999). In this chapter, we appeal to a more limited conception of institutions, which emphasizes only those institutions necessary to for us to assess the general context of economic policy making.

7. This relationship is known as the Verdoorn Law.

8. See Boyer and Petit (1991) and Setterfield (1997) for more detailed discussion of the channels through which increasing returns accrue. As will become clear below, the precise sources of increasing returns during different episodes of growth—and in particular, whether increasing returns are more or less

involving the accumulation of fixed capital or from intangible learning effects—is central to our argument about the new balance between CIP and MP in the new growth regime.

9. See Cornwall (1977) for an obvious exception.

10. Cumulative growth outcomes may, in turn, affect these structural forms, of course, so that is ultimately appropriate to think of their being a joint interaction between growth outcomes and the institutional context within which growth is occurring.

11. Indeed, our very distinction between old and new growth regimes since WWII is, as yet, tentative, because it is questionable as to whether the structural forms of the new regime and its macroeconomic outcomes are, as yet, fully apparent. Hence we may be observing an established, slow growth regime, a regime that has yet to gather its full momentum, or merely a long drawn out process of transition between regimes. See Houston 1992 on the difficulty of identifying contemporary regime changes.

12. One can only now reflect that this process was bound to change once saturation in terms of quantities, brought about by mass production, led to greater weight being attached to qualitative differences between goods in the determination of consumption decisions. The implications of this development are taken up in section 4 below.

13. For empirical discussions of the importance of non-price competitiveness in the contemporary era, see Amable and Verspagen (1995), and Fagerberg(1996).

14. We return to the themes of the complexity of intervention and of appropriate attitudes towards this complexity below.

15. As a matter of fact, developing the case for CIPs has much to do with the question of how to deal with internationalization, and not just because of the prominence of the latter in the negative case for CIPs that is under discussion here. This will become more apparent in what follows.

16. The desire of local authorities to attract "high tech" learning centers is not the only factor that motivates local development. Individual citizens increasingly identify local conditions—such as the quality of the environment and education, or the availability of social and cultural services—as the essential features for personal welfare and quality of life. Hence there has been growing political

personal welfare and quality of life. Hence there has been growing political pressure to decentralize policy responsibilities, including financial responsibilities, in order to give more power to local communities (regions, cities, etc.) and thus enable differentiation in the provision of public services according to local needs.

References.

Abramovitz, M. 1986. "Catching-up, Forging Ahead and Falling Behind", *Journal of Economic History*, 46, 385—406.

Amable B. and B. Verspagen 1995. "The Rôle of Technology in Market Share Dynamics", *Applied Economics*, 27, 197—204.

Amable, B. and P. Petit 1997. "New Scale and Scope for Industrial Policies in the 1990s". In *The Relevance of Keynesian Economic Policies Today*, P. Arestis and M. Sawyer eds., London: Macmillan.

Aoki, M. 1988. *Information, Incentives and Bargaining in the Japanese Economy*, Cambridge: Cambridge University Press.

Boyer, R. and P. Petit 1991. "Kaldor's Growth Theories: Past, Present and Prospects for the Future". In *Nicholas Kaldor and Mainstream Economics: Confrontation or Convergence?*, E.J. Nell and W. Semmler eds., London: Macmillan.

Boyer, R. and D. Drache eds.1996. *States against Markets. The Limits of Globalization.* London: Routledge.

Cornwall, J. 1977. *Modern Capitalism: Its Growth and Transformation.* London: Martin Robertson.

Fagerberg J. 1996. "Technology and Competitiveness", *Oxford Review of Economic Policy*, Vol. 12, No.3.

Fine, B. 1998. "Endogenous Growth Theory: a Critical Assessment". *SOAS Working Paper* in Economics #80.

Grossman, G. and E. Helpman 1991. *Innovation and Growth in the Global Economy,* The MIT Press.

Ioannidis E. and P. Schreyer 1997. "Déterminants Technologiques et Non-technologiques de l'Accroissement des Parts de Marchés à l'Exportation" , *Revue Economique de l'OCDE*, No. 28,1.

Hodgson G.M. 1988. *Economics and Institutions: a Manifesto for a Modern Institutional Economics,* Cambridge:Polity Press.

———— 1998. "The Approach of Institutional Economics", *Journal of Economic Literature,* March, Vol. XXXVI, No.1.

Houston, D. 1992. "Is There a New Social Structure of Accumulation?", *Review of Radical Political Economics,* 24, 60—67.

Kaldor, N. 1970. "The Case for Regional Policies", *Scottish Journal of Political Economy,* 17, 337—348.

———— 1972. "The Irrelevance of Equilibrium Economics", *Economic Journal,* 82, 1237—1255.

———— 1985. *Economics Without Equilibrium.* Cardiff University College Cardiff Press.

Kirman, A. 1998."Information et Prix". In l'*Économie de l'Information: les Enseignements des Théories Économiques,* P. Petit ed., Paris: La Découverte.

Krugman, P. 1987. "Is Free Trade Passe?", *Journal of Economic Perspectives,*Vol.1, No. 2, Fall, 131—134.

Lucas, R. 1976. "Econometric Policy Evaluation: a Critique". In *The Phillips Curve and the Labour Market,* K. Brunner and A.H. Meltzer eds., Amsterdam: North Holland.

———— 1988. "On the Mechanics of Economic Development", *Journal of Monetary Economics,* 22, 3—42.

Petit, P. 1999. "Structural Forms and Post Fordist Growth Regimes", *Review of Social Economy,* forthcoming.

Petit, P. and L. Soete 1997. "Is a Biased Technological Change Fueling Dualism?" , CEPREMAP, mimeo.

Richardson, G.B. 1995. "The Theory of the Market Economy", *Revue Economique,* 6, November.

Sawyer, M. 1992. "Reflections on the Nature and Role of Industrial Policy", *Metroeconomica,* 43, 51—73.

Schonfield, A. 1965. *Modern Capitalism: The Changing Balance of Public and Private Power.* Oxford: Oxford University Press.

Setterfield, M.A. 1997. *Rapid Growth and Reative Decline: Modeling macroeconomic Systems with Hysteresis.* London: Macmillan.

————— 1999. "Macrodynamics". In *A New Guide to Post Keynesian Economics*, S. Pressman and R. Holt eds., London: Routledge, forthcoming

Solow, R.(1956. "A Contribution to the Theory of Economic Growth", *Quarterly Journal of Economics*, 70, 65—94.

Storper M. 1996. "Institutions in the Knowledge-based Economy". In OECD *Employment and Growth in the Knowledged-based Economy*, Paris.

5 A SIMPLE THEORY OF COOPERATIVE INDUSTRIAL POLICY. MODEL BUILDING AND PRACTICAL EXPERIENCE

Wolfram Elsner

Introduction

(1) Economic structural change is frequently connected with high social costs. These costs are incurred through production capacities, qualifications, key technologies and system capabilities becoming redundant in specific regions. At the same time, such capacities and capabilities are set up very often by the same enterprises in other regions in a more up-to-date form, or with a slightly changed orientation.

While such processes are (or initially seem to be) efficient from a corporate point of view, they are, due to the social costs mentioned, highly inefficient for the economy as a whole, and in particular for the region concerned. As a consequence, regions in particular are interested in preserving and further developing such potential that is vulnerable but worth keeping. The region is thus a unit that is primarily affected, a stakeholder and a potential actor.

(2) How then can structural change be managed in such a manner as to reduce the social costs involved, especially when there is an acceleration of structural change everywhere (and the accompanying increase of social costs) and at the same time a (at least relative to the problems) decline of the ability (or willingness) to implement proactive structural policies. The active management of structural change is considered here as a counter-part to passively allowing the degrading of regions.

Admittedly, there is a trade-off between avoiding social costs and the speed of structural change (in the sense of an improvement of efficiency). In other words, the problem is an optimisation between competing targets and not that of a naive maximisation of one particular target.

(3) Managing the process of structural change for the purpose of preserving and further developing existing regional potential usually fails because obstacles or blockades, are encountered ubiquitously which have the effect of impeding action. Although individual (often even all) agents are willing to act, such obstacles have the effect that all agents taken together are incapable of action, or at least (relative to the problems involved) inadequately capable of action. Such obstacles often lead to widespread frustration and eventually to industrial policy abstinence and lethargy, or are used as an excuse for this.

(4) How then can structural change be managed so that high social costs (in the regions) are avoided, blockades are removed and a progressive structural change can be started which optimises the speed of the change against the social costs involved, improves (regional) socio-economic performance and contributes to the realisation of a maximum of social and economic interests?

An indication of the answer to this question that will be developed in this chapter is the following. This is essentially a question of the whole constellation of the various interests and agents, industrial policy instruments and institutional arrangements which enable specific cooperative processes to become effective. Concrete experience gained in the field of regional industrial policy as well as a theoretical model will be used to explain and illustrate this.

A Model of Cooperative Industrial Policy

Structural problems: An industrial policy view of market failure and public goods

(1) The logical origins of industrial policy can be traced back to the existence of systematic, permanent and unintended structural problems.

It is a well known fact that capitalistic market economies produce systematic, and in general unintended, specific permanent situations which we call structural problems which in other words incur (too) high social costs. Theoretical models define this as market failure: It is generally accepted that market prices reflect mainly information representing past and present conditions, and the time horizon of private agents is generally too short (the time preference rate of individuals generally too high) in order to adequately produce certain goods. Moreover, private capital markets are often not in a position to raise the necessary funds for particular investments by themselves, usually because of the risk involved, in other words because of the relatively low return and/or the relatively long pay-back period. All this is particularly true for goods with high positive external effects (collective goods, public goods). Private agents acting on an individualistic basis also very often do not make decisions, or even make wrong ones, due to the large degree of uncertainty involved. Strong uncertainty, which exceeds a calculated risk, can result from too little information (which is of course not costless), or also from too much information which cannot be individually processed ("bounded rationality"). The decision situation is then too complex for the individual.

(2) The Prisoners' Dilemma (PD) is a well-known and simple, but nevertheless, very relevant model which shows that individual rationality can lead to inefficient results or to specific obstacles. It illustrates how easily markets can fail when the results for the agents involved are directly dependent on the decisions of other agents (strategic interdependence, external effects). In reality, this is probably more frequently the case for markets, industries, regions and the whole economy than mainstream economists generally tend to believe. The practical relevance of strategic interdependencies and benefit-

distribution dilemmas in everyday, mainly market-related, situations should certainly be investigated in more detail.

(3) The neoclassical individual dealt within this framework can be considered as the egoistic worst case of reality which doubtlessly socialises individuals in the direction of the neoclassical individual. Even on this theoretical basis the breakthrough of social solutions, i.e. the evolution of cooperative action, can be illustrated by repeated social interaction processes. Nevertheless, it is under discussion whether evolutionary game theory, referred to below, actually presupposes a hard core neoclassical agent. I claim these agents need not only be able to know their decision sets and to employ maximisation calculations but also be able to have a vision of an alternative path and to summon up the courage to take the first step towards a potential alternative path (i.e. to make cooperative offers).

(4) The pay-off matrix of the one-shot PD illustrates, as is well known, that the individualistic utility maximisation inevitably leads to a stable sub-optimal situation.

The PD problematic can also be interpreted as the problematic involved in the production of a collective good. Under normal circumstances, the dominant strategy for both actors is not to cooperate. The result is that the collective good will not be produced. The Pareto optimum, as the "best" (or, at least: better) situation for the economy in question, however still has to be provided with practical meaning (see below).[1]

(5) A general problem related to these considerations confronting the industrial policy maker is that in reality there is incomplete information about pay-off matrices, i.e. the spectrum of alternative decisions and their effects (benefits). It is (more or less) known what has been achieved under spontaneous market conditions, but there is no knowledge available about what has never been achieved (by the market). Other experience, theoretical knowledge and fantasy have to be used then to develop possible solutions. A collective good (the Pareto-superior, or "better" situation) that has never been produced, can, before it is actually produced collectively, only be produced theoretically as a solution and as a desired objective.

In other words: market failure as well as collective goods are not (only) objectively given facts, they have to be (also) socially identified and constructed in accordance with a structural vision. With respect to the direction and effects of the economic process, market failure does not inevitably lead to objectively "inefficient" results, but to "unsatisfactory" ones, i.e. results with (too) high social costs, or (too) few social benefits.

"Structural problems" are thus (also) defined on the basis of politically and socially defined objectives and valuations.[2] They are therefore not necessarily arbitrary because they can be clarified with the help of formal and empirical analyses, including analyses using theoretical models such as for example the analysis of individualistic decision paradoxes or collective goods theory.

We will not deal however, in the following, with the problem of political decision making processes which aim at defining public structural objectives. Instead, the (regional) state will be dealt with as an external actor.

Industrial policy objectives as merit goods—meritorisation and cooperative production of "structural goods"

(1) Against this background, industrial policy is to be understood as an attempt to produce that which (up to now) has not been (reasonably) realised in the market. Accordingly, industrial policy objectives are goods which—probably due to strategic interdependencies, related external effects, benefit distribution dilemmas and related blockades— are not (reasonably) produced via the market. This may be related to the desired, or required, quantity and/or quality, at the desired price, in the desired and/or required timespan, or with the desired and/or required reliability of supply. Furthermore society and politics have to define these goods as desirable goods. In other words, solutions have to be defined (by standards of quality, quantity, price, time and supply reliability) for such goods which are undefined by the market, i.e. "no man's land" in the "solution set". It is here that we enter the field of meritorics, i.e. of merit goods and "meritorisations".

(2) At this point, the analysis of the PD provides us with the knowledge that the individual is personally interested and thus can be systematically induced to contribute to the production of the collective

good or the "better" economic situation, i.e. to the results of the cooperative solution—and that the state by no means has to bear the full responsibility and costs for the production of these goods as implied by the traditional collective good analysis.

(3) This use of individual interests and the subsidiarity role of the state is also included in the concept of the merit good and the theory of meritorics which involves a specific interaction of private and public interests. Merit goods are goods which can be produced, in principle, by individuals in the market, in other words they are basically private goods. However, due to various reasons, they are not produced in sufficient quantity, quality, at the desired/required relative price, in a sufficiently short period of time and/or with adequate supply reliability.

(4) From a game theoretic point of view, the transition from the individualistically non-achievable collective good (in the one-shot PD mentioned above) to the good which can, in principle, be produced individualistically, i.e. to a private good (and later merit good), is described by transition from the one-shot PD to the supergame. As is well known, in the supergame it is possible to produce the collective good by means of cooperation. Thus, by means of the repetition of the game, the collective good becomes, in principle, a private good.

However, from a practical point of view, the time horizon and certainty in which the cooperation takes place in a society of (more or less) neoclassical individuals still remains open. Cooperation remains basically uncertain and flawed, due to a permanent tension within the strategic interdependencies, corresponding externalities and the distribution dilemma between the agents of an (relatively) individualistic society.

(5) It is exactly this decision situation which can be changed through state decisions (meritorisations) in such a manner that individuals now no longer unintentionally remain prisoners in a dilemma situation. Instead, socially superior economic solutions are then achieved faster and with adequate certainty. The state can for instance, as the industrial policy agent, help through positive sanctioning (bonification, subsidisation) of the cooperative action to produce the socially "better" solution by having the individual agents carry out the production of the

(merit) good within a shorter time horizon and/or with better supply reliability.

In this manner, industrial policy can, in principle, also become leaner and even to be quite profane—cheaper. It can open up the possibility, and create the necessary incentives, for private actors, to participate in the realisation of (meritorised) structural goods through their own economic activities—and of course to profit individually (especially in the longer term). Industrial policy can, in this way, provide an incentive, for instance for companies, to integrate a higher degree of rationality in their decision making process with respect to the co-production of collective, or merit goods which have been publicly defined as structural objectives. The cooperation required is obviously a possible alternative of the individual agent which can be considerably facilitated by industrial policy measures.

(6) In doing so, the state has by no means to eliminate the basic dilemma situation. This could, in turn, be a relatively expensive solution, i.e. high public subsidies from the state could be required and it would be, incidentally, a (also theoretically) trivial solution. It should be noted that a kind of competitive tension between the private agents in their cooperation field as well as competition between them in fields other than the defined areas of cooperation is by no means eliminated.

The conditions under which cooperation between individualistic agents can take place and be accelerated or ensured by the industrial policy actor will be discussed in the following.

Conditions of cooperation and industrial policy instruments to promote cooperation

Cooperation as an optimal strategy

(1) The PD can be illustrated for the simplest general case as in Figure 5.1,

Figure 5.1 Prisoners' dilemma (simple general case)

	S_{21}	S_{22}
S_{11}	a, a	d, b
S_{12}	b, d	c, c

where $b > a > c > d$ holds. As is well known, the dominant strategies (s_{12} and s_{22}) form an equilibrium which is sub-optimal.

(2) If the PD is repeated an infinite, or an indefinite, number of times, then this is called a supergame. Supergame cooperation leads to a higher pay-off (continuously a) than a possible one-shot maximum pay-off (b) when non-cooperation then leads to all actors (due to a penalty, or sanction, for previous exploitation) only receiving a lower pay-off for the remainder of the game $(c)^3$.

If all actors always cooperate (strategy C), they receive:

$$C = a + \delta \cdot a + ... + \delta^{t-1} \cdot a + \delta^t \cdot a + \delta^{t+1} \cdot a + \delta^{t+2} \cdot a + ...$$

$$C = a / (1 - \delta). \tag{1}$$

If one actor stops cooperating in a particular interaction round (here it is assumed in round $t + 1$), and all actors then behave non-cooperatively (strategy D = defect), then the actor that stops cooperating receives the following pay-off:

$$D = a + \delta \cdot a + ... + \delta^{t-1} \cdot a + \delta^t \cdot b + \delta^{t+1} \cdot c + \delta^{t+2} \cdot c + ...$$

Thus, for the particular actor concerned, it is not worth deviating from cooperation when the following condition is fulfilled:

$$C \geq D \Leftrightarrow C - D \geq 0,$$

i.e. when:

$$\delta \geq (b - a) / (b - c). \tag{2}$$

If equation (2) holds, the actors are rewarded with a higher (or, at least, not lower) pay-off for cooperation than for non-cooperation. It is defined by the necessary relationship between the pay-offs a, b, and c, and the discount rate δ.

(3) The foregoing used the ideal strategy of always cooperating, and illustrated under which general condition cooperation is worthwhile. It has also to be shown, however, which strategies are optimal in the supergame when they are dependent on the strategies of other actors. In this case, the actors have to decide for each round whether they are prepared to cooperate or not. In doing so, they are aware of the behavior of the other actors in previous interaction rounds. It can also be shown in such a case that a cooperative strategy is superior to a non-cooperative strategy.

In two competitions in the 1980s, that have since become famous, Axelrod invited participants to submit strategies for the repeated PD (cf. Axelrod (1984)). In both competitions, as is well known the relatively simple cooperative strategy of TIT FOR TAT won. In TIT FOR TAT the actor begins with the action "cooperate". He then chooses the action which his opponent selected in the previous round.

Axelrod erected the realistic environment that there are not only two agents interacting in a PD-situation, but rather a large number of actors who interact for a longer period of time. The possibility thus arises that cooperative and non-cooperative patterns of behavior are employed against each other in random combinations. In this way he has initiated an evolutionary process (wherein the strategies submitted form the initial "genes pool" which included cooperative strategies).

(4) If out of a particular population, a certain percentage p represents actors who play TIT FOR TAT and $(1 - p)$ play ALL D (always defect), then TIT FOR TAT (given, for instance, the pay-offs 1, 2, 3, 4 for d, c, a, b and a discount factor of $\delta = 0.9$ as a numerical example) results—according to equation (1)—in an average pay-off of $30p + 19(1 - p)$. The strategy would thus be worthwhile if: [4]

$$30p + 19(1 - p) \geq 20$$
$$p \geq 1/11.$$

If the proportion of cooperative agents in this population is greater than $1/11$, then (in our numerical example) the group of cooperative actors can receive a greater average pay-off than the group of non-cooperative actors.

This shows that even a small group of cooperative agents can hold its own in a large group of non-cooperative agents and, in view of the higher potential level of prosperity (i.e. higher pay-offs), even multiply. Cooperation is, therefore, worthwhile for individuals in lasting social interaction processes within larger populations where dilemma-prone structures exist—in other words under quite normal social conditions. Cooperation can, in the long term, gain acceptance in society even if it is only initially implemented by a minority of agents. From an evolutionary standpoint it can be assumed that a small group of individuals in search of suitable strategies implement a strategy of cooperation purely by chance (random mutation in the genes pool), and that it then spreads by differential growth of the cooperative actors due to their higher level of prosperity.

(5) Cooperation can, therefore, obviously emerge, or spread, in an evolutionary process as a social mode of behavior, in other words as an institution. An institution is a regularity in the behavior of agents in repetitive and strategic interdependent situations when it is generally known that everyone follows the rule, everyone expects that all others follow it and everyone prefers to follow it under the condition that the others also do this. If anyone deviates from the rule, then others are aware (or become aware) of this and as a consequence others will deviate, too (negative sanction). The benefit in the case of deviation is then smaller for all agents than the benefit related to the institution (cf. for example, Schotter (1981), p. 11). An institution, thus, is a social phenomenon which transfers information, expectations, norms, beliefs and a potential sanction mechanism (cf. for a general discussion see Neale (1994)).

TIT FOR TAT illustrates clearly that an institution of cooperation owes its stability to built-in sanctions based on the principle and specific mechanisms of reciprocity (cf. also Elsner (1987), (1989)). As in the PD there is an incentive to deviate in every single interaction, the institution has to stipulate the consequences of such a deviation. One such consequence can include the sanction imposed by other actors in the next interaction round.

(6) Up to now it has been assumed that a particular actor only employs the same strategy in all interaction rounds. It will now be argued that an individual actor can change his strategy. At the beginning of the repetitive interaction he may choose the non-cooperative behavior and after a period of time may change to a cooperative one. In other words: he learns. There are many ways in which agents can adapt their behavior. They are dependent on memory, the ability to recognise the behavioral patterns of others as well as the effects of one's adaptation to the actions of the others.

Learning can be defined as the ability of an actor to memorize the events involved in several previous interaction rounds. This enables the actors to adapt their behavior to the more or less complex behavior of their co-actors. It may even be assumed that the actors have no other knowledge about their opponents, but they can always remember their previous actions. After a few interaction rounds, they will have formed a hypothesis with respect to the behavior employed by the other actors, and will have adapted their own behavior accordingly (cf., for example, Bicchieri (1993)). The learning process can be modelled as more or less complex adaptive dynamics where actors experiment with various strategies. Evolutionary game theoretic models thus show not only that cooperation can be learned, but also how it is learned. In this way, we receive an analogy to the process of cultural evolution where the objects of selection and differential growth are the social institutions and not the agents as physical units.

(7) The type of learning will change depending on the size of the group. Cooperation can, as is well known, generally become established more easily in small groups. In large groups, on the other hand, the actions of the individual actor may remain largely unnoticed as was already suggested by traditional collective goods theory. As the influence of the individual is minimal, it may consequently be pointless to give signals, or to experiment and adapt oneself (cf. again Bicchieri (1993), and Chichilnisky (1995)). Also a moderate mobility level, or spatial social stability is a well known factor working in favor of cooperation.

(8) Against this background, the region is a predestinated unit for the emergence of cooperation and for its industrial policy promotion (cf.

section b below). The criteria of the group size or of mobility/stability refer to the basic factors of region, density, frequency of contacts, or probability of meeting a person again. These are the factors which play a crucial role also in the literature on new industrial spaces, regional networks, innovative milieus, or learning regions (cf., e.g., Benko and Dunford (1991), Pyke and Sengenberger (eds.) (1992), Grabher (ed.) (1993), Markusen (1996), Maillat and Lecoq (1996)).

In the following, we will discuss how we can interpret the factor probability to meet again (contact frequency, or density) and apply it in shaping industrial policy instruments and measures.

Industrial policy instruments for promoting cooperation

a) The significance of the future and the continuity of social interaction

(1) The discount factor in the formal modelling discussed above can, of course, be interpreted as the agent's relative weighing of the pay-off from a future interaction round. A different interpretation is that the discount factor describes the probability that the interaction will continue in the next round. If it is, therefore, probable that either a particular actor is encountered once again in the future, or if future pay-offs are important for an actor, then cooperative behavior is also probable.

(2) In order to influence the magnitude of the discount rate, in other words to increase the shadow of the future (Axelrod) (better perhaps: the light of the future), Axelrod has already pointed out the following: Interactions should be permanent and take place with high frequency, they can even be divided into many small partial situations. A permanent interaction means that the probability is high that the interaction will be continued. The actor then has to place a higher value on future pay-offs in his current calculation. If, however, cooperation is desired within a short period of time, or the deadline for the interaction has already been fixed, then it makes sense not only to meet once or a few times, but rather frequently within the short period of time. If namely an interaction is to be carried out in one single step, then there

is a greater incentive to deviate as no sanction can occur in the future. If the interaction is carried out in many small partial steps, then there is certainly an incentive in each partial step not to deviate because the future pay-off (which would be lower, due to a sanction) has also to be taken into consideration in each partial step. The total pay-off can even remain unaffected. However, in order not to raise transaction costs unnecessarily, industrial policy makers should strive to increase the number of interaction rounds by multiplying the areas of cooperation of the actors rather than artificially dividing a single project into as many partial steps as possible.

(3) Axelrod already mentioned typical situations in which such conditions occur: in the case of actors who only have a few partners on a regional level, or in the case of specialist enterprises with only a few business partners. For this reason, cooperation is more probable in such cases (see below).

Such cases offer industrial policy makers the chance to increase the probability of cooperation in the region by means of shaping the regional interaction conditions correspondingly.

b)   The change of the incentive structures

(1) Another possibility for promoting regional cooperation is to change the pay-offs. This is possible through the appropriate introduction of additional incentives by industrial policy actors.

Big changes to the pay-off structure can even change the social dilemma situation to such an extent that the PD is eliminated. If the advantage of cooperation, or vice-versa the sanction for non-cooperation, is great enough to make cooperation worthwhile even in a one-shot interaction, independent of the behavior employed by the other actors, then a dilemma no longer exists. In the case $a > b$, for instance, it is not worth deviating, if both actors cooperate.

If the pay-offs are changed further, then it can always be optimal to cooperate, independent of what the other actors do. Cooperation thus becomes the dominant pattern of behavior. In the general case, the pay-offs then have to fulfil the conditions $a > b$ and $d > c$. Here we see the trivial (and expensive) solution of the cooperation problem. It would imply high bonification payments to the private actors by the industrial policy actor.

(2) So what would be the minimum requirement of the pay-off structure in the repeated PD to enable cooperation to become generally acceptable? Equation (2) defines the range which the variables have to fulfil, in order for cooperation to become generally acceptable.

As a numerical example, it will be assumed again here that the quantities b, c, and d are given like above as 4, 2, and 1, respectively, and a is unknown. The discount factor is again $\delta = 0.9$. What is the minimum magnitude of a then, in order for cooperation to become generally worthwhile? From equation (2), the minimum magnitude of a can be determined as:

$$0.9 \geq (4 - a) / (4 - 2)$$

$$a \geq 2.2.$$

If a < 2.2, then a political increase of a to a minimum of 2.2 would lead to cooperation being able to assert itself in a long-term process. A relatively small political increase of the pay-offs can, therefore, result in a situation in which cooperation is generally worthwhile.

(3) This represents another starting point for cooperation promotion through industrial policy actors. In order to promote cooperation by means of changing the pay-offs, the specific tensions in the decision structure that characterise the social dilemma interaction, as has just been illustrated, need not be eliminated. In the example given, a needs not to take the values > 4, = 4, or even 3 in order to cooperation being promoted. Cooperation can already be made more certain by relatively lean industrial policy measures.

(4) Equation (2) also shows that public subsidies for cooperative behavior can be the smaller, the higher the private actors valuate their common future expressed by δ. Furthermore it is not at all the case that bonuses to change the pay-off structure must be quantitative/financial, while increasing the importance of the common future is seen as a qualitative instrument. As will be shown below, for a real case, changing the pay-off structure can also be carried out by "qualitative" measures.

Cooperation in a regional industrial policy setting

(1) As the (regional) state strives to obtain (egoistically motivated) contributions from the private actors to the production of merit goods (industrial policy objectives), it can define the guidelines for this in the framework of an industrial policy program.

An appropriate cooperation enables, for example, (regional) enterprises to carry out cooperative projects which help to accomplish certain meritorised (regional) structural goods, i.e. (regional) industrial policy objectives such as, for instance, an improvement of the sectoral structures (in the region), the establishment of commonly utilized specific supra-company infrastructures and service facilities, e.g. of pooled consultant services for (regional) company networks, or generally speaking, the cooperative improvement of any (regional) location factors of the actors involved.

(2) Cooperative industrial policy thus implies a specific combination of privatisation and socialisation which generally takes into account that, along with systematic market failures, forms of non-rational and ineffective political action exist, that is state failures, e.g. with a time horizon which only goes as far as the next election, or with a limited personal interest on the part of politicians and administrators, or also through the current subordination of the political-administrative system to the short time structures required by the economic system. The negative effects of the latter can be limited through the described co-ordination of the actions of private and industrial policy targets and actions. Beyond concepts of public-private partnership, which usually do not clearly specify the allocation of responsibilities and costs, the conception of Cooperative Industrial Policy (CIP) offers the possibility to integrate personal interests and responsibilities of the various participants within a defined framework and to combine the respective specific strengths of private and public participants. As a by-product, industrial policy can thus be transformed from relying heavily on subsidies to being basically leaner.

(3) One prerequisite for such a dual cooperative model of industrial policy (private-private and private-state) is, of course, an ability and willingness on the part of the state to use its power in conflicts with

powerful private actors who initially will oppose meritorised goods, corresponding objectives and proactive intervention by the state, especially because of reasons of principle or of "economic order" which are in fact reasons of power (cf. e.g. Baker (1996), Pratt (1997) for the case of regional networks). However, if a long-lasting experience of superior cooperation were organized, then there ought to emerge a willingness to accept professionally competent and democratically legitimate state meritorisations as well as private-private and private-state cooperations in the meaning described.

(4) In the wake of a long-lasting cooperation, also the personal interest of the individual will be reflected and will be further pursued more as a long-term personal interest. In the wake of increasing involvement on the part of individual participants in providing solutions to socio-economic problems, it is obvious that—in a process of cultural evolution, i.e. through the emergence of a cooperation culture—not only may individualistic dilemmas be eliminated, but also the initial, more or less neoclassical actors as such. Possibly the resulting behavior patterns then extend beyond the (more or less) methodological-individualistic framework of the initial situation.

In a longer process, the existing economically superior cooperation situation, which originally was merely a goal or vision, would become dominant and the earlier inferior situation characterised by blocking actions would gradually become irrelevant and disappear behind the veil of oblivion.

Cooperative Industrial Policy on the Regional Level

(1) The region is an adequate level for the implementation of this dual cooperative approach to industrial policy—not only as a unit affected by structural change, but also as a spatial cluster characterised by relatively frequent and long-lasting interactions which, as discussed above, enables a comparatively easier establishment of cooperation. The region is, thus, a unit in which an industrial policy actor can initiate and promote such structurally-relevant cooperation between interacting regional participants by means of creating appropriate incentive

structures and through the specification of future-oriented interaction conditions.

(2) The region is an economic location of enterprises which are inter-linked with respect to communication, cooperation and supply. With its location factors, it offers important conditions for the effects (the benefits) of strategic decisions to cooperate. The (regional structural) merit good to be achieved through cooperation can be seen in context with the preservation and further development of the (regional) economic potential. It is better achieved, as has been discussed, through the active management of structural change on the basis of CIP. For the region and the private economic actors (companies, employees and other stakeholders in the regional production processes) located there, including local public participants, this means in concrete terms active improvement of the location factors through well organized cooperation processes. This ought to be the contents of a cooperatively achieved "Pareto optimum" in lasting strategically interactive dilemma-prone situations such as exist also between the participants of a region in view of their specific common location conditions.

(3) "Region" also implies that a distinction has to be made with respect to the "state". When discussing regional merit goods, then initially the regional state is the suitable political actor and cooperation partner of the private participants or of local (i.e. sub-regional) public participants. It has to be noted that not only public, or merit, goods, but also the participant "state" represent step-like structured systems with complex connections, namely spatial spill-overs. The different steps represent different regional ranges of goods as well as the state and policy instruments. This is the subject of the economic theory of federalism. It is assumed here that there is a merit good which has no regional spill-overs so that the "region" under consideration—i.e. the regional state—is the appropriate industrial policy partner of the private, or the local public, participants (which implies—for reasons of simplification—absence of inter-regional spill-overs).

This consideration does not allow, however, simple extreme decentralisation concepts motivated by simple ("pure") competition theory. A regionalization is only effective when there is sufficient control and limitation of competition between regions in the interest of inter-regional harmonisation of living conditions and other inter- or supra-regional public goods.

(4) Against this background, concrete sectoral and regional structural problems as well as concrete CIP strategies aimed at influencing structural change in the German city-state of Bremen and the German state of North-Rhine Westphalia will be used as case studies: A CIP strategy implemented by the state of Bremen on the one hand and the strategy of regionalized regional policy by the state of North-Rhine Westfalia on the other hand.

The case studies generally refer to the extensive literature dealing with networked production and interaction structures in (New) Industrial Districts (referred to above). Numerous regional analyses (especially those of the Third Italy) have shown that collective decision structures help to overcome blockades on the regional level and improve regional developments and performances. A decision-based theory of CIP, or managed cooperative development, has, however, not yet been developed in this context. Such a theory will be tentatively applied here.

Cooperative Industrial Policy in the Region: the Example of the Bremen Conversion Program—a Practical Experience

(1) The city-state of Bremen is the federal state in Germany with the highest proportion of defense-based companies and, as a consequence, has been faced with an enormous new structural problem following the ending of the Cold War. The 1990s have thus been witness to not only a substantial quantitative but also qualitative threat to regional economic potential (highly qualified jobs in different fields of technology, system capabilities etc.).

(2) Independent of the industrial policy approach to preserve and restructure regional potential, conversion reflects a traditional discussion of sectoral (namely defense) relevance. From an industrial policy point of view, it involves the maintenance and further development of regional potential through the active management of the conversion of products, technologies, organizational structures and

markets. Conversion can thus (apart from the peace-related aspect) be considered as a specific (regional) industrial policy strategy and, as such, can certainly be inter-sectorally generalized (cf. Elsner (1995)).
(3) The Bremen Conversion Program (BCP) was written with this objective in mind and was provided with a CIP strategy. The BCP has been in effect since 1992 (for detailed discussion cf. Elsner (1993), and Elsner/Accordino (1999)).

The structural problem and the relevance of the Bremen conversion approach

The conversion situation in the state of Bremen and the Bremen approach to regional conversion management can be described by the following elements:

1. High regional dependency on the defense industry in both a quantitative (jobs, real net output) and qualitative (innovation potential, level of skills, system capabilities etc.) respect as well as a high threat to regional potential owing to the structural change caused by, at times, sudden decline in defense spending. At the initiation of the conversion process in Bremen in 1990, about 16% of the industrial workforce were either directly or indirectly involved in defense-related activities; at the same time, according to estimations, approximately half of the industrial research and development personnel in Bremen was concentrated in the defense industry. An EU study carried out in 1992 showed that Bremen ranked number three in the EU amongst regions most dependent on defense.
2. The regional embeddedness of some important defense contractors located with their headquarters in Bremen.
3. The compilation of a Bremen Disarmament and Conversion Report (1990/1991) and the BCP (1992) as a social process comprising company management, chambers of commerce and employers' associations which had, until then, not involved themselves in the conversion discussion.

4. The establishment of a specific regional consultant committee for the BCP. This committee has acted as a significant integrating force and has brought together the various chambers, employers' associations, unions, universities and representatives of the peace movement with the business world (management, workers' councils representatives).
5. Planning of company conversion lines in the form of medium-term company conversion plans required by the BCP and agreed on between managements and public administration representatives.
6. The establishment of periodic evaluation, together with a consulting company, (including public reporting) and the updating of the program as an explicit requirement of the BCP.
7. The appointment of a state official responsible for overall coordination of the program, projects, participants and committees.

The general background of a tradition of conversion discussion and conversion research and, consequently, a high political emphasis on the subject in the region.
The industrial policy approach of the Bremen conversion management is based on the fact that especially the high-tech defense industry, due to specific quality requirements placed on defense equipment or due to secrecy regulations, often exhibits a rather *low* regional involvement with suppliers and little cooperation with other regional enterprises. Very often highly specialised components and semi-finished products are required that can only be obtained from a few suppliers world-wide. Conversion is, therefore, interesting from the aspect that it opens up the branch to the region.

Moreover, the defense industry exhibits, in principle, the characteristics of a regional cluster, or development core as, for example, with systems as "ship" or "aircraft", it potentially consists not only of the final assemblers but also suppliers (system suppliers and sub-suppliers) and service providers.

Due to its characteristics, it presents the opportunity of becoming a core cluster of regional development (under circumstances of non-military production).
(3) Conversion is thus a strategy designed to preserve and further develop the regional potential, in other words to produce a "better"

situation for the economy of the region (as a regional structural merit good). In view of the shrinking market for defense-related products, this strategy also provides an enhanced opportunity for regional defense contractors to manage individual structural problems in a regional environment which has been improved through cooperation. It is in this respect that enterprises have a basic individual interest in a cooperative solution. This, in turn, is made possible through rewarding a behavior which, by means of a cooperative improvement of common location factors (including a sectoral structure improved by conversion/ diversification measures), helps to improve business efficiency and, at the same time, regional economic performance and reduce regional social costs. It will be shown now how this behavior could be encouraged.

Corporate aspects: Integration of industrial policy objectives in corporate planning

(1) Against the background of dilemma-prone strategic inter-dependencies of regional enterprises (in view of their regional environment) and the meritorisation of certain effects of cooperative behavior and measures in the framework of the BCP, the question arises how the behavior patterns of individual enterprises can be changed in favor of the (initially more difficult and seemingly unattractive) conversion option.

(2) In order to make sure that the companies' organisations take into account the regional conversion objective (as a regional diversification and, thus, structure improving), a new criterion for the promotion of industrial conversion measures was introduced, namely the submission of the mentioned medium-term company conversion plans. The longer-run and structural contexts of each individual company conversion project can be better assessed and secured within this framework. Furthermore, the state official responsible for conversion can, according to the BCP, consult industrial project groups, comprising also employee representatives, for consultation about the development of industrial conversion lines. These are institutional measures for safeguarding long-term in-company structural effects. In doing so, emphasis is also

placed on the integration of R&D, training, penetration of new markets and organizational development using the medium-term conversion plans as a basis. This also serves the purpose of safeguarding the structural impacts on the company level and ensuring that they are irreversible.

(3) Owing to the special uncertainties with regard to future market developments and short-term drastically changed market conditions of the defense procurement markets, it can be assumed that the behavioral patterns of the companies were, and perhaps still are, to such an extent under-determined, i.e. the expected benefits of individualistic strategies are so reduced, that companies indeed can be influenced by the offer of comparatively small incentives in the framework of reliable medium-term agreements. This might explain the relatively surprising fact that, in intensive rounds of discussions, companies have committed themselves to agreed medium-term planning of their strategic conversion lines (and thus to the consideration of the industrial policy objectives in the company planning). The budget for the BCP between 1992 and 2001 amounts to some 50 mill. marks, which is on the one hand relatively moderate, but it nevertheless represents a continuous, agreed upon flow of medium-term funding which can be counted on.

(4) Thus, along with a comparably limited change of the (financial) incentive structure, it has been apparently possible to improve the importance of the common future. In this way the companies came to contribute to the regional merit good by indirect and direct cooperation in favor of company conversion and of a joint improvement of specific infrastructural location factors supportive to the company as well as regional conversion.

In fact, competitors have—with the aid of gentle pressure from the public actor granting support—even begun to directly coordinate actions regarding company conversion projects.

While the merit structural good, to be produced by coordinated (directly or indirectly cooperative) conversion behavior, on the corporate level is the improvement of the regional sectoral structure, the improvement of the general economic conditions of the region through cooperative improvement of infrastructural location factors is the aspect of the structural merit good which is produced by inter- and supracorporate regional networking. This will be shown in the following.

Regional aspects: Cooperative improvement of specific location factors by means of networking

(1) Regional networking is to be implemented on a continual basis in order to safeguard the corporate conversion process, to enhance it and to integrate it in the regional economy.

Support and organisation of regional networking is carried out in the framework of the BCP by, for instance, granting priority to cooperation projects (also between defense contractors and non-military firms) as well as joint projects (between defense contractors and research institutes, including if possible also non-military enterprises).

(2) Regional networking is also supported with the help of new specific (so-called soft) infrastructures which, as a whole, improve the concrete location conditions of the private participants and the region. These projects are generally developed on a cooperative basis from the very beginning.

Included amongst these projects are, for example, the establishment of a transfer institute in conjunction with a demonstration and testing facility at the central Bremen-state water sewage plant and the setting up of an environmental technology research centre at Bremen University. Some of the core expertise of Bremen defense contractors in the fields of sensor technology, simulation and systems control can be applied and further developed to the fields of waste water analysis, waste water sensor technology and processing. In this context, the Bremen Institute for Waste Water Technologies has developed specific test, research, transfer, consultancy and training facilities.

In a similar manner, a West-East Transfer Agency (WETA), set up with the help of conversion funding, supports the transfer of Bremen's corporate and regional conversion know-how in order to assist in the establishment of profitable conversion-oriented, west-east cooperation.

Regional advisory committees of the transfer institutes are ensuring this cooperation process. Moreover, various ad-hoc groups for further supra-company projects also practice cooperation in other fields.

Incentive analysis and conclusion

(1) In order to be able to assess the probability of participants taking part in cooperation processes, it is necessary to analyse the strategic incentive structure. The willingness of defense contractors, in the case discussed, to cooperate has to be the subject of analysis. With respect to corporate conversion projects the investigation is mainly concerned with coordinated behavior in favor of the superior conversion option, i.e. indirect forms of cooperation. However, in the case of individual projects as well as infrastructure-related networking, direct cooperation has also resulted.

(2) Each individual defense contractor was faced with the dilemma of whether it is in its interest to participate in conversion-oriented cooperation. If companies had not diversified their range of products, R&D and further developed their common specific location factors, then the structure of the region would have continued to be susceptible to crises. If they cooperated, in a manner which has positive effects on the sectoral structure of the region, as well as its infrastructural location factors, then all parties in the region would benefit. From the individualistic point of view of the individual defense contractor however, the greatest benefit can always be achieved when all other companies diversify to non-military products and improve the regional economic location quality by means of cooperation. The contractor in question then would be the only one that did not participate and would bear no costs of cooperative, or coordinated restructuring. This particular contractor could not be excluded from taking advantage of the improved location qualities. This is the normal dilemma which arises when producing (regional) collective goods.

(3) The potential regional economic benefit of an improved sectoral structure, as well as infrastructure, is such that it is in the interest of the regional state to meritorise it. This is done by providing financial and non-financial incentives. Those enterprises that are willing to launch new diversified activities in such a manner that the region experiences positive external effects are granted subsidies as well as better access to regional political and administrative decision-making. Advisory committees and regional councils play a significant role. Through

access to these committees, cooperating defense contractors are able to obtain, for example, additional information regarding financial support and contacts. Cooperative behavior is also rewarded through public recognition and approval by various organizations, politicians, the public administration, media and the field of science, as they all participate in the committees.

Changing the incentive (pay-off) structure, thus, is not only performed through financial subsidies but also through non-financial ("qualitative") rewards.

(4) An improved infrastructure also increases the probability that enterprises remain in the region. The prospect of having to interact with the other participating parties at some time in the future, has in turn the effect of promoting the willingness to cooperate.

Regional merit goods and industrial policy objectives, as well as cooperation in the fields of corporate and infrastructural projects thus form a complex, interactive and iterated process wherein project-related goals become instruments of cooperation, while instruments, measures, or projects become sub-goals and, namely cooperation becomes cause and effect at the same time.

(5) The effect of such CIP strategies still cannot be fully assessed. These strategies employ financial instruments as well as qualitative instruments.

It is, however, well known that the blocking of conversion as well as the relinquishing of conversion objectives due to disappointments and frustration—as has frequently occurred in other regions—has been prevented in Bremen up to now, and that regional dual cooperation structures (private-private, private-state) have become well established. As a consequence, progressive structural change—in spite of obstacles and resistance coming from national and international political and market developments—has been introduced, new options for action (especially the strategic alternative "conversion") opened and excessive high social costs (up to now) avoided.

A short incentive analysis of regionalized industrial policy in North-Rhine Westphalia

(1) Regional-oriented industrial policies have normally been made centrally mainly by state governments and the federal government (or as a common task of both) in Germany, or by the EU. This principle has been changed in North-Rhine Westphalia since the mid-eighties within the framework of a regionalized industrial policy.

The aim of the regionalized industrial policy is to improve individual, corporate and regional location factors. Furthermore, it is intended, by means of improved cooperation by large groups of participants, to create better opportunities to exploit local and regional potentials. A regional network is to be implemented to enable bundling of regional activities, measures and projects, generation of synergy effects and promotion of increased regional responsibility for the quality of regional location factors. Cross-sectional bundling of funding and resources on the state government level should lead to a higher degree of effectiveness of public industrial policy promotion. Regional participants encompass local (i.e. sub-regional) governments and private participants. It is assumed that participants from the region are better equipped to recognize the problems of the region and propose suitable solution strategies. This type of industrial policy is implemented by regional conferences that shall take place on a regular basis and are responsible for compiling regional development plans.

(2) An improved regional economic situation resulting from the cooperative development and realisation of regional development concepts represents the merit good defined by the state government. Consequently, the state government supports this form of cooperation by guaranteeing to grant Priority to cooperatively developed projects. Support is available in many various forms. Regionally coordinated projects not only receive promises of priority treatment. An inter-ministerial working group has also been established at the state level, fulfilling an advisory function to the actors who are willing to cooperate.

The state government thus employs rewards (mainly non-financial, i.e. qualitative ones) to change the incentive structure of the interacting local communities and private actors and also tries to increase the relevance of their common future through the establishment of permanent network structures in the form of periodic regional conferences.

(3) The incentive structure to persuade local actors to cooperate has, of course, to be further examined. There is an incentive for the local communities to take part in the process of cooperation, since they obviously profit from an improvement of the location conditions. On the other hand, local communities do not necessarily have to take part in the cooperation in any formal or legal sense. On the contrary, they still have the legal rights, as their traditional standard option, to continue to apply for funding individually and try to exert their own political influence vis-à-vis the state administration like they always had done before. Funding and support for individual local projects cannot be denied legally to those individualistic public local actors. Furthermore, such individualistic local actors cannot be excluded from the positive effects of improved location conditions in the region which would be a result of cooperation of others. If individual participants do not contribute to the merit good by cooperation, they can nevertheless not be excluded from an improvement of the regional socio-economic performance and thus would achieve their greatest benefit. There is, therefore, a dilemma structure for the individual participant.

(4) This dilemma situation facing the individual actor is countered by long-term regular cooperation within the regional conferences. "The state government considers the mobilisation of all possible regional forces to be long-term" the state government declared in 1995. Thus, from the point of view of the individual, it has therefore to be expected that there will be a common future. Besides rewarding cooperative behavior, regional conferences can be considered as the instrument for increasing the "shadow" (i.e. the cooperative light) of the future.

Conclusions

(1) The model of dual CIP as developed and illustrated in this chapter can offer to competitive actors, who are lastingly interactive and prone

to dilemma structures, new options for action and thus lead to "better" structural situations, paths of development and socio-economic performance in the regions. For example, regional CIP in the Bremen case study has (up to now) succeeded in persuading enterprises to take the path of conversion, even though it normally first appears more unattractive from a corporate point of view. This implies that better regional and structural options and solutions have been opened which would normally not have been implemented by enterprises. The same applies to local public and private participants in the system of regionalized industrial policy in the North-Rhine Westfalia case.

It is, therefore, to be expected that the decision situation of individual actors can, by means of CIP, be changed to the "right" direction. Cooperative behavior in the sense of the active, regionally embedded restructuring then benefits, for example, enterprises and other stakeholders in the regional production processes. This option for action has been made more attractive to them relative to traditional options. It has apparently been possible to change incentive structures in the right direction and to increase the importance of the common future. This is especially possible in a region where the probability of future interactions, cooperation and the effects of cooperative improvement of location factors are more obvious and noticeable for all involved.

(2) We are, however, far from being able (yet) to construct concretely applied PD pay-off matrices for practical forms of cooperative industrial development and policy. If there is such a thing, then the distribution of benefits in fact has apparently been changed in the right direction in the two case studies. In addition, the discount factor has apparently been increased. More complex methods of evaluation of strategies and processes of cooperative structural development and policy may perhaps make it possible, in future, to check further on such suppositions.

(3) With some certainty it can be claimed that it is not only (or mainly) the amount of money (i.e. the financial aspect of changing the incentive structure) which has played a significant role here. It can be assumed that the whole institutional and instrumental arrangement developed here, i.e. the organized permanence and multiplication of cooperative interactions with the perspective of achieving a more significant

common future, besides financial and non-financial rewards, is suitable to enable cooperation.

(4) Regional CIP is often seen as a very special field, and namely conversion as something almost esoteric. It has been tried to show in the foregoing that cooperative industrial development and policy are not only feasible, but also can help to overcome the blocking of certain typical structural situations, and can thus become a central form of a managed progressive structural change. CIP can serve to further develop industrial policies, especially development strategies of, and for, regions. This chapter, thus, has tried to extend the numerous international examples and conceptions of cooperative, interactive and network-based regional developments and revitalization of regions; it has also tried to provide a clearer logical explanation which, it is assumed, can be not only generalized but also applied to real industrial policies.

Notes

1. See for a very short discussion of potential practical interpretations: W. Elsner and J. Huffschmid (1994).

2. This point of view corresponds to the pragmatist, or instrumentalist, philosophy upon which institutionalist economics and social economics base their concepts of reasonable values and the negotiated economy (cf., for example, J.R. Commons (1934), and M. R. Tool (1986)).

3. No negotiation approaches will be considered here. A prerequisite for negotiation games is the legal commitment to implement the results of negotiation. The participants analysed here should, however, take part in the cooperation without any formal legal commitment. The point here is the relatively simple and, at the same time realistic assumption, lacking strong preconditions, that private actors involved in relevant situations act (at the beginning) quite individualistically (egoistically) and only reluctantly commit themselves formally. If, however, cooperation is able to emerge from situations lacking strong suppositions, then it can be expected it will happen more easily when socially or institutionally stronger structured situations exist, or it can be more easily brought about by policy means.

4. As can be easily seen, TIT FOR TAT results again ALL D in a pay-off of 19, while ALL D against ALL D results in 20 for all.

References

Axelrod, R.1984. *The Evolution of Cooperation.* New York: Basic Books.

Baker, P. 1996. "Spatial Outcomes of Capital Restructuring: New Industrial Spaces as a Symptom of Crisis, not Solution". In *Review of Political Economy*, 8/3, 263—278.

Benko, G. and M. Dunford 1991. *Industrial Change and Regional Development: The Transformation of New Industrial Spaces.* London/ New York: Belhaven Press.

Bicchieri, C. 1993. *Rationality and Coordination.* Cambridge: Cambridge University Press.

Chichilnisky, G. 1995. "The Evolution of a Global Network: A Game of Coalition Formation". In *Journal of International and Comparative Economics*, Vol. 4, 179—197.

Commons, J.R. 1934. *Institutional Economics*, 2 Vols. New York: Macmillan, repr. London: New Brunswick, Transaction Publ. 1990.

Elsner, W. 1987. "Institutionen und ökonomische Institutionentheorie". In *Wirtschaftswissenschaftliches Studium*, Vol. 16, 5—14.

————— 1989. "Adam Smith's Model of the Origins and Emergence of Institutions: The Modern Findings of the Classical Approach". In *Journal of Economic Issues*, Vol. 23, 189—213.

————— 1993. "Industrial Defense Conversion: Guiding the Market at the Regional Level—The Case of the State of Bremen Germany". In *Journal of Economic Issues*, Vol. 27, 1254—1262.

————— 1995. "Instruments and Institutions of Industrial Policy at the Regional Level in Germany: The Example of Industrial Defense Conversion". In *Journal of Economic Issues*, Vol. 29, 503—516.

Elsner, W. and J. Accordino 1999. "Transatlantic Comparisons of Conversion in Maritime Regions: The State of Bremen (Germany) and the Norfolk/Newport News Region, VA". (With a contribution by Heiner Heseler on Bremen's Shipyard Industry), to be published in a special issue of the International Regional Science Review (IRSR) on defense conversion comparisons across regions and continents, ed. by A. Markusen (forthcoming).

Elsner, W. and J. Huffschmid 1994. "Industrial Policy". In *The Elgar Companion to Institutional and Evolutionary Economics,* G.M. Hodgson, W.J. Samuels and M.R. Tool eds. Aldershot, Brookfield: Edward Elgar, 343—351.

Grabher, G. ed. 1993. *The Embedded Firm. On the Socioeconomics of Industrial Networks.* London/New York: Routledge.

Maillat, D. and B. Lecoq 1992. "New Technologies and Transformation of Regional Structures in Europe: The Role of the Milieu". In *Entrepreneurship and Regional Development,* Vol. 4, 1—20, repr. in: N. Hansen, K.J. Button and P. Nijkamp eds. *Regional Policy and Regional Integration,* Cheltenham, Brookfield: Edward Elgar, 485—504.

Markusen, A.R. 1996. "Sticky Places in Slippery Space: A Typology of Industrial Districts . In *Economic Geography,* 72/3, 293—313.

Neale, W.C. 1994. "Institutions". In *The Elgar Companion to Institutional and Evolutionary Economics.* G.M. Hodgson, W.J. Samuels and M.R. Tool eds. Aldershot, Brookfield: Edward Elgar, 402—406.

Pratt, A. 1997. "The Emerging Shape and Form of Innovation Networks and Institutions". In J.M. Simmie ed. *Innovation, Networks and Learning Regions?,* Bristol (Penns.), 124—136.

Pyke, F. and W. Sengenberger eds. 1992. *Industrial Districts and Local Economic Regeneration.* Geneva: ILO.

Schotter, A.R. 1981. *The Economic Theory of Social Institutions.* Cambridge: Cambridge University Press.

Tool, M.R. 1986. *Essays in Social Value Theory. A Neoinstitutionalist Contribution.* New York: M. E. Sharpe.

6 INDUSTRIAL POLICY, INDUSTRIAL CHANGE AND INSTITUTIONAL INERTIA

Michael Dietrich and John E. Burns

Introduction

This chapter discusses the nature and significance of a dynamic industrial policy, and examines the ways in which such policy might facilitate organizational and industrial change. The rationale for the chapter is both empirical and theoretical. Empirically, successful industrial policy (for instance, that in Japan and South Korea) appears strategic in nature. Theoretically, there is an emerging research tradition which views industrial policy as unfreezing strategic "lock-in" and facilitating the emergence of new developmental trajectories (see Dietrich, 1994). This chapter aims to contribute to such theoretical development.

The theoretical ideas developed in this chapter break away from the traditional (neo-classical) economic view of industrial policy as a set of policy instruments which compensate static market failures. It also contrasts with the (Austrian economics) view of industrial policy as measures to construct an economic "level playing field" from which competition is expected to promote change. Both the neo-classical and Austrian frameworks are capable of providing local solutions which, at best, apply to understanding particular strategic trajectories. In contrast, the dynamic approach presented in this chapter views industrial change as: (1) evolutionary, and (2) institutionally embedded. The meaning of, and complexities introduced by (1) and (2) will be developed in the chapter.

A dynamic understanding of industrial policy has strategic lock-in within, and between, organizations as a core feature. Traditionally, strategic lock-in has been viewed as a random process determining choice of technology (see David, 1985; Arthur, 1988; 1989). But, for present purposes such a view is regarded as overly limiting in two respects. First, lock-in is characteristic of other factors besides technology; in particular, a geographical dimension exists (Best, 1990; Porter, 1990; Krugman, 1994) where emphasis is placed on agglomeration externalities and infrastructure synergies. It follows that lock-in problems may be ubiquitous and hence present a central rather than marginal concern for national and regional policy. Second, the traditional approach to lock-in is insufficiently institutional in character.

To accommodate institutional complexity, strategic lock-in is viewed both as an organizational and a technical (inter-organizational) phenomenon. Organizational lock-in can be explained as the result of strategic leaders emerging from coordination problems amongst different firm stakeholders (see Dietrich, 1997). Put another way, organizational lock-in is suitably understood in terms of the actions and decisions of individuals (or groups) with sufficient power to control and dominate organization-specific strategy. Examples of such dominant stakeholders might be a profession (e.g., accounting) which has become institutionally embedded in particular organizations, or an overpowering leader. Coordination problems must be solved if the advantages of corporate coherence (coordination synergy, learning effects, etc.) are to be exploited. In general terms, we can conceptualize firm coherence as a particular stakeholder (or group) assuming a dominant (leader) position with other stakeholders being the followers.

Technological lock-in can be understood as a coordination problem between leading organizations which differ in terms of their leadership characteristics and coherence, hence their strategies. It is organizational lock-in which shapes these leadership characteristics; the implication, therefore, is that rather than study lock-in as an inter-firm phenomenon alone, we must also explore interaction between organizational lock-in and technological lock-in. In so doing, we focus on the importance of dominance in organizations which are channeled by more general institutional characteristics underpinned by formal rules (e.g. accounting and legal practices) and/or informal "norms".

From the perspective sketched out thus far, institutional inertia can be viewed as a central problem for industrial policy because of the way in which it influences (a) organizational activity and (b) industrial change. It follows that we must extend industrial policy beyond a narrow technological conception to include institutional factors. The framework of ideas which is developed in this chapter suggests that, in practice, there is no such thing as a "level" industrial playing field, and that recognizing market failure provides potential for change but no more.

In this contribution we examine the nature of strategic/institutional industrial policy using illustrative case study material. The chapter is organized as follows: first, we expand on the notion that strategic lock-in can be understood both in terms of its organizational and technological elements. We explore the complexities of organizational lock-in, and the influence which intra-firm dominance has in molding such complexity. Then, we discuss the technological aspects of lock-in and how this can be understood as the result of coordination problems between different firms. The second part of the chapter explores the potential dominance of the accounting profession in organizations in general, followed, third, by illustration with evidence from a case study of a UK chemicals manufacturer. This case study offers interesting insight into a "dominant profession" (i.e. accounting) shaping organizational strategy—i.e., reinforcing processes of organizational lock-in. In addition, the case study illustrates how a dominant accounting perspective within an organization can drive specific technological (in this case, research and development) trajectories. Fourth, we relate the case study material and the preceding theoretical ideas specifically to the area of industrial policy, and provide some ideas relating to implications for future research in that field.

Strategic Lock-in as an Organizational and Technological Issue

The framework of ideas developed in this chapter begins with the assumption that industrial policy measures must address strategic lock-in if the underlying aim is to influence industrial and organization-level change significantly. Strategic lock-in involves the interaction of coordination problems at two levels, namely organizational and technological, as well as interaction between the two. The institutional and evolutionary dimensions of such interaction are explored in this section.

In economic terms, strategic lock-in has traditionally been discussed in terms of the choice of a particular technology, whereby firms become tied to particular processes and/or assets linked to such processes. This view is based largely on technological factors. For example, Arthur (1988; 1989) argues that where the choice of technology follows a random walk, four self reinforcing factors produce lock-in: (1) large set-up or fixed costs; (2) learning effects; (3) coordination effects which confer external benefits from cooperation, and; (4) adaptive expectations where increased use enhances belief of further use. Technological history is then explained in terms of accidents or random events rather than actors sponsoring particular technologies. This approach gives bias to policy implications which follow from recognizing lock-in because it minimizes institutional input. As discussed earlier, to accommodate institutional complexity strategic lock-in can be viewed both in terms of its organizational and technological dimensions. We now explore these dimensions further.

(a) Organizational lock-in

Organizational lock-in can be understood as the result of a coordination problem amongst different stakeholders. A moment's consideration indicates that the same self-reinforcing mechanisms that apply to technologies also apply to complex organizations: organizational control systems have set-up costs and are subject to learning effects; coordination and cooperation advantages exist which are based to a large extent on expectations and beliefs. In general terms, therefore, we can conceptualize organizational coherence as a particular stakeholder assuming a dominant (leader) position, and developing control systems which reflect this dominant position, with other stakeholders being followers. While using different logic, Miles and Snow (1978) from a managerial perspective, suggest similar conclusions that key functions or professions might dominate organizational strategy to produce characteristically different organizational outcomes. Any particular leader-follower relationship consequently becomes locked-in, which implies that fundamental strategic change requires coordinated rather than individual efforts. An illustrative example, namely the potential dominance of accounting, is discussed in a later section of the chapter.

Recognizing the importance of dominant actors and dominant professions for shaping organizational (and industrial) strategies, we must consider the organization as a system in which decision making is not assumed to react to external stimuli alone (the perspective of conventional economic views of the organization). A dynamic view of organizations acknowledges that change (hence organizational strategy) can also evolve internally. Such a perspective relies on emphasizing learning processes within organizations.

Conceptually, it is possible to think of organizational decision making as being underpinned by "expressive rationality" (see Hargreaves-Heap, 1989), which suggests that decision making concerns itself with the choice of ends, rather than either given ends or an emphasis on procedures. Furthermore, the choice of ends encompasses genuine uncertainty and conflict amongst alternative ends—necessitating creative, proactive decision-making. This contrasts with "instrumental" and "procedural" rationalities (characteristics of conventional economic views of the organization), whereby the former views reactive decision making in terms of given ends, and the latter places emphasis on procedures used to reach an end as well as programmed decision making.

If the firm is to be considered a single unit in its own right rather than a collection of interacting individuals and groups, emphasis must be placed on its strategic framework (see Dietrich, 1994). Such a framework is necessary for controlling the way uncertainty can undermine organizational coherence; in narrow economic terms it defines a particular cost and revenue perspective. Using earlier lock-in logic, the implication here is that an organization's strategic framework revolves around dominant individuals and/or groups. Recognizing the importance of an organization's strategic framework allows us to incorporate the insights of expressive rationality because of the way in which ends depend upon dominant stakeholders. In short strategic change becomes an issue of conflict over alternative ends.

It is important to recognize that different actors can hold differing strategic perspectives, without which organizational change would lose its complexity; improved performance would either be impossible or have to rely on existing leaders changing their perspectives. Grinyer and Spender's (1979) framework of the dynamics of corporate change is useful for conceptualizing some of these ideas. They argue that corporate change dynamics can be split into three aspects as follows: first, given unsatisfactory performance, managers will initially work "inside" existing strategies by tightening existing side payments or controls. If this fails, a second more fundamental stage involves reconstructing existing strategy, but within the same underlying strategic framework (to use the term introduced above). Third, an organization can change its strategic framework, thereby radically changing its practices, managerial motivations, etc. Under such a perspective, transformation in organizational functioning (the difficulties of which should not be understated) implies the endogenization of goals, organizational practices, etc. The old knowledge base of a firm becomes more or less irrelevant, depending on how radical the restructuring. Furthermore, learning processes become imperative to strategic aims because the parameters of new strategic problems cannot be specified "ex ante", as past practice offers little relevance to current decision-making. Productive opportunities are endogenized and decision-making becomes proactive rather than reactive.

Strategic organizational change which involves changes in underlying assumptions and expectations occurs infrequently. Otherwise, firm-specific knowledge would be frequently disrupted, thereby increasing ambiguity and unpredictability (Dietrich, 1994). Furthermore, such inertia within organizations is a powerful force for resisting change. Schein (1985) suggests that organizations which rely on "negative reinforcement" (i.e. operating in standard, institutionalized ways) were more likely to have greater problems with forces of inertia than organizations which relied on "positive reinforcement" (i.e. based on learning). Nevertheless, even with positive reinforcement much organizational change is still likely to be incremental (Lindblom, 1959). In effect incrementalism seems to be merely a statement that organizations become locked-in (or path dependent) to particular trajectories, for reasons already discussed. Organizations implicitly avoid the complexities of expressive rationality, with the resulting conflict and learning, by restricting themselves to procedural considerations.

Many writers from a political economy perspective argue that organizational strategies further the interests of those in senior hierarchical positions who have effective control over practices. In the business strategy literature it is conventional to emphasize the power of various stakeholders for influencing organizational strategies; e.g., suppliers, customers, financiers, government, trade unions, etc (see Johnson and Scholes, 1989; Donaldson and Preston, 1995). Organizations become idiosyncratic, their objectives dependent upon particular organization-stakeholder interactions. However, if we move beyond the conventional business perspective we can recognize ways in which organization-stakeholder interactions might be bounded by wider (formal and informal) institutional characteristics. It follows that industrial policy can be broadened to recognize: (a) the ways in which organizational activities depend upon particular strategic frameworks; and, (b) the ways in which such frameworks depend on wider institutional factors.

This broadening of industrial policy should avoid overly static and simplified reasoning. The complexities of organizational creativity should be recognized. Although the firm and its functioning is bounded by its strategic framework, sub-unit opportunities (facilitated, for example, by decentralized creativity and entrepreneurship) still exist—channeled by the dynamics underpinning dominant organizational characteristics. Intra-organization diversity will exist in all firms except where a small organization has a dominant leader, or where a powerful, institutionalized ideology exists (Mintzberg, 1979).

Conceptualizing firms as diverse phenomena, we can assume that individuals in different sub-units will have different characteristic "mental maps" which structure their particular expectations and perceived opportunities. This implies the emergence of different strategies from learning processes and responses to environmental change. No single strategy is necessarily more rational than the rest; each merely reflects the perceptions of different individual (and collective) decision-makers. However, given the strategic framework, some strategic responses will dominate. This highlights a fundamental point, which will be related specifically to industrial policy issues later, namely that successful strategic reorientation requires a powerful coalition of interests at senior hierarchical levels and sometimes the intervention of an outsider followed by action which must have an important symbolic significance. To put this another way, where strategic reorientation is intended, the effects of different perceptions and expectations should be acknowledged in order to facilitate restructuring of sub-unit aspirations. In organizational (or, more aggregated, industrial) change, a particular ideology must effectively be "imposed" over alternative ideologies, although the formers dominance does not necessarily rid the alternatives. Conflict between alternative ideologies is, of course, always possible.

(b) Inter-organizational lock-in

Inter-organizational (which we will assume for simplicity is technological) lock-in can be understood in terms of the interaction of different strategic frameworks (and hence dominant actors and groups) in leading organizations. By assuming that individual organizations are characterized by specific, idiosyncratic alliances (see above), it follows that organizational and technological lock-in cannot simply be juxtaposed (Dietrich, 1997). Furthermore, given that each particular firm embodies its own trajectories, this undermines traditional arguments that choice of technology follows a random walk. In contrast, the framework presented here views technological choice as channeled by organizational characteristics. It follows that to generate technological lock-in (given organizational lock-in) mechanisms, processes and/or structures must exist to undermine the diversity implied by the idiosyncratic nature of decision-making, and thus promote convergent technological choices in a way that substitutes for a random walk assumption.

There would appear to be two possible ways to explain the above convergence involving: (1) markets or (2) institutions (Dietrich, 1997). Market-driven links between organizational lock-in and technological lock-in are somewhat problematic because in the context of idiosyncratic firms that have an ability to innovate there may be a number of different companies in existence which accommodate different aspects of the environment such that there need be no unique, stable equilibrium which "selects out" inefficient firms. It follows that institutional factors should be recognized as being important for linking organizational lock-in to technological lock-in.

Organizational lock-in (e.g., dominance of particular professions) can be viewed as a phenomenon which is embedded in wider institutional arrangements. For example, there is discussion in the accounting literature about how accounting's dominance within UK/US organizations has been grounded in the significance of external financial reporting and stock market concerns (see Kaplan, 1984; Johnson and Kaplan, 1987). More generally, organizational practices will be regularized by accounting and legal rules as well as evolving "informal" accounting practices. Such institutional characteristics homogenize organizational strategic frameworks, hence facilitating the development of technological lock-in that may, of course, be supported by market processes. Internationally, common institutions do not exist. Hence in this wider arena market processes may play a wider role in the linkage of organizational and technological trajectories.

The above discussion can be further conceptualized as a coordination problem at two levels. On the first level is a coordination game between firms which are grouped by institutional factors. These groupings then interact at a second level in a coordination game between technological leaders from particular groups, i.e. strategic leaders sponsoring particular technologies (Dietrich and Schenk, 1993). Following on from the discussion so far, these strategic leaders are more likely to be the dominant organizations (and managers) in particular institutional settings. Organizational lock-in can therefore significantly influence the degree of technological lock-in within a particular country, where choice of technology is dominated by leaders of organizations characterized by locked-in responses to environmental change. Rather than resulting from a random walk, the choice of technology can therefore, we argue, be more appropriately understood as the path-dependent response of dominant ideologies in leading organizations within particular settings. It follows, and as we develop later in the chapter, that industrial policy must consider the extent of, and link between organizational and technological lock-in of a particular country, in particular the path-dependent strategic characteristics of leading organizations in relevant industries. However, before we take discussion of industrial policy any further, we shall first illustrate some of the ideas and issues discussed thus far, by investigating the potential dominance of accounting in firms and drawing on case study evidence.

The Dominance of Accounting

Accounting practices represent a highly routinized part of day-to-day organizational activity (Nelson and Winter, 1982; Scapens, 1994). Through time, and with continual re-enactment of accounting practices, routines develop, and accounting begins to underpin "settled ways of thinking and doing" within particular organizations. Accounting thus becomes institutionalized in organizational settings (see Burns, 1996; 1997). Recent literature centers on the institutional aspects of accounting within organizations. For example, this work has examined: (1) the visibility which accounting provides within organizations (see Hopwood, 1987); (2) the way in which accounting underpins the meanings which organizational members attach to business phenomena (see Macintosh and Scapens, 1990); (3) the way accounting legitimates firms to the external environment (see Covaleski et al., 1993), and (4) the extent to which accounting routines underpin organization-specific know-how, thereby informing decision-making (Burns, 1997). Such research (the above is far from exclusive in this vast literature) highlights the potential for accounting—and accountants—to dominate the ideology (hence, action, thoughts, decision-making, and so on) in individual firms. This is clearly related to the discussion above concerning dominant, idiosyncratic "professional paradigms" in organizations.

Dominant accounting paradigms (characterized by emphasis on the financial or "bottom line" aspects of day-to-day business activity) has been studied previously at a "macro" level by socio-economists. For example, Fligstein's (1990) work suggested that accounting dominated the strategy of US companies, compared to engineering and production in France, Germany and Japan. Similar findings were made in Lane's (1989) comparative study of UK, French and German organizations, in which she found that UK firms were finance-orientated, while their French and German counterparts placed more emphasis on engineering, and engineering with science, respectively.

Taking the level of analysis a stage further, recent accounting research has explored the potential dominance of accounting at the "micro" level. Such work, we argue, can provide useful insight for developing our understanding of strategic lock-in within firms—thereby improving our understanding of industrial policy issues. In the next section case study evidence illustrates this. However, initially, it might be sensible to establish clearly what is actually meant by "accounting". The term is often either over-simplified or mis-understood. Essentially, the accounting in most organizations can be split into two, as follows:[1]

1. The production of primarily financial information for reports ("the accounts") which are distributed to external accounts users (e.g., shareholders, customers, suppliers, bankers, potential buyers). Traditionally, this has been called "financial accounting", although increasingly (and the term we adopt) it is specifically referred to as "external reporting", so dropping the accounting term.
2. Information provision and calculation adopted by managers to control their business, and to inform decision-making and day-to-day operational management. This is more commonly termed "management accounting", and encompasses both financial and non-financial information.[2]

Clearly, there are overlaps between (1) and (2). Much of the financial information which constitutes a firm's management accounting forms the basis of external reports, and in many companies there exists a single system of data capture which is able to provide both sets of information independently without manual adjustments. This overlap is the reason for adopting the term "external reporting" rather than "financial accounting", because the latter implies that management accounting is relatively free from financial information and that financial information is primarily produced for use by external accounts users, both of which are mistaken views.

If we are to discuss the dominance of "accounting" in firms it is important to make the above distinctions, since they imply two separate issues, namely: (1) the dominance of external reporting, and; (2) the dominance of management accounting practices within firms. The issue of dominant concerns over external reporting was discussed briefly above. However, it is the potential dominance of accounting within organizations (management accounting) which provides the key focus to what follows next.

An Illustrative Case Study—Neville Ltd[3]

This section presents evidence from the case study of a small (UK) chemicals manufacturer called Neville. The material provides illustration of some of the ideas discussed thus far in the chapter—particularly highlighting the dominance of a firm's strategic trajectories by a single profession—in this case, accounting. We also explore the effect which such domination had on the choice of technology in Neville, and, by extrapolation, the UK chemicals industry as a whole. Although studies of one organization lack a basis for general conclusions of industrial policy issues, such insight is useful for making sense of the complex interaction between organizational lock-in, technological lock-in, and industrial policy.

Neville was formed in the late-1970s and is located in the north of England. Its chemical products are very specialist, many involving "nasty" chemical processes. Traditionally the majority of its sales result from "captive" contracts (see below) spanning over five years, with large multi-national customers. There are four shareholder-directors, namely: (1) the Chairman, (2) the Technical Director, (3) the Sales and Marketing Director and, (4) the Managing Director (MD). The latter is a chartered accountant, while (1), (2) and (3) are qualified chemists. The Board consists of these four directors, plus the Financial Controller, two Operations Directors and an Engineering Director.

Neville's growth since its formation and up to the early-1990s was impressive. Turnover rose from around £1.5 million in 1983 to nearly £20 million in 1994 (with around sixty five per cent being exports). Annual profits in 1994 were in the region of £2 million and the company had no major debt. Much of this growth was due to success in "captive" work, mentioned briefly above. Captive products involve Neville being in a contract to produce a customer-specified product over a period of normally five years. This said, most captive deals involve production of a derivative of a single, very successful product. During the 1980s and into the 1990s, captives constituted around 80% of Neville's earnings. The remaining 20% was earned through sales of "multi-client"[4] products— i.e., products developed in-house by Neville's research department and aimed at attracting a variety of customers rather than single "captive" customers. The remainder of the section is split into two parts. First, we discuss how organizational lock-in developed from the domination of accounting in Neville and, second, we explain the effects which such domination had on research activity.

(a) Contribution routines

Events in 1988 had major ramifications for the way Neville was managed. In that year, two major captive contracts came to an end and were not renewed. Cash flow difficulties developed and bankruptcy became a possibility. Neville's existing bank proved unsympathetic, and the four shareholder-directors turned to a different bank for better finance terms and a "haven" period[5], thus ensuring short-term survival. This new bank offered extended overdraft facilities. Importantly, by 1990, a small number of new captive contracts had been secured, partly filling the gap left by the two major contract terminations in 1988 and, more importantly, providing breathing space. Nevertheless, fundamental lessons had been learned, and the Board members vowed never to be in such a situation ever again. The new, medium-term strategy for Neville, set at Board level, was to redress the (80/20) balance between captive and multi-client deals so that Neville would no longer be so exposed to the effects of termination of major captive deals. The intention (strategy) was to achieve a 50/50 split between captives and multi-clients by the mid-1990s, and this was to be facilitated by focusing managers more on "results" and "making money". In particular, new emphasis was placed on an accounting concept termed "contribution" in all departments within the business. Contribution is defined within Neville as sales less material costs[6], and the strategy was to achieve major improvements in contribution earnings from multi-client sales, and to question more rigorously any captive deals with low contribution earnings potential. Joint responsibility for this lay with the sales and marketing department, and the research department (see below).

By 1990, contribution underpinned the business language at various levels of the organization, was a key source of information for internal reports and calculations, and largely informed (day-to-day and strategic) decision-making. Information systems, though very simple, allowed managers and workers to make "local" calculations in contribution terms. For example, contribution per product soon became an important source of knowledge in the production department, as did contribution earnings per chemical vessel.[7] Furthermore, much of the knowledge embedded in contributions was tacit, such that people: "just know which products are making more money than others" (the MD). In this sense, ongoing re-enactment of contribution-based procedures, and the emergence of new (accounting) routines, assisted personnel to make sense of their activities as well as the activities of others.

The MD sarcastically explained that before the new contributions focus, managers were: "too detached and more interested in the color of toilet rolls than how things were going". For example, of managers in the production department, he added:

> Five years ago, these documents never belonged to Production. Well, that has gone completely. This lot now belongs to them—they generate it. And they have gone through a lot of pain over the years to get to grips with what are effectively accounting concepts. They are not complex concepts, but for a guy

whose world is production or engineering—he understands the word "yield". He does not understand how a company actually arrives at the figure. And yet, it is only a break up of very obvious data. You have to explain to people that there is no magic in accounting.

In relation to earlier discussion in the chapter, it is important to stress that the new focus on contribution earnings was driven by the MD, who imposed his personal accounting ways of thinking and doing on the rest of the business. The MD was the major force behind the development of an organizational lock-in which saw Neville's strategy constituted in, and undertaken through, accounting terms. What also needs to be stressed is the MDs mobilization of power through which he insisted that a contributions-focus should become the norm in all parts of the organization. His management skills, backed up by his professional knowledge of accounting, were popular with the other shareholder-directors. Also, the respect he had from other managers and workers in the plant was reinforced by the time he spent on site compared to the other shareholder-directors, as well as through his very strong personality. Drawing from ideas presented earlier in the chapter, it appeared that the MDs personal aspirations were endogenized within the entire organization as a result of his effective power and control over Neville's strategic development, thus channeling the decision-making processes which unfolded.

Some (very basic) training in the new, accounting (contribution-based) practices—e.g., budgets, reports and reviews—was provided. However, it was mainly through learning by doing that new accounting practices soon became routine. Though the MDs insistence (authority) virtually assured that such routinization would occur, he also played an active part (through meetings, presentations, etc.) in promoting a general perception that this was the "right" thing to do for the business. The three other shareholders were convinced of the contributions concept by its simplicity—enabling them to grasp how different parts of the business were contributing towards their investment returns. All four shareholders were nearing retirement and a desire to realize their investments was widely known. Similarly, support for the new contribution routines was explicit in interviews with managers from the sales, marketing and production departments.

In summary, it was the powerful MD who imposed an accounting focus on the rest of the organization—a focus which soon became the dominant "way to do business" in Neville, a process of organizational lock-in.

(b) Research

The strategy to improve multi-client contribution earnings brought Neville's research department to the forefront of conversation at Board level more than ever before. Pre-crisis, when Neville's growth and earnings were particularly impressive, the research department had been rather detached from the rest of the business. Their location was in a mobile building quite remote from the main offices, and from the plant. The chief chemist reported monthly to the Technical Director, but with little real accountability, and he had very little contact with other senior managers or directors. Day-to-day activity was largely dictated—either developing derivatives of existing captive products, or dealing with problems surrounding existing captives in production. There was some (but only very minor) time available for "experimentation" on new products which personnel from within the research department believed might be worthwhile pursuing.

- Post-crisis, it was decided (again, specifically by the MD) that the research department should become more "results-orientated" and view their service to the rest of Neville "more in terms of making money". In this respect, the MD intended to instill some of his personal (institutionalized) accounting ways into the research department. In terms used earlier, the research department was intended to become an integral (rather than detached) part of the locked-in focus on contribution earnings. On reviewing the research department's "hit rate" (i.e., the number of new products passing through the research department and making sale) the MD was shocked at what he deemed to be "an abysmal record". From early-1991 to April 1993, 99 new products had passed through the research department. Of these, 13 products earned total contribution of £80,000 and only one product earned what the MD described as "acceptable" contribution earnings. The MD also expressed his dismay at the 60% time-utilization within the research department—namely, hours worked on actual research as a percentage of total hours worked. And, he struggled to come to terms with the fact that no overtime had ever been worked in the research department. His reactions were not untypical of a manager with an accounting background, illustrated also in some of the comments he made. For example, referring to the findings of his investigation into the activities of the research department, he said:

> There was evidence of poor scientific approach, together with a total absence of ownership......You discover that your technical line managers aren't business men.   They just look at themselves as providing a service,.... *they needed different leadership and guidance*....to try and open the curtains and the doors in the department to bring it into the mainstream.... That is our future profit and loss account in there. That is it!   There may be lots of masturbating going on and lots of chemical thrills, but what is going on commercially? They are having a wonderful time here. But the fact is it's not ultimately generating invoices, and that's what we're about....*The speech and the patterns of thinking are not results-orientated.* If you have not got a results—and priority-orientated operation in there, then it would be more by good luck than good management that you would end up getting results.

As a consequence, it was made explicit to the chief chemist that his department had to become more results-orientated, and especially to develop (in collaboration with sales and marketing) new multi-client products with good contribution earnings potential. The MD set up spreadsheets which, with a little training, enabled the chief chemist to input (time-sheet) data and to analyze the time-utilization within his department. Also, there was to be more prioritization of products ongoing in the research department, as well as new products. This prioritization came about through consideration of a combination of factors—including potential contribution earnings, time-to-market, chemical "nastiness", technical difficulty and life expectancy.

The power of the MD, drawing on his accounting professionalism, was again a key part of the process by which the above changes were brought about in the research department. Within months, the new accounting practices had become routine—at least as far as the chief chemist was concerned. The latter presented a report of figures (e.g., hours, time-utilization, product priority-rankings) to the MD in a meeting held every month. However, away from the accounting, the implications for active research activity in Neville were quite substantial, as we now develop.

Following the strategic change, sales and marketing began to target new customers more directly than they had previously done. In the past, captive customers tended to approach Neville rather than the other way round. According to the chief chemist, sales and marketing's approach became "too bullish", offering chemicals which, technically, were non-feasible for Neville. The embedded beliefs and assumptions within sales and marketing and the research department, respectively, were quite different. Embedded in the research department were assumptions that were epitomized by statements like "chemistry is slow" and "sometimes the chemistry just does not work no matter how hard you try" (both comments by the chief chemist). Such embedded and taken-for-granted assumptions were at odds with the sales and marketing's (and the MDs) "quick-fix", accounting-driven expectations.

Contributions focus had been relatively easily instilled within sales and marketing. This process had been helped along, in particular, by the Sales and Marketing Director's personal interest in contributions made to earnings, and by the Marketing Manager's accounting knowledge from an MBA gained in 1995. Sales and marketing's approach in the early-1990s was effectively to look into as many multi-client products as possible where there seemed to be any potential market and, hence, potential contribution earnings. However, according to the chief chemist in the research department, this approach frequently over-looked technical capabilities.

However, importantly, sales and marketing was a relatively powerful department within Neville. Its director was one of the four shareholders who, along with the MD, was "seen" on site far more frequently than the Chairman and the Technical Director. Also, the Marketing Manager was very popular with, and well respected by, other senior managers and directors. Accordingly, whichever chemical products the sales and marketing department offered to potential customers, the research department were in no position to resist and *had to* undertake relevant experimentation. The chief chemist said:

> If the Marketing Department say we are doing it, we do it! They are the ultimate masters of what we are doing. They go out and say "yes" we can make this, that and the other' without actually asking whether we can or not!

The many jobs "thrown at"[8] the research department (many incidentally still derivatives of captive products) accounted for the majority of research time between 1991 and 1996. Although the chief chemist believed that his department had the expertise to develop new, multi-client products with decent contribution earnings, there was very little "free" time to do so. Domination by senior sales and marketing personnel, and a dominant drive within the business to achieve more multi-client earnings (quickly), prevented the research department from achieving significant improvements in multi-client earnings through their own experimentation.

This is an important point because, as the MD himself admitted, many interesting and potentially rewarding research discoveries appear either "by mistake" or "through experimentation" with, and by undertaking variations in, existing chemical products. Such experimentation was now very unlikely to occur; research activity had to promise decent contribution returns (in forecasts) and most of the research department's activity was dictated by sales and marketing anyway. This situation was illustrated no better than the postponement of a new chemical product in 1993 which had previously earned Neville a place in the final of a very prestigious national competition for innovation. This recognition was for developing an environmentally-friendly treatment of an extremely nasty chemical. The research department had played a major role in such development. However, the product had been very expensive to develop, and promised small contribution earnings, and was postponed.

By the mid-1990s, there had still been little improvement in multi-client earnings, captive products remained the dominant part of Neville's sales portfolio. Neville's directors increasingly looked into the possibility of improving new (multi-client) product development through acquisition of other businesses. In 1996, an acquisition was made of an organization which already had a strong portfolio of multi-client products. Within months, responsibility for pure research was transferred to this new organization and research at the original site ceased.

The case study provides useful illustrations (albeit briefly) of some of the ideas and issues addressed in earlier parts of the chapter. In particular, it provides illustration of how a profession (accounting) can, through a process of organizational lock-in, come to dominate day-to-day activity in individual organizations. In this case domination came about through the power mobilization of an MD from the accounting profession, as well as domination of research activity by a sales and marketing department driven by accounting numbers. Whilst there were positive local aspects to the changes described (e.g., enhanced commercial orientation amongst managers which, long-run, fits with organizational objectives), there were also negative aspects. For example, there were underlying clashes between different professional and functional ideologies, as well as negative implications for research activity. Conceptually, we can say that the case study described research activity which is subject to institutional rather than market-based control. Hence, we can also say that organization-technology links should be explored in ways discussed in earlier parts of the chapter rather than as random walk.

Industrial Policy

This section attempts to apply ideas discussed in earlier parts of the chapter, as well as insight gained from the case study, to the particular area of industrial policy. We can characterize industrial policies as long-run supply-side initiatives aimed at restructuring or promoting the activities of particular sectors (see Dietrich, 1994). This definition is sufficiently broad to encompass (a) neo-classical market failure logic, (b) Austrian free market arguments, as well as (c) the strategic rationale suggested here. If we can imagine a world in which the only form of lock-in is technologically based, neo-classical industrial policies might be considered appropriate because firms will respond to state-sponsored incentives in predictable ways. In a world of organizational (but not technological) lock-in, a ruthless form of developing market flexibility and competition might be considered adequate for the promotion of efficiency and economic progress. However, when organizational and technological lock-in interact, in ways described above, we are arguably entering a world in which strategic-institutional policies become necessary. Neo-classical and Austrian perspectives will, in their different ways, merely reinforce existing strategic orientations.

From a strategic-institutional perspective industrial policies are said to be measures which aim to influence developmental paths and shape the parameters within which organizational policies operate. In the context of this chapter, dynamic industrial policies can be viewed as aiming to unfreeze strategic lock-in within firms (i.e., micro-policies) to assist development of new and emerging trajectories. In this respect, there seems a definite case for proactive and selective industrial policy aimed at restructuring parts of the economy deemed to be strategically important. Arguably this is along the lines which exists in some countries. For example, the Japanese have emphasized products and sectors with high income elasticities of demand and large scope for technological advance (Donald and Hutton, 1991). Also, Germany has directed much funding towards R&D, as well as encourage diffusion and the establishment of research networks (Grewlich, 1987; Streit, 1987; Stoneman and Vickers, 1988).

The traditional, and somewhat dated, industrial policy approach of "down-loading" policies formulated in aggregated (i.e. industry- and economy-level) terms fails to acknowledge the importance of firm-specific idiosyncrasies and characteristics, which limits the effectiveness of such policies. A particular way that governments might attempt to facilitate dynamic change in firms and industries is by taking measures to promote horizontal links, hence providing the coalition of interests necessary to foster organizational and technological innovation. In particular, this might involve developing contacts which coordinate strategic change; for example, in the pre-competitive stage of technological development as has happened in the European Union (Dietrich, 1991). But, the danger in developing horizontal links is that they reinforce the status quo, competitive rivalry is reduced and firms become less willing to undertake radical redirection. Hence, while competition alone will not generate change, for reasons developed earlier, it can be an important catalyst. Without strategic redirection existing path dependencies remain unchanged.

Vertical links offer more chance to take advantage of dynamic strategies (Johnston and Lawrence, 1988). One way this can be achieved is through "top-down" policies which involve inducing leading organizations to shoulder the responsibility of innovative projects, against which "networks" are established in response to demand for the emerging core activities. Strategic government procurement has an important role to play here (Geroski, 1992), with potentially far more reaching effect than financial hand outs. One problem, however, might be that leading firms may not respond well to restructuring initiatives, particularly if top-down policies are combined with a horizontal policy. Under these circumstances, it is important to foster networking between the public and private sectors, as in Japan's case where the Ministry for International Trade and Industry (MITI) works very closely to private sector businesses (see Dore, 1986; Donald and Hutton, 1991).

The importance of public-private networking should not be under-estimated as it can be used to facilitate institutional change, and therefore indirectly affect corporate performance. This is obviously the case with credible restructuring of formal institutions, but can also be important in shifting perceptions and expectations (as happens in Japan) by helping break down the antagonism of parties which is likely to be reinforced with arms-length contacts. In short, financial inducements are unlikely to succeed in shifting path dependent organizational activity by themselves.

Referring to the case study earlier, it is not necessarily so that Neville would have increased "free experimentation" in its research and development had the UK government offered some relatively favorable financial deal. Their specific accounting routines had become embedded throughout much of the business and, imposed and continually reinforced by the MD, this was unlikely to be changed.

Financial incentives would be unlikely to dislodge such dominant strategic paths. Contribution was all that senior managers and directors were interested in, and most other workers (still aware of how close they were to losing their jobs in 1988) seemingly accepted this was the "right" way forward. While the shareholder-directors' wish to secure decent returns on their personal investments can be understood, a key message from the case study is that industrial policy measures must be very sensitive to such complex, institutional dimensions of organizational life. Favorable financial deals stood little chance of impacting on the research and development activities in Neville.

However, the significance of R&D activities of medium-sized organizations like Neville should not be disregarded, many pioneering ideas evolve from the R&D activities in small- and medium-sized organizations. The illustration provided in the case study of postponing development of an environmentally-beneficial chemical product due to poor earnings potential, suggests that existing dominant path dependency parameters would have to changed to promote R&D activity both within Neville and its industry. For example, measures could be put into place which encourage (or, indeed, *force*) the leading organizations to undertake the main share of research and development in the relevant industry. Networks could then be established to share "best practice", smaller organizations receive "sponsor" funds from the larger organizations for R&D activity, and/or private-public bodies established to coordinate the networks and share new knowledge.

A further way that governments might attempt to influence the dynamic strategies of particular organizations and industries is through "bottom-up policies" which involve improving the capacity to supply goods and services by exploiting particular comparative advantages and needs. The incidence of bottom-up policies largely takes place at the local/regional level, and involve for example: (1) inducing the birth of new organizations, and (2) fostering change of direction by small/medium organizations. Particularly in relation to the latter, and to reiterate a point made earlier, a change in direction by any organization does not necessarily result from competitive pressures. Competition, on the contrary, can offer dynamic advantages to large firms in the form of financial, marketing and/or R&D economies, rather than static efficiency advantages (see Dietrich, 1994).

An approach which might facilitate directional change for firms, while not reinforcing the comparative disadvantage of small firms, is the creation and/or support of local institutions to provide financial, marketing and/or R&D support which enable small organizations to undertake proactive rather than reactive behavior. Following Dietrich (1994) these institutions may be called "strategic havens". In Japan such protection involves cooperation between large (core) and supplying companies. In Italy (particularly Emilia Romagna) similar economic functioning is provided by public-private bodies. Strategic reorientation through institutional restructuring might be based either on direct public sector provision or through the public sector's facilitation of private sector collective bodies. Should public sector funds become involved in this process, however, it is important they are given on the understanding that their purpose is fundamentally to redirect strategy, rather than subsidize operations in the traditional sense.

The above organization-level initiatives should not, however, underplay industrial policy at the national level. Many of the embedded institutional characteristics within organizations which constrain dynamic, strategic change are grounded in norms and taken-for-granted beliefs and assumptions that exist at society level. Cowling (1987; 1990), in particular, has commented on three fundamental institutional idiosyncrasies which have constrained UK economic development in recent decades (i.e. transnationalism, centrepetalism and short-termism), thus leading to the argument for industrial policies to involve a Strategic Development Agency and a National Investment Bank which can function alongside regional-local initiatives (Cowling, 1990).

Following from the discussion in earlier parts of the chapter, we suggest further that for industrial policy initiatives to shift the developmental path of the UK economy as a whole, a dynamic approach would also entail fuelling institutional change which facilitates the emergence of new development paths in a decentralized way. To put this another way, a recommendation would be for the promotion of decentralized, quasi-autonomous activity (Lipietz, 1992), under which allocative and technical norms cease to be effective indicators of efficiency. More relevant is new development paths which do not necessarily prioritize the aspirations of senior managers and major shareholders (i.e. those with the power to influence and reinforce existing development paths in their favor). Such redistribution (in the power base of organizations) is as important an aspect of the promotion of dynamic, strategic industrial development as traditional measures which, for instance, cover new technology and knowledge diffusion.

Concluding Comments

This chapter has discussed ideas towards developing a dynamic, institutional perspective of industrial policy, with particular stress on the processes of strategic lock-in which frequently act as barrier to industrial change. The fundamental message has been for a shift from understanding and explaining strategic lock-in primarily through technological choice, towards an emphasis on the organizational and technological dimensions of strategic lock-in, as well as links between the two. It was discussed that strategy in organizations can become locked-in by the dominance of particular functions or professions, and emphasis was given to how industrial policy must consider such issues if it is to significantly affect strategic trajectories in particular organizations and industries.

Case study evidence was used to illustrate how particular professions (in this case, accounting) can become dominant in day-to-day organizational activity. More micro-level case studies of individual organizations and particular industries are required, thus contributing towards a more holistic understanding of the interaction of organizational and technological lock-in under different institutional settings. Comparatives can be made across different individual organizations, different industries and different countries (for example, as a basis for understanding European industrial policy issues). Individual (and/or comparative) micro-case studies will not provide general theories or "complete stories" of industrial policy issues. However, they can highlight important institutional dimensions to industrial policy which are likely to be overlooked by more conventional approaches.

Notes

1. See Scapens *et al.* (1996) for elaboration.

2. For example, management accounting information might have a financial element such as costs, or profit forecasts, but also a non-financial element such as quality or customer satisfaction indicators.

3. This is not the company's real name, which is concealed for confidentiality reasons. The research was undertaken between 1993 and 1998, funded jointly by the Chartered Institute of Management Accountants (CIMA) and the Economic and Social Research Council (ESRC).

4. The nicknames "captives" and "multi-clients" are used within Neville, and are similarly adopted in this chapter.

5. The term "haven" is highlighted because later discussion emphasises the importance of, what are called, "strategic havens" for proactive industrial policy. This is effectively the role that Neville was looking for from its bank.

6. A more conventional definition of contribution would be "sales less variable costs"; however, the magnitude of materials costs shaped the specific definition used within Neville.

7. A "vessel" is the large glass container in which chemical reactions are carried out in the production stage.

8. The chief chemist's description.

References

Arthur, W.B. 1988. "Self-Reinforcing Mechanisms in Economics". In *The Economy as an Evolving Complex System.* P. W. Anderson, K.J. Arrow and D. Pines eds., Redwood City: CA: Addison-Wesley.
———— 1989. "Competing Technologies, Increasing Returns, and Lock-In by Historical Events", *Economic Journal*, 99, 116—31.
Best, M.H. 1990. *The New Competition: Institutions of Industrial Restructuring.* Cambridge: Polity Press.

Burns, J.E. 1996. "The Routinization and Institutionalization of Accounting Routines", *Ph D Thesis*, University of Manchester.

———— 1997. "The Institutionalization of Accounting Routines: Keano Ltd". In *Beyond Constraint: Exploring the Management Control Paradox*, K. Vagneur, C. Wilkinson and A. Berry eds. Management Control Association, Sheffield Hallam University.

Covaleski, M., M. Dirsmith and J. Michelman 1993. "An Institutional Theory Perspective on the DRG Framework, Case-Mix Accounting Systems and Health-Care Organizations", *Accounting , Organizations and Society*, 18(1), 65—80.

Cowling, K. 1987. "An Industrial Strategy for Britain: The Nature and Role of Planning", *International Review of Applied Economics*, 1, 1—22.

———— 1990. "The Strategic Approach to Economic and Industrial Policy". In *A New Economic Policy for Britain: Essays on the Development of Industry*, K. Cowling and R. Sugden eds. Manchester: Manchester University Press.

David, P. 1985. "Clio and the Economics of QWERTY", *American Economic Review*, 75, 332—337.

Dietrich, M. 1991. "European Economic Integration and Industrial Policy", *Review of Political Economy*, 3, 418—438.

———— 1994. *Transaction Cost Economics and Beyond: Towards a New Economics of the Firm*. London: Routledge.

———— 1997. "Strategic Lock-In as a Human Issue: The Role of Professional Orientation". In *Evolutionary Economics and Path Dependence*, L. Magnusson and J. Ottoson eds. Cheltenham: Edward Elgar, 79—97.

Dietrich, M. and H. Schenk 1993. "A Bandwagon Theory of the Firm", *Working Paper, Management Report Series*, No. 157, Erasmus University.

Donald, D. and A. Hutton 1991. "Industrial Policy and Economic Performance: The Case of Japan", *Papers in Comparative Political Economy*, 1, Glasgow College: Policy Analysis Research Unit.

Donaldson, T. and L.E. Preston 1995. "The Stakeholder Theory of the Corporation: Concepts, Evidence and Implications", *Academy of Management Review*, 20(1), 65—91.

Dore, R. 1986. "Industrial Policy and How the Japanese Do It", *Catalyst*, 2, 45—56.

Fligstein, N. 1990. *The Transformation of Corporate Control.* Cambridge MA: Harvard University Press.

Geroski, P.A. 1992. "Vertical Relations Between Firms and Industrial Policy", *Economic Journal*, 102, 138—147.

Grewlich, K.W. 1987. "Technological and Industrial Policy in the Federal Republic of Germany". In *A Competitive Future for Europe? Towards a New European Industrial Policy*, P.R. Beije, J. Groenewegen, I. Kostoulas, J. Paelinck and C. von Paridon eds. London: Croom Helm.

Grinyer, P. and J.-C. Spender 1979. *Turnabout: Managerial Recipes for Strategic Success.* London: Associated Business Press.

Hargreaves-Heap, S. 1989. *Rationality in Economics.* Oxford: Basil Blackwell.

Hopwood, A. 1987. "The Archaeology of Accounting Systems", *Accounting, Organizations and Society*, 12(3), 207—234.

Kaplan, R. S. (1984). "The Evolution of Management Accounting", *The Accounting Review*, 390—418.

Krugman, P. 1994. *Peddling Prosperity*, London: WW Norton & Co.

Johnson, G. and K. Scholes 1989. *Exploring Corporate Strategy.* Hemel Hampstead: Prentice Hall, 2nd edn.

Johnson, H.T. and R.S. Kaplan 1987. *Relevance Lost: The Rise and Fall of Management Accounting*, Boston, Mass.: Harvard University Press.

Johnston, R. and P.R. Lawrence 1988. "Beyond Vertical Integration— The Rise of Value-Adding Partnership", *Harvard Business Review*, July-August, 94—101.

Lane, C. 1989. *Management and Labor in Europe.* Aldershot: Edward Elgar.

Lindblom, C.E. 1959. "The Science of Muddling Through", *Public Administration Review*, 19, 78—88.

Lipietz, A. 1992. *Towards a New Economic Order: Postfordism, Ecology and Democracy.* Cambridge: Polity Press.

Macintosh, N. and R.W. Scapens 1990. "Structuration Theory in Management Accounting", *Accounting, Organizations and Society*, 15(5), 455—477.

Miles, R.E. and C.C. Snow 1978. *Organization Strategy, Structure and Process.* New York: McGraw-Hill.

Mintzberg, H. (1979) *The Structuring of Organizations.* Englewood Cliffs, NJ: Prentice Hall.

Nelson, R.R. and S.G. Winter 1982. *An Evolutionary Theory of Economic Change.* Cambridge, Mass.: Belknap.

Porter, M.E 1990. *The Competitive Advantage of Nations.* London: Macmillan.

Scapens, R.W. 1994. "Never Mind the Gap: Towards an Institutional Perspective of Management Accounting Practices", *Management Accounting Research*, 5(3/4), 301—321.

Scapens, R.W., S. Turley, J. Burns, N. Joseph, L. Lewis and A. Southworh 1996. *External Reporting and Management Decisions: A Study of Their Interrelationship in UK Companies.* CIMA: London.

Schein, E.H. 1985. "How Culture Forms, Develops and Changes". In *Gaining Control of Corporate Culture*, R. H. Kilman, M.J. Saxton and R. Serpa eds. London: Jossey-Bass Publishers.

Streit, M. 1987. "Industrial Policies for Technological Change: The Case of West Germany". In *Industrial Policies and Structural Change*, C.T. Saunders ed., Basingstoke: Macmillan.

Stoneman, P. and J. Vickers 1988. "The Economics of Technology Policy", *Oxford Review of Economic Policy*, 4, i—xvi.

7 STRATEGIC TRADE AND INTERNATIONAL COMPETITION POLICY

Rainer Markl and Werner Meissner

1. Introduction

Tensions beween industrial and competition policy are frequent.[1] The semiconductor trade agreement between the United States and Japan—which required Japanese firms to collude in order to reduce their exports to the United States—was in conflict with antitrust policy, as were the various arrangements within the European coal and steel industry especially during the 1970s and 1980s.

US telecommunications regulation, up to the divestiture, required AT&T to provide universal service and to engage in cross-subsidization. But when AT&T moved to cripple new entrants, whose actions systemetically undermined the structure of cross-subsidization the regulators had imposed, AT&T used its antitrust exposure to come to a settlement agreement with the government. Telecommunications and antitrust policy have thus beeen at odds with each other. But antitrust policy prevailed.

On the other hand, the OPEC cartel as the most powerful anticompetitive structure of the postwar period, has not been touched by antitrust law, despite its tremendous impact on consumers welfare—worldwide. Moreover, by preventing countervailing cooperative strategies by US oil companies, US antitrust has strengthened, not weakened OPEC's power.

Retaliatory cooperative acts by US oil companies that could have served to infringe the cartel's market power are decided illegal. Hence, the most far-reaching exercise of market power in the US marketplace has been completely untouched by US antitrust laws, while these same laws have prevented' efforts to exercise countervailing market power by US oil companies.

While these few examples illustrate some areas of of tension, if not conflict, between industrial and competition policy, the principle argument plays a major role in the debate upon the scope and limits of industrial policy. A discussion, which is largely predominated by political beliefs. On the one side of the political spectrum are those which condemn industrial policy because of its anticompetitive effect. According to their view, there is no need for additional government actions on a microeconomic level. Competition policy serves the purpose. It is the best industrial policy. On the other side are those which favor industrial policy because of its benign impact on economic welfare. According to their view, competition policy is one of the key elements of industrial policy. Consequently, there is a need to integrate antitrust with other aspects of industrial policy. Welfare enhancing industrial policy measures should at least not be hampered by an antitrust law which is too restrictive.

Interestingly, both puristic points of view tend to be misleading when industrial policy affects international markets. In this case, industrial policy can easily, perhaps even unintentional, convert into strategic trade policy and if so, the overall welfare effects will at least be less clear-cut. On the other hand, domestic competition policy can be more as the simple guardian of economic welfare. The promotion of mergers and interfirm cooperations can serve as an instrument of strategic trade policy helping to shift oligopoly rents from foreign to domestic firms.

Thus, from an international point of view one has to consider a need to harmonize both policy attempts.

Besides their significance for the success of domestic industrial policy, the welfare losses from strategic trade give rise to think about preventive measures. One possible instrument to tackle the problem of strategic trade is international competition policy—a field which is about to occupy a major place on the international agenda. Yet still indeterminate in its form, one of the crucial points in discussion is strategic trade policy: Should an international competition law explicitly cover anticompetitive actions of governments or will it be sufficient to harmonize the antitrust laws of trading nations?

According to this outline, the purpose of this chapter is twofold. To shed light on the conditions of strategic trade policy and to elicit its major implications for international antitrust. To keep this task tractable, we will, however, confine our attention to three key elements of industrial policy. After a short introduction to the rationale of strategic trade policy, section II.2 is devoted to R&D subsidies. Focusing on models of R&D competition, the subsidization of private R&D efforts turns out to be a rather inappropriate measure to shift rents in favor of domestic firms. Considering, moreover, the beneficial effects of R&D subsidies with respect to the public good problem, international competition policy should generally permit industrial policy in this field.

Section II.3 is devoted to government measures that cause a reduction of private production costs. Granted to firms that are facing strong competition from abroad, this aid forms the classical case of strategic trade policy. To tackle the problem appropriately, international competition policy is forced to adopt a world welfare principle, which is by now, however, more a vision than a concrete guideline of antitrust policy.

In Section II.4 we will analyse the promotion of mergers and interfirm cooperation covering domestic as well as international collaboration. Considering the respective antitrust implications, both forms tend to give support to the idea of harmonization.

II. Industrial Policy and Strategic Trade

II.1   The game theoretic basis of strategic trade policy

Strategic trade policy is a simple exercise on the idea of subgame perfectness. At the first stage, a domestic government has the choice to undertake some policy intervention or to refrain from action. At the second stage firms simultaneously choose their actions which yield certain payoffs. An example of such a game, which covers the principle idea of strategic trade policy, is illustrated in the following figure.[2]

Figure 7.1 The game theoretic approach to strategic trade policy

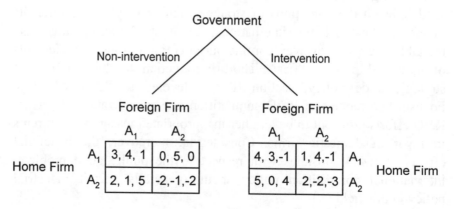

There are two firms, one domestic and one foreign, and two possible actions A_1 and A_2 among which both firms can choose. In each cell, the first number is the payoff to the domestic firm, the second is the payoff to the foreign firm and the third is domestic welfare—the payoff to the government.

Following the idea of subgame perfectness, the game is solved by backward induction. If the firms find themselves on the left side of the decision tree, the domestic firm will always choose the option A_1, because it yields the higher payoff irrespective of what the foreign firm does. The foreign firm will then choose A_2, because it yields a payoff of 5 as compared to 4, if it would have chosen A_1 instead. Thus, the Nash equilibrium solution of this subgame is the upper right cell. The domestic welfare is 0.

At the right side of the decision tree, the domestic firm chooses A_2 which is now the dominant strategy. The foreign firm will choose A_1 to avoid a loss. The solution is then given by the lower left cell. The domestic welfare is 4. Hence, the government prefers intervention over non-intervention.

First, note that government intervention is always associated with a cost: All welfare values at the right hand side are lower than the corresponding values of the left. What makes the government policy attractive, however, is the induced change of the strategic interaction between the two firms leading to a different strategy choice than without government's intervention. The result is a net welfare improvement. Pay-offs are shifted from the foreign to the domestic firm.

Second, the rationale of strategic trade policy is not restricted to any specific measures. The policy tool in question can be tariffs, quotas, voluntary export restraints, subsidies or any other of a wider range of policy instruments which serves the strategic purpose of altering the subsequent game in favor of the domestic firm. This is the reason why industrial policy can easily turn out to be strategic trade policy, even if not intended.

Third, the welfare improvement from strategic trade policy depends critically on the assumption that other countries will not retaliate. An assumption which can hardly be justified when all governments share the same incentive to act. If, however, all countries pursue strategic trade policies, the general outcome will be a welfare loss for all of them. All countries would be better off under a free-trade regime, yet they find themselves trapped in a prisoner's dilemma: The individual incentive to act non-cooperatively stays present, regardless of what the other governments do.

II.2 R&D subsidies

So far, we have not further specified the foreclosure effect which lies in the heart of strategic trade policy. In the case of R&D subsidies, the rent-shifting mechanism of governmental aid works indirectly. The model, developed by Brander and Spencer (1983), may serve here as a starting point. Considered is an industry consisting of two firms, each located in one country. There is no domestic consumption. All goods are exported.[3] Hence, domestic welfare can be identified with home firm's profit minus the cost of any policies carried out.

As in the preceding section, the domestic government moves first. It can credibly commit itself to R&D subsidies before firms are allowed to act. Firms behavior, however, is not restricted to the choice of one single action, but based on a two stage game. In the first stage firms choose R&D levels which determine the amount of cost-saving that accrues to them. In the second stage a simple Cournot output game is played.

The principle effect of the R&D subsidy is that it shifts out the R&D reaction function of the domestic firm, increasing its equilibrium R&D and reducing the R&D undertaken by the foreign firm. This leads to a cost advantage in the subsequent output market which allows the domestic firm to earn higher profit net of subsidy. Thus, domestic welfare will rise. The optimal subsidy is one that shifts the domestic R&D reaction function just enough to reach the Stackelberg leader-follower point.

Despite the beggar-thy-neighbour aspect, the overall welfare effect of R&D subsidy can be positive. The subsidy tends to increase aggregate R&D leading to more output and lower prices in the subsequent export market. Hence, there is a rise in consumer's rent in the output market which can more than offset the inefficiency from excessive R&D.

One of the less conclusive features of this model is the treatment of R&D, not distinct from any other kind of investment. In particular, one may doubt whether the argument carries over to situations where R&D competition is present. Beath, Katsoulacos and Ulph (1989) have examined this case. Their framework is built upon the theory of patent races where R&D competition takes the form of a tournament, i.e. when, roughly speaking, only the winning firm is able to realize a first-mover advantage, with no neighbouring innovation projects for rivals to move to.[4] Due to technical uncertainty, no firm can ever be sure to discover the new product or technology even in the next moment of time. Only the expected time lag before discovery can be reduced—or, which comes to the same thing, the instantaneous probability of discovery at any particular point in time can be increazed—by investing more. To win the race becomes a matter of conditional probability: The firm's own probability to complete the innovation sucessfully and the probability that no other firm has made the discovery so far.

Distinct from the Brander and Spencer analysis, the output market is not treated explicitly. Given winner's and looser's profits contribute to the firms incentive to invest which is seen as driven by two forces. The first is called the profit incentive. It corresponds with that amount of R&D investment the firm would spend if it alone were investing. The sole motivation for R&D is then the winner's profit. This investment decision is determined by the additional profits from bringing forward the likely date of innovation and the additional cost of doing so.

The second incentive is due to the race situation. It is called the competitive threat, and characterizes that R&D investment that would be chosen when the rival is almost certainly about to innovate. The strength of this force is reflected in the difference between winner's and looser's profits.

In general either of the two forces can dominate. However, one important determinant of their relative magnitude will be the ease of imitation. To see this, suppose first that imitation were very easy. In this case a firm's profit will be more or less the same, whether it wins the race or not. The competitive threat disappears and only the profit incentive is left. All in all, this constitutes a situation where there is a strong externality feature about one's R&D: The rival's effort is a good substitute for one's own. Thus, firms tend to "free-ride" on the development costs of others and this causes R&D reaction functions to be negatively sloped.

From the welfare point view, both firms invest less than optimal. A government who wants to improve national welfare will therefore try to encourage the foreign firm to do more R&D and let it bear the cost. But this is precisely what is not achieved by subsidizing domestic firm's R&D. Because of the negatively sloped reaction functions, more R&D investment of the home firm leads to lower activities of the foreign firm. Hence in a situation where the competitive threat is weak, an R&D subsidy misses its strategic goal and leads to a welfare loss.

To cover the other extreme, it is assumed that the innovation is protected by an infinitely lived, effective patent which makes imitation impossible. In this case, the looser's profit will be zero. The competitive threat exceeds the profit incentive, and the R&D reaction functions are positively sloped. However, subsidizing domestic R&D will then be harmful as well. More investment on the home firm's side will now be responded by an increase in foreign R&D. As a result, expected profits out of innovation diminish and the national welfare in both countries suffer, because firms already invest too much.

This last argument versus the strategic role of R&D subsidies requires some qualification. As Dixit (1988) and Bagwell and Staiger (1992) have pointed out, the positively sloped reaction functions in the case of complete patent protection emerge as the result of a race where R&D costs are recurrent and can be ceased when either firm has won. If, however, all R&D costs have to be sunk at the initial instant, as in Loury (1979) and Dasgupta and Stiglitz (1980), reaction functions slope downward, even when the "winner-take-all" assumption is effective. In this case, the R&D subsidy serves its strategic purpose: It shift rents from the foreign to the domestic firm.

Thus, we conclude that an R&D subsidy can be an effective measure of strategic trade policy when it is granted with respect to initial lump-sum costs. Subsidizing recurrent R&D costs, however, runs great risk that the intended result of government's intervention turns into its opposite: The strategic trade policy ends up in a welfare loss.

The theoretical basis of this view are models where R&D competition is prevalent. This stress reflects the idea that the timing of innovation gains importance the closer R&D comes to a specific output market. While basic research is essentially pre-competitive—not only with respect to output market, but also R&D competition—, it offers little opportunity to act strategically. Analyzing strategic trade policy requires therefore to shift the focus from R to D activities, with R&D competition considered as an essential characteristic of the latter.

To sum up, being aware that R&D subsidies are a rather ineffictive tool to shift rents on the D side, but on the R side a proper means to overcome the well-known public good problem,[5] there is little reason, why international competition policy should be given a hold to restrict industrial policy in this field.

II.3 Promotion of production cost savings

Compared to industrial policy measures concerning R&D, much more attention has been given to the strategic role of export subsidies. Since the pioneering work of Brander and Spencer (1985) its conlusions have been subject of intense scrutiny. This allows us to sketch the theoretical issues rather briefly.

Starting point is a simple two-stage game where the domestic government moves first by granting a subsidy to the domestic firm. In the second stage, home and foreign firm compete in the international market where they choose quantities. The major effect of the subsidy is again to alter the strategic interaction: The home firm's reaction function is shifted out and allows the domestic firm to increase its market share as the equilibrium moves to the Stackelberg leader-follower point. Because the subsidy leads to a contraction of foreign exports, the profits of the home firm will rise by more than the amount of subsidy. Hence national welfare is increased.

These results have been subject of a number critiques challenging their robustness.[6] Dixit and Grossman (1984) have criticized the partial equilibrium view that precludes from domestic competition for resources. Dixit (1984) has pointed out, that an incentive to tax exports arises, when there is more than one domestic firm. The perhaps most severe criticism comes from Eaton and Grossman (1986), who show that the sign of the policy recommendation depends critically on the Cournot assumption where the strategy variables (outputs) are strategic substitutes. If the firms would have chosen prices instead, which are strategic complements, the optimal policy is an export tax. Hence, if government lacks information about the exact nature of output market competition, the implementation of a welfare improving strategic trade policy becomes a matter of chance.

With respect to the general validity of the last argument a qualification is in order. Maggi (1996) has developed an enlarged model of strategic trade where firms choose capacities and then compete in prices. Unlike Kreps and Scheinkman (1983), the capacity is here not modeled as a rigid constraint, but an imperfect commitment device. It can vary in its strength and the resulting equilibrium ranges from Bertrand to Cournot as capacity constraints gain importance. One of Maggi's major findings is, that a small capacity subsidy increases the home country's income independent of the mode of competition. Thus, a capacity subsidy is an effective tool to shift rents, even when the government lacks information.

To sum up this draft of theoretical arguments: An industrial policy aiming at lower production costs of home firms can be an effective tool of strategic trade policy when a) the market(s) where domestic and foreign firms interact is a tight oligopoly with a high market share covered by foreign firms and b) price competition is not too harsh. Whereas informations with respect to condition a) are common, governments may have to face an informational constraint with respect to b).

To not jump to conlusions, this result gives no indication that governments might renounce strategic trade policies. First, because the subsidization of firms' productive capacities is in any case an appropriate measure of strategic trade, since it requires no further information. This argument carries greater weight as when it is concerned with subsidies to fixed R&D costs. The latter are restricted to one particular point in time—the beginning of the race—and their effectiveness requires R&D spillovers to be low.

Second, there is widespread intuition, if not clue of evidence, that condition a) and b) correspond. Hence, governments may use the tight oligopoly condition as an indicator that price competition is soft.

Third, there is a view that governments are first of all political players and not domestic welfare maximizers. Hence the presence of informational constraints need not reduce governments' motivation to pursue industrial policies. Assumed that this is true, the economic rationale can be seen as complementary, telling the government to rather choose production cost and not R&D subsidies as its means. The first offers a much better chance to end up successfully.

Taking these arguments together and taking into account the additional harm caused to foreigners, the overall welfare balance of industrial policy need not be positive. This is particularly true, when governments are trapped in a prisoner's dilemma caused by the strategic policy attempts of others. Thus, one may feel the need to control government action in this field, especially if one shares the view that governments tend to not refrain from strategic trade policy even when they risk a national flop.

International competition policy is considered a possible instrument to tackle strategic trade problems. One of its major merits is, that it allows to judge government actions from a world welfare point of view. E.g., international competition policy could encompass the right to prohibit a particular government action, when the harm caused to foreigners substantially outweighs the benefit to domestic welfare in correcting a market imperfection or otherwise protecting the national interest. Moreover, one can imagine that national industrial policy with a substantial negative external effect could become subject of a reporting and justification procedure which helps to spread information that national measures are proportionate to a proper national interest, thereby diminishing the risk of unwarranted retaliation.[7]

Though appealing from the theoretical point of view, the complication in this approach is threefold. First, it may be difficult to obtain the necessary informations. If it is assumed, that national governments lack information about output market conditions, there seems little reason to believe that this may change drastically when an antitrust authority is concerned.

Second, industrial policy measures are assumed to have long-term effects. Hence, the appropriate concept of world welfare has to be couched in a forward looking sense, with more than one single period in mind. This exaggerates the data difficulties mentioned above. On the other hand, only if all substantial present and future effects are comprehended one should allow competition policy to effectively control government actions.

Third, acknowledging the right to prohibit government actions to an international antitrust authority is likely to be interpreted as an infringement of national sovereignty. Since every nation pursues all kinds of industrial policy, it is hard to imagine how national governments could ever agree on that.

Taking all three arguments together produces the impression that the world welfare principle subject to appropriate national autonomy is more a vision, albeit an important one, than a concrete guideline of international antitrust policy. Nevertheless one can imagine steps towards this goal. The EU may serve here as an example. The Treaty of Rome requires member states to notify to the European Commission all state aids, including subsidies, which the states must then justify or eliminate. The law works reasonably well, tending to give governments an additional argument at hand to resist private-interest lobbying. This justification procedure could be extended to cover discriminative legislation as well. Nations could be obliged to publish an additional report compiling all laws that impact on international trade and discriminate against foreign goods and services, stating the justification for the discrimination.

II.4 Promotion of mergers and cooperation

From the strategic trade point of view, the promotion of cooperation beween firms can serve two objectives. On the one hand, the government strategy can aim at mergers and cooperations within the country. Provided that their establishment is associated with substantial economies of scale and/or scope and/or synergy effects, domestic firms can benefit from a cost advantage leading to an increase in their market share at the expense of foreign rivals. Thus, the principle effect is not different from the case analysed in the preceeding section: The promotion of domestic cooperation alters the strategic interaction in the international market. Home firms profits rise and national welfare is enhanced. What is lacked, however, is the accuracy of aim. The government's main instrument at hand is the faciliation of private restraints, especially in form of a permissive antitrust treatment. Its installation requires a prior private incentive which governments cannot control.

The second objective to be considered is the promotion of international cooperation domestic firms can join in and benefit from. Though rather insuspicious at the first glance, international cooperations can give rise to a substantial welfare loss to be borne by those which are excluded. This makes them distinct from all aforementioned measures of strategic policy where the incentive to seperate firms—in home and foreign—is due to government actions. In the case of international cooperations, the firms themselves decide who is in and who is out. The strategic role of the government is then restricted to assure a membership decision in favor of the domestic firm.

The following case of international R&D cooperation can illustrate the major effects.[8] To examine the strategic features properly, a few assumptions are needed, however. Firstly, suppose there is an international industry consisting of n identical firms, all located in different countries, whose sole business is to export a homogenous product to a country "n+1", which not able to produce that particular commodity by itself. Hence, the national welfare in all n countries can then be identified with home firm profits whereas any change in consumer rent is restricted to country "n+1".

Secondly, it is assumed that there exists a certain innovation project, known to all firms, that lowers production costs significantly. There is Cournot competition in the output market. Marginal production costs are constant and the demand curve is linear.[9] All firms have the same interest in realizing the associated profit stream. However, to stress the idea of an R&D race, the right to exploit the fruits from successful R&D is strictly confined to the firm that is innovating fierst.[10] Ex-post licensing is excluded. But firms have the possibility to engage in an ex-ante arrangement that offers all participating firms access to the R&D results, i.e. they can establish an R&D cooperation.[11] Let us assume that m (with $1 \leq m \leq n$) of our n firms have done so, and investigate the consequences of this decision for the other fringe firms who still act independently.[12]

According to the principle of subgame perfectness the examination starts in the product market. Since this is the final decision, it is influenced by all previous actions: the number of cooperating firms as well as the outcome of the R&D tournament, which is in turn determined by the R&D investments firms have chosen.

Without R&D all firms in the industry were facing the same production costs offering each firm a given profit. Yet, with succesful completion of the R&D project, firms profits differ. Two cases have to be distinguished. The first comes along when one of the non-cooperating fringe firms has succeeded in the R&D race. In this case the innovation is exploited exclusively by this firm. It realizes a winner's profit, whereas all others firms in the industry are loosing money. All have to face the same looser's profit, irrespective of whether they are a member of the cooperation or just another fringe firm. Thus, in this case the cooperation size has no effect on the distribution of profits in the output market. The innovator has improved its situation whereas all other firms are worse off.

If, however, the cooperation has won the race, all realized individual profits will depend on m, the number of participating firms. The more firms that join the arrangement the smaller the individual profit of the winning firm and the smaller the profit of a remaining fringe firm will be. Because of the sharing of R&D results, an increase in m implies more firms with superior technology. Assuming a standard Cournot this leads to an increase in aggregate output that harms both the remaining fringe firms and the cooperation members, which have to face an erosion of their individual competitive advantage. Thus, one can conclude that more cooperation widens the profit gap between winning and loosing for outside firms, while it narrows this gap for its members.

Even more important with respect to partial R&D cooperations is, however, that more cooperation also gives rise to a growing difference between the individual winner's profit of a cooperation member and the corresponding profit of a fringe firm. As already mentioned, due to the sharing of R&D results the profits that accrue to a single cooperation member tend to fall with rising cooperation size whereas the winner's profits of the fringe firms remain unaltered. Thus, the decision to cooperate is not costless. Cooperation members have to forego the higher winner's profits from independent R&D. Without this profit loss firms would always prefer to establish an R&D cooperation that is industrywide.

In the second stage each firm decides how much R&D to do at each instant of time. In common with most other models of R&D race, it is assumed that the relationship between the probability of discovery and

R&D efforts is time-independent and exponential, leading to constant research intensities.[13]

Secondly, all firms face the same innovation technology which is a positive, increasing and convex function of R&D efforts. Thus there are decreasing returns all around. More intense R&D is more costly, but yields a shorter time to succesful innovation.

Thirdly, it is assumed that the individual innovation processes are independent. In particular, we are precluding the abovementioned public good-case where large spillovers lead the firms to free-ride on the R&D investment of others. Hence, R&D reaction functions are positively sloped, at least between cooperation members and fringe firms.

Given these conditions, firms choose R&D intensities to maximize the expected payoff out of innovation. However, the individual payoffs are not identical for all firms. The exact formulation of the profits and the corresponding R&D reaction functions can be found in the appendix. Here it suffices to note that, according to the decision to establish an m firm cooperation in the first stage, one has to distinguish sharply between the individual payoff of a cooperation member and that of a fringe firm conducting R&D independently.[14] An independent firm has to compete with other fringe firms on the one hand and cooperation members on the other. Only if none of these competitors has succeeded first is given the fringe firm the chance to win the R&D contest. Thus, the competitive threat a fringe firm faces will be distinct leading to strong R&D investments in order to forestall the successful completion of the innovation process by its competitors.

Compared to a fringe firm, the cooperation member is in a privileged position. Because of the sharing of R&D results all participating firms are able to realize winner's profits when any of the member firms has succeeded first. Cooperation members compete only with fringe firms. Therefore, their competitive threat is reduced significantly. This offers the opportunity for the individual member firm to cut down its R&D investment, which in turn saves R&D costs.

This cost saving is the main attraction of cooperative R&D. It builds up a compensating factor to the individual profit losses in the output market that are associated with that measure. However, due to the convexity of R&D technology these cost savings will decline the more firms join in. Whereas in contrast, the combined profit losses all other cooperation members have to suffer when an additional firm is accepted will rise with m.

Hence, depending on the magnitude of either effect there is a possibility for the cooperation size to reach an upper limit before the cooperation is industrywide. This is the case of partial R&D cooperations coming into existence when the profit loss caused by more cooperation exceeds the associated benefit from additional R&D cost savings. From then on, it will be unprofitable for the existing cooperation members to admit new firms. The cooperation size will have reached its optimal level.

Distinct from cooperation members, fringe firms suffer from more cooperation. Their looser's profits melt away, increasing the competitive threat they have to face. Hence, more cooperation leads to higher research intensities—and therefore R&D costs—of those which are excluded. They have to face a profit loss which would become even greater when the cooperation size exceeded its equilibrium value.

This has two important implications. The first is most obvious: No one has an interest in more cooperation. Not the cooperation members, which have chosen the size to maximize their expected payoffs, and not the fringe firms, which would have to suffer an even bigger profit loss from that measure.

The other major implication of this property concerns the membership decision. If fringe firms suffer from more cooperation in equilibrium, one can be certain that up to that point it has always been profitable for them to join in the arrangement. They would never have chosen to stay independent, instead. This means that we can exclude the situation where fringe firms have an interest in more cooperation, not because they want to join in but because they can gain from softer R&D competition. Under the conditions described above, the decision for a partial R&D cooperation will be consistent with the individual incentives of its potential members.

Considering the results so far, the strategic element of R&D cooperations should be quite obvious. To establish a partial R&D cooperation increases the expected profits of its member firms at the expense of others that are excluded. The deterrent effect comes along with fringe firms' rising R&D intensities. This causes a decline in their expected payoffs. With fixed costs entailed in the research process, rising R&D intensities may even force fringe firms to refrain from R&D at all.

Considering the foreclosure effect of partial R&D cooperations, the incentive of governments is self-evident. They want their "national champion(s)" to be included. This raises the question of membership: How do firms decide with whom they want to cooperate and who should belong to the fringe instead?

Perhaps the most direct way to cope with that issue is to relax the assumption that all firms are symmetrical. Suppose, for example, that firms are differently efficient in conducting R&D. Then, given perfect information and differences in R&D technology that are fairly moderate and well distributed, we can expect the partial cooperation to consist of the most efficient firms. Because of lower costs, they spend more on R&D, gain the higher expected payoffs out of innovation and have, consequently, a higher incentive to cooperate.

Having this particular argument in mind, national governments are provided with an opportunity to influence the membership decision in favor of the domestic firm. By subsidizing R&D they can establish a credible pre-commitment for the national firm to become part of the arrangement.[15] As long as their subsidy does not exceed the difference in payoffs between a cooperation member and a fringe firm, the country is better off.

However, a common feature of strategic trade policy models is that all governments share the same incentive. And if all of them act accordingly, every country will face a welfare loss. This can most easily be seen when the afore-mentioned efficiency differences are weak. In that case every government will pay exactly the profit difference between member- and non-membership. Thus, the basic situation remains unaltered. All countries would be better off, without subsidizing their domestic firm.

To sum up, the promotion of domestic firms' membership in international cooperations can serve as a proper means of strategic trade policy as well as the promotion of domestic mergers and cooperation through permissive antitust treatment mentioned at the beginning of this section. However, with respect to the implications for international competition policy both cases should be analysed in turn. Whereas the latter calls for international harmonization, the first leads us back to our chief concern of whether international competition policy should be used as an instrument to impede strategic trade.

Let us start with the harmonization pressure put by governments' promotion of domestic mergers and interfirm cooperations. Virtually all nations have a cartel and a merger law, with only minor differences in substantive law between countries. What is lacked, however, is sufficient coverage and law enforcement. The cartel law may serve here as a good example. In most countries the cartel law allows exceptions, such as for crisis or depression cartels. Export cartels, however, are normally not covered by national law. In general, there are two reasons given to support this exclusion. First, harm abroad is not our business and second, export promotion enhances the country's welfare. From an international point of view, the first argument indicates the cause of the strategic trade problem and the second argument, considering its intended result, is rather weak. In the domestic context, it is the every day business of an antitrust authority to distinguish between welfare enhancing and anticompetitive arrangements. There is no reason why the tests cannot also be applied to exports.

Almost all nations prohibit import cartels, but are lax in enforcing their law. The problem can be adressed by nations' agreement to enforce their own law, and the provision of a right of action, including remedies, by harmed nations. To go a step further, nations might even agree to accept the jurisdictional legitimacy of antitrust action in the harmed country, especially when the enforcing court is obliged to apply home country's antitrust law.

While the improvement of national antitrust law can limit the strategic trade attitude towards domestic mergers and cooperations, it is certainly of no help when the government promotion of international cooperation is concerned. In that case governments grant support to influence the membership decision in favor of the domestic firm and get trapped in a prisoner's dilemma. An international competition policy, which explicitely covers industrial policy measures by governments, could be seen as a way out. However, this would not only mean to break a fly on the wheel, but also an abuse of international competition policy which should only be enforced when an action is presumed to be anticompetitive. A characteristic that can hardly be applied to government's membership payment.

However, there is a second aspect to be considered with international cooperations: The antitrust treatment of the arrangement itself which can harm competition in more than one country. In this case, enforcement at the national level by one or more countries is normally sufficient to deal with the problem provided that coverage and enforcement of national laws will be improved.

III   Conclusion

The examination of the effects of industrial policy in international markets shows little evidence that international competition policy can serve as a proper instrument to control strategic trade. In the case of R&D subsidies, we have argued that their strategic potential is rather low. Hence, there is little need to control them at all. This is certainly not true with respect to measures aimed at private production cost savings which are in the focus of strategic trade policy. Since their adequate treatment by antitrust authorities would require a test based on the world welfare effects, we consider this more as a plans for the future. Finally, the promotion of mergers and cooperations can be treated properly by national antitrust authorities provided that coverage and enforcement of national laws will be improved.

Notes

1. This statement and the following remarks are due to Jorde and Teece (1997).

2. This figure has its origin in Brander (1994).

3. This set of assumptions is common in models of strategic trade policy, though not crucial for its results. It serves to isolate the profitshifting motive from the terms of trade effect and the effect on consumer surplus. In particular, the

insights offered by the model carry over when foreign and domestic firm are active in both markets.

4. For a detailed review of different innovation race models, see Reinganum (1989). The analysis of Beath, Katsoulacos and Ulph is based on the model of Lee and Wilde (1980).

5. This argument is based on Spence (1984) who has shown that subsidies are effective in markets where spillovers are high.

6. For a survey, see Krugman (1989).

7. For a more detailed discussion, see Fox and Ordover (1997).

8. The following draws heavily from Meißner and Markl (1997).

9. These assumptions are not crucial to the existence of partial R&D cooperations. However, this standard Cournot setting is sufficient to guarantee the properties that will be derived.

10. Of course, we could have developed our arguments within a standard model of R&D cooperation as well, where joint R&D results in lower R&D costs, more investment and consequently a higher reduction of production costs excluded competitors will have to face. Models of that type are due the pioneering work of d'Aspremont and Jaquemin (1988, 1990). However, to model the innovative process as a race gives us the additional advantage of being able to incorporate not only technical uncertainty but also R&D competition in the sense that the research undertaken by one firm explicitly depends on the R&D efforts of all others. This has particular importance when it comes to partial R&D cooperations where one would expect that the decision to cooperate itself causes a reaction of those excluded.

11. Since firms are completely symmetric, one can think of an R&D cooperation simply as an arrangement to divide the combined expected payoffs from innovation, implying that not only R&D costs but also product market profits are shared equally between member firms.

12. Thus, we are restricting the analysis to the highly simplifying case where there is only one R&D cooperation possible. Fringe firms are allowed to react to this measure only in terms of R&D intensities and not by establishing a second cooperation to recoup the profit losses they had to face.

13. For a more detailed explanation and discussion of the underlying assumptions, see Reinganum (1989).

14. Since we are precluding any additional positive externalities between R&D projects that comes along when imitation is very easy, this difference will not be softened.

15. To avoid any direct effects on the subsequent R&D contest, think of the subsidy as a simple lump-sum payment.

References

Bagwell, K. and R. Staiger 1992. "The Sensitivity of Strategic and Corrective R&D Policy in Battles for Monopoly", *International Economic Review,* 33, 795—816.

Beath, J., Y. Katsoulacos and D. Ulph 1989. "Strategic R&D Policy", *Economic Journal,* 99, 74—83.

Brander, J. and B. Spencer 1983. "Export Subsidies and International Market Share Rivalry", *Journal of International Economics,* 18, 83—100.

Dasgupta, P. and J. Stiglitz 1980. "Uncertainty, Industrial Structure, and the Speed of R&D", *Bell Journal of Economics,* 11, 1—28.

d'Aspremont, C. and A. Jaquemin 1988. "Cooperative and Noncooperative R&D in Duopoly with Spillovers", *American Economic Review,* 78, 1133—1137.

———— 1990. "Cooperative and Noncooperative R&D in Duopoly with Spillovers: Erratum", *American Economic Review,* 80, 641—642.

Dixit, A 1990. "International Trade Policy for Oligopolistic Industries", *Economic Journal,* 94, Supplement, 1—16.

———— 1988. "General Model of R&D Competition and Policy", *Rand Journal of Economics,* 19, 20—32.

Dixit, A. and G. Grossman 1984. "Targeted Export Promotion with Several Oligopolistic Industries", *Discussion Paper in Economics No. 71,* (Woodrow Wilson School, Princeton University).

Eaton, J. and G. Grossman 1986. "Optimal Trade and Industrial Policy under Oligopoly", *Quarterly Journal of Economics*, 101, 383—406.

Fox, E. and J. Ordover 1997. "The Harmonization of Competition and Trade Law". In *Competition Policy in the Global Economy* L. Waverman et al. eds. London: Routledge.

Jorde, M. and D. Teece 1997. "Innovation, Market Structure and Antitrust". In *Competition Policy in the Global Economy*, L. Waverman et al. eds. London: Routledge.

Kreps, D. and J. Scheinkman 1983. "Quantity Precommitment and Bertrand Competition Yield Cournot Outcomes", *Bell Journal of Economics*, 14, 326—337.

Krugman, P. 1989. "Industrial Organization and International Trade". In *Handbook of Industrial Organization* R. Schmalensee and R.E. Willig eds. Vol. I, Amsterdam: Elsevier Science Publishers, 1179—1223.

Lee, T. and L. Wilde 1980. "Market Structure and Innovation: A Reformulation", *Quarterly Journal of Economics*, 94, 429—436.

Loury, G. 1979. "Market Structure and Innovation", *Quarterly Journal of Economics*, 93, 395—410.

Maggi, G. 1996. "Strategic Trade Policies with Endogenous Mode of Competition", *American Economic Review*, 86, 237—258.

Meissner, W. and R. Markl 1997. "International R&D Cooperations". In *Competition Policy in the Global Economy* L. Waverman et al. eds. London: Routledge.

Reinganum, J.F. 1989. "The Timing of Innovation: Research, Development and Diffusion". In *Handbook of Industrial Organization*, R. Schmalensee and R.D. Willig eds. Vol. I, Amsterdam: Elsevier Science Publishers, 850—908.

Spence, M. 1984. "Cost Reduction, Competition and Industry Performance", *Econometrica*, 52, 101—121.

Spencer, B. and J. Brander 1983. "International R&D Rivalry and Industrial Strategy", *Review of Economic Studies*, 50, 707—722.

Appendix

Let Π be the individual profit in the product market without R&D, Π_m^W the winner's profit of a cooperation member with the subscript m indicating that the cooperation has won the race and Π_{n-m}^L the respective looser's profit when the fringe firms have succeded instead, then the total expected payoff of a cooperation member will be:

(1)
$$V = \frac{\Pi_m^W/r \cdot mx + \Pi_{n-m}^L/r \cdot (n-m)y + \Pi - z(x)}{[mx + (n-m)y + r]} ,$$

with $r>0$ as the common interest rate, x denoting the research intensity of a cooperation member and y the R&D effort chosen by a fringe firm. z stands for the individual R&D cost function depending on the research intensity.

$\hat{\Pi}_{n-m}^W$ denotes the winner's profit of an independent fringe firm, $\hat{\Pi}_m^L$ its looser's profit when the cooperation has won the race and $\hat{\Pi}_{n-m}^L$ the respective profit when another fringe firm has succeeded first. Hence, the expected payoff of a fringe firm will be:

(2)
$$\hat{V} = \frac{\hat{\Pi}_{n-m}^W/r \cdot y + \hat{\Pi}_m^L/r \cdot mx + \hat{\Pi}_{n-m}^L/r(n-m-1)\bar{y} + \Pi - z(y)}{[mx + (n-m-1)\bar{y} + y + r]} ,$$

with $\bar{y}$ denoting the research effort of another fringe firm.
The Nash equilibrium in research intensities is determined by the two reaction functions

(3)
$$x \in \arg\max_{x} V \Rightarrow \Pi_m^W + (\Pi_m^W/r - \Pi_{n-m}^L/r)(n-m)y - z'(x)/m$$
$$[mx + (n-m)y + r] - [\Pi - z(x)] = 0$$

(4)
$$y \in \arg\max_{y} \hat{V} \Rightarrow \hat{\Pi}_{n-m}^W + (\hat{\Pi}_{n-m}^W/r - \hat{\Pi}_m^L/r)mx + (\hat{\Pi}_{n-m}^W/r - \hat{\Pi}_y^L/r)$$
$$(n-m-1)y - z'(y)[mx + (n-m)y + r] - [\Pi - z(y)] = 0$$

showing one firm's profit-maximizing choice to any given research intensity of the other firms.

Yet, to establish the industry equilibrium, the decision to cooperate has to be introduced. Assuming that member firms choose m to maximize their individual profits, their decision is given by

(5)
$$m \in \arg \max_m V \Rightarrow \left[\Pi_m^W/r + (\partial \Pi_m^W/\partial m)/r \cdot m \right] \cdot x$$
$$- \Pi_{n-m}^L/r \cdot y - V(x-y) = 0$$

Conditions (3), (4) and (5) build up the industry equilibrium.

8 POLICY IMPLICATIONS

OF PURELY STRATEGIC MERGERS

Hans Schenk

Introduction

The 1990s have seen a merger and acquisition wave with unprecedented peaks in both the United States and Western Europe. With around 1,000 bln US dollars in deal value on a annual basis during much of the second half of the 1990s, this fifth merger wave of the century easily matched or even outpaced the size of investments in equipment, machinery and corporate R&D. While a considerable share of merger activity consists of the getting together of firms that were already large thanks to earlier mergers, a substantial number of mergers concerns the takeover of small, innovative firms. However, if the experience of earlier merger waves is indicative—and, indeed, there are not many reasons for suspecting that it is not—then much managerial time and effort will again have been devoted to investment projects with an expected value of approximately zero or worse (Mueller, 1996; Schenk, 2000).[1]

For example, Dickerson et al. (1997) found for a panel of almost 3,000 UK-quoted firms that acquisitions have a systematic detrimental impact on company performance as measured by the rate of return on assets. Not only was the coefficient on acquisition growth much lower than that on internal growth, but there appeared to be an additional and permanent reduction in profitability following acquisition as well. More specifically, for the average company, the marginal impact of becoming an acquirer was to reduce the rate of return relative to non-acquirers by 1.38 percentage points (i.e. in the year of the first acquisition). Taking all subsequent acquisitions into account, acquiring firms experienced a relative reduction of 2.90 percentage points per annum. Since the mean return across all non-acquiring firms was 16.43%, this translates into a shortfall in performance by acquiring firms of 2.9/16.43, which is around 17.7% per annum.

This finding is not an exception. On the contrary, the most common result of merger performance studies is that profitability and productivity, variously measured, do not improve as a result of merger (see e.g. Ravenscraft and Scherer (1987) for the US; Bühner (1991) for Germany; Simon et al. (1996) for the advertising industry; and Berger and Humphrey (1992) and Rhoades (1994; 1998) for the banking industry).[2]

It is also likely that mergers and acquisitions have a negative effect on R&D investments, R&D investments relative to the industry average, and R&D output except for some industries, most notably the chemical industry (Scherer, 1984; Ravenscraft and Scherer, 1987; Hitt et al., 1991). From an economic point of view, the recurrently high incidence of mergers is therefore paradoxical. Several authors have tried to explain this apparent paradox by suggesting that hubris or the maximization of status or personal income may lead managers (a) to expand company size through merger beyond that which maximizes real shareholder wealth, and/or (b) to disregard dismal experiences with earlier mergers (for a synopsis, see Schenk, 2000). However, while possibly correct in a substantial number of cases, these explanations cannot by themselves clarify why mergers should occur in waves. Rather, they would have to be seen as contributions that have exposed conditions that should be met before a merger wave can start and continue.[3]

The following section, which draws on Schenk (1996), will therefore endeavour to develop a theory of mergers that explicitly captures the persistent and cyclic occurrence of non-wealth creating mergers. Rooted in both agency theory and the theory of games, it suggests that many mergers are undertaken for purely strategic instead of economic motives. For reasons to be developed, these so-called "purely strategic mergers" call for a special policy approach, provided that the problem is sufficiently serious. Before starting up the discussion of possible policy implications, the paper therefore first tries to delineate the welfare effects of purely strategic mergers.

A Theory of Purely Strategic Mergers

Most "important" mergers are undertaken by large firms (see note 1). These firms normally operate in concentrated industries and are usually active in several of those industries at the same time (see e.g. Karier, 1993). In the typical situation of single market or multi-market oligopoly, which involves both interdependence of outcomes and strategic uncertainty, adopting mimetic routines is a likely way for solving strategic decision making problems. According to DiMaggio and Powell (1982), for example, uncertainty or lack of understanding with respect to goals, technologies, strategies, payoffs, etcetera—all of them typical for modern industries—are powerful forces that encourage imitation. Following Cyert and March (1963), they suggest that when firms have to cope with problems with ambiguous causes or unclear solutions they will rely on problemistic search aimed at finding a viable solution with little expense. Instead of making decisions on the basis of systematic analyses of goals and means, organizations may well find it easier to mimic other organizations. Moreover, organizations with ambiguous or (potentially) disputable goals will be likely to be highly dependent upon appearances for legitimacy.

Reputation. This latter point is also implied in Scharfstein and Stein (1990). Their model assumes that there are two types of managers, "smart" ones who receive informative signals about the value of an investment (e.g. a merger), and "dumb" ones who receive purely noisy signals. Initially, neither these managers nor other persons (i.e. stakeholders) can identify the types, but after an investment decision has been made, stakeholders can update their beliefs on the basis of the following two pieces of evidence:

- whether their agent has made a profitable investment; and
- whether their agent's behavior was similar to or different from that of other managers.

Given the quite reasonable assumption that there are systematically unpredictable components of investment value, and that whereas "dumb" managers will simply observe uncorrelated noise, "smart" managers tend to get correlated signals since they are all observing a piece of the same "truth" (Scharfstein and Stein, 1990, p. 466), it is likely that the second piece of evidence will get precedence over the first. Since these signals might be "bad" just as well as "good", "smart" managers may, however, all have received misleading signals. Since stakeholders will not be able to assess or even perceive these signals they will refer to the second piece of evidence in assessing the ability of "their" managers. Now, if a manager is concerned with her reputation with stakeholders, then it will be natural for her to mimic a first-mover as this suggests to stakeholders that she has observed a signal that is correlated with the signal observed by the first-mover—which will make it more likely that she is a "smart" manager.

The more managers adopt this behavior, the more likely it will be that "bad" decisions will be seen as a result of a common unpredictable negative component of investment value. The ubiquitousness of the error in other words will suggest that all managers were victims of a "bad" signal. Erring managers will subsequently be able to share the blame of stakeholders with their peers. In contrast, a manager who takes a contrarian position will ex ante be perceived as "dumb". She will therefore be likely to pursue an investment opportunity if that is being pursued by peers even if her private information suggests that it has a negative expected value. Thus, Scharfstein and Stein's model explains why conventional wisdom teaches that "it is better for reputation to fail conventionally than to succeed unconventionally" (Keynes, 1936, p. 158). **Rational herding.** This result, however, is not generally dependent on reputational considerations. Whereas Scharfstein and Stein's model is essentially an agency model in which agents try to fool their principals and get rewarded if they succeed in this, Banerjee (1992) and Bikhchandani et al. (1992), for example, have addressed the imitation phenomenon as a consequence of informational externalities. In these models each decision maker looks at the decisions made by previous decision makers in taking her own decision and opts for imitating those previous decisions because the earlier decision makers may have learned some information that is important for her. The result is herd behavior, i.e. a behavioral pattern in which everyone is doing what erveryone else is doing.

These models are essentially models which explain why some person may choose not to go by her own information but instead imitates the choice made by a previous decision maker. Following Banerjee (1992), suppose that—for some reason—the prior probability that an investment alternative is successful is 51 percent (call this alternative i_1), and that the prior probability that alternative i_2 is successful is 49 percent. These prior probabilities are common knowledge. Suppose further that of ten firms— i.e. firms A,...,J—nine firms have received a signal that i_2 is better (of course, this signal may be wrong) but that the one firm which has received a signal that i_1 is better happens to choose first. The signals are of equal quality, and firms can only observe predecessors' choices but not their signals. The first firm (firm A) will clearly opt for alternative i_1. Firm B will now know that the first firm had a signal that favored i_1 while her own signal favors i_2. If the signals are of equal quality, then these conflicting signals effectively cancel out, and the rational choice for firm B is to go by the prior probabilities, i.e. choose i_1. Her choice provides no new information to firm C, so that firm C's situation is not different from that of firm B. Firm C will then imitate firm B for the same reason that prompted firm B to imitate firm A, and so on: all nine follower firms will eventually adopt alternative i_1. Clearly, if firm B had fully relied on her own signal, then her decision would have provided information to the other eight firms. Such would have encouraged these other firms to use their own information.

Thus, from a broader perspective, it is of crucial importance whether firm A's decision is the correct decision. If it is, then all firms will choose for the "right" alternative, but if it is not, all firms will end up with a "wrong" decision. Also, the result of this game is dependent on chance: were firm B,....,J to have had the opportunity to choose first, things would have come out entirely different. However, when translated into our merger problem, if alternative i_2 is set equal to "do not undertake a merger" then A's action ("merger") will always be the first to be observed as a deviation from actual practice, thus prompting firms B,....,J to respond. The mechanism is especially clear when a first and a second firm have both chosen the same $i \neq 0$ (where the point 0 has no special meaning but is merely defined as a point that is known, i.e. observable, to the other firms). That is, the third firm (firm C) knows that firm A must have a signal since otherwise she would have chosen $i = 0$. Firm A's choice is therefore at least as good as firm C's signal. Moreover, the fact that B has followed A lends extra support to A's choice (which may be the "wrong" choice nevertheless). It is therefore always better for C to follow A.

The main virtues of Banerjee's model are (a) that some aspects of herd behavior can be explained without invoking network externalities, i.e. without requiring that a decision maker will actually benefit from imitating earlier decision makers (which would be the case if undertaking some action is more worthwhile when others are doing related things); and (b) that it is possible that decision makers will neglect their private information and instead will go by the information which is provided by the actions of earlier decision makers (or the prior probabilities).

Cascades. Bikhchandani et al. (1992) use the metaphor of a cascade to stress essentially the same point. The process is depicted as a cascade since with increasing numbers of decision makers adopting a particular action, it becomes increasingly, i.e. more than proportionally, likely that the next decision maker will follow suit. According to Bikhchandani et al., a cascade will start if "enough" predecessors have all acted in contradistinction to a subsequent decision maker's own information and if there is no a priori reason to expect that the signals received by the earlier decision makers are less valuable than the signal received by the subsequent decision maker. The first condition is dependent on the specification of the model. The latter condition is an assumption of the model (but can be adapted by introducing variations in signal strength). Ultimately, the reason that a decision maker will tend to disregard her own information is that she is sufficiently uncertain about the value of her signal to act upon it when faced by the decisions of others. Alternatively, it could be argued that she is simply economizing on the costs which are involved with gathering and processing information. Observing the choices of others and imitating these may be a cheap and helpful alternative in the light of the many uncertainties which are involved with strategic decision making.

Regret. The models discussed so far make clear that the intricacies of information diffusion in sequential games can cause imitation despite the fact that a follower's private information would indicate a deviation from the trajectory that seems to have been started. Notice, however, that they are couched in a positive payoff framework. Furthermore, they make use of binary action sets implying that only correct and incorrect decisions are possible and that a small mistake incurs the same loss as a large mistake. The introduction of a regret framework relaxes these conditions and increases the plausibility of models of herding behavior. In a seminal series of experiments Kahneman and Tversky (1979) found that people systematically violate two major conditions of the expected utility model's conception of rationality when confronted with risk, viz. the requirements of consistency of and coherence among choices. They traced this to the psychological principles that govern the perception of decision problems and the evaluation of options. Apart from the fact that it appears to matter substantially in which frame a *given* decision problem is couched (presented; formulated), even to the extent that preferences are reversed when that frame is changed, choices involving gains are often risk averse and choices involving losses risk taking. Thus, it appears that the response to losses is more extreme than the response to gains. Kahneman and Tversky's "prospect theory", of course, is consistent with common experience that the displeasure associated with losing a sum of money is greater than the pleasure associated with gaining the same amount.

Consequently, it is likely that the contents of decision rules and standard practices will be "biased" such that they favor the prevention of losses rather than the realization of gains. Thus, behavioral norms which carry this property are more likely to be "chosen" as Schelling's focal points (Schelling, 1960). In practice, this will mean that firms are likely to adopt routines which imply a substantial degree of circumspection. A similar degree of circumspection is likely to develop if the decision maker is concerned with the regret that she may have upon discovering the difference between the actual payoff as the result of her choice and "what might have been" the payoff were she to have opted for a different course of action. Regret in this case may be defined as the loss of pleasure due to the knowledge that a better outcome may have been attained if a different choice had been made. Under conditions of uncertainty a decision maker will modify the expected value of a particular action according to the level of this regret.

Minimax regret. Dietrich and Schenk (1995) have suggested that one way of expressing this is by adopting a mini-max regret routine. Let us assume that a decision maker knows the payoffs for each decision alternative but that she is completely ignorant as to which state of nature prevails. The mini-max regret routine then prescribes to select that strategy which minimizes the highest possible regret assuming that the level of regret is linearly related to the differences in payoff. The mini-max regret criterion thus puts a floor under how bad the decision maker would feel if things go wrong. Moreover, such will protect her against the highest possible reproach that can be made by those stakeholders who assess the decision's utility on the basis of the true state of nature.

When put into a framework of competitive interdependence this develops as follows. Given a particular action of firm A which is important enough to be monitored by her peers (rivals)—i.e. a merger or an acquisition—firm B will have to contemplate what the repercussions for her own position might be. Suppose that there is no way that firm B can tell whether A's move will be a successful move. A's move could be genuinely motivated by a realistic expectation that her cost position will improve, or by a realistic expectation that her move will increase her rating with stakeholders or even her earnings. That is, A's competitiveness position vis-à-vis her peers may be ameliorated as a result of that move, say in terms of a first mover advantage. But then again, it may not. For example, A's move might be purely motivated by the pursuit of managerial goals, or it may simply be a miscalculation caused by hubris. What is firm B to do?

Suppose that A's move will be successful, but that B has not reacted by imitating that move herself (which we will call scenario α). To what extent will B regret not having reacted? Alternatively, suppose that A's move will not be successful but that B has imitated it solely inspired by the possible prospect of A's move being a success (scenario ß). To what extent will B regret this when the failure of A's move becomes apparent? Within a mini-max regret framework, it is likely that B's regret attached to scenario α will be higher than the regret attached to scenario ß. For in scenario α, B will experience a loss of competitiveness, while in scenario ß her competitive position vis-à-vis A will not have been harmed. Of course, B could have realized a competitive gain in scenario ß had she refrained from imitation, but in terms of the mini-max regret model her regret of having lost this potential gain is likely to be relatively small. The implication is that under conditions of uncertainty a strategic move by firm A will elicit an imitative countermove by her rivals—even if the economic payoffs are unknown.

The models discussed assume that a decision maker's payoffs do not depend on what subsequent decision makers do so that there is no incentive to cheat in an effort to influence a later player. Moreover, decision makers are not allowed to have heterogeneous values of adoption. Yet, these models allow us to conclude that it is likely that a decision maker who is using a mini-max regret routine will imitate actions of earlier decision makers that are regarded as significant. Thus, if—for some reason—a first decision maker within a strategic group has decided to undertake a merger, a second decision maker may follow suit even if her own information suggests otherwise. Evidently, such imitation may lead to cascades which will last very long if not forever. In a sense, mergers and acquisitions have then become "taken-for-granted" solutions to competitive interdependence. It implies that firms may have become locked into a solution in which all players implicitly prefer a non-optimal strategy without having ready possibilities for breaking away from it.

Even if some firms do not adopt mini-max regret behavior, it will be sensible for them to jump on a merger bandwagon too. For, cascading numbers of mergers and acquisitions imply that the likelihood of becoming an acquisition target increases. Thus, given the finding that relative size is a more effective barrier against takeover than relative profitability (see e.g. Hughes, 1993), firms may enter the merger and acquisition game for no other reason than to defend themselves against takeover (see e.g. Greer, 1986). Needless to say, such defensive mergers will amplify the prevailing rate of mergers and acquisitions. The cascade will inevitably stop as soon as (a) the number of potential targets diminishes, which is a function of the intensity of the cascade, and (b) the disappointing merger returns decrease the chances for obtaining the financial means that are necessary for further merger investments.

In conclusion, it would seem that the high incidence of non-wealth creating mergers is not the result of failed implementation techniques as many management scholars would like us to believe (e.g. Haspeslagh and Jemison, 1991). Rather the existence of strategic interdependence under uncertainty, conditioned by the availability of funds, may compel management's to undertake mergers even if these will not increase economic performance. Inertia may prevail for long periods, but as soon as an initial, clearly observable move has been made by one of the major players, it is likely that other players will rapidly follow with similar moves. With multi-market oligopoly omnipresent, and given the increasing weight assigned to stock market performance appraisals, the ultimate result may be an economy-wide merger boom. Mergers with these properties will be dubbed here "purely strategic mergers". These are mergers that are intended to create strategic comfort rather than economic wealth (or, for that matter, monopoly rents). It is precisely for this reason that it would be futile to wait on the so-called learning capacities of organizations to improve the economic performance of mergers.

The Welfare Costs of Purely Strategic Mergers

The previous section has developed a strategic explanation for the merger paradox. The present section discusses the potential social costs of this phenomenon and endeavours to establish whether these costs are sufficiently substantial to warrant some sort of policy action.

Traditionally, negative welfare effects of mergers and acquisitions, if any, would be expected in the area of allocative efficiency. That is, mergers might increase market concentration to such an extent that the pertinent firms would be allowed to raise prices beyond the competitive level, or restrict output, so that an efficient allocation of resources would be thwarted. Inexpedient behavior of firms in the area of mergers, however, carries important social costs even when allocative effects remain at bay. In terms of this paper, these costs would be the result of foregone improvements of, or actual decreases in, productive (or internal) and dynamic (or innovation) efficiency respectively. The finding that mergers do not lead to improvements in profitability, or merely lead to improvements that are smaller than would have been possible without merger, suggests that mergers, on average, lead to X-inefficiency (in terms of Leibenstein, 1966) or relative X-inefficiency.[4] The implications for the measurement of welfare losses can be illustrated as in Figure 8.1.

In Figure 8.1, P_m is the monopoly price which corresponds to an output of Q_m while C_c represents costs under competition (and thus the competitive price). The figure shows two options with respect to the effects of merger (for illustrative purposes, it is assumed that the merger induces a change from perfect competition to complete monopoly).

Traditionally, it is presumed that due to scale economies average costs will decline to C_m. With respect to this case, Williamson (1968) has argued that the welfare loss due to monopoly, represented by the triangle Figure 8.1.

AED, should be traded off against a welfare gain implied by C_cDBC_m (P_mADC_c representing the loss of consumer surplus that is transferred to the firm[s] with market power). However, as Comanor and Leibenstein (1969) have rightfully argued, the addition of X-inefficiency in the form of a divergence between monopoly cost and competitive cost ($C_{m'} - C_c$) implies a larger welfare loss which in the figure would be represented by AED plus $C_mB'DC_c$. If the merger will not allow P_m to exceed $C_{m'}$, then there will be a welfare loss of $C_{m'}FEC_c$.

Thus, depending on the shape of the long-run average cost curve (LRAC), a merger that will create a new firm operating beyond minimal optimal scale (MOS) may have serious non-allocative welfare consequences. If LRAC will be flat beyond MOS (i.e. if LRAC is L-shaped), implying that economies of scale have been exhausted so that improvements in size performance are no longer feasible, then any welfare losses would depend on the allocative effects of the merger only (this will be different in a dynamic framework; see further below). While allocative effects may not be detected as a result of identical ex ante and ex post price-cost margins, a merger may still create sizable negative welfare effects if LRAC curves upwards (i.e. if LRAC is U-shaped). More generally, the development of productivity and innovativeness may be harmed as merger decision making consumes an important fraction of investment funds as well as managerial time, talent, and energy, both ex ante and ex post, that cannot be spent anymore on investment projects that are more likely to create wealth in the long run, such as investment in machinery and equipment, and investment in R&D, training and schooling.

Unfortunately, it is difficult to say precisely to what extent productive and dynamic efficiency will be harmed in practice. There are, however, two reasons for expecting that the (opportunity) losses of purely strategic mergers may be significant. First, losses due to X-inefficiency extend over the entire output range rather than simply to the output contraction that would be the relevant range for determining the importance of

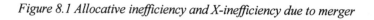

Figure 8.1 Allocative inefficiency and X-inefficiency due to merger

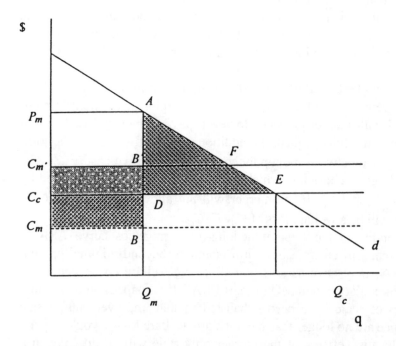

allocative inefficiencies. This is due to become relatively more important as P_m approaches C_c (or C_m). That is, in cases where welfare losses may seem small when only allocative effects are taken into account, they may in fact be large due to productive efficiency effects.

Secondly, if merger-active firms as a collectivity are sufficiently large relative to the economy as a whole then their inexpedient behavior may have macroeconomic repercussions. This latter condition would seem to apply. For, as a group, the largest one hundred manufacturers in the EU and the US—i.e. those firms that are most likely to engage in purely strategic mergers—accounted for, respectively, 28.2% and 42.3% of manufacturing employment in 1990 (data upwardly biased because the numerator, in contradistinction to the denominator, includes foreign employment). When measured as sales over GDP, the figures are 19.5 and 23.8 per cent respectively (see Schenk, 1999). Thus, the macroeconomic impact of purely strategic mergers may well be significant even if such mergers are common only among large firms.[5]

Apart from the potentially large size of the welfare effects of purely strategic mergers, one should observe, however, that these effects may not just be a matter of sub-optimal performance in a static sense. They may also affect the competitiveness of nations. Consider the following. Mergers and acquisitions are substantially more prevalent in the European Union and the United States than in Japan. When measured by numbers, and taking into account the sizes of their respective economies, Japanese firms undertake approximately ten times fewer mergers and acquisitions than US, UK and Dutch firms. When measured by value, however, the differences are likely to be much larger still. Table 8.1 shows that the values of Japanese mergers almost pale into insignificance beside those undertaken by US firms (see last column). When averaged over the seven-year period, Japanese transaction values come to only 5.1% of the American average.

Table 8.1 US and Japanese mergers compared, 1985-1991

	Transaction values ($ billions)		Index for Japan (US = 100)	
Year	US	Japan	Gross	Adjusted[b]
1985[a]	146.1	0.6	0.41	0.7
1986	206.1	2.5	1.21	1.9
1987	178.3	4.9	2.75	4.4
1988	238.5	9.5	3.98	6.4
1989	245.4	13.9	5.66	9.1
1990	160.6	12.4	7.72	12.3
1991	98.2	0.4	0.41	0.7
a: Japanese data are for fiscal years b: According to the relative levels of GNP				

Source: adapted and recalculated from OECD (1993)

Of the 100 largest manufacturers from the US, the EU and Japan in 1978, 14 US firms and 16 firms from the EU had disappeared fifteen years later as a result of merger, whereas this happened to only 4 Japanese firms. Thus, top-100 firms disappear as a result of merger and acquisition roughly 3.5 to four times as frequently in the US or the EU than in Japan (Schenk, 1999).

If the pertinent Japanese firms would rather focus their investment efforts on wealth creating projects, then this would, *ceteris paribus*, imply that western firms would be at a disadvantage. In fact, this is precisely what may have happened during the 1980s in particular. First, western firms appear to have invested less in manufacturing equipment and machinery than their Japanese rivals during the 1970s and 1980s, a period which spans at least two significant merger waves (Maddison, 1987; Schenk, 2000). Moreover, it is well known that Japanese firms have continued to invest more heavily in R&D than their western opponents. Recent calculations of the Dutch Ministry of Economic Affairs (DMEA, 1995) point out that Japanese firms have invested more than 1.8% of GDP in R&D consecutively since 1985 whereas this figure was only around 1.3% in the EU. When mergers and acquisitions peaked towards the end of the 1980s and the early 1990s these percentages were 2.2 and 1.2 respectively. Whereas investments in R&D amounted to almost 2.2% of GDP in the US on the eve of the previous mergers and acquisitions boom, this decreased to 1.7% during the early 1990s.

At the same time, US and EU firms surrendered a sizable share of the world market to their Japanese rivals. Out of the total combined worldwide sales of the largest 100 manufacturers from the US, the EU and Japan, the 100 US firms together with the 100 EU firms had a 1978 share of 87%, and the 100 Japanese firms a share of 13%. The US-EU share had declined to 78% twelve years later whereas the Japanese share had increased to 22% (see Schenk, 1996). Thus, the apparent decline in competitiveness of the West vis-à-vis Japan may well have been caused by merger predilections among those western firms that are most heavily engaged in international competition. More in particular, it seems likely that at least the cyclical part of the focus of western firms on external growth has created a relative neglect of investments in process and product improvements to the extent of allowing Japanese rivals to gain first mover advantages from new shopfloor technology and new product development, in the end allowing them to steadily eat into the world market shares of their competitors from the US and the EU.[6]

Another substantial welfare loss may result from the fact that large firms on a merger spending spree extend their activities towards small and medium sized enterprises (SMEs) as well. It is not rare to find that large firms undertake more than a few of such acquisitions on a yearly basis (e.g. Unilever undertook 158 acquisitions during 1987-1990, and of these more than three quarters concerned small and medium sized targets). These are typically the mergers that, according to Ravenscraft and Scherer (1987), fare worst of all. Acquirers frequently buy research-intensive SMEs, but soon appear to cut back on R&D expenditures. A significant number of SMEs appear to languish after having become part of a large acquirer (also see Chakrabarti et al., 1994). As small and medium sized firms in general are relatively innovative and/or efficient with respect to innovation (see e.g. Acs, 1996; Nooteboom and Vossen, 1995; Simon, 1996), one implication may be that some of society's most innovative institutions are simply eliminated from the competitive system as a result of takeover. By having stayed "alive", these firms might have been able to challenge those firms that are too occupied with merger, but in the event they were not allowed to play this role.[7]

Even apart from this, there is some evidence that concentration ratios are negatively associated with SME innovation in particular (Acs and Audretsch, 1988). Thus, even when SMEs are not swallowed up in acquisitions, mergers among other incumbents in their industry may have a significant negative impact on innovativeness.

Finally, Mueller (1999) has suggested that the vigorous pursuit of what he calls "unprofitable" mergers may be one of the factors that contribute to the decline of nations. Reporting on earlier research with Reardon and Yun, he finds that large, managerially controlled, established firms earn significantly lower returns relative to their cost of capital (i.e. the returns their shareholders can make on investments of comparable risk) than younger (and smaller) firms when annual changes in the market values of firms are regressed on their annual investments (see Mueller and Yun, 1998). During the 1980s, for example, each dollar invested by a large, established firm produced only about 69 cents of new assets. Younger firms, on the other hand, realized a return that (albeit only just) equaled their costs of capital. According to Mueller, if the economic rise of nations is caused by the rise of large, managerially controlled corporations, as some have argued (e.g. Chandler, 1990), then it would seem logical to expect that the decline of these same corporations will lead to a decline of these nations. When professional managers as well as a whole industry of investments bankers, stock analysts, lawyers "and even economists" are occupied with transfering assets instead of creating them, when casflows get used to buy existing plants rather than build new ones, then decline is almost inevitable.

Although Mueller may be stretching it a bit too far, it is evident that his propositions bear some similarity to what has already been suggested above. Noticing that, indeed, all previous merger waves were followed by years of economic distress and restructurings, it would therefore seem unjustifiable at the least to neglect the importance of the productive and/or dynamic losses that result from mergers.

Policy Implications

From the preceding section it follows that some sort of policy action, meant to prevent the widespread and persistent occurrence of purely strategic mergers, would be justified. Let me now discuss which sort of policy action might be appropriate in this respect.

Clearly, in a perfectly competitive economy, firms would not be able to undertake purely strategic mergers. That is, in the product market, firms that would invest in higher-return projects would presumably be able to outcompete rivals that would merely invest in lower-return projects. In the capital market, investors would presumably prefer firms that realize higher returns over those that do not. And in the market for corporate control, managements of higher-return firms would presumably take over those firms whose managements are apparently not able to realize the full potentials of their firms. The fact that non-wealth creating mergers keep occurring on a large scale is therefore in itself sufficient evidence of the poor operation of these mechanisms. While the takeover threat in particular is frequently regarded as the pre-eminent mechanism to keep firms alert and/or as a mechanism that takes care of replacing inefficient managements by more efficient ones (see e.g. Jensen, 1988), it would rather appear that firms' acquisitions behavior implies a perversion of this mechanism.

Policy actions should therefore focus on making these market mechanisms work more effectively and eliminating those forces that could be considered responsible for their defective operation. This would seem to extend to three domains: corporate governance policy, competition policy, and industrial policy.[8]

Corporate governance. Owners of acquiring firms would presumably be less willing to accept the managerial rationales that create merger waves if they only were better informed about what happens after a particular merger or acquisition has been realized. For, a particular firm's record in mergers and acquisitions often remains obscure as all information on acquisitions normally vanishes into consolidated reports and forms. Thus, Ravenscraft and Scherer (1987, p. 227) have recommended that acquiring companies should file with the Securities and Exchange Commission (SEC) a report "detailing all acquisitions made during the prior year, the consideration paid, the book value of the assets acquired, the method of accounting used, a description of each unit sold off during the year, and the loss or gain recorded in connection with each such divestiture". They also recommend that certain acquisitions would be designated as distinct industry segments for which disaggregated sales, assets and operating income information would have to be disclosed in annual reports. These recommendations can only be supported. Yet, shareholders might easily get caught up in the same games as their agents are playing, especially when they represent large institutional holdings. Therefore, one should not expect quick results from these recommendations. Still, and assuming that monitoring the success of mergers and acquisitions is a necessary element of good business practice and that the gathering of pertinent information should therefore simply be seen as part of normal business practice, requiring that such information would be shared with the general public would be a welcome governance innovation.

Competition policy. In a market economy there is a presumption that private agents should be free to pursue their own interests as they see fit up till the point at which this pursuit has (significantly) adverse consequences for economic welfare. It is the purpose of current competition (or antitrust) policies in both the US and the EU to prevent mergers that have, or are likely to have, such consequences (at the level of the EU, ex ante merger control has become possible only as of 1990 when the Merger Regulation, agreed in 1989, came into force). Under certain conditions (mostly relating to market share, as in the US, or size of the merger, as in the EU), mergers must presently be notified to competition authorities in order to be investigated and, possibly, challenged. These investigations, however, do not examine whether a particular merger is likely to have adverse welfare consequences as a result of productive and/or dynamic inefficiencies. Rather, the investigations are meant to establish whether a particular merger is likely substantially to lessen competition instead of measuring its effect on welfare directly. It is correct, that in the EU several more factors are taken into account, but as in the US the pertinent procedures eventually end up in testing whether a merger will substantially increase market concentration (measured by means of either a concentration ratio or the Herfindahl-Hirschman Index) beyond a certain competitive level and, if so, in estimating whether that can be sustained.[9] The underlying assumption is that growing beyond a certain threshold may deliver market power, or market dominance, which is consistently defined as the ability profitably to maintain prices above competitive levels, or above long-run average costs, for a signifant period of time (see, for example, FTC, 1997). Such market power is expected to result in a transfer of wealth from buyers to sellers or a misallocation of resources. Therefore, what is being ultimately tested is whether a merger is likely to harm allocative efficiency.

Apart from the fact that this is not an easy task (some would say: an impossible task; see for example Dewey, 1996) as a result of both conceptual and measurement problems related to delineating the relevant product and geographic market as well as to estimating demand substitutability, the likelihood of new entry, and the power of potential competition, these procedures overlook the possibility that mergers may not be motivated by either the prospect of monopoly profits or the prospect of productive or dynamic efficiency gains. The underlying presumption is that mergers which are not motivated by the prospect of financial gains will not occur or, if they do, will only be short-lived. As we have seen, this presumption cannot be sustained.

As current merger control policies are focused on only part of the potential problems that mergers may create for economic welfare, they should be qualified as half-hearted. Moreover, the part that remains un-investigated may be the more important one. It therefore follows that an adequate form of merger control should include what I call a "Full Efficiency Test" (FET), i.e. a procedure in which a proposed merger is not just tested for allocative effects but for productive and dynamic effects as well. This requirement could be seen as a natural addition to especially US merger control as the American Merger Guidelines, following Williamson (1968), already explicitly allow for an efficiencies defense since 1984. That is, if a particular merger is found to have significant anti-competitive effects, the parties to it may try to convince the authorities that the merger should be allowed nevertheless on the basis of a merger's prospective positive effects on productive efficiency (implying a trade-off of the deadweight loss depicted in Figure 8.1 as triangle AED against the rectangle C_cDBC_m). Although the European Merger Regulation does not explicitly allow for an efficiencies defense, it has become evident that productive and dynamic efficiency effects are assessed in practical cases nonetheless (see Neven et al., 1993).[10] Thus, there is no logical reason why negative or zero efficiency effects should not be allowed as arguments that count against a particular merger.

Since purely strategic mergers are likely to occur especially among large firms and—in the form of takeovers—between large firms on the one hand and SMEs on the other, all mergers that are desired by large firms should therefore be notified to the authorities. Such notifications should include an efficiencies protocol or prospectus, i.e. a memorandum that demonstrates whether and how productive and dynamic efficiencies will be realized. As it is in the merger candidates' interest to come up with a plausible efficiency protocol, it will be evident that the burden of proof in productive and dynamic efficieny cases will rest on them. The reason for excluding small mergers, i.e. mergers in which both (or all) parties are small or medium-sized, is twofold. First, mergers among SMEs are less likely to originate from the non-wealth creating strategies that are played in small number games. Secondly, SMEs are more likely to operate below MOS so that there is at least some likelihood of realizing economies of scale.[11] Notice that focusing on all mergers in which a large firm is implied would also allow an assessment of piecemeal creations of market dominance, or as it is formulated in the US, the creation of market dominance in its incipiency.

Thus, mergers that are unlikely to create productive and/or dynamic efficiencies would be blocked while mergers that are likely to have positive efficiency effects would be allowed if no negative allocative efficiency effects are to be expected. Two practical points deserve special attention, however. First, at least during the initial years of an FET-regime, the numbers of mergers that would have to be investigated may be very large, especially since takeovers of SMEs would need assessment too. A pragmatic solution, to be adapted as the FET-regime becomes more established, would be to limit screening to only those mergers that are proposed by the very largest firms from the US and the EU respectively. For example, Dewey (1996), who has made similar suggestions, proposes to limit control to those mergers that are proposed by the 500 largest US industrial firms or so. These firms should not be allowed to grow by merger "unless it can be shown that the merger is likely to confer some non-negligible consumer benefit through cost reduction, product improvement, increased research outlays or more rapid innovation" (Dewey, 1996, p. 397).[12] Mueller (1997), while keeping up a market share criterion, has proposed to disallow mergers that lead to a combined market share of more than 25% in any one market, or to total sales in excess of $600 mln, *unless* it can be demonstrated that a particular merger is likely to yield substantial efficiency gains in excess of its anti-competitive effects. Dewey's proposals imply the more radical departure from established practice but a substantial simplification of it as well, as there is no need whatsoever to assess any longer a merger's impact on competition. An added advantage would be that there is no need either to establish whether a merger is horizontal, vertical or conglomerate.[13] While Mueller's proposals still require estimating the allocative efficiency effects of a merger, though apparently only in cases where firms can come up with a plausible efficiency prospectus, Dewey's proposals would perhaps fit in best with the present paper's gist. The present EU thresholds may be adequate as far as large mergers are concerned, while the acquisitions of SMEs by large firms could be investigated at the level of individual member states.[14] Besides, and given the empirical evidence on mergers, it may be expected that the number of mergers that will have to be vetted will eventually be reduced dramatically once firms are to come up with a plausible efficiency protocol.

Secondly, one may rightfully ask whether the present investigating skills of the merger authorities would allow conducting a sufficiently sophisticated FET. As Scherer (1997) has noted, the detailed analysis of plant-specific and product-specific scale economies, and the technological and organizational determinants of productivity, does not belong to the regular bag of tools of an antitrust economist. Applying an FET would, indeed, require staff with solid management consultancy experience or training. Such skills, according to Scherer, would be expensive to obtain. While Scherer's doubts may be justified, applying an FET would be less demanding if the burden of proof is, as has been suggested here, on the shoulders of those firms that wish to undertake a merger or acquisition. Still, it would be necessary to inject more management know how into merger investigations than is presently the case. A possible solution may include hiring business school experts, however. Anyhow, assessing efficiency protocols that have been submitted by merger candidates would be much less demanding than making up these same protocols.

Also notice that the transparency of merger controls would be increased substantially by using an FET, which should be welcomed both by the firms involved and by those wishing to investigate the decisions taken by the authorities. The chances for opportunistic settlements and regulatory capture—such as documented for the EU case by Neven et al. (1993)— would be reduced significantly. Finally, a rather important advantage of the type of merger control proposed here would be that it reduces the complexities of the international gearing of merger policies, particularly of those within the Triad. Apart from the jurisdictional questions involved, there is presently much confusion over the interpretations of different merger control procedures and institutional arrangements (see e.g. Waverman et al., 1997). The steadily increasing number of international mergers and acquisitions implies that firms will increasingly have to notify their mergers to different national authorities. Moreover, given the internationalization of the world economy, it becomes increasingly possible that domestic mergers have foreign repercussions. Indeed, the recent takeover of McDonnell Douglas by Boeing became the subject of cross-atlantic confusion as the European Commission decided, for good reasons, to leave its mark on the finalization of the deal. The transparency of the pertinent discussions would have benefitted substantially of an assessment that would have included an FET.

Thus, subjecting all mergers and acquisitions undertaken by the largest firms to a Full Efficiency Test would seem to be a significant improvement over present arrangements in several respects.

Industrial policy. More would be needed, though, to address the problem in full. Governments have historically displayed a persistent love affair with mergers and corporate bigness (see e.g. Adams and Brock, 1988; for confirmation of the permanency of this, see Vernon, 1974), so that the introduction of an FET in merger control may well meet up with unjustified but vested instincts and may eventually be confronted with lax enforcement. As is evidenced by consolidation programs in the car industry, the steel industry, the aircraft industry, the transport industry (railways; airlines), electricity generation and distribution, and the telecommunications industry, merger predilections have survived the ages with governments too.

For example, the Dutch government was instrumental in the takeover of DAF Trucks by Paccar in late 1996, and attempted—though in vain—to consolidate all four electricity generators into one big firm in 1998. In 1996, it tried rather desparately to sell Fokker Aircraft to Korea's Samsung, even after it had become expressely clear that the earlier strategy of consolidating Fokker into Daimler-Benz had failed when the German conglomerate wanted to get rid again of the acquired Dutch aircraft manufacturer in which the Dutch state had a minority stake. All these mergers had at most dubious effects on productive and dynamic efficiency.

A further illustration of merger predilections at the level of the authorities is given by the (then) director of industrial policy of the European Commission who claims that mergers and acquisitions should be regarded as "important and beneficial" and worthy of encouragement (Marchipont, 1995: 32). Similarly, the US government does not even seem to have contemplated obstructing Boeing's 1997-acquisition of McDonnell Douglas which—apart from creating a near-monopolist in several fields—is likely to have at most very small improvements in productivity or innovativeness (see, for example, *The Economist* of 8 August 1998; 27 February 1999).

Consequently, rather than inducing and supporting mergers and acquisitions, industrial policies should advocate de-mergers and management buy-outs as socially beneficial corporate strategies (see Lichtenberg and Siegel, 1990; Thompson, Wright and Robbie, 1993; Schenk et al., 1997).

Secondly, governments should support the independent survival of those firms that are potentially capable of challenging the apparent *modus vivendi* of corporate capitalism, viz. small and medium sized enterprises. Such support should contribute to strengthening these firms' negotiating position vis-à-vis large acquirers. Many SMEs now succumb to acquisition proposals because these seem to offer better facilities for growth, capital in particular, than elsewhere obtainable. It is well-known that SMEs still face great difficulties in finding sufficient amounts of growth capital, especially equity, even with western economies running at full speed (for recent accounts of this long-standing problem, see Hughes and Storey, 1995; McVey, 1998). This would appear to be related to recent developments at the level of two main potential sources of investment funds: banks and venture capital firms. Increasing concentration in the financial services industry, especially acute during the 1980s and 1990s, has reinforced the orientation of banks toward the wholesale market to the detriment of the retail market (Schenk, 1995). SMEs are likely to be presented the bill of obviously merger-related diseconomies in the banking industry. Moreover, banks appear to be quite reluctant to provide funds for innovative but risky firms if these firms cannot provide hard collateral. According to *The Economist* of 25 January 1997, more than half of Europe's venture capital investment is used now to finance changes in firms' ownership (especially by means of management buy-outs) and much less to support growing, established SMEs (and only a meagre 6 per cent to finance new start-ups).

Partly in response to these problems, new stock markets have recently been launched in several European countries (such as the Alternative Investment Market in London; the Nouveau Marché in Paris; the Easdaq in Brussels; the NMAX in Amsterdam; and the Neuer Markt in Frankfurt). However, these so-called small-cap markets are typically chasing fund managers rather than retail investors which is limiting both the type and numbers of accepted candidates for quotation (see *The Economist*, 15 March 1997). This may have much to do with the fact that the small-cap markets are still tied to, or associated with the main exchanges. Yet, in general, financial markets have an advantage over banks in the case of especially new technology-based firms (NTBFs) as making up an assessment of the potentialities of such firms is frought with difficulties. By bringing together many analysts, investors and traders, financial markets are less dependent on individual judgements than banks (see e.g. Allen, 1993). Thus, it would be commendable to reform the microstructure of capital markets in such a way that the possibilities for raising growth equity would be geared more to the needs of SMEs.

In this respect, a particularly interesting initiative has recently been taken by one of the several institutions that were created in the 1970s to support regional development in the Netherlands, the Gelderland Development Authority GOM (Schenk, 1998). Assisted by academic as well as business experts, GOM is developing a stock market that is both regionally accessible for firms and entirely set up on the Internet. Between eight and ten regional counters are scheduled for the Netherlands which will assess candidates for quotation and provide guidance as well as information services to both firms and investors. On line and real time stock trading facilities—if so desired, without the inclusion of layers of middlemen—as well as pertinent information on quoted firms will be available on the Internet. Code keys and personal information are to be obtained from the regional counters while identification, clearing, account guarantees, etc., may be settled real time through a central computer. Thresholds for quotation as well as offering costs on this virtual stock market would be considerably lower than they presently are at the small-cap markets while local (investment) banks as well as other intermediary institutions can more easily separate the wheat from the chaff among candidate firms than intermediaries located in the main financial centers could ever aspire. Making use of the Internet also is likely to do away with the familiar liquidity problem of small-cap markets as there are no limits to expanding the system nationally or internationally. Still, the regional counters would enable the stock exchange to be close to the SME-sector.

The attractive element for investors is that they will not only have the opportunity to spread their risk but also to do this while requiring only relatively small initial investments. Moreover, making use of the possibilities of the Internet would also tend to reduce costs considerably as layers of floor middlemen become redundant while instantaneous settlement of trades will reduce for investors the risk of default. By widening the pool of investors, and allocating shares on a first-come, first-served basis, an Internet offering can moreover change the typical volatility of initial public offerings (IPOs) by allowing small investors the same chance as large institutional investors of getting in on the ground floor (see Ibbotson and Ritter, 1995; Röell, 1996). This would benefit dedicated investors who would be attracted by a fairer market over those who as favored investors normally have the privilege of selling for an immediate profit. Besides, an efficient system might, eventually, be able to put so much pressure on the large banks that these would be forced to increase their productive efficiency and decrease their grip on the retail market.

The concept of a virtual stock exchange, while being innovative especially when built on a regional base, would seem to be supported by recent developments in both information and communication technology and global capital markets. First, the penetration of the personal computer, and soon its descendants, into the home of the investor is relentless. Second, developments in encryption and identification technology, which allow to conduct secure and authenticated transactions anywhere in the world, are rapidly proceeding (Shuttleworth, 1998). Since digital signatures may soon replace passwords as a means of authentication, it is foreseeable that attacking databases of passwords at a brokerage or the exchange, presently an important potential source of worry, will become a thing of the past.

Capital markets, especially in the US, are presently encountering changes that would seem to support the GOM initiative too (see e.g. *Business Week*, 10 August 1998). Perhaps most notable is OptiMark's system which features a supercomputer that conducts highly sophisticated courtships between buyers and sellers in cyberspace, arranging matches in nanoseconds without layers of floor intermediaries.[15] It only facilitates trades, however, in stocks that are quoted on already-established exchanges (such as the New York Stock Exchange and NASDAQ). In the meantime, the Internet has already attracted droves of novice investors in the US and has created an entirely new industry of online brokers. More than seventy of these now offer quick trades, real time quotes, access to research, and even portions of IPOs at rock-bottom prices. E*Trade Group, the second largest on-line brokerage firm in terms of market share, is presently (early 1999) talking to other Internet brokers about the general idea of funneling trades to a common 'electronic communications network' (ECN). As yet, most ECNs are still classified by the Securities and Exchange Commission (SEC) as broker-dealers, and therefore cannot act as full-fledged exchanges, but that could change quickly.

Similarly, in Sweden, venture capitalists have created the Innovations Marknaden which channels investments from private individuals to small high tech, innovative firms openly via an electronic system. Having started in 1994, it now services more than twenty firms as well as more than 20,000 investors.

What all of this proves, is that the psychological step from trading face to face to trading purely by technology has already been taken, and that on line real time trading is technically feasible. Establishing what I call a "VERC" (Virtual Exchange with Regional Counters) would create the possibilities for SMEs as well as informal and private investors to benefit from these developments. Industrial policy encouragement of VERCs would be an initially small but significant step towards breaking away from the traditional large firm focus of present industrial policies.

Thus, supporting initiatives like the one that has been taken by GOM, as well as helping firms prepare for quotation would be an innovative challenge for industrial policy authorities and institutions at the regional level which hitherto have either been concentrating their policy efforts on supplying small-scale subsidies, taking small participations in promising ventures, or else have been on the look-out for a purpose. Public authorities could specialize in guiding firms with a public purpose towards the stock market. Where countries do not yet have regional industrial policy institutions, the virtual stock exchange may be a good reason to start developing them. Doing so would fit in well with more general de-concentrating developments in cyberspace.

Conclusions

Current merger policies heavily bear the stamp of the economics profession's most basic premise, i.e. that firms are motivated by the promise of profits. For example, the joint 1992 Merger Guidelines of the US Department of Justice and the Federal Trade Commission (revised in 1997) explicitly make clear that one of the "underlying policy assumptions" is that "Mergers are motivated by the prospect of financial gains" (FTC, 1997: Section 0.1). This chapter has argued that many mergers refute such an assumption. Neither meant to strengthen productive and dynamic efficiency nor market power, these so-called purely strategic mergers nevertheless are sufficient proof of either the pre-existence of market power or the simultaneous build-up of it. If government policies are really meant to enhance the competitiveness of firms and further economic welfare, then purely strategic mergers should be blocked.

Competition policies should therefore be equipped with a Full Efficiency Test. If stringently enforced, such a test would arguably suffice to prevent the present squandering of resources. One hundred years of experience with antitrust and competition policy, however, are not very encouraging in that respect. Partly because of this, industrial policies should focus on the support of those firms that can potentially challenge the established practices of corporate capitalism. Since many SMEs fall prey to large target-seeking and cash-rich firms, implying that potentially valuable sources of innovation get eliminated from the market, such policies should aim at decreasing the barriers which SMEs encounter when trying to enter the capital market. In this respect, the paper has suggested to support the creation of a Virtual, internet-based stock Exchange with Regional entry Counters (VERC).

Notes

1. Notice that since most merger performance studies refer to mergers in which at least one of the parties is a large and/or quoted firm, the findings cannot straightforwardly be applied to mergers within the sector of small and medium-sized, unquoted firms. Although many thousands of mergers take place within this latter category, merger registration is usually confined to those mergers that are deemed "important" which normally means mergers that are announced in the business press or mentioned in firms' annual reports. Generally, merger propensity rises with the scale of firm.

2. Notice that most studies have used control groups, so that it would be a bit too easy to justify ongoing mergers by arguing that the pertinent firms might have performed even worse without a merger. Such a proposition would imply a generalization that is unlikely in the face of the overall findings, though in individual cases it might, of course, apply.

3. Notice that the relationship between merger waves and stock market dynamics is ambiguous. Sometimes stock market cycles correlate with merger waves, sometimes they do not, while if they do it remains uncertain what causes what. Evidently, merger waves must be preceded by periods of economic prosperity. But neither historical evidence nor economic logic would lead one to qualify this as the fulfilment of a sufficient condition.

4. Notice that X-inefficiency is normally defined as being the excess of actual cost over minimum possible cost in a given situation. Thus, in principle, it could be removed by economizing on inputs (especially in the form of managerial expense) or by working harder. Our usage of the term productive efficiency is broader in the

sense that it includes excess costs which, in a given situation, cannot be removed but are simply the result of merger-induced diseconomies of scale such as control loss. Since the implications for measuring welfare losses are identical, we will not explicitly make a distinction between the two concepts.

5. It could be argued that the billions expended on mergers do not vanish from the economic process. Indeed, it may be so that shareholders at the receiving end instead of creating a consumption bubble, or overindulging themselves in Veblen-type conspicuous consumption (Veblen, 1899), will reinvest their newly acquired pecuniary wealth in investment projects that do create economic wealth. If so, then we would merely have to worry about a retardation effect. Still, such an effect may be significant.

6. From this point of view, one might even argue that Japan's financial crisis has been a sort of reverse blessing in disguise for western firms.

7. For example, in the US SMEs as a group have been found to be slightly less than 2.4 times more innovative than large firms when innovativeness is measured as the number of innovations per employee (Acs and Audretsch, 1990). Also, it appears that SMEs are able to more effectively utilize the knowledge spillovers from universities (Acs et al., 1994). It should be noticed, though, that the high average relative performance of SMEs conceals variations between industries. According to Acs (1996), small firms produced more than half of all innovations recorded in computers and process control instruments as well as in the engineering and scientific instruments industries. By contrast in the pharmaceutical preparation and photographic equipment industries, large firms appear to be more innovative. In general, however, there does not appear to be any evidence that increasing returns to R&D expenditures exist in producing innovative output. In fact, with only a few exceptions, diminishing returns are the rule.

8. Some would rightfully argue that both corporate governance policy and competition policy belong to the industrial policy domain. For reasons of clarity, however, I have chosen in this case to make a distinction between these three domains.

9. The HHI is calculated by summing the squares of the individual market shares of all participants in a particular market thus reflecting the distribution of market shares whereas the concentration ratio only reflects the shares of the top-n (usually four) firms. Since the HHI gives proportionately greater weight to the largest firms, it is not necessary to know the market shares of all participants.

10. According to Sleuwaegen (1998), the absence of an explicit efficiency defense in the EU's Merger Regulation is surprising as it is the ambition of the single market program to further the creation of European firms that are more efficient and competitive in world markets.

11. To the extent that small mergers would nevertheless tend to create market dominance, for example in regional markets, such mergers could be subjected to ex post control.

12. In this respect, also see Brenner (1990) who stresses the importance of a test for the effects of a merger on innovation performance.

13. This would correspond to the fact that it has become less meaningful to distinguish horizontal from vertical and conglomerate mergers at all now that most large firms are vertically integrated conglomerates thus making it possible for a single merger to be horizontal, vertical and conglomerate at the same time.

14. The EU Merger Regulation presently applies to mergers in which the parties when taken together have worldwide sales in excess of 5 bln euro while at least two of them have Community-sales in excess of 250 mln euro, unless all parties have more than two-thirds of their EU-sales within one and the same member state. In the latter case, the merger would be subject to national merger control. In the course of 1998, a revised scheme became effective which adds to the previous conditions that mergers should be notified to the Commission if parties have combined worldwide sales in excess of 2.5 bln euro, as well as sales in excess of 100 mln euro in each of at least three member states, while at least two of them have aggregate sales within the EU of at least 100 mln euro each, provided that at least two of the parties have sales of at least 25 mln euro in the three member states that were meant above. The new scheme has become this cumbersome as a result of negotiations between those member states (and the Commission) that preferred lowering the thresholds while others appeared quite satisfied with the 1989-regulation.

15. Notice, however, that orders which are sent to the computer are not displayed anywhere, and this could deprive the markets of crucial information. If cybermarkets cause the disappearance of intermediaries, such as the market makers who commit their own capital, markets could be hurt, especially if bull markets suddenly turn bearish and the need for intermediaries to provide liquidity becomes important.

References

Acs, Z.J. 1996. "Small Firms and Economic Growth". In Admiraal, ed. 1—62.

Acs, Z.J. and D.B. Audretsch 1988. "Innovation in Large and Small Firms: An Empirical Analysis", *American Economic Review*, 78 (4), 678—690.

———— 1990. *Innovation and Small Firms.* Cambridge: MIT Press.

Acs, Z.J., D.B. Audretsch and . Feldman 1994. "R&D Spillovers and Recipient Firm Size", *Review of Economics and Statistics*, 76 (2), 336—340.

Adams, W. and J.W. Brock 1988. "The Bigness Mystique and the Merger Policy Debate: An International Perspective", *Northwestern Journal of International Law & Business*, 9 (1), 1—48.

Admiraal, P.-H. ed. 1996. *Small Business in the Modern Economy.* Oxford: Blackwell.

Allen, F. 1993. "Stock Markets and Resource Allocation". In Mayer and Vives eds., 81—116.

Banerjee, A.V. 1992. "A Simple Model of Herd Behavior", *Quarterly Journal of Economics*, CVII (3), 797—817.

Berger, A.N. and D.B. Humphrey 1992. "Megamergers in Banking and the Use of Cost Efficiency as an Antitrust Defense", *Antitrust Bulletin*, 37 (Fall), 541—600.

Bikhchandani, S., D. Hirshleifer and I. Welch 1992. "A Theory of Fads, Fashions, Custom, and Cultural Change as Informational Cascades", *Journal of Political Economy*, 100 (5), 992—1026.

Bishop, M. and J. Kay eds. 1993. *European Mergers and Merger Policy.* Oxford: Oxford University Press.

Brenner, R. 1990. "Innovations and Antitrust". In B. Dankbaar, J. Groenewegen and H. Schenk eds., 235—257.

Bühner, R. 1991. "The Success of Mergers in Germany", *International Journal of Industrial Organization*, 9 (4), 513—453.

Chakrabarti, A., J. Hauschildt and C. Süverkrüp 1994. "Does it Pay to Acquire Technological Firms?", *R&D Management*, 24 (1), 47—56.

Chandler, A.D. 1990. *Scale and Scope. The Dynamics of Industrial Capitalism.* Cambridge, MA: Harvard University Press.

Comanor, W. and H. Leibenstein 1969. "Allocative Efficiency, X-Efficiency and the Measurement of Welfare Losses", *Economica*, 36, 304—309.

Cowling, K. ed. 1999. *Industrial Policy in Europe: Theoretical Perspectives and Practical Proposals.* London: Routledge (forthcoming).

Cyert, R.M. and J.G. March 1963. *A Behavioral Theory of the Firm*, 2nd ed. 1992, Cambridge, MA: Blackwell.

Dankbaar, B., J. Groenewegen and H. Schenk eds. 1990. *Perspectives in Industrial Organization.* Studies in Industrial Organization, Vol. 13, Dordrecht/Boston/London: Kluwer Academic Publishers

Dewey, D. 1996. "Merger Policy Greatly Simplified: Building on Keyes", *Review of Industrial Organization*, 11, 395—400.

Dickerson, A.P., H.D. Gibson and E. Tsakalotos 1997. "The Impact of Acquisitions on Company Performance: Evidence From a Large Panel of UK Firms", *Oxford Economic Papers*, 49, 344—361.

Dietrich, M. and H. Schenk 1995. "Coordination Benefits, Lock-In, and Strategy Bias", *Management Report*, 220, Rotterdam: Rotterdam School of Management, Erasmus University Rotterdam.

DiMaggio, P.J. and W.W. Powell 1983. "The Iron Cage Revisited: Institutional Isomorphism and Collective Rationality in Organizational Fields", *American Sociological Review*, 48, 147—160.

DMEA, Dutch Ministry of Economic Affairs 1995. *Knowledge on the move* (in Dutch). The Hague: Ministry of Economic Affairs.

FTC, Federal Trade Commission (1997), *1992 Horizontal Merger Guidelines [With April 8, 1997, Revisions to Section 4 on Efficiencies].* Washington: Federal Trade Commission

Greer, D.F. 1986. "Acquiring in Order to Avoid Acquisition", *Antitrust Bulletin*, Spring, 155—186.

Haspeslagh, Ph.C., and D.B. Jemison 1991. *Managing Acquisitions. Creating Value Through Corporate Renewal.* New York: Free Press.

Hitt, M.A., R.E. Hoskisson, R.D. Ireland and J.S. Harrison 1991. "Effects of Acquisitions on R&D Inputs and Outputs", *Academy of Management Journal*, 34 (3), 693—706.

Hughes, A. 1993. "Mergers and Economic Performance in the UK: A Survey of the Empirical Evidence 1950-1990". In: Bishop and Kay, eds. 9—95.

Hughes, A. and D.J. Storey eds. 1995. *Finance and the Small Firm.* London: Routledge.

Ibbotson, R.G. and J.R. Ritter 1995. "Initial Public Offerings". In Jarrow, et al., eds. 993—1016.

Jarrow, R.A., V. Maksimovic and W.T. Ziemba eds. 1995. *Handbooks in Operations Research and Management Science. Finance.* Vol. 9, Amsterdam: North-Holland.

Jensen, M.C. 1988. "Takeovers: Their Causes and Consequences", *Journal of Economic Perspectives,*2 (1), 21—48.

Kahneman, D. and A. Tversky 1979. "Prospect Theory: An Analysis of Decision Making Under Risk", *Econometrica*, 47 (2), 263—291.

Karier, T. 1993. *Beyond Competition. The Economics of Mergers and Monopoly Power.* Armonk: M.E. Sharpe.

Keynes, J.M. 1936. *The General Theory of Employment, Interest, and Money.* London: Macmillan.

Leibenstein, H. 1966. "Allocative Efficiency versus X-Efficiency", *American Economic Review*, 56, 392—415.

Lichtenberg, F.R. and D. Siegel 1990. "The Effects of Leveraged Buyouts on Productivity and Related Aspects of Firm Behavior", *Journal of Financial Economics*, 27, 165—194.

Maddison, A. 1987. "Growth and Slowdown in Advanced Capitalist Economies: Techniques of Quantitative Assessment", *Journal of Economic Literature*, 25 (June), 649—698.

Marchipont, J.-F. 1995. "La Stratégie Industrielle de l'Union Européenne: à la Recherche d'un Concept de Politique de Compétitivité Globale", *Revue d'Économie Industrielle*, 71 (1er trim.), 17—37.

Mayer, C. and X. Vives eds. 1993. *Capital Markets and Financial Intermediation.* Cambridge: Cambridge University Press.

McVey, B. 1998. "Finance and Entrepreneurship—The Role of the New Stock Exchanges in Local Economic Development", *Paper*, Third Biennial Conference of the Association of European Financial Centres, Manchester, 4—6 March.

Mueller, D.C. 1996. "Antimerger Policy in the United States: History and Lessons", *Empirica*, 23 (3), 229—253.

————— 1997. "Merger Policy in the United States: A Reconsideration", *Review of Industrial Organization*, 12, 655—685.

―――――― 1999. "On the Economic Decline of Nations". In D.C. Mueller, A. Haid and J. Weigand eds. 351―381.

Mueller, D.C., A. Haid and J. Weigand eds. 1999. *Competition, Efficiency and Welfare. Essays in Honor of Manfred Neumann.* Boston etc.: Kluwer Academic.

Mueller, D.C. and S.L. Yun 1998. "Rates of Return Over the Firm's Lifecycle", *Industrial and Corporate Change*, 7 (2), 347―368.

Neven, D., R. Nuttall and P. Seabright 1993. *Merger in Daylight. The Economics and Politics of European Merger Control.* London: Centre for Economic Policy Research.

Nooteboom, B. and R.W. Vossen 1995. "Firm Size and Efficiency in R&D Spending". In Van Witteloostuijn ed. 69―86.

OECD 1993. "Working Group on Innovation and Technology", *National Systems for Financing Innovation* (restricted draft version), Paris: Organisation for Economic Co-Operation and Development.

Ravenscraft, D.J. and F.M. Scherer 1987. *Mergers, Sell-offs, and Economic Efficiency.* Washington, D.C.: Brookings Institution.

Rhoades, S.A. 1994. "A Summary of Merger Performance Studies in Banking, 1980―1993, and an Assessment of the "Operating Performance" and "Event Study" Methodologies", *Staff Study*, 167, Washington, DC: Board of Governors of the Federal Reserve System.

Rhoades, S.A. 1998. "The Efficiency Effects of Bank Mergers: An Overview of Case Studies of Nine Mergers", *Journal of Banking and Finance*, 22, 273―291.

Röell, A. 1996. "The Decision to go Public: An Overview", *European Economic Review*, 40, 1071―1081.

Scharfstein, D.S. and J.C. Stein 1990. "Herd Behavior and Investment", *American Economic Review*, 80 (3), 465―479.

Schelling, T. 1960. *The Strategy of Conflict.* Cambridge Mass: Harvard University Press.

Schenk, H. 1995. *The Dutch Economy After the Turn of the Century. Pilot study: Financial Services and the Food Industry* (in Dutch). Rotterdam/The Hague: GRASP, Erasmus University Rotterdam/Dutch Ministry of Economic Affairs.

―――――― 1996. "Bandwagon Mergers, International Competitiveness, and Government Policy", *Empirica*, 23 (3), 255―278.

——— 1998. "Bases de una Política Industrial para una Bolsa Virtual con Accesos Regionales", *Boletín Informativo de la Fundación de Estudios Bursátiles y Financieros*, December, 20—25.

———1999. "Industrial Policy Implications of Competition Policy Failure in Mergers". In Cowling ed., 180—196.

——— 2000. *Mergers, Efficient Choice and International Competitiveness.* Cheltenham: Edward Elgar (forthcoming).

Schenk, H., J.-P. Warmenhoven, M. van Velzen and C. van Riel 1997. "The Demise of the Conglomerate Firm" (in Dutch), *Economisch Statistische Berichten*, 82 (4122), 736—740.

Scherer, F.M. 1984. *Innovation and Growth: Schumpeterian Perspectives.* Cambridge, Mass.: MIT Press.

——— 1997. "Comment on "Merger Policy in the United States"", *Review of Industrial Organization*, 12, 687—691.

Shuttleworth, M. 1998. "The Impact of the Internet, New Trading Technologies and New Levels of Competition on Stock Exchanges— What New Innovations Can We Expect in the Near Future?", *Paper*, Exchange Tech '98, Hong Kong.

Sleuwaegen, L. 1998. "Cross-border Mergers and EC Competition Policy", *The World Economy*, 21 (8), 1077—1093.

Simon, H. 1996. *Hidden Champions. Lessons from 500 of the World's Best Unknown Companies.* Boston: Harvard Business School Press.

Simon, J.L., M. Mokhtari and D.H. Simon 1996. "Are Mergers Beneficial or Detrimental? Evidence from Advertising Agencies", *International Journal of the Economics of Business*, 3 (1), 69—82.

Thompson, S., M. Wright and K. Robbie 1993. "Buy-Outs, Divestment, and Leverage: Restructuring Transactions and Corporate Governance", *Oxford Review of Economic Policy*, 8 (3), 58—69.

Van Witteloostuijn, A. ed. 1995. *Market Evolution. Competition and Cooperation.* Studies in Industrial Organization, vol. 20, Dordrecht/ Boston/London: Kluwer Academic Publishers.

Veblen, T.B. 1899. *The Theory of the Leisure Class: An Economic Study of Institutions.* New York: Macmillan.

Vernon, R. ed. 1974. *Big Business and the State. Changing Relations in Western Europe.* Cambridge, MA: Harvard University Press.

Waverman, L., W.S. Comanor and A. Goto eds. 1997. *Competition Policy in the Global Economy. Modalities for Cooperation.* London/New York: Routledge.

Williamson, O.E. 1968. "Economies as an Antitrust Defense: The Welfare Tradeoffs", *American Economic Review*, 58, 18—36.

9 CONTRACTS AND COSTS IN A CORPORATE/GOVERNMENT SYSTEM DYNAMICS NETWORK: A UNITED STATES CASE

F. Gregory Hayden and Steven R. Bolduc

Social scientists have come to understand that society is a set of integrated values, beliefs, institutions, technology, and ecological systems as explicitly laid out in Figure 9.1 (Hayden 1988, 1997). Societal integration and organization takes place through the on—going processing of overlapping institutions and their organizations. The components of transorganizational frameworks, as demonstrated in Figure 9.1, create and structure the networks within which organizations such as business corporations and government agencies function. "Trans" as used in this sense means across. Across organizational networks normative criteria are provided by social beliefs, technology, and ecological systems (Hayden, 1998). From basic criteria, numerous rules, regulations, and requirements are codified by various institutional organizations such as courts, corporations, and government agencies. Transorganizational frameworks guide multi-organization networks made up of overlapping organizations. Thurman Arnold explained in his *Folklore of Capitalism* that modern industrial systems are the integration of huge organizations that are coordinated with different kinds of organizations. Corporations, government agencies, universities, and inter-organizational compacts, for example, function together and are dependent upon each other (Arnold, 1937). They are one of another.

Much of the coordination and planning among the different organizations is finalized through multi-organizational contracts and agreements. Thus, analysis to meet the challenges of industrial policy needs to incorporate the inter-organizational forms whose content, interpretation, and final function are determined by the actions taken in dynamic transorganizational networks. For such an accomplishment, the analytical methodology needs to be transdisciplinary as is implicit in Figure 9.1.

The purpose here is methodological, substantive, and policy-oriented. The purpose is to analyze the ramifications of a cost-plus contract arrangement that is very influential in determining the costs and activities of a particular corporate/government network in the United States. The network is built around the five—state Central Low—Level Radioactive Waste Compact (CIC) to include its policymaking Commission, a number of corporations, and several government agencies. The main methodological concern is how to model a transorganizational network utilizing the knowledge of transdisciplinary models. To accomplish this, the social fabric matrix (Hayden, 1982; Groenewegen, 1988; Meister, 1990) is combined with system dynamics (Radzicki, 1990; Gill, 1996).

Both the social fabric matrix and system dynamics procedures share a similar foundation. Institutional economics is oriented to the development of understandings about system cause and effect or influence patterns. The basic notion is that system management can only proceed upon a sound understanding of this underlying causation. The social fabric matrix is a systematic procedure for identifying and developing system insights. It is in effect, an institutional pattern modeling procedure. It may also serve as a structured process to facilitate the active participation of system players in policy development. System dynamics is another kind of pattern modeling, usually orientated to the quantitative representation of systems for simulation analysis. Qualitative relationships identified through the social fabric matrix process can be translated into a system dynamics model formulation. As a two-part procedure, a preliminary social fabric matrix is applied to explore systematically the insights of system players and represent them in an entirely qualitative construct. These insights, when translated into a formal system

Figure 9.1   Relationships among values, beliefs, attitudes, technology and the
ecological system

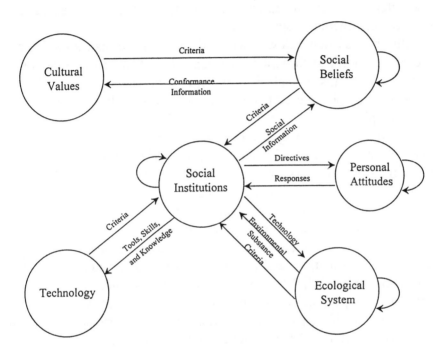

dynamics model, can be manipulated to address the concerns, expectations and ideas of system players and lead toward the development of management strategies and policies with which they have some empathy (Gill, 1996, p. 179—180).

The substantive interest is to understand both the network and the monetary costs during the future operational phase of the CIC facility (abbreviations listed at end for the readers' convenience). After a general overview of the system, the analysis is divided between the pre-operational phase and operational phase of the project. Coinciding with the last two years of the pre-operational phase is the construction phase. The latter will be explained with the operational phase cost because that is when construction costs are paid.

In the first section below a standard social fabric matrix (SFM) and digraph are utilized to explain the general context of this case study. The next section is an analysis of the pre-operational phase in which the SFM and digraph are used to demonstrate how to analyze the provisions of a cost-plus contract in order to, first, arrive at algebraic formulae of the contracts and, second, arrive at the total costs to be carried forward into the operational phase. The last section of analysis devoted to the projection of operational costs of the CIC facility. This is accomplished by utilizing the system dynamics program, *ithink*. The program serves as a vehicle for defining the digraph, and associated SFM, and for projecting an integrated set of operational costs.

Roderic Gill has explained that the SFM is to be constructed through a process of consultations and interactions with real-world system agents and documents (Gill, 1996, p. 173). The analysis here is based on a great deal of personal experience by the authors with the actors and institutions of the network. In addition, numerous primary documents have been consulted. They include the main contracts and agreements, the invoices and accounting systems, meeting minutes, the legal opinions and court decisions, legislative bills, considerable correspondence, the US Security and Exchange Commission (SEC) 10-K reports of the primary corporations, and the Safety Analysis Report (SAR), the name given to a multiple volume application submitted for a license to build and operate the CIC radioactive waste facility.

Too often, public—policy literature about transorganizations coveys the idea that overlapping organizations are collaborative and cooperative endeavors devoid of animosity. That is misleading with regard to the real world and is not necessary for modeling. In addition, such an assumption is inconsistent with the CIC case whose record is one of civil and political turmoil, a continuous parade of lawsuits, expensive overruns, renegotiations and re-formulations of contracts, an imprisoned CIC executive director, instances of raw intimidation, exploitative interest expenses on loans, and heavy social and personal burdens on various groups.

Contextual Description of The CIC Network

Because the corporate/government case of interest revolves around the Central Interstate Low-Level Radioactive Waste Compact (the CIC), a brief history is reviewed before a general overview of the network is presented.

History of Low—Level Waste Compact System

In 1980, the US Congress passed legislation for states to create a regional decentralized system of compacts for the disposal of low-level radioactive waste. Several basic premises upon which compact legislation were based have proven incorrect. First, contrary to expectations, the stream of low-level radioactive waste generated has continued to decrease since 1980 and is projected to continue to decline. Second, due to the particular characteristics of the externalities associated with federal compacts, they are not structured to be successful for the given objective (Hayden and Bolduc, 1997). Third, the compacts among the states are not regional. For example, California, the most southwestern state bordering the Pacific Ocean, is in a compact with South Dakota and North Dakota, the most northern state bordering Canada. Texas, the most southern state bordering Mexico, is in a compact with Vermont and Maine, the most northeastern state bordering Canada and the Atlantic Ocean. Consequently, the argument that a regional structure of compacts would minimize the number of miles that waste would need to be transported can not be realized.

When little progress was made toward establishing compact relationships and disposal sites, Congress, passed the Low Level Waste

Policy Amendment Act of 1985. That act generally provided states with a timetable and milestone penalties to encourage each state to either construct its own low—level waste storage facility or form a compact with other states. This was followed by a period of lawsuits in which different states challenged, in some cases successfully, different parts of the federal legislation. After that, internal conflicts within certain compacts led to the resignation or removal of some states. To date, new construction has not been undertaken by any compact.

The CIC is a compact made up of an agreement among the states of Arkansas, Kansas, Oklahoma, Louisiana, and Nebraska. The site selected for the disposal facility is near the northern border of Nebraska, a central state located north of the geographical center of the United States. Louisiana is one of the most southern states, bordering the Gulf of Mexico. Louisiana generates more low-level radioactive waste than any of the other Compact states; therefore, the site location will maximize transportation of such waste for disposal in the CIC area. In addition to the U.S. Congress and state governments, the CIC industrial system includes federal, state, and local government agencies, some of the world's largest and several of the United States' smallest corporations, and the electric generators from the five states.

Social Fabric Matrix Description

To begin to obtain an understanding of the whole system, the CIC, related agencies and organizations, and their relevant connections are articulated in the social fabric matrix (SFM) in Figure 9.2. Across the left side and top of the SFM are the social criteria and institutional components, which inform the network digraph that is uniquely associated with the SFM. Researchers utilize the SFM from left to right, so to speak, in order to discover what the row components are delivering to the columnar components in each cell. For cells where there is a delivery, or deliveries, a 1 is entered. The SFM network digraph for Figure 9.2 is found in Figure 9.3 with relevant cell deliveries on the directed edges among components.

Figure 9.2 General social fabric matrix of CIC system

Delivering Components ▼ / Receiving Components ▶		1. U. S. Congress	2. Federal Govt. Agencies	3. Non-Host State Govts.	4. Nebraska State Govt.	5. Nebraska State Agencies	6. Local Monitoring Committee	7. Boyd County Communities	8. Central Interstate Compact	9. Major Generators	10. Minor Generators	11. Contract	12. Agreement	13. American Ecology Corp.	14. Bechtel	15. Other Subcontractors	16. Sub-subcontractors	17. Operational Phase
U. S. Congress	1.		1	1														
Federal Govt. Agencies	2.			1	1				1					1				1
Non-Host State Govts.	3.								1									
Nebraska State Govt.	4.				1				1									
Nebraska State Agencies	5.					1								1				1
Local Monitoring Committee	6.																	
Boyd County Communities	7.																	
Central Interstate Compact	8.						1		1		1	1	1					1
Major Generators	9.								1				1					1
Minor Generators	10.																	1
Contract	11.								1	1				1	1			
Agreement	12.								1	1				1				
American Ecology Corp.	13.				1				1				1		1	1		1
Bechtel	14.													1			1	
Other subcontractors	15.													1			1	
Sub-subcontractors	16.															1		
Operational Phase	17.								1					1				

Figures 9.2 and 9.3 are jointly utilized to provide an overview of the general network for this corporate/government case study. They emphasize the pre-operational phase of the development process with only one entry serving as the subsequent operational phase. A more refined elaboration on both phases will be presented later. The institutional component that created the compact system is the US Congress. To make it function, Congress directly delivered rules, regulations, authority, and responsibilities to federal government agencies and to the five CIC states. Primary responsibility was placed on the US Nuclear Regulatory Commission with concurrent jurisdiction and responsibility residing with the US Environmental Protection Agency, the US Department of Energy, and the US Department of Interior. These federal agencies, in turn, promulgate rules, regulations,

Figure 9.3   General social fabric digraph network of CIC system

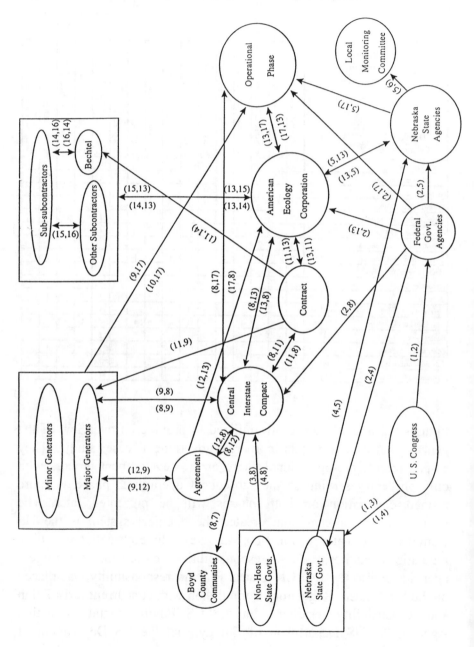

requests, and inspections that are delivered to the CIC states [cell (2,4)]; to Nebraska state agencies [cell (2,5)]; to the CIC [cell (2,8)]; and to American Ecology Corporation (AEC) [cell (2,13)]. Similar deliveries will be made to the same institutional agencies and organizations during the operational phase of the facility.

The five state governments provide a small percentage of the funds necessary for the administration of the CIC [cells (3,8) and (4,8)]. The four states without the site provide $75,000 annually to the CIC with the resulting $300,000 delivered to Boyd County Communities [cell (8,7)]. Boyd County, Nebraska is the proposed site for construction of the low-level radioactive waste disposal facility.

The most powerful organizations in the network are the major generators that own the nuclear power plants in the five states; the most important institutional document is the "Agreement" between the major generators and the CIC. The major generators are Nebraska Public Power Districts, and Omaha Public Power District in Nebraska, Wolfcreek Nuclear Operating Corporation in Kansas, Arkansas Power and Light Co. in Arkansas, and Gulf States Utilities Co. and Louisiana Power and Light Co. in Louisiana. The first two are owned and operated by government, while the latter four are private corporations. The nuclear power plants in Arkansas and Louisiana are owned by Entergy Corporation. Entergy is one of the 250 largest corporations in the United States, operates power generation facilities in several countries, and is currently negotiating to acquire the electric facilities from the British government. Entergy provides leadership among the major generators. The significant influence of the major generators is due to the fact that they provide the funds to the CIC so the CIC can pay AEC for the development of the facility.

The Agreement is a loan agreement between the major generators and the CIC with a stipulation that interest on the loan is to accrue during the pre-operational phase and then be repaid during operations. During the latter period, principal and interest is to be paid to AEC [cell (17,15)] which pays it to the CIC [cell (13,8)] which in turn, pays back the loan principal and interest to the major generators [cell (8,9)]. During the operational phase, both the major and minor generators of radioactive waste such as hospitals, research centers, and universities are to deliver waste to the disposal facility in Boyd County [cells (9,17) and (10,17) respectively].

In addition to the Agreement, another organizing document in the network is the "Contract" between the CIC and AEC. Both organizations provide provisions and negotiations to the Contract [cells (8,11) and (13,11)] and both are governed by these negotiated provisions [cells (11,8) and (11,13)]. The Contract establishes AEC as the developer and the CIC as the provider of funds that are obtained by the loan Agreement with the major generators. The funds are then sent to AEC, which in turn, sends most of them to Bechtel National Inc., the subcontractor. The importance of the major generators is also recognized in the Contract even though the generators are not a party to the Contract [cell (11,9)].

A major problem was created when the Contract established AEC as the developer rather than allow CIC to remain the developer and itself contracting with AEC to perform particular functions as determined by the CIC. Consequently the CIC is left without research and planning functions, and administrative control. Instead, AEC, the corporation that the CIC hired, determines what is to be accomplished and requests that the CIC give its approval and pay the invoices. Given the provisions of the Agreement and the Contract, the CIC has no alternative because the CIC does not have the millions of dollars to hire planners, engineering firms, test well drillers, monitors, and so forth to inspect and evaluate the developer's work.

A connection not recognized by the Contract is a connection to the Nebraska State agencies that have been granted authority to license and regulate the development and operation of the facility by the Nuclear Regulatory Commission and by the Nebraska state government. The lead state regulatory agency is the Nebraska Department of Environmental Quality (NDEQ). Since it is not a signatory to the Contract, the Contract has established provisions that NDEQ has not approved, nor will approve, in the operational phase [cell (15,17)]. This arrangement has led to conflict and lawsuits, and will continue to do so in the future.

An odd arrangement is the establishment of NDEQ as a subcontractor to AEC. Thus, NDEQ is dependent on the corporation it is mandated to license and regulate for the funds necessary to undertake the licensing and regulation activities. NDEQ will continue to perform licensure and regulation functions during the operational phase [cell (5,17)]. In addition, NDEQ will regulate the volume rates that AEC can charge on waste deposited at the facility.

The payments to NDEQ for reimbursable costs [cell (13,5)] that are provided by AEC, are also obtained from the major generators through the CIC. Included each year in the invoices from NDEQ to AEC is $100,000 for the Local Monitoring Committee (LMC) in Boyd County [cell (5,6)]. These funds are provided, according to legislation, so that the LMC can monitor all aspects of the system. Such monitoring activities have included research, data collection, advocacy, lawsuits, attendance at meetings, lobbying of legislation, and so forth. LMC's information is delivered to all organizations in the system. These informational deliveries are not shown in Figure 9.2 and 9.3 because the main interest here is the cost aspects of the system.

The network recipient of the most funds is Bechtel National, Inc. Approximately 80 percent of the $81 million that has been expended to date on the project has gone to Bechtel, one of the world's largest engineering services and construction corporations. According to Laton McCartney in *Friends in High Places*, Bechtel prefers a contractual arrangement whereby a smaller firm serves as the main contractor that actually signs the contract for development and construction, and Bechtel establishes a subcontract with the smaller firm to do the work and receive most of the money. That is consistent with the arrangement Bechtel has in the CIC network. AEC, a small corporation in desperate financial condition, has a "Technical Services Agreement" with Bechtel with the latter to do the planning, engineering design, and construction of the CIC facility. The Technical Services Agreement [11,14], is recognized by the Contract between AEC and the CIC.

This SFM description clarifies that it is not possible to understand any part of the system without knowing the contextual environment in which the system exists. While remaining cognizant of the surrounding network, the following sections will further refine and elaborate particular parts of the system with a final goal of projecting costs of operating the facility.

Pre-operational Phase Expenses Without Construction Costs

Although the main interest of this chapter is to model the costs during the thirty-year operational phase of the CIC facility, the network of the pre-operational phase costs are also visited because costs will be carried over to the operational phase from the activities of the pre-operational phase. The costs are to be amortized and repaid from disposal charges assessed on users of the storage facility during the operational phase.

As defined in this section, the pre-operational phase of the CIC project includes all activities prior to the beginning of facility operation with the exception of facility construction (construction payments are not incurred until the operational phase). In preparation for planning discussions regarding future litigation and budgets, AEC presented a projected schedule of the licensing and development process to the CIC. The projected date for commencement of operations, approximately January 2002, assumed that NDEQs schedule of license application evaluation is maintained and results in application approval (1997 Pre-construction Plan 2.0, 1996). Thus, the pre-operational phase is from 1987 through December 2001. The SFM and accompanying digraph in Figures 9.4 and 9.5 are used to analyze contracts to determine cost functions. Although the SFM of Figure 9.4 is devoted to the pre-operational phase, the operational phase (row and column 20) is included as a component because it receives accumulated costs from the pre-operational phase as well as from the construction phase. The main contracts of concern are the Contract between AEC and the CIC, and the Agreement between the major electric generators of the five states and the CIC.

SFM of Contract between AEC and The CIC

The Contract consists of the Contract itself, signed in 1987, and three subsequent amendments. Since it is the main determinant of costs and distribution of funds among parties of the CIC process, an in-depth analysis of the Contract is needed. But how? What kind? Attorneys analyze contracts for conformity to law. Contractors and subcontractors are only concerned about the costs they are allowed in the part of the contract directly affecting them. Economists seldom read contracts;

Figure 9.4 Social fabric matrix of contracts and costs during CIC pre-operational phase

Delivering Components		A. Sub-subcontractor w/o adder	B. Sub-subcontractor w/ adder	C. Bechtel's operating expenses less payroll & property	D. Bechtel's home-office payroll	E. Bechtel's non-home office payroll	F. Bechtel's equipment costs	Bechtel National, Inc.	American Ecology Corporation (AEC)	Central Interstate Compact (CIC)	Major Generators	Operational Phase
		10.	11.	12.	13.	14.	15.	16.	17.	18.	19.	20.
Contract 4.01 (a)(i)(A)(B)(D) & (E)(1) & (2)	1.	1										
Contract 4.01 (a)(i)(C)(D) & (E)(1)(2)	2.		1									
Contract 4.01 (a)(i) & Technical Service Agreement II & III	3.			1	1	1	1	1	1	1		
Contract 3.05, 3.07 & 6.01	4.								1	1		
Contract 3.02 (b), 4.01 (b), 4.02, & Amend. 3 (4) & (9) (6.01)	5.								1	1		
Agreement & Contract 2.01 (a)(b), 3.02, 3.03, 4.01 & Amend. 3	6.									1		
Agreement & Contract Amend 3 (2)	7.											1
Agreement & Contract 2.01 & 4.02	8.									1	1	
Agreement & Contract 2.01 & 6.01	9.									1		
A. Sub-subcontractor without adder	10.							1				
B. Sub-subcontractor with adder	11.							1				
C. Bechtel's operating expenses less payroll & equipment	12.							1				
D. Bechtel's home-office payroll	13.							1				
E. Bechtel's non-home office payroll	14.							1				
F. Bechtel's equipment costs	15.							1				
Bechtel National, Inc.	16.	1	1						1			
American Ecology Corporation (AEC)	17.								1	1		1
Central Interstate Compact (CIC)	18.									1	1	1
Major Generators	19.									1		
Operational Phase	20.											

*Figure 9.5   Social matrix digraph network of contracts and costs during CIC
pre-operational phase*

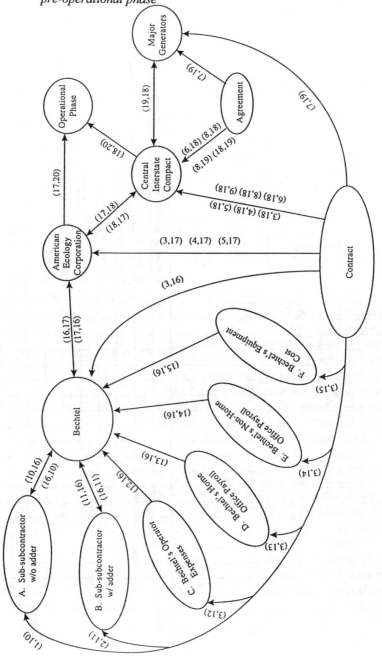

rather they do statistical studies on the ex-post financial flows. How do we get an ex-ante analysis of consequences? As is usually the case, the Contract's text does not contain mathematical or arithmetic expressions. Can we translate the textual provisions into the mathematical expressions helpful for analysis? Although such analysis has not been done before, a SFM analysis is completed in order to discover how different contract articles, sections, and terms define costs; what criteria are provided regarding cost criteria and requirements; and how the Contract defines the relevant relationships among different parties.

The SFM requires researchers to move cell by cell and identify whether there are deliveries in the cells in order to provide an explication of those deliveries. In some cases, the conversion of cellular information to a mathematical expression allows for more precision in explaining a particular delivery. To use the SFM, the Contract is thoroughly analyzed to discover the major criteria, requirements, and institutions. As discovered, they are entered in the SFM as the row and column components. Then, the SFM is used to explain what each row component delivered to each column component as relevant to our problem area.

Social belief criteria are expressed through the rules, regulations, and requirements of the Contract. These criteria are expressed in the matrix (Figure 9.4) as the sections in the Contract from whence they gain their legitimacy. For example, Article 4.01 in Figure 9.4 indicates that the criterion is found in Article 4, Section 1, of the Contract. The social institutions in Figure 9.4 are those recognized in the Contract. They include corporations such as AEC and Bechtel, accounting categories such as subcontractors' costs, and so forth. In comparing Figure 9.4 with Figure 9.2, it becomes evident that the SFM components in Figure 9.4 are refined subdivisions of the Contract and Agreement components of the SFM in Figure 9.2.

A complete SFM of the Contract and Agreement is not included in Figure 9.4 for a number of reasons. First, our main interest is in the operational phase. Second, receiving columns 1 through 9 are excluded because they demonstrate inter-contractual legal deliveries not immediately pertinent to the cost analysis. Symbols A through F designate both the category of the contractor and the invoice expenses of the same contractor. For example, A is the expenses on the invoice of a sub-subcontractor A sent to Bechtel. The components and cellular information included are sufficient to explain how formulae (1), (2), and (3) below can be derived from the SFM. Figures 9.4 and 9.5 are limited to defining Bechtel's part of the cost-plus formula. By explaining that part of the SFM, we learn how the cost-plus adder clauses build through the Contract process to define formulae (1), (2) and (3). Cost categories G through N (see Table 9.1) are here excluded because the inclusion of cost categories A through F for Bechtel are sufficient for demonstrating how the analysis can be completed for contractual provisions. This is done through understanding the cellular deliveries as follows:

Cell (1,10) Contract's Delivery to A: The delivery of interest in cell (1,10) for defining costs is the coefficient delivered to sub-ubcontractor A from the Contract. That coefficient is the coefficient that may be used to multiply costs before sending the invoice to Bechtel for reimbursement. A is the expenses of a sub-subcontractor whose contract with Bechtel does not allow for a cost plus adder, thus, the coefficient delivered in cell (1,10) is 1.

Cell (2,11) Contract's Delivery to B: The Contract terms in row 2 of the SFM are delivered to B. B is the expenses of a sub-subcontractor who may add 10 percent to its cost before sending its invoice to Bechtel. Thus the coefficient delivered in cell (2,11) is (1 + .10).

Cell (3,12) Contract and Technical Service Agreement's Delivery to C: The CIC/AEC Contract and the Technical Service Agreement between AEC and Bechtel join together to determine the relevant delivery in this cell. C is Bechtel's own operating expenses, exclusive of payroll expenses and capital equipment costs that are delivered internally to Bechtel. The Contract delivers a coefficient of (1 + .10), thus, the C expenses on the invoice can be increased by 10 percent.

Cell (3,13) Contract and Technical Service Agreement's Delivery to D: D is Bechtel's home-office payroll expenses for the project. Due to contractual deliveries, they are increased by about 41.5 percent, and in turn, 78 percent of that total is added for a coefficient of (1+ .415) [1 + .78].

Table 9.1 Cost-plus percentages that multiply CIC costs

Percentage	Definition of Terms
PV = 110% of A	A is cost of sub–subcontractors without cost-plus contract
+ 121% of B	B is costs of sub–subcontractor with cost-plus contract adder equal to 10%
+ 116% of C	C is Bechtel's operating expenses, exclusive of payroll & capital costs
+ 291% of D	D is Bechtel's home office payroll
+ 233% of E	E is Bechtel's non-home office payroll
+ 116% of F	F is Bechtel's capital equipment bought by CIC
+ G	G is stipulated sum or unit cost contract awarded by Nebraska DEQ
+ (1 + a) of H	H is cost-plus contracts awarded by Nebraska DEQ
+ DEQ	DEQ is in-house costs of Nebraska DEQ
+ 105% of I	I is stipulated sum or unit-cost contract awarded by DEQ
+ 108 % of J	J is AEC's operating expenses exclusive of payroll and equipment costs
+ 258% of K	K is AEC's home office payroll
+ 210% of L	L is AEC's non–home office payroll
+ 108% of M	M is AEC capital equipment bought by CIC
+ N	N is lobbying and extraordinary legal expenses of AEC

Cell (3,14) Contract and Technical Service Agreement's Delivery to E: E is Bechtel's non-home office payroll expenses for wages and salaries. The contractual delivery is $(1. + .415) [1 + .425]$ whereby E is increased by 41.5 percent, and that total is increased by 42.5 percent.

Cell (3,15) Contract and Technical Services Agreement's Delivery to F: The coefficient delivered in Cell (3,15) is one which is to be applied to F. F is capital equipment that is bought by the subcontractor, Bechtel, who selects the equipment and owns it.

Cells (10,16 and 11,16) Sub-subcontractors Deliveries to Bechtel: The sub-subcontractor's expenses, multiplied by the contractual coefficients delivered to them (as explained above), are delivered as invoices to Bechtel. They are, therefore, A and B $(1 + .10)$ when delivered.

Cells (12,16), (13,16), (14,16), and (15,16) Bechtel's Internal Cost Categories Deliveries to Bechtel: Bechtel's own expenses are delivered to Bechtel with their coefficients as defined above. They are: $C(1 + .10)$, $[D(1 + .415)][1 + .78]$, $[E(1 + .415)] [1 + .425]$, and F.

Cell (3,16) Contract and Technical Service Agreement's Delivery to Bechtel: Cell (3,16) provides the contractual authority for Bechtel to apply the coefficient $(1 + .05)$ to invoices it receives from sub-subcontractors A and B. and $(1 + .08)$ to its own internal expenses as they are bundled and presented with their own internal coefficients as presented in the cellular explanation just preceding this one.

Cell (3,17) Contract and Technical Service Agreement's Delivery to AEC: Cell (3,17) delivers to AEC the coefficients to apply to invoices received from subcontractors such as Bechtel. The nonfactual authority is provided for AEC to multiply subcontractor's invoices by $(1 + .05)$ and to multiply its own expenses by $(1 + .08)$.

Cell (16,17) Bechtel Delivery to AEC: Given the authority explained above to utilize the contractually defined cost-plus coefficients, Bechtel sends an invoice to AEC as follows:

$\{A + [B(1 + \cdot 10)]\}\{1 + .05\} + [C(1 + .10)] + \{[D(1 + .415)][1 + .78] + [E(1 + .415)][1 + .425]\}\{1+.10\} +F(1 + .10)$

The aggregating character of the Contract becomes clear with some very large cost-plus adders being authorized, often without a rational economic explanation. D, for example, is increased by 41.5 percent and that total increases by another 78 percent, as was explained above. That total, with adders, is increased again by 10 percent before sending the invoice to AEC. E is treated similarly. F is an equipment gift to Bechtel, ultimately paid for by the CIC. Bechtel selects the equipment, gets to own it, and in addition adds 10 percent onto the cost of the gift.

Cell (3,18) Contract and Technical Services Agreement Delivery to The CIC: Cell (3,18) establishes the authority for the cost-plus invoices to be submitted to the CIC for reimbursement.

Cell (17,18) AEC Delivery to The CIC: With regard to the Bechtel part of the cost-plus process, AEC takes the invoices sent form Bechtel, adds another 5 percent of that total, as provided in cell (3,16), and sends the total invoice to the CIC for reimbursement. Thus, the Bechtel part of the formula becomes:

$$\{\{A + [B(1 + .10)]\}\{1 + .05\}\}\{1 + .05\} + [C(1 + .10)][1 + .05] +$$
$$\{\{[D(1 + .415)][1 + .78]$$
$$+ [E(1 + .415)][(1 + .425]\}\{1 + .10\}\}\{1 + .05\} + [F(1 + .10)][1 + .05]$$

As clarified in the discussion of cell (3,16), AEC may also add a 5 percent adder to the costs of other subcontractors as well as add an 8 percent adder to AECs own expenses. Therefore, the total invoice, PV, sent to the CIC is as found in formula (1).

$$PV = \{A + [B(1 + .10)]\}\{1 + .05\}\}\{1 + .05\} + [C(1 + .10)][1 + .05] \qquad (1)$$
$$+ \{\{[D(1 + .415)][1 + .78] + [E(1 + .415)][1 + .425]\}\{1 + .10\}\}\{1 + .05\}$$
$$+ [F(1 + .10)][1 + .05] + G + [H(1 + a)] + DEQ + [I(1 + .08)] + \{[J(1 + .365)][1 + .75]$$
$$+ [K(1 + .365)][1 + .425]\}\{1 + .08\} + [L(1 + .08)] + M + N$$

PV stands for the present value of the invoices sent to the CIC. In addition to the Bechtel part of the formula contained in Figure 9.4, all contractors, subcontractors and sub-subcontractors are included (symbols G through N are defined in Table 9.1). When the formula is solved, the percentage coefficient for each term is as found in Table 9.1.

Examples from Table 9.1 can be used to indicate why the costs of the project have become so exorbitant and why cost overruns have been common. For example, sub-subcontractors a not allowed a cost-plus adder, yet their costs, A, invoiced to the CIC are 110 percent of costs because Bechtel and AEC are allowed to include their own percentage adders. Bechtel's home of lice payroll, D, is invoiced at 291 percent of cost, their non-home of lice payroll by 233 percent, and so forth. The information in formula (1) and Table 9.1 also clarifies that all incentives are in the Contract are to increase cost functions without disincentives or penalties for increasing cost functions. The Bechtel part of formula (1) has the highest cost adders and it is also the part that has received the most payments from the CIC, to date about 80 percent of approximately $81 million. Table 9.2 is an example of how a $1,000,000 budget of direct costs becomes a budget of $2,269,850.63 when all adders, summing to $1,269,850.63, are added as defined by formula (1).

Cells (6,18), (7,19), (8,18) and (8,19) Contract and Agreement Deliveries to The CIC and Major Generators: The Agreement between the CIC and the major electric generators in the five states of the CIC establishes the authority for the major generators to provide the financing source for the project's expenses. This Agreement is also recognized in the Contract, giving AEC the authority to submit invoices and expect the financing from the major generators for the paying the invoices. The major generators agreed to finance the amount of the invoices submitted to the CIC from AEC. Thus, the costs are really being financed by the electric ratepayers. The interest rate delivered by the Agreement to the major generators is the prime rate in the United States plus 6.5 percent. The financing is an accrued interest arrangement whereby interest accumulates and the interest rate is applied to the accruing interest as well as to the principal. When the facility begins operations, the loan plus accrued interest will be amortized for repayment as part of the charges to those depositing radioactive waste at the facility.

Cell (18,19) The CIC Delivery to Major Generators: Cell (18,19) is the delivery of notice from the CIC to the major electric generator to send a financial sum equal to the invoiced expenses that have been submitted from AEC for reimbursement.

Cell (19,18) Major Generators Delivery to The CIC: The delivery in cell (19,18) is the delivery of loanable funds from the generators to the CIC to pay AEC's invoices.

Cells (19,17), (17,16), (16,11) and (16,10): Delivery of Payments to Pay Invoices of AEC, Bechtel, A and B: The cells are the monetary payment flows for reimbursement of invoices as the money is loaned by

Table 9.2 Example of direct costs equal to $ 1,000,000 to demonstrate Bechtel part of formula

Term	Explanation	Sample Budget	Bechtel Formula	Bechtel Amount	American Ecology Corporation Formula	American Ecology Corporation Amount	Central Interstate Compact Formula	Central Interstate Compact Amount	Cost plus Adders:
A	Sub-subcontractor without cost-plus contract	$25,000.00	A	$25,000.00	A(1+.05)	$26,250.00	[A(1+.05)][1+.05]	$27,562.50	$2,562.50
B	Sub-subcontractor with cost-plus contract, adder=10%	$75,000.00	B(1+.10)	$82,500.00	[B(1+.10)][1+.05]	$86,625.00	[[B(1+.10)][1+.05]][1+.05]	$90,956.25	$15,956.25
C	Bechtel operating expenses, exclusive of payroll & capital costs	$150,000.00			C(1+.10)	$165,000.00	[C(1+.10)][1+.05]	$173,250.00	$23,250.00
D	Bechtel's home office payroll	$500,000.00			{[D(1+.415)][1+.78]}(1+.10)	$1,385,285.00	{{[D(1+.415)][1+.78]}(1+.10)}(1+.05)	$1,454,549.25	$954,549.25
E	Bechtel's non-home office payroll	$200,000.00			{[E(1+.415)][1+.425]}(1+.10)	$443,602.50	{{[E(1+.4150][1+.425]}(1+.10)}(1+.05)	$465,782.63	$265,782.63
F	Bechtel capital equipment bought by CIC	$50,000.00			F(1+.10)	$55,000.00	[F(1+.10)][1+.05]	$57,750.00	$7,750.00
G	Stip. sum or unit-cost contracts awarded by Nebraska DEQ						G	$0.00	$0.00
H	Cost-plus contracts awarded by Nebraska DEQ						H(1+a)	$0.00	$0.00
DEQ	In-house costs of Nebraska DEQ						DEQ	$0.00	$0.00
I	Stip. sum or unit-cost contracts, awarded by AEC						I(1+.05)	$0.00	$0.00
J	AEC's operating expenses exclusive of payroll and capital costs						J(1+.08)	$0.00	$0.00
K	AEC's home office payroll						[[K(1+.365)][1+.75]](1+.08)	$0.00	$0.00
L	AEC's non-home office payroll						[[L(1+.365)][1+.425]](1+.08)	$0.00	$0.00
M	AEC capital equipment bought by CIC						M(1+.08)	$0.00	$0.00
N	Lobbying and extraordinary legal expenses of AEC						N	$0.00	$0.00
	TOTAL	$1,000,000.00						$2,269,850.63	$1,269,850.63

Conclusion: $1,000,000 budget increases to $2,269,850.63 due to cost plus adders of $1,269,850.63. This total does not include interest adders in finance agreement the major generators to the CIC which pays AEC who pays Bechtel who pays subsubcontractors.

Cell (18,20) The CIC Delivery to Operational Phase: Cell (18,20) is the delivery of formula (2) to the facility operational phase of the CIC for amortisation of the financing from the major generators. Formula (2) is as follows:

$$FV = \sum_{j=1987}^{y} PV_j (1 + r + .065)^{y-1} \tag{2}$$

FV is the future value of the financing from the major generators. The letter j indexes the year in which the PV on the invoice was paid; the first year being 1987. The letter y is the year to which the loan is being accumulated; the last year being 2001. PV_j is the total value of major generator financing to pay costs in year j. The prime interest rate is r, and .065 is the interest rate added to the prime rate as specified in the Agreement. The estimated total owed to the major generators at the end of 1996 was approximately $120 million; this includes the amount of the loan and the accrued interest for the period 1987-1996 (Hayden and Snider, 1996). The accumulation is not only significant but continues to grow exponentially. It will continue to grow in this fashion until the facility begins operation in January 2002. To find that amount, the total owed was projected forward, at the same rate as it has increased from 1987 through 1996, to December 2001. The total delivered in cell (18, 20) is to be amortized and paid in the operational phase. It is projected to be approximately $325 million at the end of 2001.

Cell (5,17) and (5,18), Contract Delivery to AEC and The CIC: Provisions in the Contract between AEC and the CIC provide that in the initial period of the contract, a small part of project costs are financed by AEC. The Contract delivers those provisions in cells (5,17) and (5,18). From 1987 to 1992 that financing contribution amounted to about $6.2 million.

Cell (17,20) AEC Delivery to Operational Phase: Between 1987 and 1992 the contribution from AEC for financing pre-operational cost amounted to about $6.2 million. Both the CIC and AEC have responsibilities in the collection of the loan plus accrued interest in the operational phase of the facility. Together they deliver the results of formula (3), as follows:

$$FV_{AEC} = \sum_{j=1987}^{y} AECPV_j (1 + .20)^{y-j} \qquad (3)$$

where FV_{AEC} is the future value of the financing from AEC to include accrued interest; j is the year in which AECPV was contributed, first year being 1987; and y is the year to which the loan is being accumulated. AECPV is the total value of financing contributed to pay costs in year j, and .20 is the interest rate paid on AEC financing until January 1997. According to the CIC correspondence, the total of principal plus accrued interest in December 1996 was $21,427, 401. Beginning in January 1997, that amount has been carried forward using the new interest rates for an expected amount to be owed to AEC in December 2001 equal to approximately $33.4 million. That amount is delivered to the operational phase for amortization and repayment from operational revenues.

The SMF has provided a means to describe the general context, to articulate particular socioeconomic components embedded in that context, to define connections among the components, and to convert cellular information to mathematical expression where appropriate. The analysis completed above allows us to see how the cost-plus formula builds through the Contract and Agreement to create a financial burden to be carried forward to be amortized and paid during the operational phase. The total delivered to the operational phase is about $504.1 million. It includes the major generator financing ($325 million), AEC financing contribution ($33.4 million), construction loan ($91.6 million), financial assurance loan ($41.5 million) and AEC's subsidiaries' interest ($12.6 million). Major generator financing and AEC financing were explained above. The others will be explained below. In addition, the analysis above pinpoints the particular provisions in the Contract and Agreement that need to be renegotiated to reduce the financial burden.

Operational Phase

According to Pre-construction Plan 2.0, developed for the CIC by AEC and Bechtel, the operational phase of the facility is planned to begin on January 2002, assuming the NDEQ licensing process is followed, and the license is granted. Again, the plan is for the facility to operate from 2002 to 2031. The purpose of this section is to estimate the allowable yearly costs during the operational phase in order to determine the consequent fee that waste generators will need to pay for waste storage. As explained earlier, some costs accrued in the pre-operational phase are to be amortized and paid during the operational phase. The cost of facility construction, which occurs the two years prior to operations commencing, is also amortized to be paid by storage fees. Moreover, since $4.5 million in funds for re-mediation and possible early closure of the facility are to be in place the day operations begin, that amount is also to be borrowed. According to the SAR this loan of financial assurance funds will be amortized according to the same parameters as the construction loan.

To discover the corporate/government network that processes these costs, a SFM of the institutions involved is constructed in Figure 9.6. Because the delivery of contractual provisions has already been explained and demonstrated in the pre-operational SFM of Figure 9.4, this SFM does not include the contractual criteria, rules, and requirements found in the Contract, Agreement, and SAR. The SFM will be reported, modeled and, analyzed with the assistance of the system dynamics program, *ithink*. The SFM network digraph will be the system dynamics format of the *ithink* program.

System Dynamics Network and Analysis

System dynamics is an intellectual evolution from systems theory (Hayden, 1989). Crucial to dynamic modeling is an understanding that the behavior of a system depends on its structure and the connections among the parts. A fundamental concept is that systems are structured so that the system provides for what is called feedback among the component parts. This means that one component influences another

Figure 9.6 Social fabric matrix of institutional components during CIC operational phase

Delivering Components	Preoperational Phase					Operational Phase																	
Receiving →	1.	2.	3.	4.	5.	6.	7.	8.	9.	10.	11.	12.	13.	14.	15.	16.	17.	18.	19.	20.	21.	22.	23.
1. Major Generators Financing						1																	
2. Construction Debt							1																
3. Financial Assurance Debt								1															
4. AEC Financing									1														
5. AEC General Interest										1													
6. Major Generators Amortization																			1				
7. Construction Amortization																			1				
8. Financial Assurance Amortization																			1				
9. AEC Financing Amortization																			1				
10. General Interest Amortization																			1				
11. Depreciation Schedule Application																			1				
12. Rate Setting Process																							
13. CIC Debt Fund																							
14. CIC Administration													1										
15. Community Improvement Account													1	1		1		1					
16. Boyd County Agencies													1	1	1								
17. Nebraska State Agencies																							
18. American Ecology Corporation											1				1					1			
19. AEC Charges & Payment Fund													1	1	1	1						1	
20. AEC Waste Storage																						1	
21. Waste Generators																							
22. Major Generators																				1			1
23. Subcontractors																							

component, which influences another component, maybe in another part of the system, which in turn influences the original component (Radzicki and Sterman, 1994). Such "feedback" patterns are emphasized in system dynamics. "System dynamics models represent change as a function of the interplay between underlying patterns of positive- and negative-polarity feedback" (Gill 1996, p. 168). Negative feedback guides systems to stability and sustainability while positive feedback leads to growth and decay.

Several system dynamic programs have been developed. The authors, however, have found the modeling capabilities of *ithink* to be the most consistent with the theories and process concepts of the social sciences and institutional economics. In the explanation and diagrams below, circles are rules, regulations, requirements, or criteria—those expressions of social beliefs. The circles with "spigots" are the regulations, or regulators, that either regulate the level of deliveries between institutions or deliver regulations to influence other regulations. The rectangles are the SFM institutional components from Figure 9.6. The directed double lines represent the delivery flows among institutions, and the single-line directed arcs represent deliveries of rules, regulations, requirements, and criteria for the regulation of flows among institutions. The cloud-looking symbols are utilized to indicate that the source or destination of a delivery is not being explained by this model. (The symbols are in Appendix D).

Operational Phase Network

The analytic approach begins by presenting the highest level framework and proceeds to explanation and analysis of the particular sections which are the working parts of the whole. The high level, found in Figure 9.7 presents the main sections, or sectors, of the problem of concern. They are the Waste Generators, the CIC, AEC (divided between the production operation in Boyd County and the pecuniary operation of the corporation), subcontractors to the AEC, Boyd County Agencies, and Nebraska State Agencies. The heavy lines in Figure 9.7

Figure 9.7 High level mapping of CIC network structure

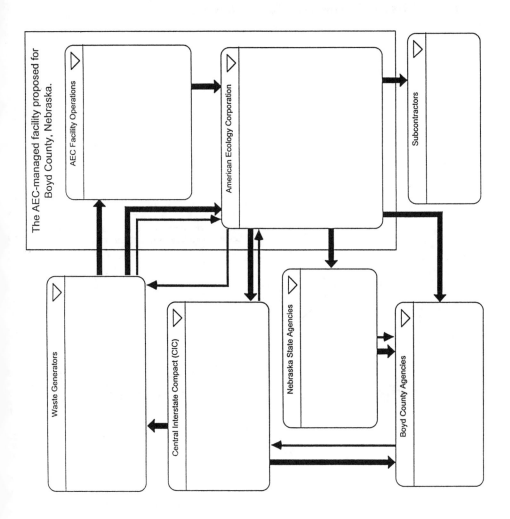

indicate the general flows among sectors; the thinner lines represent deliveries of rules, regulations, or criteria. Articulation of the sectors will begin with an explanation of the radioactive waste stream delivered from the generators to the AEC facility.

Figure 9.8 Total radioactive waste flow of CIC states

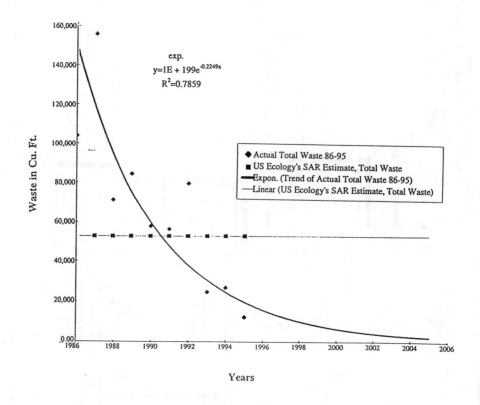

Waste Stream

As has been confirmed by numerous studies, the annual level of low-level radioactive waste continues to fall in the five-state region of the CIC and in the United States since 1980 (Coates, Heid, and Munger, 1994; Hoffman and Hayden, 1996; Chem-Nuclear, 1997; and Fuchs, 1996). Figure 9.8 is a summary of the waste flow in the CIC area since

1986. As is evident, total waste fell from a high in 1986 to a level of approximately 12,000 cubic feet in 1995. Statistical projections and technological assessments by nuclear engineers and economists predict the waste stream to continue to decrease.

The dramatic decrease in the waste stream is due to the development of new processes and the application of new technology. The history of low-level waste generation and disposal is one of increasing public concern for safer storage and disposal. Reconstructed, improved, and more secure facilities resulted in increased disposal fees charged to waste generators. In turn, generators responded to the increased fees by finding new ways to decrease the volume of waste through innovations in production technology and in compaction of waste generated (Jackson, 1996). As the volume of waste generated diminished, fewer units of waste were available over which to spread disposal facilities' overhead costs. Consequently, unit costs increased, providing generators further incentive to reduce waste volume still more. As will be discussed below, the combination of declining waste volume, increasing facility costs, and the contractual requirement that disposal fees be sufficient to cover unit costs has resulted in estimated disposal fees for the CIC facility mach higher than industry norms.

Furthermore, the cycle of innovation creates a problem with regard to the SAR that assumed a constant annual 55,000 cubic feet stream of waste (see Figure 9.8). A review of the waste stream of 5,000 cubic feet per year is a sound assumption for modeling purposes, erring on the side of adequacy. Thus, in Figure 9.9, the waste stream from the Waste Generators sector is 5,000 cubic feet per year. This reduction is waste volume calls for a reduction in the facility construction scenario, as will be discussed below.

Pre-operational Debt Owed to Major Generators

As explained above, the total principal and interest that accrued during the pre-operational phase to pay project expenses, is to be amortized and paid from waste stream charges. The major generators have been financing the payments of non-construction expenses during pre-operation with a cost-plus interest rate of prime plus 6.5 percent. The

Figure 9.9 CIC operational cost network

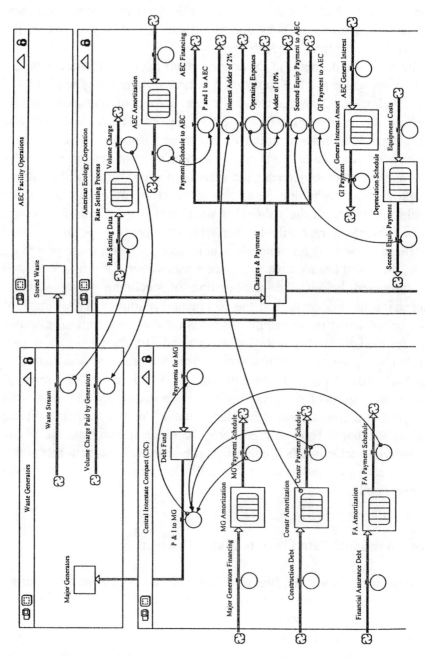

Figure 9.9 CIC operational cost network (continued)

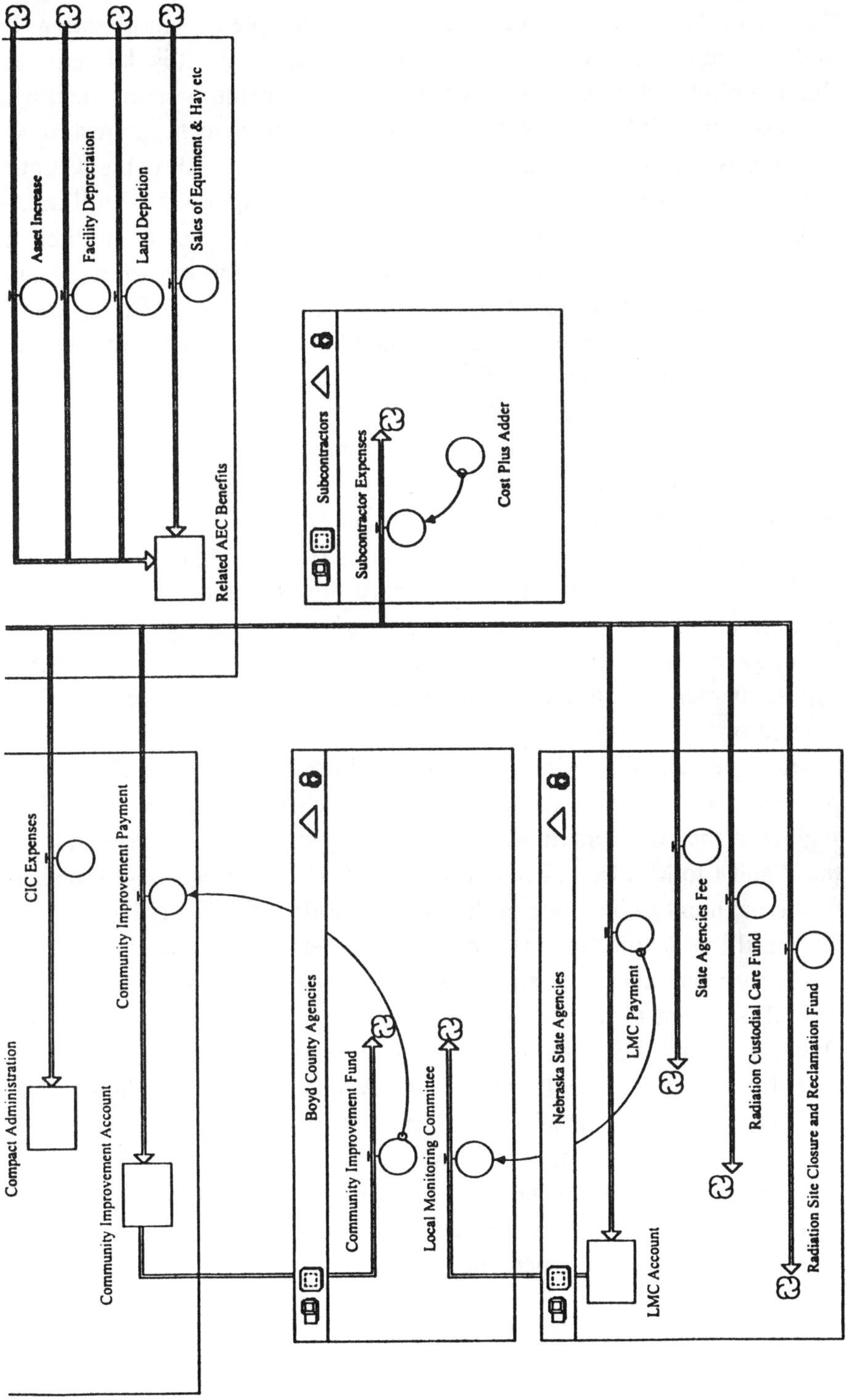

financing plus accrued interest will equal approximately $325 million at the end of 2001 and then becomes the new principle for amortization. It is delivered to the CIC, as demonstrated in Figure 9.9. It is delivered to the double-lined rectangle labeled, Major Generators Amortization. interest since 1987 and will continue to receive such interest until operations begin in 2002. The interest rate was 20 percent until December 31, 1996. At that date, the original principal of $6.2 million.

According to the Agreement, the loan is to be amortized at an interest rate of prime plus 6.5 percent. The prime rate for the past thirty years has averaged about 9 percent, thus, consistent with the SAR, 9 percent is used as the prime rate. The double-lined rectangle is used to indicate that a programming sub-model is being used to transform a delivery in some way. A sub-model, which is a transformation processing station, usually represents an institutional component or components that have the responsibility and/or authority to apply the requisite rules, regulations, and their coefficients to the original delivery. The sub-model for the major generators financing is found in Appendix A. As is evident upon inspection, it is a standard amortization routine. In this case, it is utilized to determine the yearly payment to amortize the major generators' loan according to the requirements of the Agreement. (Subsequent amortization sub-models are similar to the one presented in Appendix A.)

After the transformation process, the information about the yearly payments is delivered as MG Payment Schedule (Figure 9.9). The regulator then delivers those instructions, by the arc, to the regulator on the P and I to MG flow. This informs AEC (Figure 9.9) about the size, of the payment to be made each year to amortize this debt. The loan of $325 million is amortized at a rate of 15.5 percent with level payments for thirty years using the amortization function from Appendix A. The annual payment to be collected for the loan is about $51 million. The flow lines from AEC charges and payments to the CIC Debt Fund and then from the CIC Debt Fund to the Major Generators (Figure 9.9) indicate the yearly flow of the loan payment. The loan payment for each of the thirty years is found on row 30 of Table 9.3 According to the Agreement, any year in which that payment is not made, the unpaid amount is added to the remaining principle and the begins to accrue interest at prime plus 6.5 percent.

AEC Contribution to Financing Pre-operational Expenses

As explained above, a contribution was made by AEC for the financing of pre-operational expenses. This began in 1987 and reached the full contribution of $6.2 million in 1991. This amount has been accruing plus accrued compound interest had grown to $21.4 million. From January 1, 1997 until October 30, 1997, the interest rate is to be prime plus 3 percent. From then until December 31, 2001 the interest rate is to be equal to prime. The total that will be owed to AEC on January 1, 1997 will be approximately $33.4 million. According to the third amendment to the Contract, that amount is to be delivered to the operational phase, amortized, and repaid from surcharges on the disposal fees. As demonstrated in Figure 9.9, the AEC financing total is delivered to the AEC Amortization sub-model. The sub-model then delivers to the AEC Payment Schedule instructions to the P and I flow to AEC. The loan is amortized at an interest rate of prime plus 2 percent, or 11 percent, which results in level payments of $4.1 million for the thirty-year life of the facility (see Table 9.3, row 31).

Construction Loan

Construction is to be completed by Bechtel. The plan in the SAR was for the facility to be constructed in three phases. However, due to the decrease in the amount of waste generated in the region, the first construction phase is all that will be considered in our analysis. The construction phase to be completed during the two-year period prior to operations provides for sufficient capacity. Its costs and the loan arrangement are determined according to the SAR, the 1997 Pre-construction Plan, and the Contract. The total includes a 5 percent adder paid to AEC for the construction work completed by Bechtel, and interest that accrues on the loan during construction. The total to be amortized is $91.6 million.

Because of the destitute financial condition of AEC, it is assumed that the funds for the construction loan will also come from the major generators. As was the case for the pre-operation loan, the CIC will

Table 9.3 Total costs during operational phase, 2002 through 2031*

Cost Classifications (year)	2002	2003	2004*	2011	2012	2013*	2027	2028	2029	2030	2031	Totals
1 Direct Costs												
2 Salaries and Benefits	2,495,252	2,595,062	2,698,865	3,551,522	3,693,583	3,841,326	6,651,934	6,918,012	7,194,732	7,482,521	7,781,822	139,946,069
3 Office Supplies	167,481	174,180	181,147	238,377	247,912	257,829	446,476	464,335	482,908	502,225	522,314	9,393,142
4 Travel and Relocation	139,567	145,150	150,956	198,648	206,594	214,857	372,063	386,946	402,424	418,521	435,261	7,827,618
5 Office Costs - Lincoln	58,618	60,963	63,401	83,432	86,769	90,240	156,267	162,517	169,018	175,779	182,810	3,287,600
6 Office Costs - Boyd County	33,496	34,836	36,229	47,675	49,582	51,566	89,295	92,867	96,582	100,445	104,463	1,878,628
7 Office Security	167,481	174,180	181,147	238,377	247,912	257,829	446,476	464,335	482,908	502,225	522,314	9,393,142
8 Legal Costs	34,892	36,287	37,739	49,662	51,648	53,714	93,016	96,736	100,606	104,630	108,815	1,956,905
9 ANI Insurance	37,683	39,190	40,758	53,635	55,780	58,011	100,457	104,475	108,654	113,001	117,521	2,113,457
10 Other Insurance	—	—	—	—	—	—	—	—	—	—	—	—
11 Offsite Monitoring Access	1,396	1,451	1,510	1,986	2,066	2,149	3,721	3,869	4,024	4,185	4,353	78,276
12 Boyd County Facility Costs	376,552	372,745	390,674	536,424	557,881	580,197	1,004,713	1,044,901	1,086,697	1,130,165	1,175,372	21,087,270
13 Subtotal: Direct Costs	3,512,418	3,634,045	3,782,426	4,999,739	5,199,729	5,407,718	9,364,418	9,738,994	10,128,554	10,533,696	10,955,044	196,962,106
14 Subcontracts:												
15 Radiological Lab	586,182	609,630	634,015	834,320	867,693	902,401	1,562,666	1,625,173	1,690,180	1,757,787	1,828,098	32,875,996
16 TLD	16,748	17,418	18,115	23,838	24,791	25,783	44,648	46,434	48,291	50,222	52,231	939,314
17 Bioassay	13,957	14,515	15,096	19,865	20,659	21,486	37,206	38,695	40,242	41,852	43,526	782,762
18 Wholebody Counter	17,446	18,144	18,869	24,831	25,824	26,857	46,508	48,368	50,303	52,315	54,408	978,452
19 Crane Service	34,892	36,287	37,739	49,662	51,648	53,714	93,016	96,736	100,606	104,630	108,815	1,956,905
20 Site Maintenance	13,957	14,515	15,096	19,865	20,659	21,486	37,206	38,695	40,242	41,852	43,526	782,762
21 Engineering Services	139,567	145,150	150,956	198,648	206,594	214,857	372,063	386,946	402,424	418,521	435,261	7,827,618
22 Subtotal: Subcontracts	822,749	855,659	889,885	1,171,028	1,217,869	1,266,584	2,193,313	2,281,046	2,372,288	2,467,179	2,565,866	46,143,808
23 US Ecology Overhead	1,060,482	1,102,902	1,147,018	1,509,397	1,569,773	1,632,564	2,827,072	2,940,155	3,057,761	3,180,072	3,307,274	59,477,079
24 10% Cost Adder	539,565	559,261	581,933	768,016	798,737	830,687	1,438,480	1,496,020	1,555,860	1,618,095	1,682,818	30,258,299
25 Total Operations Costs	5,935,214	6,151,866	6,401,262	8,448,180	8,786,108	9,137,552	15,823,283	16,456,215	17,114,463	17,799,042	18,511,003	508,048,891
26 Community Improvement Fund	2,791,344	2,902,998	3,019,118	3,972,953	4,131,871	4,297,146	7,441,267	7,738,917	8,048,474	8,370,413	8,705,229	156,552,361
27 Local Monitoring Committee	100,000	100,000	100,000	100,000	100,000	100,000	100,000	100,000	100,000	100,000	100,000	3,000,000
28 State Agencies Fee	279,134	290,300	301,912	397,295	413,187	429,715	744,127	773,892	804,847	837,041	870,523	15,655,236
29												
30 MG Loan Payment	51,051,900	51,051,900	51,051,900	51,051,900	51,051,900	51,051,900	51,051,900	51,051,900	51,051,900	51,051,900	51,051,900	1,531,557,000
31 AEC Loan Payment	3,842,000	3,842,000	3,842,000	3,842,000	3,842,000	3,842,000	3,842,000	3,842,000	3,842,000	3,842,000	3,842,000	115,260,000
32 AEC General Interest	1,455,500	1,455,500	1,455,500	1,455,500	1,455,500	1,455,500	1,455,500	1,455,500	1,455,500	1,455,500	1,455,500	43,665,000
33 Construction Loan Payment	14,388,800	14,388,800	14,388,800	14,388,800	14,388,800	14,388,800	14,388,800	14,388,800	14,388,800	14,388,800	14,388,800	431,664,000
34 2% Adder on Const. Loan Interest	283,960	283,369	282,685	273,818	271,654	269,155	147,771	126,070	101,005	72,056	38,619	6,801,276
35 Financial Assur. Loan Payment	6,514,200	6,514,200	6,514,200	6,514,200	6,514,200	6,514,200	6,514,200	6,514,200	6,514,200	6,514,200	6,514,200	195,426,000
36 Rad. Site Closure & Reclam. Fund	4,465,455	4,644,073	4,829,836	6,355,734	6,609,964	—	—	—	—	—	—	60,222,689
37 Radiation Custodial Care Fund	—	—	—	—	—	—	—	—	—	—	—	—
38 Institutional Control	1,764,000	1,834,560	1,907,942	2,510,722	—	—	—	—	—	—	—	21,178,773
39 Remedial Action	—	—	—	—	619,784	644,576	1,116,196	1,160,844	1,207,278	1,255,569	1,305,792	18,455,983
40 Second Equipment Payment	44,103	86,197	130,578	281,078	298,505	313,803	561,572	584,035	607,397	631,692	656,960	11,313,803
41 CIC Expenses	885,723	921,152	957,998	1,260,660	1,311,087	1,363,530	2,361,193	2,455,641	2,553,867	2,656,021	2,762,262	49,675,737
42												
43 TOTAL COSTS	93,801,334	94,466,914	95,183,731	100,852,841	99,794,559	93,807,877	105,547,809	106,648,014	107,789,731	108,974,235	110,202,789	2,993,269,152
44 Waste Stream (cubic feet/year)	5,000	5,000	5,000	5,000	5,000	5,000	5,000	5,000	5,000	5,000	5,000	150,000
45 Disposal Charge per cu. ft. ($)	18,760	18,893	19,037	20,171	19,959	18,762	21,110	21,330	21,558	21,795	22,041	

*Representatives years are included in the table; other years are available from the authors.

serve as a conduit; borrowing from the major generators and loaning to AEC. Consistent with other funds borrowed from the major generators, the interest rate is expected to be prime plus 6.5 percent, or 15.5 percent. The construction loan is delivered to the CIC via the Construction Loan sub-model in Figure 9.9 for amortization calculations.

In addition to the construction loan being amortized over thirty years an adder of "an amount equal to two percent (2%) of the interest portion of said payments . . ." (Contract; 3rd Amendment 9, (6.01) a.4) is to be paid to AEC. The sub-model delivers the instructions for the annual loan payment to the CIC and the 2 percent adder to AEC (row 5, 33 and 34 of Table 9.3).

As indicated in Figure 9.9, the debt created by the financial assurance loan is delivered, via another amortization sub-model, to the CIC for collection. The FA Amortization sub-model (Appendix D) determines the yearly payments and delivers notice of that information to AEC, in Figure 9.9, for repayment. The yearly payment is reported in row 35 of Table 9.3 as about $6.5 million.

AECs General Interest Expenses

AEC has reported in their SEC 10-K Report that they are capitalizing interest expenses incurred by their corporation in general, as part of the development costs of their projects in Boyd County, Nebraska and Ward Valley, California. None of this interest was incurred for the CIC project in Boyd County because all costs have been reimbursed including land and equipment costs. Only one of AECs subsidiaries, US Ecology, is involved in the CIC project. The interest that is being capitalized on the Boyd County project is related to borrowing under the Company's credit agreement with its bank lender in an attempt to keep AEC out of bankruptcy. AEC expects the capitalized interest, none of which was incurred for the Boyd County project, to be included in the rate base charged waste depositors as indicated in Figure 9.9. This General AEC Interest flow is delivered from outside the operational phase to the General Interest Amortization sub-model for calculation of the yearly payment. An average of the past two years was used as the expected added capitalization for each of the years during 1997 through 2001. One-half was allocated to Ward Valley and one-half to the CIC project. This made for a total of about $12.7 million that will accumulate through 2001. Since other AEC contributions to be repaid are amortized at prime plus 2 percent, that rate (11 percent) is used for determining the loan payment schedule. The payment schedule is then conveyed to the payment process as indicated in Figure 9.9. The annual payment is about $1.4 million, as reported in row 32 of Table 9.3.

Operating Costs

The costs explained above did not occur during the operational phase. Next, the costs that are to occur during the operational phase are discussed.

Direct Costs: The direct operating costs, along with their total are listed in rows 2 through 13 in Table 9.2. They are taken directly from the SAR. The assumption of AEC, in the SAR is that direct costs will remain at the same level and mix throughout the thirty-year period. Therefore, the only growth in those rows is a 4 percent annual increase due to inflation.

Of special interest is that the various direct-cost categories include equipment and small tools such as trucks, computers, office equipment, lab and calibration tools, and so forth. Therefore, this equipment is paid for in full when operating expenses are paid. The reason this is of special interest is because AEC is paid for this equipment a second time when AEC is paid an amount equal to the cost of small equipment according to what is called depreciation, as discussed below.

Subcontracts: The subcontractor's expenses during operation along with their total are found in rows 14 through 22 in Table 9.3, as reported in the SAR. The SAR explains that they are to be projected forward with an inflation rate of 4 percent.

AEC Overhead: An overhead charge of 42.5 percent of salaries and benefits is made by AEC. The annual payment to AEC is equal to the amounts found in row 23 of Table 9.3.

AEC adder of 10 Percent: AEC, according to the Contract, is to receive a 10 percent adder (row 24, Table 9.3) applied to the total of direct costs, subcontractor costs, and overhead; equal to the total of row 13 plus row 22 plus row 23.

As indicated in Figure 9.9, the total operating expenses are paid from charges on the waste stream and paid to AEC. These expenses are reported in row 25 of Table 9.3.

Second Payment for Equipment and Tools

According to the Contract, AEC is to be paid an amount equal to a depreciation schedule as applied to the full cost of equipment and tools bought during operation. So, in addition to using the depreciation as a tax deduction, AEC will get paid that amount. That means AEC is getting paid twice for the equipment and tools. For example, if a $25,000 truck is bought, AEC gets paid $25,000 immediately through reimbursement by the CIC. Then a five-year depreciation schedule is utilized as a means to get paid an additional $5,000 per year for five years, or $25,000. Moreover, AEC is allowed to retain the sale price of the truck when sold after it is five years old and to deduct the value of depreciation on its tax return. .

The depreciation schedule utilized here assumes straight-line depreciation and a five-year useful life. The sub-model detailed to calculate the depreciation amount is shown in Appendix B. The delivery of the annual payment to AEC is indicated in Figure 9.9, and the total of this delivery is indicated in row 40 of Table 9.3.

Nebraska State and Local Agencies

As demonstrated in Figure 9.9, the facility is expected to generate funds for state and local agencies. One such fund is for community improvement in Boyd County, which is to paid to the CIC, which will, in turn, make equal payments to Boyd County. The total grows at 4 percent per year to cover inflation, as found in row 26 of Table 9.3. Another fund is established to support the Local Monitoring Committee (LMC). Its funding is a level $100,000, without adjustment for inflation (row 27 of Table 9.3). It is paid by AEC to NDEQ, which in turn makes the payment to the LMC. Lastly, reimbursement of NDEQ expenses is represented as a delivery to Nebraska State Agencies. It is adjusted by 4 percent annually for inflation; (see row 28 of Table 9.3).

Radiation Site Closure and Reclamation Fund and the Radiation Custodial Care Fund

Nebraska law requires that funds be available for remedial, or corrective, action during the operational phase, and for site closure and stabilization after operations; a portion of these funds are initially front-loaded with monies from the financial assurance loan. The funds are collected as a surcharge on waste disposed at the facility. The Radiation Site Closure and Reclamation Fund (RSC&R Fund) provides for site closure, while the Radiation Custodial Care Fund (RCC Fund) provides for both remedial action and long-term institutional care. Because of the reduced waste stream, figures reported in the SAR have been adjusted as discussed below.

Radiation Site Closure and Reclamation Fund: To accommodate the lower waste stream, a smaller facility than originally proposed will be sufficient. Therefore, a facility consistent with only the first phase of construction is assumed. The cost of closing a facility of this size, as estimated in the SAR, is accepted and then adjusted for inflation. This leaves about $60 million to be collected via waste volume charges in the first eleven years. Consistent with the plan proposed in the SAR, the $60 million is collected over years one through eleven of operations to satisfy the requirements of the RSC&R Fund. This is indicated in row 36 of Table 9.3. Consistent with state guidelines that these funds be "outside the licensee's administrative control," Figure 9.9 represents payments for this fund as being delivered to the sector labeled Nebraska State Agencies.

Radiation Custodial Care Fund: The RCC Fund is administered in two components; remedial action and institutional care. As presented in the SAR, the necessary funds for remedial action are to be collected during years eleven through thirty. For institutional care, funds are collected in years one through ten. A portion of the financial assurance loan is targeted for the institutional care component of the RCC Fund.

Consequently, given adjustments for inflation, for the smaller facility size, and for the diminished waste stream, about $21.2 million is to be collected for institutional care, and about $18.4 million will be collected for remedial action.

Table 9.3, rows 38 and 39, indicate the projected surcharges as required by Nebraska law. Similar to the delivery of the RSC&R Fund, Figure 9.9c represents the RCC Fund payments as a delivery from AEC to the Nebraska State Agencies, consistent with NDEQ guidelines.

The CIC Administrative Expenses

The Contract provides that the CIC Commission may obtain funds from a surcharge to be levied on the users of the facility in order to pay the expenses of the Commission's administration of the Compact. Such charges have been represented in Figure 9.9. The administrative costs in 1996 were more than $700,000. For calculations here, however, $700,000 has been projected forward at an annual inflation rate of 4 percent. The payment amount is indicated in row 41 of Table 9.3.

Related AEC Benefits

Although not explicit in Figure 9.9, given the structure of the Contract, AEC can make a profit without the project being financially viable. AEC gets paid the adder equal to 2 percent of the interest owed on the construction loan, the adder of 10 percent of operating expenses, and gets paid twice for equipment and tools purchased. They can benefit as long as the major generators are willing to continue to finance losses even if there is no inflow of waste. The provisions of the Contract do not require that the facility have a positive cash flow before AEC can make a gain.

Other related benefits indicated in Figure 9.9 are as follows: the assets of AEC have been increased as the CIC pays for the land, equipment, and facility development and AEC takes ownership of the same. AEC has not had to pay interest on the asset gain. AEC, therefore, is receiving an implicit interest benefit. Since the facility has been given to AEC, it can be depreciated for tax deductions. The land value, according to AEC's SEC report, will be depleted for tax purposes Finally, the salvage value of equipment and other miscellaneous sales such as the hay crop, are also benefits to AEC. In addition, the Contract allows AEC any other income they might be able to get through the rate-making process. The provisions of the Contract do not require AECs gains be reduced if the facility is not financially successful.

Financial Death Cycle

As indicated in Figure 9.9, the Rate Setting Process sub-model (Appendix C) connects the payments to be made with the waste stream upon which the volume charges are to be assessed. The Contract provides that the disposal price is to be determined by dividing the costs by the amount of waste deposited at the facility. The results from those calculations are found in row 45 of Table 9.3. The charges necessary to cover contractual costs are greater than $18,500 per cubic foot for every year. In comparison, Coates *et al.* found that for the compact system to work, charges could not be more than $250 per cubic foot of waste (Coates, Heid and Munger, 1994). For private sector comparisons, Envirocare of Utah charges about $125 per cubic foot for the lower spectrum of low-level radioactive waste. Chem-Nuclear Systems of South Carolina charges about $340 for the full range of low-level radioactive waste. The Central Midwest Compact, made up of Illinois and Kentucky, estimated their expected operational costs to be $600 per cubic foot and consequently decided the project was not financially viable. Thus, the estimated rates for the Boyd County facility indicate a death cycle—a financial death cycle.

The system is in a financial death cycle according to a two scenarios. The first is the economic character of demand, and the second concerns the exponential growth rate on unpaid loans. Knowledge of demand curves informs us that as prices are increased to try to cover exorbitant costs, the quantity of the good or service demanded decreases. If the decrease in quantity demanded is substantial relative to the increase in price, then revenues decline. This is the case for monopolies because the elasticity of demand for monopolies is greater than unity for the relevant range of operation.

The AEC facility in Boyd County is a monopoly low-level radioactive waste facility. Given the cost situation that has been created by the CIC, the unit price on waste deposited at the facility must be extremely high. This causes total revenue to fall, thus causing prices to be increased as required by the Contract, thus, causing revenues to fall further, and so forth. The facility, as indicated by the cost data in Table 9.3, is too expensive for use. To attempt to cover costs by raising disposal prices further contributes to a financial death cycle.

The second way in which the death cycle is manifested is through the expansion of costs as amortized loans are unpaid. Since the unit disposal price is too high to call forth sufficient revenues to cover costs, it will not be possible to meet scheduled principal and interest payments on loans. The unpaid portion will then be refinanced at the high interest that will further increase the payments to be made. However, this merely adds to the payment amount, previously not payable due to insufficient revenue. The debt continues to grow, contributing to the conditions of a financial death cycle.

Concluding Remarks

This SFM analysis has allowed us to observe the working of a corporate/government network, to confirm the validity of some well-known system principles, to discover new principles in a system network, to model operational costs of a particular case with the assistance of the system dynamics program *ithink*, and to thereby discover a financial death cycle that resulted when analysis and democracy have been excluded from policy and decision making.

One of the most important principles confirmed is the consequence of continuous circular cumulative causation whereby the feedback cycles of a system continue to reinforce each other, propelling a system farther and farther along a particular path as explained by Nobel prize economist, Gunmar Myrdal. When a system begins to deteriorate, the forces that are creating the deterioration continue to re-circulate and accumulate greater and greater capacity for destruction. This happens because system provide feedback among the component parts such that any impact on a system which is inconsistent with the welfare of the system becomes magnified through the feedback process.

The CIC project is a refulgent example of the principle of continuous circular cumulative causation. Its basic contractual structure is designed to reinforce destructive characteristics. There are positive incentives to create high costs; to the high costs are added high cost-plus adders, to which high interest rates are then applied. All of these high costs require high waste-volume charges which will decrease use of the facility, which will then lead to accumulated high unpaid costs, which circle back through the system to make waste-volume charges increase further. This has continued to the point that the CIC project is not financially whole.

Closely related to continuous circular cumulative causation, and also confirmed, is the principle that positive feedback leads to growth and decay, while negative feedback is necessary for stability and sustainability. In the case studied here, the positive cost-plus incentives and interest adders encourage that energies and resources continue to be devoted to increasing costs, to the point the system is not financially viability. Negative incentives to encourage the reduction of cost functions, and penalties if performance milestones are not reached, are necessary to build a financial process that is sustainable, but are here absent.

The analysis of this corporate/government network confirms and magnifies the finding Henry Maine made late in the last century when he stated that the base of society had evolved from status to contract. The contractual element has grown in importance, and the battles over contractual form have a great influence on the working of the modern business and industrial process.

This study presents a new way to analyze the legal contracts that guide a system, a way that allows for connections to be made between contract provisions and the consequential flows and deliveries. Such an analysis becomes increasingly important as interest grows in monitoring costs of government contracts. Refined studies that uncover the direct and indirect consequences of particular contractual provisions can be made with the SFM analysis as was demonstrated with the analysis of the CIC pre-operational phase. Analyzing contracts is like eating bear meat—the more you chew the bigger it gets. Thus, an improved method for the analysis of contracts is a welcome addition to the social science tool kit.

We have also seen that social beliefs are not vague abstractions, but are criteria embedded in rules, regulations, requirements, as expressed and enforced in contractual obligations. Moreover, beliefs are divided and developed among a whole array of institutions and organizations, and refined by the institutional process throughout the network.

Policy scientists cannot determine efficiency criteria until social beliefs are known. This leads to the instrumentalist question: which belief components are appropriate to use in determining efficiency? In turn, this leads to the issue of social conflict and power. John R. Commons emphasized that the real social beliefs of a system are those that are enforced. This, he emphasized, determines reasonable value. His conclusion, is inadequate for a number of reasons. First, he was really stating, tautologically, that what exists is best. Second, in the case analyzed above, the enforced belief components led, not to reasonable consequences, but rather to a financial death cycle. Third, his prescription can be interpreted to mean that who ever has the power to establish and enforce the rules, regulations and requirements should be considered as enforcing efficiency and reasonable value. Such a prescription cannot be endorsed by instrumentalists. Those who have the power may enforce a system that is quite inconsistent with general social beliefs. Therefore, policy scientists can not avoid the issue of power and social conflict when evaluating for efficiency.

The system analyzed above functions the way it does because particular groups had the power to establish and enforce particular social rules and requirements that led to socially undesirable consequences. For example, when the two-to-three hundred percent cost-plus adders were established and enforced in the pre-operation phase Contract formulae, the operational phase was predestined for failure. The positive feedback was established within a swirl of social conflict manifested through political and judicial battles. The SFM analysis of networks allows for the tracing of connections between system components and system consequences. This allows for instrumental decisions about system efficiency. It also allows for the observation of socioeconomic power at work.

Policy studies have generated numerous hypotheses about social conflict, especially with respect to alliances among corporate interests and government. But such hypothesis are seldom modeled or explained with real-world examples. The SFM and *ithink* analysis allows for explicit modeling of a real world example and generates information about how those with power alliances have established a real-world network.

In addition, the computer model developed for this case can be utilized for future analysis and deliberations. It allows for the determination of impacts throughout the system to be measured when particular changes are contemplated. Thus, the impacts of alternative provisions in the Contract and the Agreement can be traced throughout the model. New sectors and new concerns can be added. For example, new engineering designs can also be used to help discover the systems that are viable.

References

Antonucci, G. 1997. *Pre-requisites for a Stable Disposal Future at Barnwell.* Presented to the Low-Level Waste Forum. Chem-Nuclear System.

Arnold, T. 1937. *The Folklore of Capitalism.* New Haven: Yale University Press.

Coates, D., V. Heid and M. Munger 1994. "Not Equitable, Not Efficient: US Policy on Low-Level Radioactive Waste Disposal", *Journal of Policy Analysis and Management*, 13, No. 3, 526—538.

Fuchs, R.L. 1996. *State-by-State Assessment of Low Level Radioactive Waste Received at Communal Disposal Sites.* DOE/LLW-237. Washington, DC: US Department of Energy.

Groenewegen, J. and P. Beije 1989. "The French Communication Industry Defined and Analyzed Through the Social Fabric Matrix, the *Filière* Approach, and Network Analysis", *Journal of Economic Issues*, 23, December, 1059 -1974.

Gill, R. 1996. "An Integrated Social Fabric Matrix/Systems Dynamics Approach to Policy Analysis", *System Dynamics Review*, 12 (Fall), 167—249.

Hayden, F.G. 1982. "Social Fabric Matrix: From Perspectives to Analytical Tool", *Journal of Economic Issues*, 16 September, 637—661.

————— 1988. "Values Beliefs, and Attitudes in a Sociotechnical Setting", *Journal of Economic Issues*, 22, June, 415—426.

————— 1989. *Survey of Methodologies for Valuing Externalities and Public Goods*. Washington DC: US Environmental Protection Agency.

————— 1996. "Report on the Financial Condition of American Ecology Corporation." Lincoln, NE: Office of the Nebraska Commissioner, Central Interstate Low-Level Radioactive Waste Compact.

————— 1998. "Normative Analysis of Instituted Processes". In *Institutional Theory and Applications*: *Essays in Honour of Paul Dale Bush*, S. Fayazmanesh and M.R. Tool eds. Cheltenham: Edward Elgar Publishing Ltd.

Hayden, F.G. and S.R. Bolduc 1997. "Political and Economic Analysis of Low-Level Radioactive Waste", *Journal of Economic Issues*, 31, June 605—613.

Hoffman, D.J and F.G. Hayden 1996. "Waste Stream Analysis of the Proposal Low-Level Radioactive Waste Site in Boyd County, Nebraska." Lincoln, NE: Office of the Nebraska Commissioner, Central Interstate Low-Level Radioactive Waste Compact.

Jackson, S.A. 1997. *LLWnotes*. Washington DC: Afton Associates Inc. 11, June.

Kuzelka, R. 1996. "American Ecology Financial Information", *Memo to F. Gregory Hayden,* Lincoln Nebraska: Central Interstate Low-Level Radioactive Waste Commission, September.

————— 1996. "US Ecology Equity Contribution Information", *Memo to F. Gregory Hayden,* Lincoln Nebraska: Central Interstate Low-Level Radioactive Waste Commission, November.

Maine, H.S. 1861 (1986). *Ancient Law: I   onnection with the Early History of Society and its Relation to Modern Ideas*. New York: Dorset Press.

McCartney, L. 1988. *Friends in High Places: The Most Secret Corporation and How It Engineered the World*. New York: Simon Schuster.

Meister, B. 1990. "Analysis of the Federal Farm Policy Using the Social Fabric Matrix", *Journal of Economic Issues*, 24, March, 189—224.

Melman, S. 1983. *Profits Without Production*. New York: Knopf.

Nebraska Department of Environmental Quality. *Title 194-Rules and Regulations for the Disposal of Low-Level Radioactive Waste*.

Nebraska Department of Health. *Title 180, Nebraska Administrative Code*, chapter 1-Regulations for the Control of Radioation.

Radzizki, M.J. 1980. "Institutional Dynamics, Deterministic Chaos, and Self-Organization Systems", *Journal of Economic Issues*, 24, March, 57—102.

Radzizki, M.J. and J.D. Sterman 1994. "Evolutionary Economics and System Dynamics". In *Evolutionary Concepts in Contemporary Economics* R. England ed.,Ann Arbor: University of Michigan Press, 61—89.

Safety Analysis Report (Rev. 8). License Application submitted by US Ecology to the Nebraska Department of Environmental Quality, Lincoln NE.

Technical Service Agreement Between US, Inc. and Bechtel National, Inc. For Engineering, Procurement, and Construction Management Services for the Central Interstate Low-Level Radioactive Waste Disposal Facility. Lincoln, Nebraska: Office of US Ecology, Inc.

**Appendix A   Amortization of Major Generators Financing
                     Contributions**

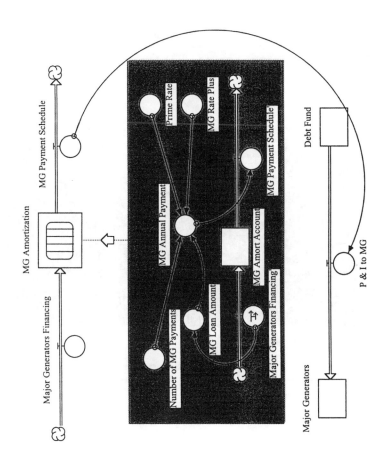

Appendix B Depreciation Payment on Equipment

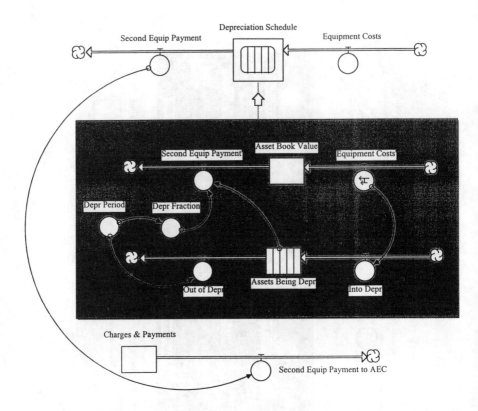

Appendix C Rate Setting Process

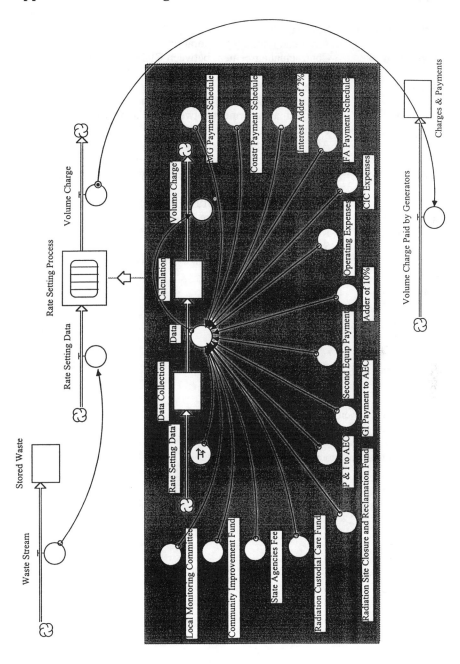

Appendix D Abbreviations and Symbols

A through N	See Table 9.1
AEC	American Ecology Corporation
Agreement	Contractual agreement between CIC and the major generators
Bechtel	Bechtel National, Inc.
CIC	Central Interstate Low-Level Radioactive Waste Compact
Contract	Contractual agreement between CIC and AEC
FA	Financial assurance
GI	AEC general interest
ithink©	Name of system dynamics computer program
LMC	Local Monitoring Committee of Boyd County, Nebraska
MG	Major generators
NDEQ	Nebraska Department of Environmental Quality
RCC Fund	Radiation Custodial Care Fund
RCC&R Fund	Radiation Site Closure and Reclamation Fund
SAR	Safety Analysis Report
SEC	US Securities and Exchange Commission
SFM	Social Fabric Matrix
P and I	Principal and Interest

– Institution or organization

– Flow delivery

– Regulator on a flow delivery

– Rules, regulations, requirements, or criteria

– Arc indicates delivery of rules, regulations, requirements, or criteria

– Programming submodel, or a transformation process station

– Source or destination of flow delivery not modeled in the system

10 SMALL AND MEDIUM-SIZED ENTERPRISES (SMEs); EMPLOYMENT CREATION AND INDUSTRIAL POLICY

Paul Schreyer

Introduction

High and rising unemployment rates in the early 1990s have moved the employment question centre-stage in the policy debate. The effects of the business cycle as well as underlying structural questions have been the subject of a large body of research and policy recommendations. Among the structural aspects, the relation between firm size and employment creation has attracted policy makers' attention, triggered by empirical work by David Birch (1979), who pointed out that, in the United States, the small business sector had been a major source of net job creation. Birch's work and the rising interest by policy-makers in employment issues led to further studies of the subject, both in the United States and in other countries. Some studies confirmed Birch's results, others did not, leading to a debate among researchers that focused mainly on methodological and statistical issues which turned out to be very important. At the same time, policy makers paid increasing attention to SMEs' actual or perceived job creation capacity and a substantial number of support programmes and policies for SMEs emerged. However, policy implications from the empirical work on MEs and job creation are not straightforward, partly because they are not placed and interpreted within an explicit theoretical framework.

This chapter aims at advancing the discussion in this respect. It does so by taking another look at the empirical evidence on gross and net job creation rates, and the characteristics of these processes (sections 2 and 3). It then places these stylised facts within a theoretical framework to examine whether there is consistency (section 4). Once the coherence between theory and empirical observation is established, it turns to a number of policy conclusions (sections5 and 6).

2. SMEs in the Economy—Static Picture

The term "SME"—small and medium-sized enterprises—covers a variety of definitions and measures. In OECD Member countries, employment is the most widely used criterion for determining firm size. SMEs are usually defined as firms with fewer than 500 employees, although a number of countries—including those in the European Union—use a lower cut-off point of 250.

It is apparent that SMEs play an important role in all OECD economies: they make up over 95 per cent of enterprises and account for 60 to 70 per cent of jobs in most OECD countries. The share tends to be somewhat lower in manufacturing, although it varies between 40 to 80 per cent of employment in manufacturing, see Table 10.1 (p. 288 and 289). The overall share of small firms in employment and output may be even higher given that establishments or firms in the service sector are normally of smaller average size than in manufacturing. Table 10.1 also illustrates the variability across sectors: for example, wholesale and retail trade and hotels and restaurants are dominated by SMEs. In construction SMEs account for 80 to 90 per cent of all employment. The fact that these industries loom large in overall employment underscores the importance of SMEs as sources of employment.

Furthermore, the share of large firms in employment and output has tended to show a certain decline. The average establishment size manufacturing has fallen since the early 1980s in Canada, the United Kingdom and the United States, has remained constant in Germany, and has risen in Japan.

While this is valid information, it tells us little about one aspect of small firms and employment that policy-makers care about: job creation. Note that the share of SMEs in employment in Table 10.1 reflects a static concept but that the share of SMEs in job creation is a dynamic notion, requiring different types of statistical information. It is worth pointing out that the comparison of two static pictures between different points in time does not help, either: to show that the share that SMEs occupy in employment has risen over time is not sufficient to conclude that size class has shown superior performance in job creation. For example, it does not take much to show that the share of SMEs can increase as a consequence of large firms' downsizing—a situation that reflects large firms' adjustments rather than small firms' job creation capacity.

This example can be generalised to state that any static consideration in this context, though interesting in its own right, hides important aspects of job dynamics, in conjunction with establishments or firms entering or exiting an industry, expanding or contracting. These flows need consideration to obtain empirical observations that are pertinent to the policy question: who creates most new jobs and what can be done to support this process?

3. Job Creation and Destruction—A Dynamic View

Evidence on net job creation by firm size

In a dynamic context, the importance of smaller establishments in job creation is typically assessed on the basis of net employment changes. Net employment changes are the difference between gross job creation (the sum of employment growth due to the creation of new firms[1] and the expansion of existing ones) and gross job destruction (the sum of

Table 10.1 Distribution of employment by firm size and sector

	Year	Employment size class					
		1-9	10-19	20-99	100-499	500+	Total
		Percentages					
United States Manufacturing	1993	3.5	3.9	14.6	16.5	61.5	100.0
	1988	3.1	3.7	14.5	16.1	62.6	100.0
	1993	28.6	17.0	30.7	12.5	11.1	100.0
	1988	25.5	16.5	31.7	14.8	11.5	100.0
	1993	13.1	9.9	22.2	11.8	43.0	100.0
	1988	13.6	10.4	23.2	11.9	40.8	100.0
	1993	12.5	5.5	13.8	12.2	56.1	100.0
	1988	12.3	5.7	14.3	12.4	55.3	100.0
	1993	10.7	7.7	18.8	13.1	49.6	100.0
	1988	10.5	7.8	19.3	13.3	49.0	100.0
Canada Manufacturing	1992..		11.4	20.3	22.0	46.3	100.0
	1989..		9.9	21.3	22.8	46.0	100.0
	1992..		56.0	26.7	12.3	5.0	100.0
	1989..		51.0	29.4	14.5	5.1	100.0
	1992..		33.6	25.7	13.2	27.5	100.0
	1989..		28.9	24.5	12.9	33.7	100.0
	1992..		17.8	12.1	9.7	60.4	100.0
	1989..		17.2	14.4	10.8	57.6	100.0
	1992..		25.5	20.8	15.1	38.6	100.0
	1989...		23.5	22.0	16.3	38.2	100.0
Japan Manufacturing	1993	12.5	10.4	30.8	24.6	21.7	100.0
	1986	13.7	11.0	30.6	23.5	21.3	100.0
France Manufacturing	1992	8.1	5.0	22.4	23.6	40.9	100.0
	1990	10.1	5.1	22.0	23.1	39.7	100.0
Construction	1992	29.0	11.5	27.5	14.0	18.0	100.0
	1990	33.9	10.8	26.7	12.8	15.8	100.0
Wholesale and retail trade, hotels and restaurants	1992	32.9	10.3	25.8	12.4	18.5	100.0
	1990	38.6	9.8	23.7	11.2	16.8	100.0
Finance, insurance and real estate	1992	15.9	7.2	19.6	17.9	39.4	100.0
	1990	19.7	7.4	18.9	17.4	36.6	100.0
Total non-farm business sector	1992	18.2	7.1	21.7	17.1	35.9	100.0
	1990	22.0	7.0	21.0	16.2	33.7	100.0

Table 10.1 Distribution of employment by firm size and sector (continued)

	Year	Employment size class					
		1-9	10-19	20-99	100-499	500+	Total
		Percentages					
Germany							
Manufacturing	1992	7.8	6.2	16.3	21.6	48.2	100.0
	1988	6.1	6.1	16.1	21.5	50.1	100.0
Construction	1992	27.1	21.6	28.0	13.7	9.6	100.0
	1988	22.8	20.4	31.9	15.3	0.6	100.0
Wholesale and retail trade,	1992	37.8	12.6	19.2	11.9	18.5	100.0
hotels and restaurants	1988	29.0	14.6	22.2	13.5	20.7	100.0
Finance, insurance and	1992	28.3	10.8	16.0	16.7	28.2	100.0
real estate	1988	21.3	10.3	16.9	17.9	33.6	100.0
Total non-farm business	1992	21.1	10.2	18.2	17.0	33.5	100.0
sector	1988	15.3	10.2	19.2	18.0	37.2	100.0
Italy							
Manufacturing	1991	24.2	14.8	24.4	16.9	19.7	100.0
Construction	1991	52.3	16.0	19.5	7.9	4.3	100.0
Wholesale and retail trade,	1991	74.6	9.7	8.8	3.1	3.8	100.0
hotels and restaurants							
Finance, insurance and	1991	49.5	7.0	9.4	9.0	25.2	100.0
real estate							
Total non-farm business	1991	44.2	11.4	15.9	10.1	18.4	100.0
sector							
United Kingdom							
Manufacturing	1991	13.3	4.7	14.4	17.0	50.7	100.0
	1988	10.9	4.0	17.0	17.8	50.3	100.0
Construction	1991	58.3	6.1	12.3	10.2	13.1	100.0
	1988	58.2	7.4	12.9	9.6	11.9	100.0
Wholesale and retail trade,	1991	31.3	8.8	19.6	26.9	13.5	100.0
hotels and restaurants	1988	33.8	9.0	19.4	24.2	13.6	100.0
Finance, insurance and	1991	25.6	5.0	13.5	12.3	43.5	100.0
real estate	1988	17.8	4.2	11.7	20.3	46.1	100.0
Total non-farm business	1991	25.2	6.0	15.0	17.8	36.0	100.0
sector	1988	24.0	5.9	15.7	19.3	35.2	100.0

Notes: 1 Measured in average labour units. Smallest size class: 0-19
2 Underlying statistical unit: establishment. Smallest size class is 4-9 employees.
3 Classes 2+3+4 of NACE 70.
4 Class 5 (building and civil engineering) of NACE 70.
5 Class 6 (distributive trades, hotels, catering and repairs) of NACE 70.
6 Class 8 (banking and finance, insurance, business services, renting) of NACE 70.
7 Classes 2-8 of NACE 70.
8 Includes size class zero.

Sources: OECD, SME database; Eurostat (1996) Enterprises in Europe.

employment losses due to the exit of firms from industries and the contraction of existing units). Disaggregated by size class, it has been found that from the mid-1980s to the early 1990s, in all countries, small establishments (fewer than 100 employees) displayed more rapid net employment growth than larger ones (OECD (1994)). However, there are several ways in which this should be put into perspective:

First, it is not surprising that small enterprises/establishments play an important role in the job creation process since they account for between 40 and 80 per cent of total manufacturing employment. To see whether their role is disproportionately high, net job creation has to be expressed in relation to the size of employment in small and large establishments. As shown in Table 10.2 (p. 292-295), net job creation rates are in fact often higher for smaller size classes. However, for a number of countries it was found that the highest net job creation rates were among very small firms whereas small to medium-sized firms (between 20 and 50 employees) did not perform better than large firms.

Second, nearly all young firms are small and constitute a dynamic element of the small firm sector because they are in an early phase of their life cycles and young firms are more likely to grow than older ones. At the same time one notes that by no means all small firms are young.

Third, methodology matters. An important technical issue in studies on net job creation rates is how firms are allocated to size classes: for example, a firm can be considered "small" if it corresponds to the criterion "small" in some *base year*. Any subsequent job creation is then attributed to the size class "small", irrespective of whether the firm has moved to a different size class by the end of the observation period. Alternatively, a firm can be considered "small" if it corresponds to the criterion "small" *on average*, over the entire period. It has been shown that net job creation rates of small and large firms are highly sensitive to such changes in the size class allocation of firms, a methodological point that has raised a substantive amount of discussion. Opinions are still divided on this matter, although most authors acknowledge the importance of this methodological matter.

Two views prevail:

In one view[2], employment often fluctuates from year to year, owing to variation in demand and other factors. In this case, average rather than current plant size provides the appropriate indication of the production unit's intended scale of operations and minimises the measurement error time will be so because they are in a transitory downturn, so that the random component is negative. However, these "small" firms will return to their "typical" size in the future. The result is that, overall, small firms will appear to grow disproportionately and the performance of large firms will appear to be rather poor. Note that this view, implicitly or explicitly, subscribes to the existence of an equilibrium path that firms follow, at least in the long run. It also implies that at least part of the observed turbulence in gross job flows is "noise", caused by shocks (exogenous, such as business cycles or endogenous such as productivity shocks or adjustment costs) that prevent firms to embark immediately on their equilibrium path of expansion or contraction. This observation is of consequence to the discussion of turbulence later on which in turn has strong policy implications.

Another view sees a more turbulent system in which change is the normal state of affairs and owners or entrepreneurs adjust employment to maximise profits: they increase employment as demand increases and workers are available and decrease employment as demand drops to reduce costs. To capture changes precisely, frequent observations are needed. The most appropriate measure of size may be the one taken at the beginning of each year (base-year size) over the observation period. This is the firm's size before employment is adjusted in response to changing cost factors or market opportunities.[3] This view corresponds to a more evolutionary vision of the market process or, in its purest form, to an Austrian vision of markets (a recent overview can be found in Kirzner (1997)): in an environment of permanent change of tastes, technologies and institutions, firms discover opportunities as they are active in the market place and aim at exploiting them. Uncertainty (as opposed to risk) and idiosyncrasy prevail and characterise the market process. The notion of competition is linked to this process and, by definition, there can be no equilibrium state or path towards which firms or industries would converge. Note that as a consequence, the rationale for choosing average size as the criterion for allocating units to size classes, loses its relevance.[4]

Table 10.2 Job creation rates and distribution of gross job flows

	Gross job creation[1]		Gross job losses[2]		Net job creation
	Percent of initial employment[3]	Distribution by size class	Percent of initial employment	Distribution by size class	Percent of initial employment
Canada 1978-1992					
Base year size allocation[4]					
0-19 employees	26.7	48.0	-18.6	37.0	8.1
20-49	14.9	13.0	-14.6	14.0	0.3
50-99	13.0	8.0	-13.8	9.0	- 0.7
100-499	11.1	13.0	-11.9	16.0	- 0.8
500+	5.9	17.0	- 7.1	23.0	- 1.2
Total	13.4	100.0	-12.1	100.0	1.3
Average size allocation[5]					
0-19	23.4	42.0	-20.2	40.0	3.3
20-49	15.9	14.0	-14.2	14.0	1.7
50-99	14.4	9.0	-13.0	9.0	1.4
100-499	12.2	15.0	-11.2	15.0	1.0
500+	6.8	20.0	- 6.6	22.0	0.1
Denmark 1985-86	13.4	100.0	-12.1	100.0	1.3
Base year size allocation[4]					
1-9	30.3	40.7	18.6	33.2	11.7
10-49	15.5	30.8	11.5	30.3	4.0
50-99	13.2	9.2	11.9	11.0	1.3
100-499	12.6	14.1	10.4	15.5	2.2
500+	7.6	5.2	11.0	10.0	- 3.4
Total	17.1	100.0	12.9	100.0	4.2
1989-1990					
Base year size allocation[4]					
1-9	25.1	40.7	21.4	33.3	3.7
10-49	12.5	31.9	14.5	35.3	- 1.9
50-99	10.3	8.9	13.1	10.8	- 2.7
100-499	9.4	13.1	11.1	14.8	- 1.7
500+	7.0	5.4	7.8	5.8	- 0.8
Total	13.9	100.0	14.5	100.0	- 0.6
Finland 1986-1991					
Base year size allocation[4]					
1-19 employees	..	52.7	..	38.4	..
20-99	..	24.7	..	26.9	..
100-499	..	17.3	..	23.9	..
500+	..	5.3	..	10.8	..
Total	..	100.0	..	100.0	..

Table 10.2 Job creation rates and distribution of gross job flows (continued)

	Gross job creation[1]		Gross job losses[2]		Net job creation
	Percent of initial employment[3]	Distribution by size class	Percent of initial employment	Distribution by size class	Percent of initial employment
Italy 1984-1992					
Base year size allocation[4]					
1-19 employees	..	65.4	..	56.2	..
20-99	..	17.5	..	20.0	..
100-499	..	9.0	..	11.0	..
500+	..	7.8	..	12.8	..
Total	..	100.0	..	100.0	..
Japan 1987-1992					
Base year size allocation[4]					
30-99 employees	..	45.5	..	50.9	1.2
100-199	..	18.3	..	17.5	1.4
200-499	..	17.4	..	15.0	0.2
500-899	..	7.7	..	5.8	1.6
900-1499	..	4.7	..	3.2	1.6
1500+	..	6.5	..	7.6	0.3
Total	..	100.0	..	100.0	1.2
Germany 1978-93					
Base year size allocation[4]					
1-19 employees	14.7	12.3	14.0	10.0	0.7
20-49	9.0	18.6	8.0	14.2	1.0
50-99	6.6	13.4	6.5	11.7	0.1
100-249	5.5	18.7	5.3	15.6	0.2
250-499	4.5	13.2	4.8	12.5	- 0.3
500-999	3.3	8.6	4.6	10.7	- 2.3
1000-2499	2.7	7.0	4.9	10.9	- 3.6
2500-4999	1.2		4.8		- 0.8
5000+	1.7	8.2	2.5	14.3	..
Total	..	100.0	..	100.0	
Average size allocation[5]					
1-19 employees	12.1	10.1	15.6	11.2	- 3.5
20-49	9.3	19.5	8.2	14.2	0.7
50-99	7.1	14.4	6.7	11.8	- 0.1
100-249	5.4	18.6	5.4	16.0	0.0
250-499	4.4	13.0	4.8	12.5	- 0.5
500-999	3.4	8.9	4.5	10.4	- 1.1
1000-2499	3.5	9.2	4.7	10.4	- 1.2
2500-4999	1.3		4.3		- 3.0
5000+	1.7	6.2	2.5	13.5	- 0.9
Total	..	100.0	..	100.0	..

Table 10.2 Job creation rates and distribution of gross job flows (continued)

	Gross job creation[1]		Gross job losses[2]		Net job creation
	Percent of initial employment[3]	Distribution by size class	Percent of initial employment	Distribution by size class	Percent of initial employment
New Zeeland 1987-1992					
Base year size allocation[4]					
1-19 employees	..	55.6	..	41.8	..
20-99	..	26.2	..	30.4	..
100-499	..	13.8	..	18.5	..
500+	..	4.4	..	9.3	..
Total	..	100.0	..	100.0	..
Netherlands 1979-1991					
Average size allocation[5]					
10-99 employees	12.9	..	11.2	..	0.6
100+	4.6	..	6.1	..	- 1.4
Sweden 1985-1989					
Base year size allocation[4]					
Simples	5.2	45.4	4.2	42.4	1.1
Tops	2.5	6.6	2.5	7.8	0.0
Branches	3.0	48.0	2.7	49.8	0.3
Total	3.7	100.0	3.2	100.0	0.6
United Kingdom 1985-1991					
Base year size allocation[4]					
1-19 employees	15.0	50.4	10.7	45.4	4.7
20-49	8.2	9.5	7.7	11.3	0.6
50-99	8.1	8.0	5.7	7.2	2.6
100-499	7.4	12.7	5.7	12.8	1.7
500+	4.0	19.4	3.7	23.3	0.3
Total	8.2	100.0	6.4	100.0	1.9

Table 10.2 Job creation rates and distribution of gross job flows (continued)

	Gross job creation[1]		Gross job losses[2]		Net job Creation
	Percent of initial employment[3]	Distribution by size class	Percent of initial employment	Distribution by size class	Percent of Initial employment
United States 1973-1988 Average size allocation[5]					
0-19 employees	18.7	10.7	23.3	11.8	- 4.5
20-49	13.2	12.5	15.3	13.0	- 2.1
50-99	12.2	14.0	13.5	13.8	- 1.3
100-249	9.6	19.5	10.7	19.5	- 1.1
250-499	7.7	13.6	8.7	13.6	- 1.0
500-999	7.0	10.4	7.6	10.1	- 0.6
1000-2499	6.3	8.5	7.3	8.8	- 1.0
2500-4999	6.1	4.7	7.5	5.1	- 1.3
5000+	5.4	5.0	5.6	4.6	- 0.2
Total	..	100.0	..	100.0	..
United States 1987-1992 Base year size allocation[4]					
30-99 employees	..	34.4	..	27.7	0.5
100-199	..	19.8	..	17.8	- 0.3
200-499	..	21.1	..	21.0	- 0.8
500-899	..	9.3	..	9.8	- 0.9
900-1499	..	5.0	..	6.2	- 1.6
1500+	..	10.3	..	17.5	- 2.8
Total	..	100.0	..	100.0	- 1.0

1. Gross job creation = employment gains from business openings and expansions.
2. Gross job losses   = employment losses from business closures and contractions.
3. For most countries gross and net job flows are measured on an annual basis. For any two years, gross job flow rates are measured as a percentage of the employment in the first year. The percentage reported in the table corresponds to the mean of these annual gross or net job flow rate. No annual measurements were available from the studies concerning Japan, Sweden, the United Kingdom and the United States (1987-1992). In these cases, annualised gross or net job rates are reported in the Table.
4. Base-year size allocation: the employment gains or losses of a firm or establishment between years are allocated the size class to which the firm or establishment belonged in the initial year.
5. Average size allocation: the allocation of a firm or an establishment to a particular size class is determined by the average size of the firm between two or more periods. Accordingly, employment gains or losses are allocated. Average size allocation reduces the regression-to-the mean bias.

Source: Schreyer (1996).

Gross job creation and destruction

Despite its obvious policy interest, the customary estimation of net employment growth conceals the separate processes of job creation and destruction. Plants of all sizes incur both job gains and job losses Table 10.2. Some idea of these dynamics is given in OECD (1994). The data paint a picture of the concentration of gross job gains and losses in very small and small establishments. Establishments employing fewer than 20 workers seem to account for between 45 and 65 percent of new job gains and 36 and 56 per cent of annual job losses.

Moreover, several regularities have been observed in studies of job dynamics, across countries, sectors and for different periods:

- Both job creation and job destruction tend to be concentrated among a comparatively small number of firms: a small share of all firms with exceptional growth patterns accounts for large part of employment creation (see e.g., Haltiwanger, 1996; OECD, 1996a; Storey, 1988). Similarly, a comparatively small share of all firms contracts very rapidly and job destruction is concentrated there.
- Information on job creation and destruction reveals a considerable amount of churning in all labour markets. Annual job turnover rates—the sum of newly created jobs and jobs that have disappeared—are of the order of 20 per cent per year and by far exceed net job creation rates (OECD, 1996; Boeri , 1994).
- Job turnover rates are of similar order of magnitude in countries as diverse as France, Sweden and the United States. There is no apparent evidence of a correlation between job turnover rates and net job creation rates (Figure 10.1).
- The remarkable churning is also documented by measures of firm demography: as a rule of thumb, and with variations between countries and industries, fifty percent of all start-ups do not survive their fifth birthday and only some 25 percent remain after more than eight years (OECD, 1996a).

These empirical regularities make it worth investigating what the possible links are between the presence of SMEs, firm dynamics,

Figure 10.1 Net job creation rates and turbulence

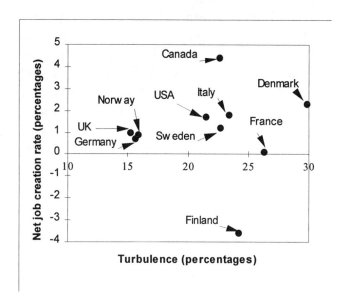

Source: Boeri (1994).

growth and employment. Specifically, the pervasiveness of "turbulence" across countries, industries and over time is an issue of interest. One obvious interpretation is that turbulence, mainly apparent among small units, is an indication of the degree of entrepreneurship: the search for new processes, market niches, differentiated products, customer orientation, as well as new relationships with large firms. High firm (and therefore employment) turnover may thus be viewed as a process of trial and error, with some enterprises failing almost from the start, some being limited by the life span of an innovation, and others enjoying sustained success. Most of the stylised facts above are consistent with this line of reasoning, with one important exception: one measure of turbulence, job turnover,[5] is of similar size across countries and appears to be unrelated to countries' performance, whether measured as growth rates of output, employment growth or the

development of unemployment (see Figure 10.1). There are three possible interpretations of this evidence:
(i) there is a causal link between turbulence and performance but the intensity of the link varies between countries: the same search intensity in country A and country B gives rise to a greater success rate in country A, because opportunities are different, or because institutions and other framework conditions are more favourable in A; (ii) there is no link. Turbulence is "noise" in a statistical sense, caused by external shocks and essentially a phenomenon that prevents enterprise and employment dynamics to approach a state of equilibrium where entry, exit, expansion and contraction are either absent or occurring in a smooth, foreseeable manner;   (iii) turbulence is mismeasured: job turnover or firm turnover are inadequate indicators for the hurly-burly of the market place.

From a policy perspective, the answer to this question has considerable implications. If (i) applies, policies would have to be directed towards improving opportunities, institutions and framework conditions for an ongoing search process with a view to rendering it more successful;   if (ii) applies, policies would be directed towards reducing turbulence. As the latter would have few positive effects but entail well-identified costs (bankruptcies, sunk costs at start-ups etc.), it would be consequent to support market participants at the margin, and small firms in particular, given that the latter are most exposed and more vulnerable to exogenous shocks. If (iii) applies, policy-makers should decide to spend more on measurement.

Unfortunately, a well-founded empirical answer to this question requires significant work based on resource-intensive use of longitudinal micro-level data in several countries—an enterprise for medium or long-term research. In the short run, and for the purpose of this chapter, a different methodology has to be used. The approach is essentially one of envoking plausibility, established through the use of a simulation model that allows to carry out several checks.

First *the quality check*: instead of using indicators of a search process and indicators of performance and combining them empirically, we *postulate* a search process. An simple, explicit search model is constructed, rooted in straightforward economic theory and using plausible parameter values. The "quality" of the model will be checked by its capacity to reproduce a series of stylised facts (mainly the ones outlined above) that have solid empirical footing. If the model passes this quality check, it certainly shows that a search process is not inconsistent with empirical observations.

Second, the *uncertainty check*: we artifically restrain the functioning of the search process in the model (everything remains unchanged, only uncertainty is reduced). If this has visible implications for the performance variables (in particular in the sense that the stylised empirical effects cannot be reproduced now) this will be taken as an argument that a search process under uncertainty constitutes a necessary element in the dynamics of job creation.

Third, the *parameter check*: small parameter variations are introduced into the model to examine whether they can visibly affect net job creation rates without changing the order of magnitude of measures of turbulence. The objective is to show that it is possible, within a simple search model, to generate observations that resemble cross-country comparisons. If a certain parameter constellation is interpreted as country-specific and if different parameter constellations reproduce the same qualitative picture as their empirical counterparts (turbulence rates are of similar magnitude across countries but quite different performance in growth or job creation), we will draw the conclusion that: such an outcome is not in contradiction with an underlying search model but that, despite this coherence, there is not necessarily a stable relation between turbulence and gross job creation that would justify cross-country regressions, which in one way or another assume common and stable inter-country parameters.

4. Turbulence as a Search Process: A Simulation Model

Main features[6]

Pool of potential entrants. There is a (fixed) pool of potential entrants, each endowed with a certain level of entrepreneurial, managerial or innovative capacity. This is akin to the basic assumption of the theory of firm selection proposed by Jovanovic (1982).

Search process. At the heart of our argument is the explicit modelling of a search process where entrepreneurs (potential entrants) are at the search for an "idea", in the form of a new product or process. There is uncertainty[7] involved, modelled as a realisation from a stochastic process. Importantly, it is assumed that the position of the distribution from which a potential entrant draws his "idea", is positively related to the entrepreneur's qualification: the higher qualified a potential entrant, the greater his chances to pick a good idea. The quality of the idea is captured through a parameter that shifts the entrepreneur's demand function. The better the idea, the higher the price that can be charged and the more likely is entry.

Bounded rationality. A second element of the search process is the assumption that firms do not take decisions under full information. Rather, all they have at their disposal, is knowledge about the average market price in the preceding period, their own cost function and an expectation about the position of the demand function for their specific product. However, as demand depends, among other things, on the entrepreneur's price relative to the overall market price (whose future realisation is unknown), entry and operations are risky because ex-post, sales, prices and profits may turn out to be less than expected. If profits are negative, the competitor leaves the market and becomes again a potential entrant in future periods.

Technology path. Once entry has taken place, the entrepreneur is "stuck" with the idea that he drew just before entry. However, his environment evolves in several ways. First, his demand function moves over time—outwards, if he is highly qualified, not at all if he is unqualified. The rationale behind this formulation is to acknowledge managerial capacity to make more of a good idea and to expand demand. Unqualified entrepreneurs may have drawn a brilliant idea, perhaps even making profits but their demand function does not shift outwards and their demand does not expand.

The second change in the environment comes via process innovation, modelled as a gradual improvement (i.e., lowering) of the marginal cost parameter. Here, several forces are at play: for once, a general advance in production technology, and available to everybody. However, we assume that highly qualified entrepreneurs can benefit to a greater degree from this potential for cost improvement than can less qualified incumbents. Then, there is an element of learning-by-doing which enables fast-growing firms to move faster towards the technological frontier than slowly growing firms with comparatively less cumulative output. All firms are permanently challenged by the possibility of a new entrant with a successful idea, possibly combined with strong managerial capacities.

The model makes one important shortcut: expansion and contraction are all measured as volume output growth and gross job flows are assumed to be proportional to gross output flows and labour productivity does not change. However, as improvements in marginal total costs are part of the model, this assumption only constrains labour productivity—it implicitly permits changes in total factor productivity.

No attempt was made to provide a closed analytical solution to the model. Simulation techniques were used to observe industry behaviour and to see whether reasonable parameter values were capable of reproducing the stylised facts outlined above. As the simulations involved the use of stochastic variables, each single run produced different outcomes. 100 simulations were carried out per parameter, and results are presented as medians over all runs. Each simulation comprised a period of 30 time units, best interpreted as years.

Results

Quality check. The quality check has been defined as the model's capacity to generate, under reasonable parameter values, the stylised facts known from the literature. Except under implausible parameter constellations, the search model always generates relatively large measures of turbulence. Gross job creation and gross job destruction occur simultaneously and account for rates of turbulence that significantly exceed the rates of net job creation. The model also replicates the empirically observed concentration of job creation and job destruction in a small number of firms (Table 10.3). For example, in the baseline case, just over 6 percent of all expanding firms accounted for half of total job creation. A similar relation is found for job destruction. As the simulation model incorporates a random variable,

Table 10.3 Overview of studies on job creation: qualitative results

Country/Author	Period	Sector	Allocation to size class	*Gross* job creation rates	*Net* job creation rates
Canada Picot, Baldwin, Dupuy (1994)	1978-92	business sector	base-year	fall with firm size	fall with firm size
	1978-92	business sector	average	fall with firm size	fall with firm size
	1978-92	manufacturing	base-year	fall with firm size	fall with firm size
	1978-92	manufacturing	average	fall with firm size	fall with firm size
Denmark Leth-Sorensen, Boegh-Nielsen (1995)	1985-86	business sector	base-year	fall with firm size	fall with firm size
	1989-90	business sector	base-year	fall with firm size	only micro-firms show high net job creation rates – no systematic relationship for other size classes
Germany Wagner (1995)	1978-93	manufacturing	base-year	fall with firm size	highest net job creation rate in 20-49 size class
	1978-93	manufacturing	average	fall with firm size	no relationship
Japan OECD (1995)	1987-92	manufacturing	base-year	..	no systematic relationship
Netherlands Broersma and Gautier (1995)	1979-91	manufacturing	average	fall with firm size	job creation rates in firm with less than 100 employees exceed job change rates of firms with more than 100 employees
Sweden Davidsson (1995)	1985-89	business sector	base-year	fall with firm size	smallest firms show largest net creation and destruction rates
United Kingdom Gallagher *et al.* (1995)	1982-91	business sector	base-year	fall with firm size	highest net job creation rates for micro enterprises, weaker performance of 20-49 size class
United States Haltiwanger (1995)	1973-88	manufacturing	base-year	fall with firm size	fall with firm size
	1973-88	manufacturing	average	fall with firm size	no relationship
United States Dennis *et al.*	1977-90	business sector	base-year	fall with firm size	fall with firm size
United States OECD (1995)	1987-92	manufacturing	base-year	..	fall with firm size

Source: Schreyer (1996).

identical parameter constellations yield different outcomes. Despite a large variance of these outcomes, the basic features tend to persist.

Uncertainty check. Under the uncertainty check we restrain the degree of uncertainty in the simulation model. Formally, this is done by reducing the variance of the probability distribution governing the process of "idea" drawing.[8] A series of simulation runs with all parameters except the variance of the probability distribution identical to the baseline cases does not reproduce the stylised empirical facts. In particular, we note that, for a significant number of periods (20 out of 30) there is either no entry into the industry and, once it occurs, it is concentrated among a very limited number of firms that either all enter or all exit simultaneously. The effect is an implausibly large rate of turbulence (over 80 percent); strongly at variance with empirical observations. The intuition behind this process is that, with risk reduced or eliminated, success of product or process innovation is entirely driven by the entrepreneur's qualification: those potential entrants with the greatest human capital enter first. They are never driven out of their position because now, other potential entrants further down in the ranking of managerial capacity are not able to "draw" a better idea and challenge the incumbents' position. This observation confirms the usefulness of the simulation model to demonstrate how uncertainty[8] and the ensuing turbulence can become a necessary condition to emulate the features of a market process.

Parameter check. The parameter check has been set up with the intention to examine the sensitivity of model outcomes with respect to small parameter variations. In the logic of the argument, we are looking both for robustness and reactivity: *robustness* where the *qualitative* aspects of the model results (e.g. high concentration in job creation or large turbulence but small net job creation) are concerned—after all, much of the case we are making here hinges on the capacity of the model to reproduce empirical stylised facts; *sensitivity* where the *quantitative aspects* of the model results are concerned: if small parameter changes bear visibly on the level of, say, net job creation rates and turbulence, then we should not expect strong econometric results from simple, linear cross-country correlations.

Indeed, simulations presented in Table 10.4 indicate that, for example, a smaller price elasticity of demand (-1.1 instead of -2.0) generates a much smaller turbulence (11 instead of 22 percent); net job creation rates drop from 2 to 1 percent. Further examples of small parameter changes confirm that, while turbulence and net job creation rates remain within reasonable bounds, there is no simple, observable relation. This leads to the impression of the absence of a link between the two, as in the empirical case shown Figure 10.1. However, we have shown that all artifically generated results stem from an explicit search model in which turbulence plays a vital role. In other words, one should not *expect* a simple or stable relationship between the variables. At the same time, it would be erroneous to play down the importance of the search process on the grounds that its indicator, turbulence, is not readily correlated with the performance measure, net job creation.

5. Policy Conclusions

The red thread throughout this chapter has been a vision of the process of growth and job generation among small firms as one of continuos search, trial and error. Using empirical evidence and results from a simulation model, we tried to substantiate this view. A number of policy implications follow:

Facilitating search processes

From the above discussion, it is quite apparent that reducing turbulence among small businesses may not be a well-chosen policy objective, given that it is a necessary companion of any successful search process. Rather, what follows for policy is that it should support the functioning of the search process, through appropriate institutional, legal and administrative framework conditions for firms and potential entrants. If specific action is called for small firms, it should be to *help them to find out* about the viability of their goods and services but not to help them *with* the goods and services themselves. It should be noted that turbulence and churning are also signs of considerable heterogeneity

Table 10.4 Simulation results

	Turbulence	Net job creation rate	Concentration: % of firms that account for about 50% of		Average of largest market share
			gross job creation	gross job destruction	
Quality check:					
baseline	24.0%	2.6%	6.5%	9.8%	25.2%
Uncertainty check:					
Reduced uncertainty (smaller variance of probability distribution)	85.3%	1.7%	17.8%	16.1%	3.7%
Parameter check:					
Inelastic demand	11.2%	0.9%	4.5%	5.0%	28.5%
Rapid overall technology growth	32.2%	1.9%	6.5%	10.1%	26.3%
- Low fixed costs of entry	20.4%	2.9%	5.6%	8.5%	28.9%
- Low fixed operating costs	15.7%	1.7%	5.1%	6.6%	29.4%
- Rapid overall demand growth	23.9%	2.7%	6.5%	10.0%	25.3%

Note:

Turbulence	= gross job creation rate + absolute value of gross job destruction rate.
Gross job creation rate	= jobs created between t and t+1 as a percentage of total employment in year t.
Gross job destruction rate	= jobs lost between t and t+1 as a percentage of total employment in year t.
Net job creation rage	= gross job creation rate minus gross job destruction rate.

Source: author's calculations

among firms—a fact that makes targeted policies hard to formulate and implement (Haltiwanger, 1996). Consequently, policies with "framework" character tend to be more efficient and easier to implement. With these preliminaries in mind, we turn to the policy discussion of the three aspects of the search process: entry, search; exit.

Entry: there are several areas of government action to facilitate entry. First, the removal of entry barriers, such as regulations that make entry costly (e.g., compliance with administrative procedures for start-ups) or arrangements that protect incumbents (e.g., monopoly rights in certain industries). Secondly, and based on the observation that well-educated persons are more likely to start a new business that others, the long-term support through educational policies. A specific aspect of this is financing of basic research in universities which may help to broaden the pool of potential successful entrepreneurs through researchers who are ready to set up small technology-based firms. Third, establishing the necessary infrastructure to facilitate financing of start-ups and young firms, for example through the institution of venture capital markets[9].

Search: much of what has been said for entry applies to government action towards facilitating the search processes in the market: education and support of lifelong learning of the workforce, support of research and of the diffusion of knowledge about innovations and technologies. Widening of the scope of technology diffusion policies seems important, given the increasing importance of the services sector as a key user of information-based technologies and as a source of technical progress. Policies in place have generally been shaped by the needs of manufacturing sectors and it may be necessary to review the effectiveness of technology diffusion policies in building on and encouraging the interaction between manufacturing and services.

Exit: as exiting is an integral part of enterprise dynamics, governments should take no specific measures to prevent firms from exiting. There is a difficult choice, however, in that exiting is the part of the entrepreneurial process that may entail direct costs for society, either the taxpayer or other enterprises that may suffer from a client's bankruptcy. Legal arrangements are important but cannot resolve a basic conflict between protecting other market participants and minimising negative incentives both for potential entrants and for those who exit but may want to try another entry. There are also the costs of worker displacement, in the case of exit and the need for readjustments of the workforce. Again, education and lifelong learning can somewhat accommodate that process but certain costs remain.

There is another, quite different aspect to exiting: firms may cease to exist because they are sold, merged or otherwise transformed because, in this case, their exit is a sign of success and, generally, neither their product nor their accumulated knowledge leave the market. Statistical problems of tracing such transformations aside, efficient exit mechanisms (trade sales, initial public offerings and repurchases) are crucial, in particular for the functioning of venture capital industries.

Help fast growers or laggards?

If job creation is concentrated among a small share of fast growing firms, should policies aim at supporting such fast growing firms or rather try and stimulate growth among those that do not grow? The answer is probably "neither", both for theoretical and practical reasons. Generally, the track record of governments to pick winners has not been very impressive and it is quite likely that fast growers actually grow with or without government help. Active support of laggards, on the other hand, implies large-scale and costly policies to improve company profitability. From the theoretical point of view that has been adopted throughout this chapter, the effectiveness of such policies is questionable, and empirical evidence (Keasey and Watson, 1993) suggests that improved profits are "simply a windfall gain by the owner-managers [that] is removed from the business in the form of increased directors' fees. Although it is possible that increases in the profitability of existing small firms may encourage new entrants, the lack of easily available financial information on small firms suggests that this is unlikely (p. 93)."

From size to age?

Recent work by Haltiwanger et al. (1996) for the United States has brought up a different issue in the SME-job creation debate. Haltiwanger et al. point to two age-related patterns in job creation: one is that net job creation rates decline with plant age; the other is that employment volatility declines with plant age. These patterns should not come unexpected, given that young firms are nearly always small. However, small firms are not necessarily young. The distinction is important because, if age rather than size was the criterion, policy should focus less on small firms and more on young firms. Put differently, a policy in favour of SMEs would be replaced by a policy to promote entrepreneurship, for example, through the removal of regulatory barriers to firm creation. In many ways, this links up with the theoretical stance taken in this chapter: entry, displacement, search, fast growth and exit drive overall performance—and young firms and entry opportunities are key in this process. Yet, more empirical evidence on the significance of age as opposed to size is needed before clear policy conclusions can be put forward.

Improving SME statistics

Demand for reliable, relevant and internationally comparable data on SMEs has been rising. Statistical offices have started to collect and publish relevant data but serious shortcomings persist. International comparability has remained weak, due to divergence of definitions for size-class and treatment of underlying units (firms, establishments) and variation in industry classification and time periods used for data collection. Many interesting issues in conjunction with SMEs can only be addressed with sets of micro-level, longitudinal data that allow the tracing of individual firms or establishments over time. In addition to problems of comparability, the sheer volume of the data sets involved, as well as questions of confidentiality, have prevented rapid progress of international studies.

More generally, there is a conflict of interest between obtaining comprehensive and timely information about SMEs and limiting the administrative burden associated with responding to statistical question-naires. As a result statisticians must increasingly endeavour to exploit creatively the existing statistical or administrative sources to obtain better information on SMEs and to minimise future response burdens.

6. Conclusions

This chapter started from several empirical observations on the dynamics of job creation. In particular, it stated that relatively small net job creation rates are always accompanied by sizeable turbulence, a measure for the combined size of gross job creation and destruction. Another well-established fact is that turbulence is greatest among small firms who are also large contributors to net job creation. Whether this contribution is more than proportionate, has been a long-standing point of discussion.

The turbulence associated with net job creation is interpreted as a sign for an ongoing search process, a measure of trial and error, necessary for discovery, innovation and growth. Idiosyncrasy of behaviour, heterogeneity across establishments and a large variance among rates of success and growth are part of this image, and fit well with the empirical observations, including the fact that job creation and destruction tends to be concentrated among a small number of very rapidly growing or very rapidly contracting firms.

If such a search process is at the heart of market dynamics and turbulence is its indicator, then surely we should be able to observe a close correlation between turbulence and performance of industries or countries. Unfortunately, cross country comparisons yield no conclusive picture. However, this chapter shows that this is insufficient to refute the hypothesis of an underlying search process: a simulation model is used to show that an explicit search process is perfectly capable of generating observations for different industries or countries that present a picture of seemingly uncorrelated behaviour between turbulence and net job creation.

This examination of the turbulence hypothesis has several policy implications:

In their SME policies, governments should be concerned about the functioning of market processes, or the ease with which firms can enter, search and exit. This is quite different from proposing that incumbent SMEs receive specific support to improve their profitability, simply because they are small and because they exist.

In many ways, it might be preferable to substitute the notion of entrepreneurship policy for the notion of SME policies: the latter make "size" their criterion, the former the "readiness to enter and to search". Although the two criteria often coincide (new entrants, and fast growers are nearly always small), entrepreneurship is what is sought, not a specific size.   Large firms can be highly entrepreneurial, thus contributing to performance and growth. Alternatively, "age", could be a criterion that is closer to the notion of entrepreneurship than size and, indeed, certain empirical studies have shown the relative importance of young firms in net job creation.

One of the implications of entrepreneurship policies is that direct government support targeting specific firms is unlikely to succeed—on the other hand, establishing institutions and rules to permit, for example, venture capital, business angels and secondary markets to develop, is at the very heart of entrepreneurship policies. Essentially, government becomes a facilitator—a role that includes areas such as promoting—again, through appropriate rules and institutional settings—the interchange between potential start-ups and universities, or the protection of intellectual property rights.

Another major policy challenge is education and training.   Most studies on small business come up with the conclusion that success of entrepreneurs, either in their search for ideas or in their dealing with the capital market, or in their management functions is linked to the entrepreneur's human capital.   Finally, entrepreneurship has also a cultural and social component and governments should reflect on the values attached to entrepreneurship—in some cases, there may be room for actively promoting the social acceptance and desirability of entrepreneurship.

Notes

1. In what follows, we shall simply use the notion "firm" to denote the statistical unit underlying empirical studies of job creation. However, it is well understood that the distinction between "firm", "stablishment", "local unit" etc. is of great importance for empirical results and their interpretation.

2. This discussion draws on OECD (1996a).

3. For empirical results with different size allocation methods see for example, Davis et al. (1994), Konings (1995), Picot and Dupuy (1995) or Wagner (1995). A full treatment of the question can also be found in Kleijweg and Nieuwenhuijsen (1996).

4. Another measurement issue has to do with the metric of firm size. Traditionally, firms have been grouped into size classes with employment as the criterion. Employment size classes have also been the most widely used classification criteria in studies of net job creation. A recent Canadian study, however, has shed some doubts on this choice, or rather on the robustness of this criterion. Baldwin (1996) uses relative wage rates to create a measure of employment that is adjusted for wage differentials. When this is done, small producers no longer outperform large producers in terms of job creation over the 1970s and 1980s in the Canadian manufacturing sector.

5. Job turnover is defined as the sum of all jobs created in a period plus all the jobs lost in the same period. The job turnover rate which is the measure of turbulence in what follows, expresses job turnover as a percentage of the total number of employed.

6. For a full exposition see Annex.

7. We maintain, however, that the mean of this distribution shifts with each entrepreneurs qualification/capacities.

8. The literature (Knight, 1921) makes a clear difference between risk and uncertainty: there is risk when decision-makers know what they are ignorant about; there is uncertainty when decision-makers do not know what they are ignorant about. Risk is typically modelled with a probability distribution known to the entrepreneur. Our present model uses a probability distribution to characterise the random process of generating ideas, but does not assume that the potential entrant is aware of this distribution. Formally, there is no maximisation of expected profits, given the probability distribution. Hence, our model incorporates an aspect of uncertainty—at least where the entrepreneur's information set is concerned.

9. Venture capital, a specific type of finance available to fund high-risk projects in young companies that are not quoted on the stock market, is a strategic resource for new technology-based firms (OECD, 1996c). The venture capital industry is at different stages of maturity in the OECD area and in many countries its underdevelopment constitutes a bottleneck in the innovation system. It is well established in the United States, where it is oriented to technology-based activities and finances a significant share of early stage investment. The European venture

industry is younger, oriented towards mainstream sectors and later-stage investment, and generally dominated by banks—even in the United Kingdom which has the most developed venture capital industry in Europe.

References

Audretsch, D.B. 1995. *Innovation and Industry Evolution.* MIT Press.

Boeri, T. 1994. "Why are Establishments so Heterogeneous?", *Small Business Economics 6.*

Birch, D.L. 1979. *The Job Generation Process.* Program on Neighborhood and Regional Chang, Cambridge, Mass.: MIT.

Davis, S.J., J.C. Haltiwanger and S. Schuh 1994. "Small Business and Job Creation: Dissecting the Myth and Reassessing the Facts", *Business Economics,* July.

——— 1996. *Job Creation and Destruction.* MIT Press.

Dupuy, R. and G. Picot 1995. "Job Creation by size Class: Recent Evidence from Canada", paper presented at the OECD Industry Committee Working Party on Small and Medium-sized Enterprises High-level Workshop on *SMEs: Employment, Innovation and Growth,* Washington D.C.

Geroski, P.A. 1995. "What Do We Know About Entry?", *International Journal of Industrial Organization 13.*

Jovanovich, B. 1982. "Selection and Evolution of Industry", *Econometrica* 50(2).

Keasey, K. and R. Watson 1993. *Small Firm Management, Ownership, Finance and Performance.* Blackwell Publishers.

Kirzner, I. 1997. "Entrepreneurial Discovery and the Competitive Market Process: An Austrian Approach", *Journal of Economic Literature* Vol. XXXV.

Kleijweg, A. and H. Nieuwenhuijsen 1996. "Job Creation by Size Class: Measurement and Empirical Investigation", *Statistics Netherlands Working Paper.*

OECD 1996a. *Technology, Productivity, Job Creation.* Paris.

——— 1996b. *Employment Outlook.* Paris.

———— 1996c.*Venture Capital and Innovation.* General Distribution Document, Paris.

———— 1997. *Small Businesses, Job Creation and Growth: Facts, Obstacles and Best Practices.* Background Paper for the 1997 G7 Denver Summit.

———— 1994. *Employment Outlook.* Paris.

Schreyer, P. 1996. "SME and Employment Creation: Overview of Selected Quantitative Studies in OECD Member Countries", *STI Working Papers 4*, OECD.

Storey, D. 1988. *Fast Growth Small Businesses: Case Studies of 40 Small Firms in Northern England.* Research Paper 67, London: Department of Employment.

Wagner, J. 1995. "Talkin" bout Job Generation: Firm Size and Job Creation in Germany", *Working Paper of the University of Lüneburg.*

Annex: Simulation model

Qualification and pre-entry draw. For the hypothetical industry under consideration, there is a pool of N^{max} potential entrants. Each entrepreneur i is endowed with a certain amount of human capital (managerial capacities, education etc.). These capacities, characterised by the variable ξ_i, are distributed as:

$$\xi_i = \begin{cases} i^{-\theta} \\ 0 \end{cases} for \begin{cases} i = 1, 2, \ldots N^{max} \\ i > N^{max} \end{cases}.$$

Without loss of generality, ξ_1, the highest qualification, is normalised to unity. $\xi_{N^{max}}$ is then the lowest qualification, relative to ξ_1. It is assumed that the ratio $\xi_1 / \xi_{N^{max}}$ is exogenously determined, partly through government action such as education policies. Then, for given $\xi_{N^{max}}$ and N^{max}, the distribution parameter θ can be evaluated as $\theta = -\dfrac{\ln \xi_{N^{max}}}{\ln N^{max}}$.

Each potential entrepreneur who is not active in the market, is at the search for an idea to come up with a new or diversified product. This search process is random and the potential entrant can be more or less lucky in his search. However, the probability with which he will find an idea that is good enough to allow entry, depends on his human capital ξ_i.

We postulate a market with features of asymmetric monopolistic competition where each supplier faces a demand curve specific to his differentiated product, but not independent of what happens in the rest of the market. Specifically, let the demand function for I's product be:

$$D_i = \Phi_{io} \left(P_i / \overline{P} \right)^\alpha$$

D_i denotes demand for producer I's differentiated product; P_i is the price for good i, $\overline{P}$ a price index for the entire market, α the negative price elasticity of demand, assumed to be identical across products. Heterogeneity of demand functions enters via Φ_{i0}, a parameter that shifts the entire demand function. As an outward shift of demand can be interpreted as product innovation, it is straightforward to use Φ_{i0} as the random variable that each potential entrant draws and which, along with other factors, determines entry.

The draw of Φ_{i0} is based on a lognormal distribution whose mean is ξ_i, the qualification parameter. The expected value of drawing a larger Φ_{i0} then rises with the entrepreneur's human capital. More formally, Φ_{i0} is

distributed as $F(\Phi_{i0}) = \dfrac{1}{\sigma \Phi_{i0} \sqrt{2\pi}} \exp\left(\dfrac{(-\log \Phi_{i0} - \xi_i)^2}{2\sigma^2}\right)$. Equipped

with this draw, the entrepreneur takes an entry decision, based on available information on the market. Once he enters, the entrepreneur is bound to his initial Φ_{i0} (although it evolves, as will be described below); if he stays out, he can continue to draw in the subsequent period.

Entry decision. A potential entrant, after having drawn an idea in the form of a realisation of Φ_{i0}, decides whether or not to enter the market. This decision hinges on the possibility to end up with a profit in the case of entry. As outlined earlier, the decision is taken under limited information which extends only to past market prices, the demand function, and the cost parameters for production. The entrepreneur neither factors in strategic interaction between producers nor is he aware of the shape of the probability distribution of Φ_{i0} (whose knowledge might induce him to wait or to go ahead). This assumption of limited information is both practical for purposes of modelling and closer to an evolutionary approach where discovery processes are essential. If entry takes place, the entrepreneurs expected profits are $\Pi_{i0} = P_{i0} D_{i0} - C_{i0}$, where P_{i0} is the price that could be charged, given demand $D_{i0} = \Phi_{i0}(P_{i0} / \overline{P}_{i,t-1})^\alpha$ and total costs $C_{i0} = \gamma_i D_{i0} - F_0 - F$. γ_i is the marginal variable cost of production, F_0 the fixed cost of market entry, and F the fixed cost of production. Maximisation of the profit equation, subject to cost and demand functions, yields the well-known expression for the product price as a mark-up over marginal costs:

$$P_{i0} = \frac{1}{1+1/\alpha}\gamma_i.$$

Insertion of this expression into the demand function and the profit function yields a value for Π_{i0} whose sign determines entry[1].

Post entry. If entry occurs, the new market participant, as well as all incumbents, set their market prices as $P_{it} = \frac{\alpha}{1+\alpha}\gamma_{it}$. The assumption of marginal cost that are independent of the scale of production permits this choice of prices irrespective of quantities sold. Note that the latter depend on $\overline{P}$, the market price which is determined simultaneously and which is itself a geometric average of all prices quoted on the market. In line with index number theory, each price enters the market price index with its current-price share s_{it} in industry turnover:

$$\log(\overline{P}_t) = \sum_{j}^{N} s_{it}\log(P_{it}) \text{ , with } s_{it} = \frac{P_{it}D_{it}}{\sum_{j}^{N}P_{jt}D_{jt}} = \frac{\Phi_{i0}\gamma_{it}P_{it}^\alpha}{\sum_{j}^{N}\Phi_{j0}\gamma_{jt}P_{jt}^\alpha}.$$

Given P_{it} and s_{it}, $\overline{P}_t$ can be derived and, consequently, D_{it} and Π_{it}, the actual profits realised during period t. Π_{it} determines also market exit: competitors leave the market if $\Pi_{it} < 0$.

Technology. Little has been said so far about the technology (cost) parameter γ_{it}, defined as marginal costs of production. There are two dimensions to γ_{it}, one of technology diffusion and one of technological progress through learning by doing. Consider these in turn; the technology diffusion aspect arises because a certain amount of knowledge about efficient production processes is publicly available. This effect is captured

by $\tilde{\gamma}_{it} = \gamma_0 \left(\dfrac{1}{A+\xi_i}\right)^t$ which describes the evolution of the technological

frontier over time: minimum attainable marginal cost $\tilde{\gamma}_{it}$ is driven by general technological progress, A, and by the entrepreneur's individual capacity to benefit from it, expressed through ξ_i, his human capital.

The second technology dimension is one of learning-by-doing, whereby a larger amount of cumulated production facilitates the entrepreneur's adjustment process towards an evolving technological frontier $\tilde{\gamma}_{it}$. This adjustment process is characterised as:

$$\gamma_{it} = \beta_{it}\left(\tilde{\gamma}_{i,t-1} - \gamma_{i,t-1}\right) + \gamma_{i,t-1} \qquad \text{with}$$

$$\beta_{it} = \left\{1 - \left(\sum_{\tau=0}^{t} D_{i,t-\tau}\right)^{-1}\right\} \quad for \left(\tilde{\gamma}_{i,t-1} - \gamma_{i,t-1}\right)\begin{Bmatrix}<0\\ \geq 0\end{Bmatrix}.$$

Hence, the adjustment parameter β_{it}, which can only take values between zero and one, rises with a firm's cumulative experience. If a firm's actual marginal cost parameter γ_{it} has caught up with the technological frontier $\tilde{\gamma}_{it}$, the adjustment factor equals zero.

Demand. Akin to the technology component, demand evolves over time. Its dynamics are governed by an expression for long-run demand, $\tilde{\Phi}_{i,t}$, which hinges on each entrepreneur's initial "draw", Φ_{io},, the overall (macro-economic) demand growth G, and, again, the entrepreneur's human capital: $\tilde{\Phi}_{i,t} = \tilde{\Phi}_{i,t-1}(G + \xi_i)$. The actual demand parameter $\Phi_{i,t}$ evolves according to an adjustment mechanism, where the speed of adjustment depends again on the entrepreneur's capacities:

$$\Phi_{i,t} = h_i\left(\tilde{\Phi}_{i,t-1} - \Phi_{i,t-1}\right) + \Phi_{i,t-1} \text{ with } h_i = \begin{Bmatrix} \xi_i \\ 0 \end{Bmatrix} for \left(\tilde{\Phi}_{i,t-1} - \Phi_{i,t-1}\right) \begin{Bmatrix} > 0 \\ \leq 0 \end{Bmatrix}.$$

Parameters. Starting with the following parameter constellation, the model was run for 30 periods, i.e., until to $t = 30$. As each run involved the drawing of random variables from a normal distribution, no run yielded identical results. Hence, for each parameter constellation, 100 runs were carried out and empirical results as shown in Table 10.4 were evaluated as the median of all 100 runs. Key parameters underlying the baseline results are:

Number of potential entrants (N^{max})	Periods	Price elasticity of demand (α)	Overall market growth (G)
100	30	-2.0	1%
Lowest/highest qualification ratio ($\xi^{N max} / \xi_1$)	Fixed cost of market entry (F_0)	Fixed cost of operation (F)	General technological progress (A)
0.3	5	10	1%

Note

1. Note that for this entry decision, the market price that enters the calculation of demand D_{i0}, is last period's market price. The actual market price, after everybody has taken his entry decision, may turn out to be quite different.

11 POLICIES FOR SMALL AND MEDIUM-SIZED ENTERPRISES (SMEs)

Patrizio Bianchi

1. Traditional Approaches to SMEs and New Tendencies

In the past, SMEs were considered unproductive, marginal firms. They were assumed to be either enterprises at the very beginning of their life-cycle, working especially in infant industries, or unsuccessfull stories, surviving at the margin of the modern economy.

In both cases they were not able to sustain a regular competition from big business, and therefore, in the case of a sudden opening of the economy to international trade, they had to be protected by the government either to stimulate infant industries or to save employment in traditional sectors.

This strong assumption was motivated by the so-called Fordist paradigm, affirming that—if technology is given, product is homogeneous, and demand is steady or steadily increasing—there are economies of specialization implying decreasing marginal costs as output rises. However in the mid-1950s Bain and Sylos Labini proved that incumbent companies increase their strategic dimension beyond their minimum efficient scale, in order to pre-empt the market and therefore to deter new entries. Various cases have also shown that large scale is not *per se* efficient, if the increased size involves organizational costs larger than market transaction costs. Moreover where demand is unstable, products are mature and therefore can be differentiated and where technology changes rapidly, the existing economies of scale cannot be efficient because they are based on asset specifity that is not only sunk but also rigid. In that case, smaller firms, which are more flexible both in using process technology and in differentiating products, can be more competitive than a rigid mass-production company, operating with highly specific, but rigid assets and having high internal bureaucratic costs.

Furthermore, a variety of cases throughout Europe, especially in Italy and Germany, showed that territorial agglomerations of firms can performe very efficiently if a process of inter-firm specialization starts and determines a network of activities which are highly complementary.

In the 1980s, the so-called industrial districts emerged as a mode of production having a remarkable resilience to global pressure. Several authors explored the European and especially Italian cases, showing that in Europe industrial districts performed very well in the following sectors: knitwear and garment production, shoe manufacture, ceramic tile production, upholstered furniture, but also motor-cycle, machinery for packaging, wood-processing and farming, machine tools production, and also biomedical products and food processing (Cossentino, Pyke and Sengerberger, 1997) American authors confirmed that this mode can work also for very advanced sectors such as defence, electronics and movie production.

The success of these cases, and the evidence that large firms restructured their activities to be competitive in the global context, by cutting jobs instead of creating new employment in new industrial and service sectors, induced several countries and international institutions to revise the issue.

It was made evident that most European countries have rooted their growth on a wide basis of clusters of SMEs. In fact, in Europe SMEs are anything but marginal, low-productive operators[1].

SMEs have created and preserved jobs while large enterprises were not able to maintain employment levels between 1988 and 1993. This evidence is particularly clear for Mediterranean countries, where there are 65 enterprises per 1,000 inhabitants, whereas in the other member states this ratio is below 40.

Finally, it is evident that the term "Small firms" is very ambigous, because we can identify an SME as a rural family activity, devoted simply to guaranteeing the survival of the family, or a very inefficent company which failed to grow up, or a firm offering services at a very local level, or we can consider an SME as a new enterprise rapidly growing up or a component of a successful network, competing at international level. Thus, the real policy issue is to identify the conditions to create such clusters and to allow SMEs to become a corner-stone in the process of local development.

The recent diffusion of successful SMEs in South Europe and the discovery of several embryonic districts in emerging industrial countries induced international institutions to support policies for SME growth in developing countries.

2. Conditions for SMEs' Efficiency and Policy Orientations

In the context of trade liberalization, SMEs can perform a triple function of:

1. starting an endogenous process of economic development, by enlarging the number and variety of economic actors;
2. spreading industrial development over wider areas of the country;
3. contributing social stability to the entire economy, by multiplying the independent centres of production and distribution of wealth.

The three aspects above mentioned are crucial for designing a process of sustainible development, that is to say an economic growth which produces and distributes wealth without breaking off the entire society, because it can generate a process of development with equity.

A proper policy orientation favouring the development of SMEs can contribute considerably to the social and economic stability of individual countries, by:

- favouring self-employment, especially among young people and women;

- developing activities that at present have low productivity levels and are directed towards local markets;
- generating networks of specialised enterprises forming a bridge between local and global economies;
- contributing not only to the reduction of unemployment,but creating a variety of new activities;
- consolidating an economic and social system that is able to take full advantage of an integration policy within an open and competitive context.

Nevertheless, several international experiences show that SMEs can be active and dynamic actors in integrated and sustained development, only if they can increase continuosly their own skills and, therefore, their own efficiency. This means that SMEs can be competitive if they can substitute dynamic economies of scale for static economies of scale.
The principle of economies of scale means that the unitary cost of production declines as the volume manufactured rises. Static economies of scale means that processing a larger amount of materials at the same time, the unitary costs decrease. The source of efficiency of static economies of scale is given by the relative specialization of skills and technical assets employed in the process. Dynamic economies of scale means that repeating overtime a series of production functions involves the capacity to improve skills and asset specificity, reducing the timing of replicating functions and stimulating the capacity to generate new functions.

1. This is possible if the entrepeneur and his productive organization can focus capacities and competences over a number of limited functions, so that they can learn progressively more efficient ways to reproduce the process.
2. This is reliable if an SME operates in a cooperative context, in which other enterprises produce and sell goods and services that are complementary to those that it offers;
3. This process of clustering of complementary activities is efficient if a large number of institutions, not necessarily governmental, are developed to organise the collective life in which individual businesses are involved, from the financial system to the education system, from the diffusion of innovation to the promotion of new

business initiatives on the part of actors particularly hard hit by prolonged unemployment, such as women and young people.

4. This requires that central and local institutions guarantee the necessary legal context, services and adequate infrastructure for the development of this network of enterprises;

5. In other words, the real subject of the economic process is not the individual SME, but the grouping of SMEs, organized either by the progressive evolution of local history, or by explicit policy intervention in clusters.

6. These clusters can be organized on the basis either of a territorial agglomeration, or of sectoral affinity. Whereas the two aspects tend to coincide, the cluster assumes the typical form of the industrial districts, largely studied by a rich literature from Marshall to Becattini and forward (Cossentino, Pyke and Sengenberger, 1997).

A grouping of small enterprises is efficient, could be a reliable means for accelerating local development and could also be an international competitive actor, if the whole economic and social system becomes efficient. Otherwise its growth, and even its conception, may be impeded by obstacles that could actually block the more general development of the country and its capacity to insert itself in a global economic context. It becomes necessary to examine not only the situation of individual SMEs in the various countries, but also to evaluate the overall industrial structure of industry, available services and the general state of the economy of the country in question.

Therefore, attention should be paid not only to the efficiency of the administrative structure, both central and peripheral, that is to how the government is organised, but also the so-called "governance", that is, the collection of subjects, public, private, intermediary and associative that shape local society. It is also necessary to discover how the banking and financial system works, how the education system operates and, more generally, how the "national and local innovative systems", or the combination of non-governmental institutions and organisms participating in the development of human resources, research and the diffusion of innovation functions. Finally, infrastructure and public utilities must be examined.

3. National and Community Policies to SMEs

A comprehensive SME related policy first of all calls for a clear distinction among the different typologies of small enterprises. As an example there is a strong difference between the treatment of small rural enterprises, having the duty of providing subsistence to a wide local population, and enterprises which—even if small—are committed to high-tech production to be offered on the open market. There is substancial difference between an isolated craftsman and a small firm working as a subcontractor of a large firm.

We can stress that a special duty of policy makers is to recognize these differences and to try to diffuse innovative routines throughout the different groups of firms. It is clear that a large number of SMEs remain confined to the very local economy, and that they survive managing a mix of local commerce and simple crafting. Nevertheless, a number of SMEs must be competitive in the open economy, in order to support the process of trade liberalization of the country, of starting up of new private activities, and also to diffuse new practices which can improve the efficiency of the entire economy.

Since the success of a policy strategy for SMEs' development implies the reinforcement of relationships within firms, among firms, and between the firms' system and the institutional environment, the design and implementation of economic policy concerning small and medium-sized firms requires a clarification of the role of the state in the specific context of the normative and regulatory system which regulates social and economic life. In brief, in a market opening context the role of the state needs to be strengthened in order to stimulate market forces and especially the local potential.

Thus, there are two relevant levels of policy design and implementation. We can define thereas macro and micro industrial policies: the macro industrial policies establish the legal and regulatory framework for the development of market forces; the micro industrial policies define specific interventions to accelerate the process of industrial development, through an increase in the competitivness of the firms.

- The macro level defines the entitlements regulating who may take part in the game, creates the normative system which governs the behavior of all actors, and sanctions free-riders and abuses of dominant positions.This means that the first set of policies supporting SMEs' development is the creation of the market itself. This means to create a positive legal environment, and to liberalize the domestic market, because it should create a wider extent of the market, favouring specialization and agglomeration of interests. The risk is due to the possibility of further concentration among large companies which could limit the market room for SMEs. A further necessary set of policies is given by competition policy, managed by independent authorities, to avoid price and market discrimination toward SMEs.

- The micro level establishes the capabilities with which the actors take part in the economic arena, which means that micro policies not only include local firms, but also local educational institutions, infrastructures, etc. Together policies on both levels, macro and micro, must be integrated to create the positive externalities needed for growth in order to avoid the formation of groups resistant to change.

A summary of policy measures implemented by government in the European countries and by the European Commission identifies seven policy fields. European governments and the Commission developed these measures according to the specific local problems and the governance systems working locally.

The seven policy fields are:

- start-up of new firms
- modernization of subcontracting
- support to export activity
- removal of finance discrimination to SMEs
- sustaining of education and training
- adoption of new technologies.

The variety of tools is very wide; financial aids, fiscal support, information and counselling, training and the creation of specific centres to sustain technology diffusions have been variously used by national, regional and local authorities (see Table 11.1).

Table 11.1 Policies in favour of small and medium-sized enterprises in Europe

Objectives	Financial subsidies	Tax breaks	Information and consultancy	Training	Other
Start-up of new enterprises	all	B, F, L, N	all	B, Dk, D, Gr, Ir, I, L, N, P, UK	B, F, D, UK
Development of sub-contracting	I, EC	none	Gr, Ir, I, N, P, S, UK, EC	None	F, L
Export support	all EC	Ir, P	all EC	Dk, D, Gr, L, S, UK	none EC
Development of financial activities	all EC	Dk, F, D, L, I	F, D, P, S	None	none
Employment support	B, Dk, D, Gr, Ir, I, L, N, P, S, UK, EC	B, F, P	Dk, F, D, Gr, I, L, P, S, UK	F, D, Gr, L, N, P, S, EC	Gr, Ir, UK
Development of education and of professional training	B, D, Gr, Ir, L, N, S, UK, EC	none	F, D, S, EC	B, Dk, D, F, Gr, Ir, L, N, P, S, UK, EC	none

Key: B-Belgium; Dk-Denmark; F-France; D-Federal Germany; Gr-Greece; Ir-Ireland; I-Italy; L-Luxembourg; N-Netherlands; P-Portugal; S-Spain; UK-United Kingdom; EC-European Commission

The European Union is explicitly oriented to supporting the creation of networks of innovators which could lead the opening process through an industrial reorganization of firms which redefine their own introducing such an industrial strategy into the European Community context.

This strategy is applied at the territorial level to favor the growth of the less favoured areas, such as defined by the so-called structural policies of the EC; it is used for innovation policy and human resource development in education and research policy; it is adopted for developing small and medium sized firm clusters.

Moreover, all the member-countries of the EU support start-up and development of new and small and medium-sized firms. Most financial incentives have been established during the 1980s but in most of the cases, these direct financial support schemes have been integrated and in several cases substituted by Information and Counselling services and courses to train the new entrepreneurs to manage their own business. Equally, most of the countries have programmes supported by the Commission to support the creation of new firms by women, young people, returning migrants.

Public support for exports is provided by all the European governments. Also, in this case there is a clear trend from financial aids provided by central government to information and counselling services provided by the local authorities, through specialized promotion agencies.

In the sector of finance there are a variety of national measures to respond to the evidence that in Europe the financial sector is not instrumental in helping new and small firms to develop. The EU Commission intervenes stimulating the diffusion of seed capital funds, venture capital programmes, mutual guarantee schemes, cooperatives, mutual societies and associations.

The EU report on State aids to industrial sectors showed clearly that there is a clear tendency from financial support to service supply, and from central government to local authorities. A major determinant of this reordering of national policies has been the increasing role of the European Union, which has controlled the incentive schemes given by national governments, and at the same time has designed a clear model of intervention through the relaunching of the structural policies. Structural policies, which define areas of economic underdevelopment and of industrial decline, pushed national, local authorities and private actors to work together in designing and managing local plans for economic and social growth .

The EU Commission has promoted a variety of integrated programmes devoted to improving the environment of SMEs and to improving the access of SMEs to finance and Research and Development activities. These integrated programmes offer a wide range of incentives and services, which can be used by the local authorities to create the local conditions for helping SMEs to improve their productivity and competitivness and enter new sectors. Recently the Commission organized the different programmes within a Multiannual Programme for SMEs. The Third Multiannual Programme covers the period 1997-2000 (Commission, 1996). This multiannual programme is part of the Commission's Confidence Pact on Employment, agreed with the social partners, to develop the full potential for job creation in Europe.

The limit of this approach is that all these programmes, and the approach based on the possibility to work together for creating a social environment inducing economic development, requires a strong awareness of the local community. Whereas economic crisis stems from a social disease, it is necessary to work for rebuilding the local identity, for calling all the local actors to work together for growth.

The strong relevance of SMEs for growth and employment has been stressed by the G7 Group. In the 1995 meeting held in Brussels, G7 along with the European Community decided to identify a number of selected projects concerning market globalization and the development of information society. Among these a specific project was devoted to SMEs and the diffusion of information society, in order to accelerate the creation of a global marketplace for SMEs, by using new information technologies (G7, 1995). Along this path, a massive attention toSMEs has been paid to SMEs in the First Action Plan for Innovation in Europe, adopted on the 20th November 1996. A further mention of the role of SMEs has been recognized by the G8 Group (the 7 largest industrialized countries plus Russia) in the Denver Meeting (June 20-22, 1997), encouraging government to support diffusion of best practices of SMEs in the G7 countries as useful examples for developing and transition-market economies (G8, 1997, point 10).

4. SMEs in Developing and Transition Economies

Although representing considerable structural diversity, particularly due to the dominating presence, or absence, of raw materials and oil and mineral extraction industries, the economies of the emerging countries seem to be characterised by a strong dualism between the presence of a few industrial giants, usually directly or indirectly controlled by the

State and in some cases by multinational companies, and an enormous variety of small and very small enterprises. The latter may be rural, manufacturing or commercial, and have often emerged from an informal sector in which the various activities are continually mixed.

In almost all of these countries manufacturing contributes to the national revenue by providing just under 15 to 20% of total national revenue, leaving agriculture, commerce, the oil and mineral extraction industries and the public sector to account for the remaining 80 to 85%. In fact, viewing the situation "in the field" it becomes much less schematic. The same enterprises often engage in production and commerce, agriculture and artisan activities, just as public employees often have second jobs in private services or the commercial sector.

Therefore, in all the developing and transition-market countries there is a large number of small and very small private companies, almost all having fewer than 10 employees, that are beginning to be recognised by national governments as important elements, not only because they employ a large part of the working population, but also as an important part of a development that is no longer based on chemical or steel industries, directly connected with the processing of mineral products, or with heavy industry, connected with military production.

In most of the transition-market economies a large number of service companies were born in the last ten years, to respond to a variety of local demand. The emerging demand for personal services and consumer goods is a proper context to develop new firms. Nevertheless, most of these companies develop their activities for export. In several cases, these firms are supported by European investors, who have transferred their operation to these countries. For instance, several Italian textile and garment companies have transferred their production or have activated subcontractors in Slovenia, Hungary, Slovakis and Rumania.

In many developing countries, SMEs producing consumer goods, often in traditional sectors, such as textiles, clothing or in the more innovative sectors, such as that of pharmaceutical products, are aiming their activities more toward exports. For example, the textiles/clothing sector accounts for approximately 30% of Tunisian exports. In Jordan there is a growing pharmaceutical sector, also oriented to export to developed countries like the United States. In several countries in Asia, like India, there are important areas of electronic and informatic production, but in most of the cases those firms are insulated with respect to the entire economy, like islands in a wide sea of inefficent craft and small firms, simply devoted to provide means of survival to local population.

Therefore, it is important to distinguish between the vast area of small and very small businesses operating essentially on the local market, that is, those which limit both their production and their market to the local, or sometimes national situation, and that small, but fundamental, group of companies operating on the international market.

The first enterprises are important because they constitute an important base of socio-economic stability and provide the majority of jobs. The second are important because international competition forces them to seek production quality, efficiency and innovation, so that these companies can become catalysts for modernisation throughout the production system. However, these two groups of SMEs risk being separated in a national context which is closed towards international trade, while—as confirmed by various European experiences—they must necessarily be linked in a context of transition.

The opportunity for increasing the number of companies able to compete on the international level primarily depends on the possibility of allowing the largest number of companies to expand from local production to the international market, enabling them effectively to become a catalyst for the whole production system. At the same time, local business in general needs to be encouraged to grow, so that it can adequately compete against products that are easily imported in a situation of rapid market opening.

Let us identify three major aspects of policy-making for SMEs:

1. opening and liberalizing the economy;
2. new entrepreneurship and the role of the financial market;
3. innovation, education and the basic infrastructure.

5. Opening the Economy and Liberalization of the Legal Context

An open and competitive economic context is essential for the development of systems of competitive SMEs, in that it offers companies the possibility to extend their markets and, as a result of greater competitive pressure, to introduce increased efficiency and technical specialisation. Nevertheless, it must be pointed out that the management of a process of economic opening is extremely complicated and not without risks. Fragile economies, given by only a few large enterprises working in the national public utilities and several SMEs used to operate in very limited local markets, both traditionally protected by the state, risk becoming further depressed and marginalised if their needs for adjustment and requalification are not adequately met. A deep analysis of the case of Argentina shows clearly that a rapid process of opening and liberalizing the economy transferred capital (both international and national) to the non-market companies operating public utilities in a monopolistic context, and crowded out small firms, which were under competitive pressure by international competitors (Chudnovsky, 1996).

Therefore, the risk involves the management of an exceptional transition phase characterised by growing unemployment, while the active and autonomous role of the State in the economy is reduced.

Most of the countries have clearly understood the problems and have initiated policies to accompany the process of opening and liberalising of the internal market with large-scale efforts to promote investment. Additionally, increasing attention is being paid to the problems of adapting internal production to international standards.

The Tunisian government has, for example, set up a vast programme of "Mise à Niveau", whose objective is to adapt and prepare Tunisian industry for international competition and for progressive integration with the EU. The problem of "mise à niveau" involves not only the manufacturing industries themselves, but it also affects the services offered by private enterprises and the public system. Therefore, reorganisation must progressively involve the whole economic structure of the country.

Emerging countries show, with only a few exceptions, that one of the main difficulties encountered by companies in this phase is the complexity and inefficiency of public administration. The main effect of this situation is that there is very limited mobility between a formal sector of micro-industries and a vast informal sector comprised of very small firms that have no incentive to emerge from the so-called "informal economy".

The subject of the informal economy deserves further consideration. An important policy for the consolidation of systems of SMEs regards an attempt to make a large part of the informal activities more "formal". Apart from the aspects of tax and regulation evasion, the development of a vast informal economy can become a barrier to development, since it generates interpersonal and inter-group dynamics, often on the verge of being illegal, that are not subject to any kind of control and that are often alternatives to the relationships that the government intends to regulate in order to open and modernise the economy of the country. In several transition-market economies this is a growing up problem. Various governments have repeatedly tried to drastically reduce the informal economy.

Several experiences have demonstrated that a policy of consolidation of the industrial clusters of SMEs requires a gradual, but steady action to recuperate and formalise informal activity, through an ad hoc simplification of the regulatory procedures, a functional taxation system, and measures of technical support allowing this activity to be consolidated and inserted permanently into the sector of formal activity.

In almost all these countries agencies have been set up to attract and encourage investment, benefits initially being made available only to foreign operators, and later extended to include national operators.

Moreover, in the majority of cases the main means of investment support, including that of SMEs, have been the creation of Free Zones or "new urban communities", which offer simplified administrative mechanisms, numerous tax exemptions and easier access to banking services.

Similar cases, experimented in several parts of the world such as in China, Egypt, Tunisia, and Mexico, demonstrate that the creation of zones, and therefore of companies functioning under a special regime, can be catalysts for development only if they become the nodes of development networks that extend throughout the country, acting as areas of practical experimentation which is then generalised to companies throughout the country. The risk is that these free zones become areas out of the national regulation system, having their own evolutionary pathway, which are not able to rejoin the rest of the country, and therefore, simply accepting a process of breaking off from the society.

In any case the European Community testifies that the most difficult aspect of economic integration is not the management of the tariff rebate, but is the process of institutional harmonization and the quality improvement of the bureaucratic efficiency.

6. Promotion of New Entrepreneurship and Financial Problems

In most of both developed and developing countries, a major problem is given by the possibility to accelerate the start-up of new companies operating in new industries and capable to compete internationally. In those countries having a very advanced corporate governance, like the United States, financial markets provided instruments which are able to select and promote new companies. Venture capital companies, guarantee funds and a very active scouting by merchant banks define a very positive environment, which has the final advantage of a rich capital market. In several other also developed countries there are different circuits; in France, Italy, Germany, Japan there are different corporate governance models, with banking playing a different role. In several countries government has to develop incentives to stimulate new enterprises, because the capital market is not working properly.

Nevertheless, these actions for SMEs are useful if they also act on the entrepreneurs themselves and if they allow new social actors to become entrepreneurs in order to widen the number, quality and experience of enterprises. It is therefore also necessary to set up cultural actions for the promotion of "doing business" as a form of self-realisation, not only economic, but also personal and social. Promoting models of small enterprise compatible with open competition is useful not only with respect to the creation of new enterprise, but may also favour the transition of the vast informal sector, that is often characterised by traditional business forms, towards more structured forms able to work toward development.

In this context, maximum attention must be given to young people and women. In Europe, these are the two principal categories that contribute to so-called long-term unemployment; in fact, also in all the emerging countries, these are increasingly young people and women with an intermediate education, who have difficulty finding adequate employment in the informal sector or in traditional industries.

On the other hand, by encouraging the entry of young people and women into the production system, in both manufacturing and services linked to production, existing situations can be changed and bridges can be created between the various parts of national system of production. For example, Morocco has introduced simplified credit lines for the young promoters of new businesses and for the employment of young people.

The experiences launched by many international organisations in this field demonstrates the need to encourage the affirmation of some highly successful cases in which young people and women have set up their own autonomous activities, in order to be able to show that these projects are feasible and to procure examples of experiences that can be reproduced in other contexts. In these cases, however, the development of intermediate support structures should be favoured in order to transform individual cases into generalizeable methodologies to be applied, for example, to associations of young entrepreneurs or associations of women entrepreneurs. Algeria among the developing countries provides a good example of the latter.

An Italian law, law 44/1986, creating an agency for young entrepreneurs promotion, is based on the conviction that young people do not set up new businesses because they lack access to support structures with experience and ability to guide them. The goal of this initiative is to provide the young entrepreneur with a tutor to assist him in launching his new activity. This experience is also useful for entrepreneurs who intend to radically improve their professional experience. However, it is well known that owners of small businesses rarely accept minority partners who dictate how they should run their business. In Europe the development of private venture capitalists or of public structures providing similar services often encounter distrust among entrepreneurs, who are accustomed to planning and operating on their own.

The EU has developed various programmes on start-up pilot schemes and Seed Capital programmes (Commission, 1995, 1996b).

The considerations made above tend to clash with a financial system that has not yet shown itself capable of supporting the process of transformation and modernisation outlined for the next few years and that, in particular, has not yet given adequate support to the process of SME development.

In fact, almost each developing country has tried to compensate for the shortage, and in many cases the absence, of financial institutions principally oriented towards responding to the needs of SMEs by activating specific lines of credit and favouring the creation of guarantee funds.

In several cases, government created national banks and financial institutions allowing credit access to small enterprises, such as the Credit Guarantee Corporation in Egypt, or the various funds operating in Morocco, such as FOPRODI and FONAPRA. In India there is the Small Industries Development Bank of India-SIDBI, established in 1990 as a subsidiary of the Industrial Development Bank of India. It is the principal financial institution for promotion, financing and development of small scale industries, and it coordinates the functions of other institutions engaged in similar activities throughout India.

For these institutions, international organisations have set up supporting initiatives essentially designed to develop the financial sector as a whole. However, it would be opportune to address these interventions to designing financial packages, specifically directed towards the problems of SMEs. These would also encourage forms of association between companies in different countries, and encourage long-term joint ventures, gradually developed through progressive integration based on transnational projects.

7. Innovation, Education and Basic Infrastructures

In the particular case of SMEs it should be remembered that, in small enterprises, the most qualified managerial functions tend to coincide with the entrepreneurial figures or their family members, so that, in the first place, attention needs to be devoted to the education of entrepreneurs themselves, their heirs, to young people and to women who wish to become entrepreneurs. Above all, training should not only be strictly linked to production itself, but should also include professional training in entrepreneurship. For this purpose local training programs should be combined with the possibility of exchanges with similar institutions in other countries and with in-house training courses given by companies in industrialised countries.

Various EU programs are specially devoted to this issue, like COMETT, EUROTECNET, LEONARDO. These programmes introduce young people into enterprises in other countries so that they may learn techniques and organisational methods which can be later adapted to their businesses in their countries of origin (Commission, 1995).

The development of a dialogue between enterprises and the educational system nevertheless risks being limited to short-term needs if relationships with basic research are not also included. Educational systems are still very differentiated throughout the world for both teaching organization and linkage with the production system.

A comparative analysis of the educational structures of developed countries reveals a complex situation, with very different levels of schooling, education expenditure and educational organisation (OECD, 1992). This situation is enormously differentiated in the developing and transition-market economies. For example, it should be remembered that in countries like Egypt and Algeria, the rate of illiteracy reaches almost 50% and that—in these countries as in most countries of developing—the rate of illiteracy among women is extremely high.

The universities' structures themselves also vary considerably from country to country. However, they are generally well respected. In Israel, in particular, there is a structure consisting of universities that are very highly regarded by the international scientific community. In Cyprus university courses have only recently been established, although they are quickly acquiring a good reputation. The Palestinian Authority only acquired control of the educational system in 1994.

In almost all the other countries a consolidated university system exists, with various universities generally considered to be quite good, especially in the more traditional sectors, such as medicine and engineering, which traditionally attract many students because they are considered to guarantee "good" careers.

In many countries a system of technical schools and training centres is also present and aims to provide training more directly connected to the world of production. Similar programs subsidised by international institutions and the cooperative efforts of various industrialised countries are by now widespread and provide training schemes directed at tackling highly specific problems. These programs also work on the restructuring of professional training centres, on the development of training courses for adults, on education for the creation of cooperatives, on the reorganisation of technical schools and on teacher training.

However, there is a general sense of dissatisfaction with the fragility of the relationship between the educational system, in particular universities, and companies, especially small enterprises. At the same time there is a growing number of young people with educational levels so high that they are unable to find suitable jobs and, almost universally, companies complain that the shortage of qualified personnel is one of the most serious constraints to their development.

These problems are not limited to any particular area. All over the world the organisation of the educational system is being put into question, reproposing the need to intensify relations between companies, universities and scientific research.

In many developing countries central organisations for research already exist; for example, the Royal Scientific Society of Jordan, founded in 1970, that now employs around 600 researchers in 30 labs, working on a variety of research projects. In Brasil there exist several universities strongly connected with the local development authorities.

With this respect the major problem is nowadays the reorganization of the national innovation system in the past socialist countries, which used to have different structures for reasearch (the national academies for research), for teaching (the universities), and for R&D activities (the research centres depending from the central administration).

The possibility of establishing an applied research structure, which is not directly connected to the actual demands of individual enterprises, appears to be an essential element in guaranteeing that the national innovative system of the country will be able to make long term plans, and will be able to participate in the international exchange of technology without having to assume a passive role.

In any case, the spread of innovation to the entire production and administrative system of these countries remains a fundamental problem and, therefore, concerns not only the nucleus of enterprises already directing their activity towards the international market, but also all the enterprises, including SMEs, that together shape the structure of the production system in the country. In this phase of expansion, it is essential for the range of intermediate institutional organisations— associations, service centres, NGOs, etc.—to operate as nodes in an information network connecting enterprises, schools, universities and research centres, and providing entrepreneurs with a simple, friendly introduction to the innovation system.

There is a final set of problems that is vital to the development of SMEs—the state of physical infrastructure and public services, or utilities. SMEs may grow if "externalities" are such that individual firms do not have to bear all the costs of production alone but can rely on production factors available in the community. SMEs are the parties hardest hit by inadequate, or non-existent, public services, just as they are heavily disadvantaged by a physical infrastructure that does not allow them to carry out their activities with continuity and certainty.

In this context the perspective of market globalization implies a considerable effort of "mise à niveau" not only on the part of individual enterprises but also of the countries' infrastructural systems. Infrastructure linked to communications, and in particular to telecommunications, becomes particularly essential for the effective insertion of regions and groups of firms in the global economy.

The development of the so-called Information Society has allowed for the creation of long-distance production and commercial relationships, but these connections must be stable and reliable in order to become stabilising and permanent factors in company development. For example, the relocation of production, even to remote areas, especially in the clothing sector, is becoming increasingly frequent. However, high quality production requires careful control of production quality and variety, that the parent company needs to be able to monitor continuously, especially if production is designed for distribution on the world market.

It is evident that the development of local abilities, skills and the need for good and, above all, reliable infrastructure is absolutely essential to a strategy of stable and constant development.

The principal physical infrastructures required by companies are urban structures, which have often been degraded by processes of accelerated and uncontrolled urban development. In some cases, such as in Casablanca, there has been large scale intervention, in the form of the widespread housing construction. In other cases, such as in Egypt, new areas have been built relatively distant from the capital city. These problems of urban congestion not only negatively affect the cost of industrial areas, but also the possibility of setting up relationships of trust that link small enterprises and that may form the necessary conditions for the development of production complementarities vital to the creation of SME clusters.

8. Some Final Remarks

SMEs are important not only because they constitute a large proportion of national production in the developing countries, just as in highly industrialized countries, but also because the goal of encouraging the development of SMEs entails an examination of how the whole economic and administrative structure of a country effectively encourages growth. SMEs grow if the whole system of the country is oriented towards growth.

As far as enterprises are concerned, it should be noted that, two separate subsystems may be created within the same country, one for enterprises that are concentrated in local production and localised market relationships but that provide the majority of jobs, and one for enterprises that are part of a system of international relationships, that do not diminish the unemployment problems of the country to any great extent, but which develop product innovations, and compete with foreign enterprises in technical terms and organisational models.

The risk is that the two groups of enterprises do not communicate with each other, creating a dualistic economy and a broken society. Proper network policies for linking SMEs operating in different contexts and searching for complementarity can work as a bridge between different parts of the economy in the stage of accelerating globalization.

The object of industrial policy is not only to stimulate individual capacity, but also to networking those individual capacities in the social and economic fabric of society, to build a governance system that could be the basis for a sustainble social development.

Note

1. In 1993 there 17 million of these SMEs in the European Community (after 1993 European Union), but ther only 12,000 large enterprises, with more than 500 employees. For every 1,000 inhabitants there are almost 50 enterprises. In the period 1987-1992 SMEs increased by 2,5%. 67 million jobs were provided by SMEs in 1993; 2.6 million new jobs with respect 1988. Among these 68 million

jobs, about 30 million are provided by micro firms having less than 10 employees. These data are provided by the European Observatory for SMEs, Second Annual Report, 1994, p. 9—10.

References

Acs, Z.J. and D.B. Audretsch 1990. *Innovation and Small Firms*, Cambridge, Mass. MIT Press.

Bianchi, P. 1996. *Euro-Mediterranean Parnership and SME Development:Towards Shared Growth Thorough Complementarity.* Proceeding of the Workshop on the Development of Small and Medium Size Enterprises, Milan, June 4-5-6.

————— 1997. *Industrial Policies and Economic Integration. Learning from European Experiences.* London: Routledge.

Chudnovsky, D. et al. 1996. *Los Limites de la Apertura. Liberalizaciòn, Reestructuraciòn Productiva y Medio Ambient.* Buenos Aires: CENIT-Alianza Editorial.

Commission of the EU 1995. *Report on the Coordination of Activities in Favour of SMEs and the Craft Sector.* Brussels.

Commission of the EC 1996. *Maximising European SMEs Full Potential for Employment, Growth and Competitiveness.* Proposal for a Council Decision on the III Multiannual Programme for SMEs in the EU 1997-2000), Bruxelles.

Commission of the EC 1996b. *The First Action Plan for Innovation in Europe. Innovation for Growth and Employment.* Brussels, 20 Novembre.

Cossentino, F., F. Pyke and W. Sengerberger 1997. "Local and Regional Response to Global Pressure: the Case of Italy and its Industrial Districts", *International Institute for Labour Studies*, Research Series, 103, Geneva.

European Observatory for SMEs 1994. *Second Annual Report by European Network for SMEs Research.* Brussels.

G7 Group 1995. *Information Society Conference.* Executive Summary, Brussels, 25-26 February. G8 Group 1997. *Confronting Global and Financial Challenges.* Denver Summit Statement by Seven, 21 June, and Communique, 22 June Denver.

Kosakoff, B. 1993. *El desafio de la Competitividad. La Industria Argentina en Trasformacion.* Buenos Aires: CEPAL Alianza Editorial.

OECD 1992. *Education at a Glance.* Paris.

12 REGIONAL PATHS OF INSTITUTIONAL ANCHORING IN THE GLOBAL ECONOMY. THE CASE OF THE NORTH-EAST OF ENGLAND AND ARAGÓN

Arnoud Lagendijk

Introduction

Drawing on recent developments in the literature on spatial-industrial networking, governance and regional industrial policy, this chapter will discuss changes in industrial policy and business support at the regional level. Over the last decade, regions, to use the expression of Hay (1994, p. 1), have become "strategic sites of economic intervention". Regions are seen as the sites where, by the mobilisation of internal resources and the creation of "customised spaces" for external investors, clusters of related firms and support organisations can be created able to compete in an increasingly global market place. Throughout the developed world, tendencies can be observed towards regionalisation of industrial policy and the creation of regional institutional capacity to facilitate local processes of networking and clustering.

The empowering of regions will be elucidated here applying an institutional perspective. The core argument of the chapter is that the role of institutional capacity and the salience of the region in creating economic competitiveness should be seen at the cross-roads of two processes of change: (1) the move towards a "networked economy" characterised by core-ring structures, and (2) associative tendencies in the regional institutional structures leading to new forms of territorial governance. In doing so, a perspective emerges which tries to understand regional development as a complex and articulated process of positioning in the global economy, and which focuses on the institutional capacity underpinning this process. The policy implications of such a perspective are that new initiatives should go beyond attracting and "embedding" foreign investments and support to SMEs, and develop more integrative sector or cluster based initiatives that take account of the positioning of the regional economy in global value chains. The perspective will be applied to recent developments in Aragón and the North-East of England. The case studies will focus, in particular, on how the institutional systems have evolved and to what extent they support more strategic approaches towards regional industrial policy.

The chapter is structured in six parts. Section one presents the institutional perspective and explains the approach followed in the study. Section two and three discuss the emergence of the "networked economy" and new governance structures along industrial and territorial lines. These two lines are brought together in Section four with an orientation on the development of peripheral regions. Section five presents the case study results, followed by the conclusions in the last section.

1. Parallel Shifts in the Organization of Industrial and Territorial Systems

Scholars have addressed recent changes in industrial and territorial development by invoking concepts of networking and "governance". On the one hand, students in the field of industrial geography have shifted their attention from the spatial conditions of industrial location to the role of the geographical environment or "milieus" in the growth of local industrial agglomerations (Malmberg et al., 1996; Lagendijk, 1997).

With more emphasis on inter-firm networking and the organizational characteristics of industrial agglomerations, spatial economic development is increasingly caught in terms of networks, production systems, industrial districts, clusters, and regional innovation systems (Cooke and Morgan, 1993). Regional policy, accordingly, is seen in the context of the evolution of the governance of industrial development rather than the provision of spatial incentives.

Writers in the field of regional geography and political theory, on the other hand, have developed their perspective on regional industrial policy from the changes perceived in the nature and role of government at different spatial levels. Originally, this literature was grafted onto a conventional political science model. Following the stages of policy design, implementation and evaluation, such a model was used to examine discrete policy areas, such as land use planning, infrastructural projects, local employment and training schemes, and investment subsidies. The move to a more entrepreneurial approach in regional policy, with emphasis on close interaction between public and private partners and a much greater variety in the kind of supply-side measures undertaken to promote economic development, has changed this approach. Research is increasingly focusing on the institutional and organizational underpinning of regional policy formation, which includes the role of not only public and semi-public organization, but also business associations, chambers of commerce, educational organizations, etc., and the formal and informal networks between them. This literature has also been inspired by the trends towards regionalization of core policy areas which has taken place throughout Europe, and the impact of European policy and programmes on the shaping of regional policy and its institutional underpinning. The result is the emergence of a territorial governance approach as the basis for a new conceptualization of the local state and its position in both local and supra-regional socio-economic networks (Hay, 1994).

The parallel shift towards a governance approach in industrial and political geography should be seen within the context of wider economic and political developments associated with the transition from a "Fordist", commodity based era of production to a system based on "Schumpeterian" competition in which *innovative capabilities* play a dominant role. From an industrial dimension, the governance perspective is part of what is seen as the emergence of a "networked economy" (Harrison, 1994). Firms derive their competitiveness from their position in more or less decentralized industrial systems that combine the innovative and productive capabilities of related firms and organizations. Sectors, or to use other fashionable terms, filières, industrial clusters, value chains, are thus seen as essential sites of political economy (Hollingsworth et al., 1994). Within political science, the rise of the governance approach is associated with the move from a concern with political modes to social modes of economic coordination (Jessop, 1995). Because such modes of coordination are based on an intensive process of networking and institution building between business, public organizations and other social partners, regions, rather than nations, are seen as the appropriate strategic sites of coordination. The role of proximity in the shaping of common identities, norms and values, the sharing of information and the setting of common goals and principles play an important role in this resurgence of the region. The result is one of the paradoxes of current processes of economic change: increased global economic integration is reviving the position of the region in shaping economic competitiveness.

An institutional approach to regional industrial policy, accordingly, should be situated at the interface between industrial and spatial modes of governance, that is, in particular, at the intersections of industrial filières and regional socio-economic systems. One of the problems in describing and analysing industrial and spatial modes of economic coordination is the great variation in governance structures and processes between different sectors and regions. Indeed, the development of governance structures should be seen as an ongoing process of customization and adaptation rather than the move towards new types of coordination models (Heinze and Schmid, 1994). In most cases, the effectiveness and success of governance structures depends on striking the right balance between the capacity to change and the stability of the underlying routines of communication, decision making and action. An institutional approach can help to describe the main characteristics of governance structures in terms of its underlying routines, patterns of behaviour and impact on business behaviour. Within the context of regional development, the key challenge is to describe and analyse the interfaces between industrial networks and chains on the one hand, and the networks governing the creation of business support and industrial policy on the other.

One of the core messages of this chapter is that networking is not seen as intrinsically good. Much of the literature on regional development and policy has heralded the concept of networking both as a crucial element in the creation of innovative capacity and as the way forward to establish new forms of regional industrial policy. As will be shown below, this concept of networking has been associated with the *embedding* of business activity in the local economy, and with associative models in regional policy making. Networking will here be conceived much more from a political economy perspective, in which the impact of networking processes is seen as dependent on the power relations and strategies which characterise the agents involved. In this context, networks are regarded devices of manipulations and controlling processes of competition as much as structures in which new capabilities can be created and coordinated between independent agents.

While a thorough analysis of such networks and their institutional set-up requires ideally a highly sophisticated methodology, the present study only allowed for a rather pragmatic and narrower approach. The object of analysis is a description of the position of and the relationships between organizations involved in the setting of regional industrial policy and business support, assisted by general observations about the kind of routines and cultures underpinning organizational behaviour and institutional change. The analysis focuses on the intermediate regional organizations, such as economic development and promotion agencies, local business association, branch federations, and training agencies. Such organizations form part both of wider industrial networks, underpinning the development of supply chains, alliances and networks at regional, national and international level, and of the local socio-political networks aiming at local economic development. While organizational bridges admittedly form just one element, they are seen here as an important window on the complex interaction between industrial and territorial trajectories.

The next two sections will discuss the two main dimensions of governance distinguished so far, industrial and territorial, placed within the context of regional development. After that, they will be brought together and be applied to the case study of two peripheral regions.

2. The Role of Industrial Governance at the Regional Level

From an industrial perspective, the emergence or "revival" of the region as a strategic site of economic development and policy has been related to fundamental changes in the organization of industrial production. These changes are generally seen against the background of the trends towards decentralization of production, towards an increased importance of inter-firm relationships, and the orientation on "core-activities". To understand the move towards a more decentralized organization of production and its perceived link with spatial agglomeration, initially inspiration was sought in the revival of transaction costs economics. More recently, the general trend has been to subscribe to a more social view of economic activities, with a strong emphasis on the role of networking and the importance of governance structures (Lagendijk, 1997). Within this perspective, however, a bifurcation may be observed between two bodies of literature which differ sharply in their interpretations of the nature and virtues of decentralized production. The two views are labelled here as the "romantic" and "critical" view.

A romantic view of the revival of regional economies

One view that has had a great impact on thinking about the revival of regional economies stresses the role of entrepreneurship and increased workers participation in creating new forms of localised innovation and competitiveness . Backed by studies on the development of industrial districts and on the alleged success of small firms in creating employment, writers such as Sabel (Sabel, 1995) and Brusco (1995) have expounded a highly romantic view on the nature of the new Post-Fordist, flexible economy (Ernste, 1994). The basis for this romantic view is the concept of the "integral economy", characterised by the social integration of production and conception, and the integration of highly demanding customers and specialist suppliers along the filière, as a major source of creativity and innovation. The integral economy is one in which the relational structure is dominated, to use Hirschman's terminology, by voice and loyalty rather than "exit". The community, as the bearer of new forms of social interaction and identity, and not the company is the basis of economic development and competitiveness. The integral economy is driven, in particular, by small firms deeply embedded in local socio-economic networks. The integral economy will be born in a community "in which people are linked by the bonds of a shared history and values, where specific institutions work to the benefit of people and where codes of behaviour, lifestyles, employment patterns and expectations are inextricably implicated in productive activity" (Brusco, 1995, p. 6). Apart from supporting a high degree of flexibility and creativity, and hence success in the global economy such institutions and codes will secure that everybody will be able to participate in the integral economy. Because of its social embedding, economic benefits derived from the regions competitive position will thus be spread throughout the community.

From different sides, the idea of the integral economy, and related concepts such as "innovative milieu" have incurred considerable criticism. Storper (1995) summarises some of the main arguments on empirical grounds. There is too much focus on the role of SMEs, on success cases embodying extreme cases of localization, on market niches, and, particularly in the evidence on industrial districts, on traditional sectors. From a conceptual perspective, what is clear is that the industrial district and milieu approaches have given much insight into the role socio-economic networks and local institutions can play in supporting local industrial dynamics and competitiveness. However, in doing so, it has adopted a rather crude view of the external position of the regional economy. What is most surprising is the way industrial district advocates have tended to play down the specific role of large firms, especially multinationals, in shaping local economic development, arguing that their establishments will follow the same logic of developments and spatial embedding as local firms (Malmberg, et al., 1996). The long-standing literature on how firm-specific advantages of multi-plant firms affect their home and host territories, especially with respect to resource development and market access

(Dunning 1992; Humbert 1994), thus seems to be refuted. To contradict this myth of pervasive local embeddedness, evidence on recent developments in the Italian industrial districts actually shows how important the role of larger firms can be and how they often impose substantial changes on the local organization of production (Harrison, 1994; Bianchi, 1994). In some cases, this has even induced trends towards disintegration of local networks or the move to stronger tiering, and thus produce a reality far removed from the utopian picture of the integral economy.

Towards a critical response of the locally embedded economy

The "romantic view" emphasises flexibilization, innovation and demand differentiation as the drivers of new forms of localised industrial governance. The critical view takes, in contrast, a different starting point. While technological and organizational aspects play a fundamental role in the emergence of the "networked economy", the driving factor is the changing nature and level of competition, and the way this has changed the strategic behaviour of firms. Increased competitive pressures, combined with the trend towards more market differentiation, have forced firms to become leaner at the production and administrative side, while they tend to devote more resources to management and the development of financial and marketing competencies. Indeed, as Auerbach (1988) explains in much detail, there is a two-way relationship between the more volatile market environment that arose in the 1970s, and a rise in managerial and organizational competencies throughout the developed world. Following an institutional approach to economic change, Auerbach endorses the notion that the rising importance of management cannot be explained just in terms of its contribution to efficiency. What is essential is how management changed the organization of businesses, improving its dynamic responsiveness to market challenges, and how it manipulated the market and the wider environment in which it operated, in order to preserve market share.

Rising management competencies thus have not only transformed the internal organization of the firms, they have also reshaped the nature of the markets and filières in which businesses operate. "Leaner" firms depend more on the production and design capabilities of suppliers, on the services offered by consultancies and financial institutions to upgrade their own performance, and on more distinctive customer relations. So managing the network around the firm is a crucial aspect of business growth and survival. The position of firms within filières has become a more complex and multifaceted matter, which has underpinned the emergence of a more "organized" market (Eliasson, 1989; Beije and Groenewegen, 1992). Firms now have to manage and secure their position in the filière by engaging in a whole range of sophisticated strategies. This may involve managing collaborative manufacturing and innovation, supply chain management, joining supplier clubs, acquiring certifications from organizations such as the ISO and particular customer awards such as Ford Q1. Indeed, as for instance recent developments in the automotive supply chains show, suppliers are now involved in lengthy so-called "inquiries" which are launched as part of the conception of new models by car producers. Price, rather than a signalling devices, has become a critical target of management and inter-firm coordination. One of the paradoxes of the "organized market" is that cost reduction capacity and reputation, rather than price as such, are vital elements in the market positioning process. In essence, this reflects a transition from a commodity to a capability-based market organization.

Because of this emergence of this positioning game, competition has become more network or group based (Gomes-Casseres, 1994). In many lines of production and services, firms are increasingly engaged in collective "projects" as part of team-based competition strategies (Powell and Smith-Doerr, 1994). Such projects, which may involve a new final product, the application of a new technology or marketing strategy, or the transformation of a supply chain, reflect the need for regular, coordinated upgrading of products and processes in times of ever shorter product cycles and increased product differentiation. An essential management task in the "networked economy" is thus the development of a positional strategy. Firms need to identify the production chains or distribution channels they want to be part of, and the creation of an image and reputation as attractive and capable project partners. While processes of learning and innovation are essential for business survival, their parameters are defined by the strategic direction of the firm in the wide network it is operating.

Industrial governance at the regional level: core-ring, hubs-and-spokes

Harrison (1994) has used this more critical perspective on industrial governance to challenge the romantic story of revitalised industrial agglomerations. In Harrison's perspective, most of the businesses and industrial systems that dominate the economy are characterised by a "core-ring" structure. Power, and the way is contested, play an important role in the networked economy (Eccles and Nohria, 1992). As marketing and technology gatekeepers, large firms can control access to networks they play a dominant position in. Power is concentrated in the hands of the managers of the large corporations, but production is organized in a decentralized way, with ring organizations being controlled by core organization. Such control should not be read as simple exploitation, but as a complex relationship. Core firms are not just after the complementary technology or production capacity, but after engaging the ring firms in a process of co-development, while maintaining strong, although often negotiated, cost-reduction pressures.

There are, of course, large differences in production systems, and the prevalence of "core-ring" structures does not exclude the fact that groups of SMEs, at least temporarily, may gain market share without being part of oligopolistic structures dominated by large firms (Storper and Harrison, 1991). Nevertheless, what this critical perspective reveals is that the development of regional economies cannot be seen separate from the role of large core firms. The case of industrial districts in Italy has already been discussed, while other success models, such as Silicon Valley, have always been dependent on the role of larger firms. He thus concludes: "Everywhere in the world, we can now find examples of a shift away from agglomerated, fragmented, systematically powerful, mainly small firm production systems to core-ring systems-some agglomerated and some dispersed, but commonly organized around powerful lead firms" (Harrison, 1994, p.147).

In Europe, the process of economic integration is particularly seen as environment for further industrial concentration and creating "core-ring" structures across Europe than for the widespread growth of new industrial agglomerations, as corroborated by the unprecedented wave of mergers and take-overs which has characterised the continent over the last decades. This process represents a further tying-in and subjugation of localities to European and global networks, through the operations and linkages of large firms: "corporate activity is increasingly being articulated on a European-wide scale, with local fortunes more or less tightly locked into this process of economic integration" (Amin and Malmberg, 1992, p. 407). However, the role of corporate power should not be interpreted from a hierarchical perspective, as in conventional corporate geography, but from a network perspective. Large corporations are spiders in the webs which are stretched out at different spatial levels, and which display a great variation in the interdependencies between the participating firms and organizations. What is interesting is that in this system *voice* often still plays an important role. However, rather than being a manifestation of a socially embedded production system, voice represents a management device used by core firms to control and upgrade the subordinate value chain.

Different concepts have emerged to describe regional industrial systems and the way they are linked into the global economy. Based on research in the US, some authors have recently identified a variant of an industrial agglomeration labelled the "hub-and-spoke" district, in which the hubs present large corporations or core organizations such as a university (Gray et al., 1996). "Hub-spoke-districts" are dominated and driven by the market power and strategy of large core firms rather than a local process of networking. Regions benefit from the hubs more via the impact on the local labour market and the local industrial culture than via the inter-firm linkages. Given the fact that these "hubs" embody a vital, and in most cases sustainable, connection between the local and global economy "hub-and-spoke" districts are seen as in many ways superior than conventional industrial districts.

The idea advanced here, in summary, is that the "networked economy" is a highly complex world, in which economic fortunes depend on the particular properties and trajectories of business and supporting organizations and how these are positioned in larger networks and supply chains. Regional economic prosperity thus depends on a whole range of actions which underpin the position of regional economies in different international chains of production, or, to use the words of Hay (1995, p.389), on the "ability of local economies to construct complementary modes of insertion within national and supra-national economic dynamics". To gain more insight into how such ability is created, the discussion will now turn to the issue of territorial governance.

3. The Development of Territorial Governance

The new forms of regional policy emerging over the last decades can, to a large extent, be related to the image of the changed context and nature of production as sketched before. The shift towards a supply-side, capability-oriented approach has triggered a whole set of initiatives, which vary from business-level benchmarking and support for exporting etc., to the development of sector or "cluster" focused strategies (Enright, 1994). The concept of networking and the aspiration to build trust in the local economy has led to the emergence of brokering services and specialised support geared to business networks or clusters (Rosenfeld, 1996). All these initiatives represent a strong drive to adopt "hands-on" approaches that respond effectively to the needs and possibilities of particular businesses to improve their position in external markets and filières. The result has been a heterodox economic policy framework, which is more context-sensitive, production systems oriented and based on ongoing adjustment capacities (Storper and Scott, 1995). "Hands-on" approaches also reflect the fact that, given the absence of clear development models and methods, and the variation in challenges local businesses are facing, there needs to be scope for experimentation. Not only are different types of projects tried out in specific areas, also the whole institutional setting of policy-making is often considered as being subject to constant change.

Towards an associative model of regional industrial policy

Not only the contents and objectives of regional industrial policy have changed, however, but also the institutional basis of regional policy itself. The general context for change has been a change from the "developmental" to "entrepreneurial" models of policy-making (Amin and Malmberg, 1992). This has been accompanied by a shift in the locus of policy making from government to more decentralized governance systems. The responsibility for the development and provision of particular policy issues has often been handed over to (semi) private organizations, such as regional development agencies that are in charge of strategic planning issues. The most pro-active and successful of these organizations are generally embedded in wider networks with other social partners, either at the associative level, such as Chambers of Commerce, business associations, unions, community organizations, etc. or individual organizations such as large firms and key local business and public figures. Regional industrial policy itself, accordingly, has become a product of an articulated governance structure, which can be described as an associative model of regional policy making (Cooke, 1995).

The emergence of the entrepreneurial models of spatial governance is the outcome of a complex process, which can be seen as both a "push from below" and "pull from above". The push from below refers to the emergence of "growth coalitions" at the local level, which underpinned the processes of regional institution building. In the regions which now have become the models of the revived industrial agglomerations, an important drive to associative governance models was the capacity to exploit the new possibilities created by the shift towards a more flexible, network-based economy. One of the most articulated concepts to explain this collective capacity is Putnam's (1993) "social capital" which emphasises the role of civic engagement, collaboration and the tradition of associational life. In other regions, associative tendencies have often been related to the impact of negative phenomena such as economic downturns and industrial crisis, which triggered the need to formulate a regional response to industrial decline and rising unemployment. In these cases, regions often had to undergo a process of breaking down regressive, but powerful coalitions before new governance structures could be built to steer the process of industrial restructuring (Bianchi and Miller, 1994). In many cases, regional governance structures have evolved around the success of agencies in attracting foreign investment (Cooke, 1995).

The "pull from above" stems from the changes in the national and international context of regional policy. Many national governments have devolved some part of the responsibility of industrial policy to regional levels, notably supply-side instruments such as infrastructural development, business support and employment programmes; there have also been radical changes in the way regional policy is funded. Mimicking changes in the business world, national governments and international organizations such as the EU have moved from a redistributive model of budget allocation to a project-based, "challenge" culture, in which funding is obtained through competitive bidding. Funding conditions often require the creation of partnerships between private and public bodies, and, in the case of some EU initiatives, links with organizations in other member states. It has even been suggested that the provision of structural funds should be made contingent on the existence of regional collaborative networks among firms, chambers of commerce, research institutes and other interest groups (Rhodes, 1995).

Some authors have gone at great lengths to stress the positive aspects of the regional associative model and to promote it as a way to come to a creating more effective forms and organization of regional industrial policy and development. Sabel (1992), for instance, argues that, through the creation of trust, and the integration of social partners, a kind of "community capitalism" can be created with the capacity to resolve problems and create appropriate standards of conduct at the community level. From a more historical perspective, Putnam (1993) stresses the fact that horizontal networking will create an institutional basis underpinning principles of solidarity and collective responsibility. Hirst (1994), in his work on associative democracy, believes that effective coordination can be secured by a system of open communication in a regionalised, decentralized governance system supported by a minimal state. So the essence of the associative model as allegedly developed in industrial districts and agglomerations is the blending of political, social and business "voices" fostering the development of a flexible, innovative, well integrated production system. That is, in line with the idea of the integral economy, industrial and territorial governance structures have in effect become one and the same.

A critical view of the associative tendencies in regional governance

Other authors have challenged the positive premises of the associative movement. Initially, critics were wary of the move towards and impact of an "entrepreneurial" stance in regional industrial policy. This was seen as ineffective and detrimental particularly from a cohesion perspective. Amin and Malmberg (1992, p. 413) speak of a new local "boosterism", generating the "horrifying prospects of becoming the playing field for a thousand-and-one different and fragmenting entrepreneurial ventures, bound together by nothing more than the profit-seeking adventurism of the private sector". Regions would engage in a competitive race in which they would all try, in a "boilerplate" fashion, to copy the models represented by what are seen as the success regions, inducing institutional competition and interregional poaching (Storper and Scott, 1995). Rather than targeting development, entrepreneurial drives would primarily induce regions to sell themselves as attractive places for external investors and visitors: "entrepreneurial cities and regions, (...) are engaging in frenzied construction of science centres, recreational theme parks and conference centres and organizing urban spectacles in an attempt to strengthen their position in the race for the global dollar, yen or ECU investment" (Dunford and Kafkalas, 1992). What is particularly challenged in the optimistic accounts mentioned above is the one-sided emphasis on the virtues of associational life. Amin (1996, p. 327), for instance, remarks about Putnam's view on the merits of civic engagement that it underestimates the significance of social contestation: "It presents a kind of paradise on earth, with citizen, state and economic networks intertwined in civilised harmony and mutual regard".

It has been relatively easy for the critical view to repudiate the optimist associative approach; however, it has found it more difficult to come up with a convincing alternative model. Accepting that Keynesian and corporatist models are too rigid to address current economic problems (Amin and Hausner, 1997), a search has gone on for structures which involve the participation of intermediate organizations, but which can deal with a range of critical governance questions. Crucial issues are: How can the accountability of decentralized governance systems, and legitimacy of their action be secured (Hay, 1994; Batt, 1994). How can it be prevented that such systems fall prey to the interests of the most powerful, most aggressive groups in the local community (Amin, 1996)? How can it be avoided that such systems start to act as "regressive" (Bianchi and Miller, 1994), or poorly coordinated coalitions that lack the capacity to reform?

The answer to these questions is that associative structures need to be subjected to some form of regulation and evaluation that are neither fully centralist nor just spontaneous. With respect to evaluation, Sabel (1994) indicated that there was need for "monitoring" the development of individual projects and of the wider evolution of regional institutional settings, to facilitate institutional learning. Such "learning by monitoring" should be organized in an accountable, democratic way, facilitating the establishing of new institutions as well as, which is often more difficult, the abolishment of old ones. Sabel also points out that "monitoring" should not be just listening to firms, but that a wider representation is required. The role of the state should thus not be minimal or "lean", as for instance Hirst (1994) and other associational writers advocate, but "reflexive" (Amin, 1996). A reflexive state is one which accepts and empowers new forms of governance, but which keeps its role as central arbitrator for transparent and democratic control of institutional change.

A country which has had much experience with institutional development at the sub-national level, and where much has been written about this topic, is Germany. Heinze and Schmid (1994), for instance, observe the development of new forms of "meso-corporatism" at the Länder level. With reference to Sabel's "learning by monitoring", these institutional forms are seen as applying "weak" regulatory instruments in the context of customised governance structures to improve the supply side of the economy and manage processes of structural change. One tendency in "meso-corporatism" is that it is increasingly forged on a alliance between business and the state, while the role of unions and other social interest group tends to be more marginalised. To counter this development, Batt (1994) advocates the creation of regional development agencies (RDAs) as the "institutional expression of regional political networks". As central moderators and facilitators, such agencies should act as a pivot in regional negotiation and mobilising networks to establish a co-operative and consensus based framework for industrial policy. How this should be organized in practice is however difficult to say. One suggestion is that, as part of a commitment to full representation of all social partners, RDAs should organize "round tables" and regional conferences to secure democratic control and address problems of inclusion and exclusion (Ache, 1997).

A last point that can be made here is that some of the more idealistic interpretations of the strengths of regional associative governance overlook the role of the central state in determining the scope and resources of regional governance. The ability of regions to develop substantive industrial policy and action depends on the kind and depth of policy areas devolved, and the size and nature of funding attached. Some authors have even argued that, rather than as a way to improve the policy effectiveness, devolution has presented a way for national governments to wash regional problems, and expenses off their hands (Alonso, 1996; Grabher, 1995). This means that national governments, as well as bodies such as the European Commission, have often given little guidance to the process of local institution building, and have paid insufficient attention to questions of accountability and problems of interregional competition and poaching alluded to before. The creation of competitive funding regimes has not been very helpful either in this respect. Many local agencies have become trapped in a constant search for new, fashionable projects, which face the danger of losing support before they can demonstrate their value. Funding conditions and the "competitive bidding" culture also compel them to orchestrate a constantly changing map of partnerships and policy alliances (Garmise et al., 1995). The result is that, parallel to developments in business sector, regional organizations have to invest in a kind of Machiavellian strategies to prove their value in the world of project execution and management, rather than in developing regional development strategies.

4. Institutional Capacity for Inserting Peripheral Regions in Global Filières

The discussion so far can be summarised in three points. First, institutional capacity is *generated* within the context of regional governance structures. Such structures emerge from associative tendencies between regional institutions, which should, to be sustainable, be guided by some system of democratic monitoring and control. Second, against the background of a trend towards a more global and networked economy, the core *objective* of institutional capacity is to improve the position of the regional economy in international filières. A key objective of institutional capacity is to generate adequate responses to changes in industrial governance at different spatial levels. This may involve assisting the creation of local networks, as well as support to the positioning of local firms in external networks and supply chains. *Positioning*, finally, should be interpreted as a multifaceted process. It refers to the acquisition of the right capabilities, reputation and routes of access to match the requirements of network partners, particularly those of dominating "gatekeeper firms".

The development of institutional capacity has been discussed here against the background of a changing nature and setting of regional industrial policy. It can be argued that the role of regional policy will differ according to the type of region. In core regions, which already have strong positions in international filière, there will be less incentives to develop the kind of institutional strategies alluded to here than in peripheral regions. However, the most backward regions, on the other hand, lack the essential ingredients to play a more than a marginal role in the international economy. So the best test ground for the creation of institutional capacity can be found in intermediate regions, e.g. peripheral regions with an industrial past. In particular, such regions may provide suitable environments for experimentation with new institutional settings and various types of policy initiatives targeted on upgrading the industrial base. The two regions to be analysed here, the North-East of England and Aragón, belong to this category.

While it is common in the literature to define regions in core-periphery terms, it is important to note that thinking about peripherality has changed significantly in recent times. In the heydays of "Fordism", peripherality was associated largely with a specialization in routine activities requiring simple, standardised inputs, notably low skilled labour, as part of firm-controlled spatial divisions of labour. In many industries, in addition, peripheral areas were used by multinational firms to extend the life of obsolete designs and capital goods (Lagendijk, 1993). The trends to more globally integrated markets and production chains, with higher demands of quality and flexibility, has reduced or even eradicated the differences in the style of organization of production between core and peripheral regions. The recent establishment of state-of-the-art car assembly and component plants in Latin America and backward areas of SE Asia has by some authors even been interpreted as a sign of the end of peripherality (Sabel, 1995). Here a more modest view will be advocated, which draws on the core-ring concept mentioned before. Peripheral areas still house the more routine and lower "value added" activities, but this should be seen more from a network perspective. Both through relationships between local firms and external customers, and through the local establishments of foreign plants, peripheral economies are now more tightly integrated in global filières and their drives to higher quality, agreed regular price reductions, shorter product cycles etc. This theme will be further explored in the case studies.

5. Two Case Studies of Regional Industrial Policy

Aragón and the North-East of England both occupy peripheral positions in the European economy. Both have gone through a period of industrial crisis and decline, although they still display above average shares of industrial production. The North-East of England was once one of the most industrialised regions in Europe, which lost a large part of its industries, notably in heavy metal production, shipbuilding and mining, in the post-war period. Aragón, in Northeast Spain, has had a modest industrial development, with a specialization in metal production, which was lost in the 1960s and 1970s. Forming part of a larger research focusing on regions with a strong industrial presence (in particular, automotive production), these regions have been chosen for several reasons. They are of comparable size in population (over 1 million), they have some degree of regional identity, and they have both recently gone through a process of strengthening the role of local institutions.

In both the North-East and Aragón the development of regional industrial policy and business support has evolved along two dimensions: (1) attracting foreign investments, and (2) the development of indigenous firms, notably SMEs. The first strategy has been prominent in the North-East for more than a decade, and has resulted in a strong inflow of foreign investors, e.g. Nissan, Samsung, Fujitsu and Siemens (although the latter's state-of-the-art chip plant, considered as a jewel in the "investment crown" when it opened two years ago, is now bound to close)In Aragón, the foreign investment strategy has been historically weak but recently obtained major priority. The presence of major firms such as Samsung, Siemens and Nissan in the North-East, and Opel in Aragón played an important role in shaping local agents' perception of the role of foreign investment in improving the regional economy, for instance by using existing investments for further external promotion of the region, presenting foreign plants as examples of best practices in management, quality control, just-in-time, etc. and the development of supply chains and specific sector or cluster initiatives.

Specific interests in the development of SMEs, on the other hand, stem from the perception that the indigenous sectors are presently underperforming and may be contain vital growth potentials once certain hurdles are overcome. In both regions, the poor performance of indigenous firms is attributed to two core factors. First, the lack of entrepreneurial spirit causing a low level of business start-ups and a low propensity to pick up and develop new technologies. Second, the absence of a culture of trust and collaboration, which could form the basis of networking process which could support processes of specialization in a kind of "industrial district" fashion. This awareness has encouraged business support agencies to develop different agendas to assist local firms, varying from direct support to start-ups, improvement of skills, management, marketing, etc. to more elaborate attempt to encourage inter-firm networking.

Institution building and the attraction of foreign investment

While the major themes and objectives of regional industrial policy are broadly similar, the institutional setting in which policies and initiatives develop varies widely between the two regions. In Aragón, industrial policy is primarily a responsibility of the regional government (DGA), although many programmes are duplicated at other spatial levels (councils, districts, and provinces). The DGA acquired basic competencies from Madrid in 1984 (health, education, environment, housing, industry, and agricultural reform), and became more focused on economic support in 1988. The recent territorial reform (1997) in Spain has completed the devolution process, with a greater local responsibility for economic affairs. The DGA forms a spider in a web of regional agencies, in which the other main centres of control are the local banks, the University, the local Business Federation (CREA), the Chamber of Commerce and the banks (Fig. 2). The North-East, on the other hand, lacks a regional government, and has even gone through a period in which the position of local government has weakened. The main trend since the early 80s has been to transfer responsibilities from local authorities to semi-private organizations that operate as little "platoons" from central government (Hay, 1994). The result has been a complex map of institutional linkages, in which the key role is played by the local offices of central government (GONE), the Training and Enterprise Councils (TECs) and the Northern Development Company (NDC). Although the local authorities are represented in the latter, their role has increasingly been marginalised.

Apart from the politics of devolution and central control, institutional developments have been shaped by the availability of funds. Aragón was so unfortunate to have its 1988 regional product just above the eligibility limit for Objective One, which some commentators attribute to the presence of Opel. Only some parts of Zaragoza can claim Objective Two funding, while most rural areas are eligible under 5b. More dramatic is the fact that due to overspending and a persistent economic crisis in the late 80s-early 90s, accumulating debts forced the DGA to reduce its support to regional development (Bandres, 1994; Mené Marcén ,1994). One of the consequences was a cut in the budgets for regional technology centres. Together with the political turmoil that followed the budget crisis, the regional capacity to develop and implement a coherent and effective form of regional industrial policy was thwarted. General poor economic performance, moreover, undermined the position of support organizations issuing soft loans (such as ARAVAL). Only organizations with a wider funding basis and a strong business support, such as the organizations in the agricultural sector (e.g., DAYSA), could sustain their level of service.

In contrast, the North-East has been able to draw from a variety of funds, due to its eligibility for various regeneration programmes of the central government, and, most importantly, for Objective Two funding from the EU. The latter has facilitated the establishment of a whole range of regional agencies focused on technology transfer (RTC North, the local Innovation Relay Centre), informatics, technological support for specific sectors and business support. EU funding has also obliged the region to establish a central coordinating mechanism, the Programme Monitoring Committee, with a regional representation (Figure 12.1).

A third factor that has influenced local institution building is the need to respond to industrial crisis. A long history of industrial decline and rising chronic unemployment triggered the establishment of the Northern Development Company (NDC) in 1987. Inspired by the successes of the Welsh Development Agency and Scottish Enterprise in attracting foreign investments, NDCs initial mandate was to promote the region as an attractive location for foreign investors. With the help of NDCs promotional activities, the North-East, with less than 5% of the national GDP, managed to attract more than 10% of total foreign investments into the UK between 1990 and 1993. More recently, it has broadened its activities towards "after-care" services, such as aid to business expansion, and training and through the establishment of the Regional Procurement Office. In Aragón, the awareness of crisis and structural economic problems is of a more recent date. Looking in particular at experiences in Catalonia, the DGA established a regional development agency, the *Instituto Aragonés de Fomento* (IAF) (1990) with the mandate to develop and implement a strategic plan for the region. Apart from its strategic function, IAF has initiated several programmes, such as EXPORTA, an export promoting programme aimed at SMEs, and PRIMA, a quality awareness and enhancement programme. Compared with its peers in Spain, however, IAF is strongly limited in staff and other resources it can draw on.

A crucial factor in explaining the different paths of institutional developments is the difference in the attitudes and perceptions in the economic development and support sector in the two regions. This is

Figure 12.1 A regional network in North-East of England

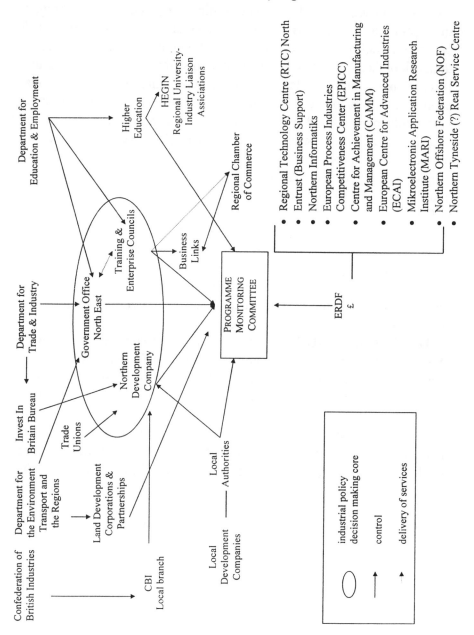

partly the result of different histories of institutional development, but also as a consequence of different administrative cultures. In Aragón, the operations of the DGA and related organizations are very much based on a traditional civil service routine and mentality. The territorial dimension, i.e. questions of the spatial distribution of resources and income, plays an important role in general thinking about regional economic development. This culture translates into an orientation on thoroughly planned and phased initiatives, which are limited in scope and size, and are not always seen as adequately targeted on meeting the needs of the local economy (Serrano Sanz and Bandres Moline, 1992).

In response, the business federation has made a case for a better coordination of regional industrial policy, by strengthening the role of IAF and by a stronger orientation on business needs. According to Hidalgo Arribas (1995), the region should "get its act together" in attracting foreign investments, in which it has been lagging behind most other Spanish and European regions (Gil and Suarez, 1995). There has also been a call for aligning the educational system more to the needs of business by raising the level of vocational training and apprenticeships (CREA, 1994).

The behaviour of NDC and other development corporations shows a sharp contrast with the Aragonese case. NDC, in particular, is constantly involved in gathering intelligence about foreign investors from outside and inside the region. This information is used to manipulate investment behaviour, to broker between firms inside and outside the region, and to influence local decision making processes that may affect business investments. One key element of the intelligence is to understanding how local firms can meet the requirements for becoming preferred suppliers to larger firms, by acquiring the right certifications and being aware of the consultation procedures applied by customers. NDC's approach contrasts sharply with the information strategy in Aragón, which relies more on statistical data and strategic input from consultancies (see, for instance, Instituto Aragonés de Fomento, 1992). NDC is driven by the need to stay at the competitive edge of regional promotion for external investors, by accommodating to the requirements of foreign investors which are looking for sites, and increasingly, those which are established in the region. As a consequence, NDC is part of process in which foreign investors such as Nissan and Siemens are reconfiguring part of the local institutional structure. While NDC is important as a general point of contact, more specific relationships have been developed with organizations such as the TECs, the universities, colleges, and technology centres, for instance to address issues of education and training.

Such issues are not only in the interests of the foreign companies. The presence of flagships such as Nissan and Siemens provide local organizations with a trigger and focus to engage in new projects and build new partnerships. In Aragón such tendencies have only emerged recently, and have so far only had a limited effect. Opel and a groups of other foreign investors have been involved in the development and running of the IAF Quality programme (PRIMA), in which they act as levers to bring local firms on board. Opel has also been a founder of a national training centre in the region, to meet training needs in the automotive and wider manufacturing sector.

Sector and cluster oriented initiatives have become more important in both regions. Already in 1987, a joint NDC-DTI initiative led to the establishment of the Northern Offshore Federation (NOF). With 450 members, and a wide range of support and lobby activities, the NOF has become a model sector organization in the UK. NDC itself, moreover, is presently being reorganized along sectoral lines, focusing on automotive, off-shore, food and drink, and electronics. At present, NDC is in the process of setting up a new sectoral organization targeted on the food and drink industry along the lines of the NOF. Although the recent sectoral orientation flows out of the endeavours to embed foreign investors more deeply in local economic networks, its remit is wider. With foreign investors and large firms as crucial hubs, the objective is to improve the integration of the local production system as a whole, in a "hubs and spokes" fashion. On the one hand, this involves improving the performance of the overall system, by the exchange of information and brokering between firms, and the detection of "holes" in existing supply chains for which new investments may be sought. On the other hand, sectoral organizations or divisions can detect the needs of associated firms in terms of training needs, infrastructure, inputs from other industries, etc. and liase with other organizations to develop adequate supply strategies. In Aragón, IAF, has started developing a stronger orientation, although so far this has mainly involved the indigenous sector, such as the wine sector and olive production.

Support to SMEs

Attracting and embedding foreign investors in the regional economy can offer an important basis for developing an entrepreneurial approach in regional development, and for developing thinking in terms of supply chains and networking. Because of the nature of the targets involved, i.e. large powerful firms, there is a strong incentive to mobilise resources around one focal organization, such as NDC or IAF, which negotiates with business and other local organizations. Looking at the support to SMEs, a much more diffuse pattern emerges. Support to SMEs has been an area where national and European programmes and funding opportunities have erupted. On the whole, the initiatives developed show little cohesion; they strongly differ in objectives, approaches, target groups, life span etc. In the UK, moreover, many initiatives have been organized at the national level with little attention for specific regional context. In Spain, initiatives have proliferated at all levels of government: local, regional and national level. An internal survey of the National Institute for SME Support (IMPI) in the early 90s came to an estimation of around 1000 initiatives, most of which had very limited resources.

Within this context, it is not unsurprising that observers see the support to SMEs in Aragón and the North-East as fragmented and unstable. In Aragón, support to SMEs is seen as strongly deficient (Hidalgo Arribas, 1995). There have been some successful ventures, such as the establishment of the CEEIA, the European Business and Innovation Centre in Aragón. The CEEIA is a business centre for business start-up environment, offering a wide range of on-site business services, and limited business venture capital, to firms located on the site. In general however, business support initiatives seem to be too limited in scope and not be able to reach firms effectively. In the North-East, one of the problems is that, due to a proliferation of initiatives and an increased competition between agencies to find "customers" to sign up for new projects, a kind of "support fatigue" has emerged. The funding regime has created an environment that cultivates short-term initiatives, and a tendency for individuals in the system to invent constantly new initiatives for which they can take credit. In particular support for innovation has been fragmented, organizationally and financially, between various organizations (Charles, 1996). Like in Aragón, agencies find it increasingly difficult to "reach" the local firms, that is, to match the right needs and find firms prepared to spend time on the project. While changes in the organization of business support and the inflow of funding has allowed the development of institutional capacity, it has so far lacked the coordination and strategic insight to really transform the local business system.

As a response to this situation, the last years have seen calls for and the first steps towards a more coordinated approach. In Aragón, the calls stem in particular from the local business federation (Hidalgo Arribas, 1995), which urges the local government to pay much more attention to local firms. It is hoped that, with the budget crisis under control and a trend towards more co-operation between IAF, sector organizations and the local and regional business federations, a more effective economic strategy will emerge. In the late 80s, three sectoral technology support organizations were established, for wood, metal, and agro-industrial production, but lack of funding has meant that these have not come off the ground.

In the North-East, on the other hand, coordination has been driven by changing conditions in the provision of structural funds and by the impact of EU programmes such as STRIDE. Under the supervision of the local DTI office, STRIDE was used to pull together various strands of technology support within a common framework, North East Technology Support (NETS) (Charles, 1996). NETS provided a platform for a more strategic approach for technology support to SMEs, and played an integrative role in the applications for ERDF funding in the early 90s. Other bottom-up attempts to more coordinated approaches in technology support have led to the establishment of various sector-oriented organizations funded under ERDF (see Figure 12.1).

Because of these initiatives, a trend may be observed in business support away from the short-term, "individualistic" approach. Rather than paying lip-service to the concepts of industrial districts and networking, as has been the general case so far, real attempts are made to bring local firms together and to foster collaboration and the creation of trust. Several organizations in the North-East (Tyneside TEC, Entrust, North Tyneside Real Service Centre) have developed *business clustering* projects, in which firms form associations to undertake collective marketing and develop other joint strategies. The North Tyneside Real Service Centre has been particularly successful in bringing SMEs together and in setting an example for other organizations in the region and beyond. Through the "clusters", in particular, SMEs have been able to explore new markets and to acquire a better position in international markets. The main problem for such a more "sustainable" approach is to secure long-term funding. In Aragón, IAF has recently invoked the help of a Catalonian consultancy to develop cluster initiatives.

Questions of monitoring and democratic control

There is no doubt that the institutional development in both regions has provided an environment for experimentation, both at the level of projects and the broader institutional setting. How is this development accounted for, how is it monitored? At this point, the two regions differ considerably. In Aragón, the fact that IAF and other organizations depend on an elected regional government provides a formal basis for democratic control. Little has been done, however, in the planning and implementation of regional strategies to involve the social partners on a more direct basis. Aragón has a regional platform with representatives from the government, business federations, and unions, which regularly produces a comprehensive, but non-binding three-party document on local economic development (*see Acuerdo de Desarrollo Económico y Social de Aragón, 1996*). Ironically, IAF commissioned Anderson Consultants to produce, with help of foreign agencies such as Scottish Enterprise and NOMISMA, its own strategy document (Instituto Aragonés de Fomento, 1992). However impressive this effort has been, the lack of embedding of the plan in regional socio-economic has, in the view of other social partners, resulted in a poor follow-up in terms of implementation and assessment. Not unsurprisingly, one of the core recommendations in the three-party document is a stronger representation of business and labour in regional policy.

The North-East lacks a democratically elected regional government. It even lacks a central body that is in charge of developing a regional development strategy. In the future, this might change with the expected founding of a Regional Development Agency and the possible creation of a Regional Assembly. At present, however, control and monitoring reside, largely in an ad-hoc manner, in a peculiar combination of the localised control of the central state (notably through Government Office North-East and the TECs), the funding regime imposed by ERDF (see Figure 1 and the various platforms where different organizations and social partners meet. Business interests are in general well presented, although often more through direct contact than through representative organizations. Local authorities and unions play a more marginal role. The Universities offer some reflection on regional developments in the region. They are represented at various platforms and have developed a strong interest in regional issues over the last years (Goddard et al., 1994). On the whole, however, developments are driven largely by the capacity of particular agents to acquire funding, and to establish a reputation on the grounds of immediate successes gained in either attracting investments or bringing local firms on board of particular projects.

As part of the development of a regional economic strategy in the context of wider structure of territorial governance, therefore, one of the key tasks of a future RDA will be to develop a proper way of assessing, and to some extent guiding, projects, partnerships and new institutional ventures. The challenge will be to impose some kind of democratic control and monitoring while keeping open the possibilities for agencies to be engaged in different types of networks and projects. For both the regions discussed, this presents a considerable challenge.

6. Conclusion

While the importance of the (supra)national institutional context and constraints cannot be ignored, regions have become more important in the development of new approaches to industrial policy and business support. This chapter has attempted to analyse the empowerment of regions from an institutional perspective, taking as a starting point the intersection between industrial and territorial forms of governance. On the one hand, the industrial dimension of governance has been described in terms of an increasingly "networked" economy, in which it is vital for firms to develop the right strategies and capabilities to position themselves in networks and production chains at different spatial levels. On the other hand, the territorial dimension has been understood in terms of the associative tendencies at the regional level that has triggered collaboration between business and a variety of local organizations. In this context, regional institutional capacity was seen as the ability of local governance structures to support local networking processes, which may for instance revolve around major hubs created by external investors, and to assist local firms in acquiring positions in international filières.

In coming to this conclusion, a critical stance has been taken towards the issue of the social integration of production at the regional level. Rather than emphasising the virtues of social embedding of production in local socio-economic networks, the role of institutional capacity is seen in the context of increased competitive pressure, and the development of "ring-core" networks at different spatial levels. This is not a denial of the importance of institutional strategies to improve voice, create joint understanding, and trust between local firms. However, rather than seeing the latter as working towards a kind of industrial district model along the line of the "integral economy" philosophy, it is part of an articulated strategy to strengthen the capacity of local firms, either individually or jointly, to relate to international filières. The context of this process is not the image of a "milieu", not a smooth blending of local economic networks in a harmonious social and political system, although such patterns may appear, sporadically, in certain locations. The context is a harsher reality of tiered supply chains, of hub-and-spoke systems, of shifting coalitions of firms that try somehow to survive in an increasingly competitive economy.

At the level of the region, one suggestion was that the competitive challenges could be met by a kind of "high road" approach aiming at mobilising internal resources rather than importing growth from outside. Harrison (1994, p. 181), in his view of a "high road" strategy, gives the following recommendation: "the trick is to move the whole system above a threshold—to achieve a critical mass of participants committed to collaborative production relations and a long-term planning horizon". The evidence in this chapter has indeed indicated some moves from attracting foreign investments towards growth strategies, notably in the form of sector and cluster strategies. What has been argued too is that a path towards upgrading and learning should be underpinned by a profound and shared understanding of where the regional economy is moving, that is, a concept of the strategic positioning of the regional economy in global production chains. It will also require an understanding of how "high road" strategies can be developed without constraining the growth opportunities of other regions.

What an institutional analysis can throw light on is, besides the institutional analysis of firms, networks, filières shown in other chapters of this book, is the particular routines and paths developed at the regional level which influence the position of local business in the wider economy. This chapter has sketched some of the ideas that may underpin such an approach. There is, undoubtedly, need for a more rigorous definition of concepts and methodologies. There is also need for further unpacking of the complex relationships between different levels of analysis, which will require a further dialogue with institutional conception of the national and global economy. For the sake of regional prosperity in Europe and beyond, however, this clearly provides a challenge that should be further explored.

References

Ache, P. 1997. "Forum Mittelstand — An Initiative to Create Innovative Milieus amongst SME in NW?" *Paper* presented to the EUNIT International Conference on Industry, Lisbon: Innovation and Territory, March.

Alonso, W. 1996. "On the Tension between Regional and Industrial policies", *International Regional Science Review* 19 (1&2), 79—83.

Amin, A. 1996. "Beyond Associative Democracy", *New Political Economy* 1 (3), 309—333.

Amin, A. and J. Hausner 1997. "Introduction". In *Beyond Market and Hierarchy: Interactive Governance and Social Complexity*, A. Amin and J. Hausner eds., Aldershot: Edward Elgar, 1—31.

Amin, A. and A. Malmberg 1992. "Competing Structural and Institutional Influences on the Geography of Production in Europe", *Environment and Planning* (A) 24 (3), 401—416.

Auerbach, P. 1988. *Competition. The Economics of Industrial Change*. Oxford: Blackwell.

Bandres, E. 1994. "Diez Años de Hacienda Autónomica en Aragón", *Papeles de la Economía Española* 59, 259—266.

Batt, H.-L. 1994. *Kooperative regionale Industriepolitik. Prozessuales und Institutionelles Regieren am Beispiel von Fünf Regionalen Entwicklungsgesellschaften in der Bundesrepubik Deutschland.* Frankfurt am Main: Peter Lang.

Beije, P.R. and J. Groenewegen 1992. "A Network Analysis of Markets", *Journal of Economic Issues* 26 (1), 87—114.

Bianchi, G. 1994. "Requiem for the Third Italy? Spatial Systems of Small Firms and Multi-regional Differentiation of the Italian Development", *Paper* presented at the 34th European Congress of the Regional Science Association, August 23—26, Groningen, The Netherlands.

Bianchi, P. and L. Miller 1994. *Innovation, Collective Action and Endogenous Growth: an Essay on Institutions and Structural Change.* Mimeo: University of Bologna.

Brusco, S. 1995. "Global Systems and Local Systems", *Paper* presented to the OECD International Seminar on Local Small Firms and Job Creation, Paris, 12 June.

Charles, D.R. 1996. "Building Technology Networks in the North East", *CURDS Working Paper*.

Cooke, P. 1995. "Introduction". In *The Rise of the Rustbelt*, P. Cooke ed. London: UCL Press, 1—19.

Cooke, P. and K. Morgan 1993. "The Network Paradigm — New Departures in Corporate and Regional-Development", *Environment and Planning D-Society & Space* 11 (5), 543—564.

CREA 1994. *Adecuación des Sistema Educativo a las Necesidades del Desarrollo Regional.* Zaragoza: Confederación Regional Empresearios de Aragón.

Dunford, M. and G. Kafkalas 1992. "The Global-Local Interplay, Corporate Geographies and Spatial Development Strategies in Europe". In *Cities and Regions in the New Europe: the Global-Local Interplay and Spatial Development Strategies.* M. Dunford and G. Kafkalas eds. London: Belhaven, 3—38.

Dunning, J.H. 1992. "The Competitive Advantage of Countries and the Activities of Transnational Corporations." *Transnational Corporations* (February), 135—168.

Eccles, R.G. and N. Nohria eds. 1992. *Networks and Organizations: Structure, Forms and Action.* Boston MA.: Harvard Business School .

Eliasson, G. 1989. "The Dynamics of Supply and Economic Growth — How Industrial Knowledge Accumulation Drives a Path-Dependent Economic Process". In *Industrial Dynamics: Technological, Organizational and Structural Changes in Industries and Firms* B. Carlsson ed. Dordrecht: Kluwer Academic, 21—54.

Enright, M.J. 1994. "Regional Clusters and Economic Development: a Research Agenda", *Paper* presented to a Conference on Regional Clusters and Business Networks, New Brunswick, Canada: Fredericton, 18—20 November 1993.

Ernste, H. 1994. "Changing Rationality of Regional Development", *Paper* presented at the 34th European Congress of the Regional Science Association, August 23—26, Groningen, The Netherlands.

Garmise, S.O., K. Morgan and G. Rees 1995. "Networks and Local Economic Development: Evidence from Southeast Wales and the West of England", *Paper* presented for the ESRC Conference on Local Governance, Exeter, 19—20 Septembre.

Gil, A. and C. Suarez 1995. "Las Empresas Industriales Aragonesas en 1992: Analisis de los Aspectos Estratégicos". In *Actas del III Congreso de Economia en Aragón* (:) 489—507.

Goddard, J., D. Charles, A. Pike, G. Potts and D. Bradley 1994. *Universities and Communities.* Newcastle upon Tyne: University of Newcastle.

Gomes-Casseres, B. 1994. "Group versus Group — How Alliance Networks Compete", *Harvard Business Review* 72 (4), 62.

Grabher, G. 1995. *The Embedded Firm: on the Socioeconomics of Industrial Networks.* London: Routledge.

Gray, M., E. Golob and A. Markusen 1996. "Big Firms, Long Arms, Wide Shoulders — the Hub-and-Spoke Industrial District in the Seattle Region", *Regional Studies* 30 (7), 651—666.

Harrison, B. 1994. *Lean and Mean. The Changing Landscape of Corporate Power in an Age of Flexibility.* New York: Basic Books.

Hay, C. 1994. "Moving and Shaking to the Rhythm of Local Economic Development: Towards a Local Schumpeterian Workfare State?" *Lancaster Working Papers in Political Economy* (Political Economy of Local Governance Series) 49, 1—18.

———— 1995. "Re-Stating the Problem of Regulation and Re-Regulating the Local State", *Economy and Society* 24 (3), 387—407.

Heinze, R.G. and J. Schmid 1994. "Industrieller Strukturwandel und die Kontingenz politischer Steuerung: Mesokorporatische Strategien im Vergleich", *SIT Working papers* 94-2, Bochum: Ruhr-Univ.

Hidalgo Arribas, M.A. 1995. *Cumbre Empresarial Aragón y el Desafío económico.* Zaragoza: Confederación Regional Empresarios de Aragón.

Hirst, P. 1994. *Associative Democracy.* Cambridge: Polity Press.

Hollingsworth, J.R., P.C. Schmitter and W. Streeck 1994. "Capitalism, Sectors, Institutions and Performance". In *Governing Capitalist Economies— Performance and Control of Economic Sectors* R.J. Hollingsworth, P.C. Schmitter and W. Streeck eds. Oxford:Oxford University Press, 3—16.

Humbert, M. 1994. "Strategic Industrial Policies in a Global Industrial System", *Review of International Political Economy* 1 (3), 445—463.

Instituto Aragonés de Fomento 1992. *The Strategic Plan for Aragón. Towards the Century XXI* (Executive Summary). Zaragoza: Gobierno de Aragón.

Jessop, B. 1995. "The Regulation Approach, Governance and Post-Fordism—Alternative Perspectives on Economic and Political-Change", *Economy and Society* 24 (3), 307—333.

Lagendijk, A. 1993. *The Internationalization of the Spanish Automobile Industry and its Regional Impact. The Emergence of a Growth Periphery*. Amsterdam: Thesis Publishers.

———— 1997. "From New Industrial Spaces to Regional Innovation Systems and Beyond. How and From Whom Should Industrial Geography Learn?", *EUNIT Discussion Paper Series* 10, 1—30.

Malmberg, A., Ö. Sölvell and I. Zander 1996. "Spatial Clustering, Local Accumulation of Knowledge and Firm Competitiveness", *Geografiska Annaler* (B) 78, 85—97.

Mené Marcén, E. 1994. *Objetivos e Instrumentos de la Política Regional: la Aplicación de la Política de Incentivos en la Comunidad Aragonesa*. Zaragoza: Gobierno de Aragón.

Powell, W.W. and L. Smith-Doerr 1994. "Networks and Economic Life". In *Handbook of Economic Sociology* M. Smelser and R. Swedberg eds. Princeton, N.J.: Princeton-Sage, 368—402.

Putnam, R. 1993. *Making Democracy Work: Civic Traditions in Modern Italy*. Princeton, N.J.: Princeton University Press.

Rhodes, M. 1995. "Regional Development and Employment in Europe's Southern and Western Peripheries". In *The Regions and the New Europe. Patterns in Core and Periphery Development* M. Rhodes ed. (European Policy Research Unit Series.) Manchester and New York: Manchester University Press, 273—328.

Rosenfeld, S.A. 1996. "Does Cooperation Enhance Competitiveness — Assessing the Impacts of Interfirm Collaboration", *Research Policy* 25 (2), 247—263.

Sabel, C.F. 1992. "Studied Trust: Building New Forms of Cooperation". In *Industrial Districts and Local Economic Regeneration* F. Pyke and W. Sengenberger eds. Geneva: International Institute for Labour Studies, 215—250.

————1994. "Learning by Monitoring". In *Handbook of Economic Sociology,* N. Smelser and R. Swedberg eds. Princeton, N.J.: Princeton-Sage, 137—165.

————1995. "Experimental Regionalism and the Dilemmas of Regional Economic Policy in Europe", *Paper* presented to the OECD

International Seminar on Lcal Small Firms and Job Creation, Paris, 1—2 June.

Serrano Sanz, J.M. and E. Bandres Moline 1992. "Aragón. Los Límites de la Euforia", *Papeles de la Economía Española* 51, 154—168.

Storper, M. 1995. "The Resurgence of Regional Economies, Ten Years Later: The Region as a Nexus of Untraded Interdependencies", *European Urban and Regional Studies* 2 (3), 191—221.

Storper, M. and B. Harrison 1991. "Flexibility, Hierarchy and Regional Development: the Changing Structure of Industrial Production Systems and their Forms of Governance in the 1990s", *Research Policy* 20, 407—422.

Storper, M. and A.J. Scott 1995. "The Wealth of Regions — Market Forces and Policy Imperatives in Local and Global Context", *Futures* 27 (5), 505—526.

13 ANYTHING NEW IN INDUSTRIAL POLICY? — MYTHS AND EMPIRICAL FACTS. THE CASE OF SOME GERMAN REGIONS

Friedhelm Hellmer, Waltraud Bruch-Krumbein and

Wolfgang Krumbein

Introduction

Times are tough for those supporting interventions through industrial policy; an obvious conclusion when taking into consideration the prevalence, even in major parts of the social democratic parties, of neo-liberal concepts. Those calling for innovation-oriented political guidance of the structural change are clearly outnumbered by their opponents who advocate market-oriented regulation.

In this chapter we will discuss the (im)possibilities of industrial policy in general and the meso economic regional policies in particular. Our analysis is based on two empirical studies[1]. The two case studies refer to two broader issues in the debate on the transition after the unification in Germany .

The first issue came about after the unification when the de-industrialization in the former East German regions (Länder) took place. Is it possible to correct those negative developments in a market economy with open borders and more or less autonomous private actors?

The second question is about the potentialities of a specific regional industrial policy as an instrument to solve the structural economic problems demonstrated in high levels of unemployment and persistently weak growth rates. These structural problems have shifted the debate from the macro to the regional level: is it possible to improve the competitiveness of regions through regional industrial policies?

In the first part of this chapter we will present two case studies that give us an insight into what really changed in Germany in the domain of regional industrial policy during the last decade. In the second part we discuss the issue why frequently propagated conceptions for intra-regional network creation (which would make industrial-political interventions easier, at least) are not materialized in reality. In the third part. we point out that the East German Länder's measures against de-industrialization (the so-called revitalization aids) can be understood from a practical policy point of view, but differ substantially from the measures advised in the more theoretical debate. In the conclusions a few provocative theoretical statements are made suggesting that the ongoing changes are far from the scope often suggested and that our empirical research does not support the claim that a new type of "post-Fordist industrial policy" is emerging.

1. Promotion of Networks in Upgrading Regions?

Regional industrial policy has gained new impetus through the discussion on the limited effectiveness of centralist interventions, as well as through the so-called industrial-district debate. Luhmann's thesis on a general non-viability of political regulation due to the increasing functional differentiation of modern societies and the operational self-containment of social systems, holds the greatest challenge for all concepts of political regulation (Luhmann, 1984, 1989). While that premise is shared or taken into account by the representatives of theory of action/institutionalism (Scharpf, 1991), as well as of enlightened systems theory (Wilke, 1992), the conclusions regarding regulative policy are different. The rejection does not refer to political regulation per se but to centralized hierarchical regulation. It is assumed that to be successful under the current social conditions, regulation must follow a decentralized, non-hierarchical functional logic.[2] Instead of the ineffective hierarchical centralist approach, a more decentralized regional type of regulation of the market is needed.

These regulative insights appeared to be further verified by economic regionalization tendencies. The debate on the so-called industrial districts centered on the issue of a "re-emergence of regional economies" (Sabel, 1989, see also Storper and Scott, 1990). It is argued that economically successful regions are characterized by more or less distinct vertical disintegration and, correspondingly, territorial integration of organizational relations or regional networks. The small-business networks of the so-called Third Italy were regarded as the prototypes of successful regional economies (Pyke, Becattini and Sengenberger, 1990).[3] In the meantime, regionalization or establishing regional networks has become one, if not the adequate answer to the socio-economic decentralization demands to be met in order to solve social problems.[4] This development is often discussed against the background of supposedly far-reaching social changes, i.e. the transition from Fordism to post-Fordism.[5]

Against this background, hopes for regional networks have given a strong impetus in Germany to the Federal states' various efforts for regionalization, although this approach seems to create quite some difficulties even in North Rhine-Westphalia, the Land which has made the best progress towards regionalization (Kemer and Löckener, 1995). With regard to the corresponding political efforts in Lower Saxony, the results tend to be equally sobering.[6] The question here is whether these modest successes in setting up regional networks are due to insufficient political implementation alone, or whether the underlying factor is a deep-rooted overestimation of the underlying economic regionalization tendencies as the basis for the development of regional networks.

Empirical evidence on regional economic cooperation[7]

As opposed to the discussions on industrial districts as the prototypes of economically successful regions characterized by well-developed cooperation relations in the form of regional networks, we will discuss in the following some findings in German Länder that show a strong continuity of long term relationships indicating that no big changes towards another type of regionalization has taken place. In our study we focused on the so-called "normal regions": not the economically prospering regions, or regions in a deep crisis, but the ones with an "average" mix of sectors.[8]

To identify economic cooperation relations, we will broadly outline the development and structure of corporate inter-organizational relationships. One dimension for defining how companies reorganize their external relations is their relationship towards suppliers. In contradiction to academic discussions[9] which often regard single sourcing as the pioneering factor, the businesses covered by our case studies follow that trend only in exceptional cases. With regard to the most important suppliers (e.g. of highly specialized components) there are no hierarchical tendencies (as assumed in a pyramidal hypothesis (with a downward shift of the cost pressure). All in all, the relationship with suppliers is marked by a high degree of continuity in the form of long-term market cooperation,[10] with prices and quality demands being the crucial factors. A certain importance is also attached to personal relations and mutual trust. This does not mean that the relations are being rearranged; instead, it reflects a long-standing tradition.

It would seem sensible to assume that the furthest-reaching changes take place in the field of streamlining, i.e. of the reduction of corporate production levels, which prove to be the interface for the direct correlation between in-house restructuring measures and changes in the supply relations. While the lean-company philosophy is well-known in almost all companies, external restructuring in the form of outsourcing internal company functions is relevant only in big enterprises. Since the great majority of the companies studied in our cases are innovative small and medium-sized businesses, outsourcing plays a comparatively small part in the overall analysis. The main reason for its modest significance to small and medium-sized businesses lies in the fact that the field of technology-intensive small and medium-sized businesses primarily contains businesses whose internal structures show many elements of a "lean company". The young businesses, in particular, have not become "lean" through comprehensive reorganization accompanied by the corresponding friction, but have been able to follow, as early as during the consolidation phase, a philosophy of creating flat hierarchies and focusing on core competencies.

Consequently, clear strategies for reducing the production range, which are connected with a reorganization of the supply relations, are only found in few large-scale companies, the number of which is below average in the regions we studied.

To sum up it can be asserted with regard to the customer/supplier relationship that the relations are not characterized by drastic changes in terms of setting up supply networks. The greatest efforts in that respect have been made in few large-scale companies that, in normal regions, are of little relevance to value added chains.

On the purchase side we can observe a prevalence of the kind of manufacturer/user relations that is regarded typical in machine tool making (with the exception of mass producers), and which is also covered by the stand "market-style cooperation". Compared to the supplier relations, the purchaser relations show a stronger tendency towards intensification, which is based on the competition parameters time, quality and service.

Within the context of our case studies and against the background of a propagated enhanced status of the regions, the crucial factor to us seems to be the spatial arrangement of the business relations we have looked at so far. From the point of view of space we found that the supplier relations are basically market-oriented, purchases are made there where technical competence is available or where the most favorable supplier is situated. Even in a close relationship, physical proximity to suppliers is less important than technical competence and price level. The spatial distribution of customers is similar, with strong national (or partly international) tendencies; to focus on regional customers is usually regarded as too risky. Even in the case of outsourcing corporate functions, this normally does not take place in the immediate vicinity. It is shown exemplarily by our empirical findings that value added chains are supra-regional, with their essential scope of action limited to the national or, if extending further mainly to the European economy. Production clusters concentrated in specific regions are not characteristic for the "normal" regions we studied.

Along with market-style cooperation, there are farther reaching forms of cooperation on the level of innovation generation. These partnership cooperations take place primarily with manufacturers of complementary products. We should also keep in mind that these forms of cooperation are by no means an entirely new phenomenon but can be found in the past as well. Noticeable from our research is at best the great number of statements confirming this kind of cooperation. The crucial factors for a successful outcome are technological competence of the partners and a high level of trust, which can only be reached through close personal relations. While technical competence is the very precondition, the success of a cooperation depends on mutual trust.

These cooperation relations are located mainly at the national level: criteria for choosing adequate partners, technical complementarities and the quality of personal contacts have priority over geographical proximity.

On the whole, we conclude that companies' relations in "normal" regions have not substantially changed into more regionalization. They are to a great extent characterized by continuous instead of sudden changes. At least regarding normal regions, it is not possible to verify that the regions have gained an enhanced status, which is all the more true for the few far reaching types of cooperations that do exist. Obviously, the national economy continues to be of the greatest relevance for economic exchange. Most of the changes take place within the scope of the innovation model regarded as typical for Germany, the strength of which is incremental innovation (the so-called diffusion oriented model, Soskice, 1996).

A second dimension of regional interaction lies where policy, economy and science intersect. Here we focus on the field of innovation generation.

All in all, the data on hand do not indicate a general trend on the part of the companies towards utilization of the broad range of technology-oriented potential existing in the regions (i.e. university and non-university research institutes, technology transfer and support centers, technology centers, innovation consulting centers). Instead, utilization and/or cooperation is limited to the occasional case, with the spatial arrangement depending on the corresponding goal, which is on the one hand the solution of specific technical problems (1) and on the other hand the diffusion of know-how and experience (2).

(1)   With regard to the solution of specific technical problems, it can
       be substantiated that the companies, when seeking to get in touch
       with a technologically competent partner, do not turn to   the
       comprehensive range of intermediary organizations which is now
       in existence. Moreover, of the small degree to which intermediary
       organizations are used in our example,[11] the concrete form of the
       cooperation depends on the function. The joint handling of
       problems, with the partners having an interdependent
       relationship, is based on cooperative interaction, the
       preconditions of which are face-to-face contacts based on mutual
       trust and a willingness to compromise and to follow the rules.
       Even though these are typical features of a network, a joint
       problem management does not take place within networks of
       pluralistic constellations, but in a partnership formed by a single
       company with a single scientific institution. The underlying
       structure is closed, initially excluding further participants.
       As stated above also in the case of technology diffusion the
       cooperation takes place on the national level. Consequently,
       physical proximity is not considered as vital for joint problem
       handling (even though it is regarded desirable by companies as it
       helps save time); here, too, technological competence is the
       prevailing criterion for choosing a partner.

(2)   Physical closeness, on the other hand, plays an important part in
       the diffusion of knowledge and experience (as well as in
       activating so-called "tacit knowledge") between public and
       private actors. In this field, there is already a number of structures
       that formally operate as associations or limited companies.

In analyzing the structures, it can be determined that the
amalgamations, instead of embracing the surrounding regions, are
geographically orientated towards larger centers where research
institutions are located. This means that there is no exchange with
companies and technology-oriented partners in the closer geographical
surroundings. Therefore, one can only speak of local or municipal
initiatives. At the interface of policy, science and economy in "normal"
regions there is no empirical proof of a new way of thinking and acting
in regional contexts, a position that is often encountered in

regionalization discussions. The constitutive element of the initiatives is project orientation, i.e. they are orientated towards a specific project that is not necessarily directly relevant for production, however. Cooperation is thus based on a common aim, the concrete output of which consists in mutually exchanging experiences and information. When taking a closer look at the details of these organizational structures, it can be said that these include a wide spectrum of public as well as private actors.[12]

Regarding the activation of so-called "tacit knowledge", there are approaches that could point into the direction of network establishment. But compared to the high value given to them in the industrial districts debate, the facts at hand, also regarding the interface of policy, science and economy, are not confirming. Here, again, there are only faint signs of anything new. All in all, the relations are characterized by continuous changes within the framework of incremental policy innovation.

Some "network-oriented" conclusions for industrial policy

The findings of a tendency towards network relations is not confirmed by our study of regions in Germany that are not typically innovative or in a phase of strong restructuring, but that have a "normal" mix of sectors. Regional networks tend to be exceptions; in the great majority of normal regions, they can be found in rudimentary forms at best. This also invalidates the conceptional hope that is based on a supposed quasi-automatic economic trend towards an "upgrading of the regions", which would result in substantially increased room to manoeuver in regional industrial policy. Even when taking into account the political level, the picture remains the same: there is little news here[13] neither in terms of inter-connections between policy and economy on the regional level. Extensive networks integrating economic and political processes (and, in addition, socio-cultural developments) seem to belong to the realm of myth.

So if no drastic changes in the economic problems of the great majority of the regions can be substantiated, it seems reasonable to assume that regional industrial policy, too, is facing the old familiar problems. While political scientists keep pointing to problems such as vertical and horizontal political inter-connection and integration of political fields, it is also important in this context to highlight the difficulties related to the structure of the participants. When assuming (as we do) that regional policy should be based on a consent reached by all significant regional actors, the results of our studies show that the fairly unsatisfactory involvement of companies in regional developments is hardly a mere coincidence. Given that the economic priorities of enterprises are on the national level, entrepreneurs could hardly be expected to have a broad interest in regional industrial policy. Since the industrial policy of the Länder is characterized by a pragmatic approach towards employers' interests, it is understandable why the Länder tend to be comparatively slow to push forward new forms of regional industrial policy (or a general regionalization policy, Kruse, 1990): neither the economic problems nor interests quoted above suggest increased regionalization efforts.

The above statements do not mean that regional industrial policy is not viable and should not be pursued at all. If the overall analysis shows that economic problems in the great majority of the regions do not correspond to frequently made assumptions, this only means for the time being that there is no such thing as an economic automatism creating an increasingly better basis for regional industrial-political efforts.[14]

Instead of taking economic "trends" as a starting point or making them the focus of hopes for efforts in regional industrial policy, our line of reasoning would be to highlight existing socio-political interests of the local districts. There seems to be powerful advantages of good inter-district cooperation in fields such as traffic, waste recycling and promotion of economic development in general.[15]

2. Revitalization-Subsidies as Industrial Policy

"Industrial policy" in the east of Germany?

With respect to the result of industrial policy in eastern Germany the situation is fairly clear: after the German unification, the East has been de-industrialized to a large degree. With just over one million, the percentage of employed persons liable to social security and working in processing industries was down at 18.7 % (as opposed to Western Germany where the percentage still amounted to at least 32.6% of all employed persons) (Bundesanstalt für Arbeit, 1997). These figures make it hard to imagine that a successful industrial policy in the broader sense of fostering industrial development had been pursued in the new Federal states.

Whereas Eastern Germany has been the subject of industrial policy on a massive scale. However, the reason for the massive intervention was not to upgrade the region through the building of networks. The political programs for the eastern part of Germany were a response to the privatization policies of the "Treuhandanstalt" (THA), the organization responsable for the transition. That those projects have not been successful, but not only politics is to blame for that. Already at an early point in the discussion,[16] there was hardly any doubt that the disastrous development in the East was largely due to the decision of a more general nature, namely to expose east German industries to the strong competition within the European Union, as if that industry was ready to face that situation. Because of that exposure without the necessary safeguards, German industries of the former centrally planned economy had no chance to develop into a strong competitive industry. What was left for politics to do was to remedy the negative consequences. There was no other choice left.[17]

However, the small room for industrial policy to manoeuver in Eastern Germany was not used to preserve a minimum of core industries. To save these cores, the Länder did initiate various projects[18]—in response to the privatization policy of the Treuhandanstalt (THA)but their success was poor as indicated by the fact that all the supporting schemes were more or less abandoned shortly after they had been introduced. Instead, government's industrial policy led to excessive funding of a few more or less spectacular large-scale projects. In the course of subsidizing the microelectronics industry in Dresden (Saxony), the THA granted in 1993 a generous start-up payment of DM125 million for the Zentrum Mikroelektronik Dresden (ZMD), the core institute of the wound-up Robotron research center. Later on, over DM1.7 billion were spent on establishing Siemens subsidiary SIMEC and AMD subsidiary FAB 30. AMD. An additional loan of the same amount was received from an international banking group, 65% of which was guaranteed for by Federal Government and Land (Wirtschaft and Markt, 1997).

The support for the Eastern German chemical industry is another example of this kind of large-scale project funding. DM30 to 35 billion was spent according to a statement in mid-1996 of a committee member of the Federal Institute for Unification-related Special Tasks (BvS)[19] (Der Spiegel 32/1996), with as much as DM9.5 billion of it being spent on subsidizing the takeover of former East Germany combinates Buna, Sächsische Olefinwerke and a part of the Leuna-Werke by the US group Dow Chemical in mid-1997 (Frankfurter Rundschau of 11/9/1995). Financing of the Eastern German chemical industry locations on such a scale can in no way be explained in an economically rational way. Two factors account for the large subsidies: first, the Federal Government had difficulties in coming up to the Chancellor's promise to preserve industrial cores, and responded by promoting "model projects"; second, the selected form of support is a continuation of Bonn's strategy to give priority (notwithstanding the usual lip service to medium-sized businesses) to large-scale projects and big companies.

For the time being, it still remains to be seen where this strategy to finance large-scale projects will lead to. The microelectronics industry in Dresden seems to make better progress than the chemical industry in Saxony-Anhalt with more investments in R&D in Dresden. Furthermore, there is indeed some interlinking between the microelectronics industry and local public research and training institutions. The chemical industry in Saxony-Anhalt, on the other hand, has four optimally equipped industrial centers which compete for a small number of investors. Research and development has been built up only on a comparatively small scale, a development which does not fit the concept of "securing industrial locations through consistent promotion of innovative pilot projects" (Kern and Voskamp, p. 289).

Another industrial-political measure designed to preserve industrial substance and/or to induce founding of new businesses, is the so-called ABS: "associations for job creation, employment and structural development". These associations should be monitored critically. While they should not be underestimated with respect to their significance for structural policy (at least in terms of qualification, area and building redevelopment as well as their function as catalyst for regional networking), they have mostly played a minor role in preserving industrial sectors and capabilities (Bruch-Krumbein and Hochmuth, 1997).

Revitalization-subsidies of the Länder: an unknown form of industrial policy

As the revitalization of collapsing enterprises was not possible, the Eastern German Länder were concentrating on saving existing industrial enterprises from bankruptcy. Almost unnoticed by the public a specific form of industrial-political intervention, the so-called restructuring subsidies,[20] was developed, which has grown into probably the most important instruments in Eastern Germany today.

That the Treuhandanstalt was closed down at the end of 1994 corresponded with the Federal Government's objective to withdraw from industrial policy, which had de facto been pursued on a massive scale, in the East of Germany.[21] This withdrawal meant that the responsibility for developing the remaining industrial basis was passed on to the Länder. Due to the THA Act, however, the Federal Government was not able to deny any kind of assistance whatsoever: the THA had been placed under the obligation to take responsibility for the respective businesses even after their privatization or re-privatization. Therefore the THA transferred to the Eastern German Länder funds amounting to DM500 million for so-called restructuring measures of former THA enterprises. These funds are to be regarded as loans repayable to the Federal Government after a period of 10 years. To guarantee non-THA businesses equal treatment, the Länder agreed to increase these funds by at least half their amount. Revitalization schemes or measures were developed in order to tackle the crucial impediments to the development of Eastern Germany's industrial plants: poor management and lack of equity capital.[22] In this way it was possible to realize, with the aid of Federal money, the industrial-political programs initiated by the Länder in 1991.

The measures to overcome these impediments consist on the one hand in providing fast and unbureaurocratic help to cure liquidity problems by means of the restructuring fund,[23] and on the other in supplying management aid either copied from existing Western German promotion programs or newly developed for Eastern Germany.[24]

The resources from the restructuring fund can be allocated in a revolving system over a period of 10 years. They are supposed to increase through loans or dormant holdings the capital resources of those small or medium-sized businesses which have no access to the usual ways of capital acquisition due to a lack of securities. Return capital as well as interest and partnership remuneration paid within the first five years may also be re-allocated if a crucial precondition is fulfilled: the respective house banks need not take part in the procedure so they are 100% exempted from liability. In that way, the instrument remains applicable in a very flexible and unbureaucratic manner. Possible losses are covered at 80% by the successor organization of the THA, the Federal Institute for Unification-related Special Tasks (BvS) and at 20% by the respective Land.

Restructuring funds are given to:

- businesses in an existence-threatening financial state which already exhausted all other support options. By drawing up a restructuring scheme it must be proven that there are "promising future prospects";
- small and medium-sized businesses to which EU guidelines on subsidies are applicable: up to 250 staff, maximum turnover DM40 million, not more than 25% ownership of one or more companies (combine clause).

It is very difficult to define the status of restructuring policy within the framework of overall industrial policy. Taking the capital flow per fund it is clear that the joint task "Improvement of Regional Economic Structures" (Gemeinschaftsaufgabe-GA) continues to be the key instrument for supporting the Eastern German economy. In 1995 and 1996, GA resources amounting to DM4.3 billion and DM6.5 billion respectively were granted to industrial enterprises in the new Länder and Berlin (East). This corresponds to a total of almost DM11 billion for 1995 and 1996 (data by Bundesamt für Wirtschaft, 1997). Compared to that amount, the restructuring fund appears to be fairly modest with

DM750 million made available in 1995 and 1996. On the other hand, there are indications that demand for resources from the restructuring fund is increasing.

While all Eastern German Länder have adjusted to the worsening situation by setting up restructuring funds, the support apparatus and the decision where to put the main emphasis differ from state to state (for details Bruch and Krumbein; Hochmuth and Ziegler, 1996). The programs and measures have been and still are subject to EU approval within the framework of subsidy control.

The programs have sharply varying ranges: while it is probably true that the respective regulative views of the regional governments were not crucial to the actual decision (on whether restructuring programs should be launched at all), they did influence to a great extent the different approaches. We believe that the most comprehensive scheme has been developed in Saxony-Anhalt, where political action is not limited to restructuring measures but also includes restructuring policies. According to the results to date, which are very contemporary however, a successful method in this context is the provision of rescue schemes: clusters of core firms in the process of being liquidated are maintained in cooperation with the trustee in order to be sold to investors. The chances of survival of these companies are then improved through well-directed area and facility management. Similar to Brandenburg and Thuringia, Saxony-Anhalt attempts to support important enterprises in trouble through minority shares.

Other significant innovations in industrial policy can also be observed in Saxony-Anhalt: in the form of an expert panel, the responsible office, the Task Force, has been integrated into the ministry of trade and commerce. That department is staffed with economists with Treuhand experience, i.e. the usual administration-oriented organization and qualification pattern has been deliberately avoided. Even consulting and related management aids (coaching) which are increasingly offered in (almost) all new Länder to tackle the obvious deficits in management are better aimed and organized here: financial assistance is only granted when the applicant is willing to receive consulting and coaching. Who is responsible for the respective consulting has not been left to chance either: a specialized institute has been commissioned to carry out that task.

A few requirements for industrial policy regarding Eastern Germany

The phase Germany's Eastern parts are currently going through may also be interpreted as a period of transition towards industrial-political normality. In view of the special conditions after the German unification, which can definitely be called historic, the Federal Government was the first to face the challenge of restructuring the GDR economy in accordance with market principles. That phase of a centralized industrial policy based largely on the actions of the Treuhandanstalt, on sponsoring large-scale projects, and on attempting to link structural and labor policies must be regarded a failure (with the exception proving the rule, here, too). The Federal Government has been successively retreating from Eastern industrial policy areas— which is by no means tantamount to a sudden total withdrawal. Instead, along with a variety of tasks in labor policy and the remaining functions of the Treuhand successor organizations, the Federal government continues to be in charge of saving what is left of old industrial structures. The latter, however, takes place within the traditional framework, with the Federal Government setting the outline conditions (incl. financial ones) and delegating the corresponding implementation tasks to the Länder.

This new political constellation (or better: the return to familiar processes and structures) and continuing economic problems have led to an increased need for action in the new "Länder", to which the ministries of trade and commerce have responded—even though in different ways—by initiating a far-reaching research and learning process. Meanwhile, even a few Western German "Länder" have come to profit from that development by adopting certain models or concepts. Another observation to be made in this context is that this increased pressure obviously helps to overcome traditional regulative barriers. And there is another indication of a transition towards industrial-political normality: in the conflict between many market economists' love of and need for order and consistency and practical furtherance of industries, it has always been the pragmatic observance of industrial interests that prevailed in Western Germany.

When considering the volume of funding spent on large-scale projects and GRW subsidizing as a benchmark, stabilization subsidies may almost be ignored—but should not be underestimated with regard to their sometimes fairly experimental methods, innovative conceptions and, in the end, possible success. It is not impossible that the policy of granting stabilization subsidies could eventually go beyond the strict limits of an emergency policy. This may be the case when the stabilization subsidies are further developed into instruments for political regulation of fundamental problems in a capitalism-bound economy. When this happens, the main targets will be to improve the financial basis of that policy, to guaranty its existence independent of economic and political cycles, and to maintain and strengthen cross-links to other political fields such as labor policy and other service oriented policies (consulting etc.).

The phase Germany's Eastern parts are currently going through may also be interpreted as a period of transition towards industrial-political "normality". After the German unification, the Federal Government was the first to face the challenge of restructuring the GDR economy in accordance with market principles. That phase of a centralized industrial policy largely based on the policy of the Treuhandanstalt, on sponsoring large-scale projects, and on attempts to link structural and labor policies, can generally be regarded a failure. The Federal Government has withdrawn from direct intervention in Eastern industrial policy areas. Instead, along with a variety of tasks in labor policy and the remaining functions of the Treuhand successor organizations, the Federal government continued to be in charge of saving what was left of old industrial structures. The latter, however, takes place within the traditional framework with the Federal Government setting the general conditions (incl. financial ones) and delegating the corresponding implementation tasks to the Länder.

3. Some Further Theoretical Ideas

In spite of their rather different subject-matters, both these examples from current industrial policy have significant common features: there are some new developments to report indeed, but their extent is much smaller than frequently expected. As far as the stabilization policy in Eastern Germany is concerned, there is an unmistakable shift towards familiar political patterns with a specific division of responsibilities between Federal Government and the Länder as well as orientation towards short-term pragmatic policies. This transition to industrial-political normality does by no means exclude innovative moments, as we see them in the orientation towards inter-sectoral, all-encompassing policies and in new flexible methods. As for regional industrial policy via network promotion (a desired discontinuity!), it does not seem to exist in any extent worth mentioning. In the majority of the German regions, the alleged trends towards an economically generated "upgrading of the regions" are most likely to be mere myths cut adrift from any empirical facts. Regional industrial policy can neither be based on new problem areas, nor can it give a new qualitative impetus as political conception; it remains limited to old conceptional schemes and instruments for regional promotion of economic development and regionalization policy which are continually open to reform.

Continuous developments can be localized, with regard to both examples, under a different aspect as well. The innovations and reformatory efforts which positively do exist follow the pattern of incremental political innovation fairly characteristic of Germany (as opposed to the US model of innovation through comprehensive qualitative breaks). The problems in the two areas we studied are well-known, too: the integration of political fields happens only partially, the structures of actors are prone to creating slowing effects, vertical and horizontal political integration is limited to a minimum, and funding proves to be insufficient. Finally, pragmatic approaches towards short-term issues and interests continue to prevail over fundamental regulative targets and objectives.

All in all we have come to the following results: even though there is always something new to report, these new elements tend to re-adjust sooner or later to the context of known contents and procedures. Vital are not qualitative breaks but continuous developments. At this point it would seem reasonable to approach a further-reaching theoretical issue: if our two studies, which are certainly not representative, paint a picture of continuous developments that contradicts common situations appraisals (or better: sentiments) proclaiming the beginning of a new era, drastic breaks, qualitatively new developments an the like, then perhaps it is the term "break", which is used extensively in social sciences to characterize the current situation[25], that needs to be reevaluated. This discrepancy at least gives reason to consider further empirical studies and theoretical research on the topic. Regarding two fields we consider especially important, we attempt to make a short thesis-like assessment which aims to contribute to a more extensive discussion.

Regarding the globalization discussions, there are frequent claims that the world economy has reached a new scale, which national policies and economies must be subordinated to[26]. We have the impression that numerous recent contributions (also within the framework of the debate on industrial locations) reflect an increasing tendency to question the term "globalization". A comprehensive new quality of globalization can hardly be substantiated. First of all, it must be stressed that the export ratios of goods and services did not regain their 1914 level until the mid-eighties (see Hoffmann, 1997). Second, the exchange of goods and services as well as direct investments are not characterized by globalization but - if at all - by triadization (HWWA 1995; Borrmann et al 1995), and third, even the multinational groups, which are without doubt the leading global actors, cannot be considered "stateless" or "footloose" enterprises (for a summary, see Krätke, 1997; Wade, 1996). These "large-scale" findings correspond to a remarkable extent with our "small-scale" empirical studies: changes do take place, but within a smaller scope and over longer periods than usually assumed by contemporary analysts: the order of the day is not "break" but "continuity". [27]

The thesis on a steeply declining autonomy of nation states is first of all supported by means of the globalization argument (which is not all too conclusive in our opinion).[28] Secondly, it is argued that the nation states are loosing regulatory authority due to a shift of such authority to the European Union. We believe that it is still too early to make final assessments in this context. It should be left to future developments to show whether or not the argument of Kohler-Koch (1996) turns out to be the right one after all: according to Kohler-Koch, there is no zero-sum game going on; instead, the very existence of the EU may put the nation state in a position to regain room to maneuver. The third and final argument regarding the autonomy of nation state theses is simply this: the undermining of the nation states' freedom of movement in the wake of any regional upgrading would presume that the later could also be proven. The contributions to the debate on where business takes place clearly indicate, as do our own studies, that enterprises currently operate not on a regional but rather on a national level and, with a slight upward trend, in the EU countries. As opposed to mainstream thinking, we believe the following conclusion currently comes closest to empirical verification: a major loss of influence of the nation state still remains to be proven. In this context, too, there are many indications of continuity and slow changes, and few signs of far-reaching sudden breaks.

Against the background of these two central conclusions,[29] we may ask: are we really on the threshold of a new era, which will overcome the globally prevailing Fordism developed since World War II in favor of a post-Fordism itself still to be exactly defined? Is it reasonable to agree to the (previously quoted) nicely phrased statement by Leborgne and Liepitz, which claims that new historic structures are presently developing from the "ruins of Fordism"? On the basis of our studies and the further-reaching considerations, we would definitely answer no. It is more likely that future developments might result in a form of neo-Fordism which, even in its terminological version, does imply changes—changes, however, within the overall framework of continuous developments. Empirical facts in both economic problem areas and industrial-political action are presently pointing to new developments rather than far-reaching historical breaks.

Notes

1. We refer to two empirical studies carried out in the years 1994 to 1997 at the Institut für Regionalforschung (Institute for Regional Research) at Göttingen University, partly in cooperation with the "Wirtschafts- und Sozialwissen-schaftliches Institut in der Hans-Böckler-Stiftung".

2. In this respect, Wilke uses the term context regulation, which means basically "reflexive decentralized regulation of the contextual conditions of all subsystems and autonomous self-regulation of the internal processes within each subsystem" (ibid. 341).

3. Meanwhile there is a large number of empirical studies available on genetically and structurally widely varying regions such as Baden-Württemberg (mechanical engineering, automotive components, textiles), Jütland (textiles, furniture, mechanical engineering), Småland (metalworking), or high technology regions like Silicon Valley, Orange County, and regions around Route 128, all of which have been subsumed to the term "industrial district". While that term has become increasingly extensive, we confine the term industrial district to networks of small and medium-sized businesses (see also Grabher 1994, p. 69), i.e. the most advanced form of vertical disintegration and territorial integration of organizational relationships.

4. This trend may also be due to the belief that it appeared to be possible to combine emancipatory prospects of man with functional requirements of economics. Regionalization became the ultimate way of social modernization (Heinze et al., 1997).

5. Since it has reached a considerable scope by now, it is not possible here to give an adequate overview on the different aspects to the debate on regulative policy (see Danielzyk and Oßenbrügge (1996)). Independent of this special theoretical variant, e.g. Mayntz (1993) assumes that "(...) networks may represent a qualitatively different type of social structure" (ibid. 44).

6. We have arrived at that assessment through a number of discussions with parties involved and by closely observing the regionalization process in Lower Saxony, all of which has shown that it has not yet been possible, apart from major breakthroughs as achieved in the token project RESON (Lompe et al., 1996), to meet the targets that were once fairly ambitious.

7. Our statements are based on a project carried out from the beginning of 1995 to the middle of 1997 within the framework of the "Arbeitsgemeinschaft Sozialwissenschaftliche Technikforschung Niedersachsen (Workgroup for Social Science Research into Technology in Lower Saxony)" under the title "Kooperation als externe Voraussetzung technisch-organisatorischer Innovation (Cooperation as external precondition for technical-organizational innovation). Sectors studied were mechanical engineering, electrical and precision-engineering/optical industries in the Lower Saxon regions of Oldenburg and Southern Lower Saxony. On the corporate level, the information is based on interviews with the

managements of businesses of all three industries. The business size varied within a scope of 50 to 1100 staff, with the emphasis on the 50- to 120-staff businesses. Approximately, the products consist of 50% customer-specific single or small-range products and of 50% standardized products with high technical standards. In addition, we talked to relevant persons from the corporate environment. All in all, we carried out 37 expert interviews on the corporate level and 34 expert interviews with persons from the corporate environment. (Hellmer et al., 1999)

8. The standardization as "normal region" serves for filling the gap the industrial district discussion left open by preferentially analyzing economically prospering or crisis-prone regions. This means that normal regions are simply the great majority of regions in Germany characterized by an "average" mixture of the sectoral economic structure. Furthermore, one of the intentions of the industrial districts-debate is taken up: to explain the reasons for economic developments—however, the "normal region" approach does not intend to give reasons for extraordinary success typical for industrial districts, its aim is rather to explain economic development along general, average lines: this refers to quantitative indicators of general economic development such as gross value added, unemployment and employment rates (the latter in its structure as well as in a temporal perspective) on state and federal level.

9. For instance, the intensive discussion on the lean production concept (Womack et al., 1991).

10. By "market cooperation" we understand any economic relationship mainly based on the market and its control mechanisms (price, contract, fixed exchange ratios).

11. See i.a. Rehfeld (o.J.); Bruch-Krumbein/Gutberger/Kollros (1995).

12. As far as the structure is concerned, the amalgamations can be better described as closed circuits, although a general openness to all sides is always stressed. The actors involved are restricted by various exclusion criteria such as formal membership that must be approved by the board of directors or the general meeting, as well as financial shareholdings.

13. We are putting the emphasis here on presenting the economic results of our studies. Yet analyzing the political level leads to similar conclusions. If at all, network creation is only to be found in small-scale projects, normally failing because of the well-known self-interest of local governments.

14. The remaining economic argument is that the regions, and certainly a few companies or industries, could be interested in enhanced regional networking if certain favorable preconditions are given. If regional networking is successful in these rather rare cases, both the region and the companies can benefit from it (which is at least one thing the industrial district debate has shown.

15. Consequently, all exemplary measures of innovative regional policy which seem to be successful at integrating different political areas (see Neumann, 1996), e.g. in Nuremberg, are not based on exploiting economic positivism but on political-administrative efforts.

16. See Priewe and Hickel 1992; Ludwig 1994; for the risks relating to financial policy, see Czada, 1995.

17. However, this did not take place either; instead, the neoliberal policy of the Federal Government and the Treuhandanstalt (THA) further accelerated the negative developments that had set in. The policy of fast privatization led to the collapse of many businesses, either during privatization or eventually some time after.

18. Namely ATLAS in Saxony, Arbeitsgruppe Industriepolitik in Saxony-Anhalt, ANKER in Mecklenburg-Western Pomerania, B-9-Modell in Berlin, ZEUS and Industriepolitischer Gesprächskreis in Brandenburg, Entwicklung Industrieller Zentren und Landesfonds in Thuringia (for details, see Nolte and Ziegler, 1994).

19. The Federal Institute for Unification-related Special Tasks (BvS) is the successor organization of the THA.

20. The following statements are based on a study carried out by the Institut für Regionalforschung at Göttingen University (IfR) and the Wirtschafts- und Sozialwissenschaftliche Institut (WSI) in the Hans-Böckler-Stiftung in the summer of 1996 (see Bruch-Krumbein W./Hochmuth E./Ziegler A., Sanierungsbeihilfen für Betriebe in den ostdeutschen Bundesländern. Eine Haandreichung für die Praxis, Göttingen und Düsseldorf 1996) and the Berlin expert conference of IfR, WSI and IG Metall on "Restructuring in Eastern Germany" of 06/05/1996.

21. According to Sturm (1991), the Treuhandanstalt was without doubt an industrial-political instrument, even though Treuhand representatives kept denying to have any tasks related to industrial or structural policy. De facto, the THA has altered industrial and regional structures to a large degree (Nägele 1994; Voskamp et al., 1993).

22. The experts do generally agree with this diagnosis (see the lectures of practicians of different institutions at the conference "Restructuring in Eastern Germany" of 6/5/1997; on problems of equity capital see Deutsche Bank 1997, and on management problems see Deutsches Institut für Wirtschaftsforschung, Institut für Weltwirtschaft an der Universität Kiel, Institut für Wirtschaftsforschung Halle, 1996). From the point of view of employers, the impediments are not so much the result of subjective deficits as of too heavy wage cost burdens, insufficient funds as well as sales problems and strong competitive pressure (see Deutsches Institut für Wirtschaftsforschung, Institut für Weltwirtschaft an der Universität Kiel, Institut für Wirtschaftsforschung Halle, 1997).

23. Other important instruments of restructuring policy are Land securities, Land holding companies, and the Holding Fund East.

24. At the expert conference "Restructuring in Eastern Germany" of 6/5/1997 it was nevertheless verified that the Federal Government has been increasingly withdrawing from financing the management aids.

25. Exemplary in this context are Leborgne/Lipietz (1994) who speak of the "Ruins of Fordism" (ibid: 109) as the starting point for future developments.

26. See et al Ohmae, 1994; 1995; Reich, 1993; Dicken, 1992; Dunning, 1993; Luttwak, 1994; Narr/ Schubert, 1994; Altvater/Mahnkopf, 1996; Thurow, 1996. It is not possible here to deal in detail with every single aspect of the different positions. The 'most advanced' globalization versions are described by Hirst/Thompson (1996) as follows: "It is widely asserted that we live in an era in which the greater part of social life is determined by global processes, in which national cultures, national economies and national borders are dissolving. Central to this perception is the notion of a rapid and recent process of economic globalization. A truly global economy is claimed to have emerged or to be in the process of emerging, in which distinct national economies and, therefore, domestic strategies of national economic management are increasingly irrelevant. The world economy has internationalized in its basic dynamics, it is dominated by uncontrollable market forces, and it has as its principal economic actors and major agents of change truly transnational corporations, that owe allegiance to no nation state and locate wherever in the global market advantages dictates." (ibid.: 1).

27. Even as regards in-house economic changes, it is becoming increasingly inappropriate to announce the 'end of mass production' (see Strutynski 1996). There has been recent talk by renowned analysts that even the industry that is exemplary in far-reaching changes—the automotive industry—"is proclaiming a

modern form of Taylorism with regard to work organization, declaring structure-preserving working-time policy the binding guideline" (Schumann/Gerst, 1997, p. 161). Also largely ignored are empirical studies of the Fraunhofer Institute for Systems and Innovation Research (ISI) in Karlsruhe (see i.a. Dreher, 1995) pointing out the small significance of new production models in Germany. Again: no break towards new forms of operation!

28. An important detail should be added: the thesis on the loss of the nation states' autonomy in interest rate policy, which belongs to the standard repertoire of contemporary analysts, does not agree with the increasing margins between interest rates between important global actors. Just take a look at the interest rate developments in, say, Switzerland, Japan, Germany and the USA! The Bundesbank pointed out in a remarkable study within the Bundesbank report (see Deutsche Bundesbank 1997) that the German interest rate only responds in the short term to sudden global market fluctuations, and that after a period of ca. half a year the long-term interest-setting factors begin to show effect.

29. There are certainly plenty of other issues to be dealt with in a comprehensive systematic analysis: ecology, the dismantling the welfare state, Keynesian economic policy, socio-cultural developments.

References

Altvater, E. and B. Mahnkopf 1996. *Grenzen der Globalisierung. Ökonomie, Ökologie und Politik in der Weltgesellschaft,* Münster.

Borrmann, A., B. Fischer, R. Jungnickel, G. Koopmann and H.-E. Scharrer 1995. *Regionalismustendenzen im Welthandel-Erschei-nungsformen, Ursachen und Bedeutung für Richtung und Struktur des internationalen Handels,* Baden-Baden.

Bruch-Krumbein, W. and E. Hochmuth 1997. *Fünf Jahre ABS-Gesellschaften. Die sächsischen Gesellschaften des Sondervermögens.* Göttingen (forthcoming).

Bruch-Krumbein, W.; E. Hochmuth and A. Ziegler 1996. *Sanierungshilfen für Betriebe in den ostdeutschen Bundesländern - eine Handreichung für die Praxis,* Göttingen, Düsseldorf.

Bruch-Krumbein, W.; J. Gutberger and H. Kollros 1995. "Wirtschaftsnahe Kooperationen zur Erschließung von Innovationspotentialen in den Regionen Lüneburg und Südniedersachsen". In *Regionale Trends. Institut für Regionalforschung* e.V. eds. Göttingen.

Bundesamt für Statistik 1997. *Statistik der Gemeinschaftsaufgabe "Verbesserung der regionalen Wirtschaftsförderung".*

Czada, R. 1995. "Der Kampf um die Finanzierung der deutschen Einheit". In *Einigung und Zerfall. Deutschland und Europa nach dem Ende des Ost-West-Konflikt.* 19. Wissenschaftlicher Kongreß der Deutschen Vereinigung für Politische Wissenschaft. Opladen.

Danielzyk, R. and J. Oßenbrügge 1996. "Lokale Handlungsspielräume zur Gestaltung internationalisierter Wirtschaftsräume — Raumentwicklung zwischen Globalisierung und Regionalisierung". In *Zeitschrift für Wirtschaftsgeographie*, Vol 1/2.

Der Spiegel 1996. *Menschenleere Projekte*, 36/1.

Deutsche Bundesbank 1997. "Die Bedeutung internationaler Einflüsse für die Zinsentwicklung am Kapitalmarkt". In *Deutsche Bundesbank Monatsbericht,* Juli.

———— 1997. "Ertragslage und Finanzierungsverhältnisse ostdeutscher Unternehmen im Jahr 1995". In *Deutsche Bundesbank Monatsbericht,* Juli.

Deutsches Institut für Wirtschaftsforschung, Institut für Weltwirtschaft an der Universität Kiel, Institut für Wirtschaftsforschung Halle 1996. *Gesamtwirt-schaftliche und unternehmerische Anpassungsfortschritte in Ostdeutschland*, Dreizehnter Bericht, Halle (Saale).

———— 1997. *Gesamtwirtschaftliche und unternehmerische Anpassungsfortschritte in Ostdeutschland*, Fünfzehnter Bericht, Halle (Saale).

Dicken, P. 1992. *Global Shift. The Internalization of Economic Activity,* Liverpool.

Dreher, C.; J. Fleig; M. Harnischfeger and M. Klimmer 1995. *Neue Produktionskonzepte in der deutschen Industrie-Bestandsaufnahme, Analyse und wirschaftspolitische Implikationen.* (Technik, Wirschaft und Politik. Bd. 18. Schriftenreihe des Fraunhofer-Instituts für Systemtechnik und Innovationsforschung (ISI)). Heidelberg.

Dunning, J. H. 1993. *Multinational Enterprises and the Global Economy,* Wokingham.

Frankfurter Rundschau 1995. *Brüssel genehmigt Milliardenspritze für Ost-Chemie,* 9 November.

Friese, C., F. Hellmer and H. Kollros 1996. "Kooperation als externe Voraussetzung technisch-organisatorischer Innovation". In *Arbeitsgemeinschaft Sozialwissenschaftliche Technikforschung Niedersachsen* eds. Ergebnisse, Zwischenberichte und neue Projekte, Göttingen.

Grabher, G. 1994. *Lob der Verschwendung,* Berlin.

Heinze, R.G., C. Strünck and H. Voelzkow 1997. "Die Schwelle zur globalen Welt: Silhouetten einer regionalen Modernisierungspolitik". In U. Bullmann and R.G. Heinze (Hrsg) *Regionale Modernisierungspolitik — Nationale und internationale Perspektiven,* Opladen.

Hirst, P., G. Thompson 1996. *Globalization in Question,* Cambridge.

Hoffmann, J. 1997. "Gewerkschaften in der Globalisierungsfalle"? In *PROKLA-Zeitschrift für Kritische Sozialwissenschaft,* Vol. 106.

HWWA 1995. *Grenzüberschreitende Produktion und Strukturwandel — Globalisierung der deutschen Wirtschaft,* Hamburg.

Jürgens, U., W. Krumbein eds. 1991. *Industriepolitische Strategien— Bundesländer im Vergleic,* Berlin.

Kern, H. and U. Voskamp 1995. *Bocksprungstrategie — Überholende Modernisierung zur Sicherung ostdeutscher Industriestandorte?* In J. Fischer and S. Gensior eds. Netz-Spannungen, Berlin.

Kohler-Koch, B. 1996. "Der Nationalstaat im Übergang zum 21. Jahrhundert: erfolgsträchtig oder überholt?" In K. Armingeon ed. *Der Nationalstaat am Ende des 20. Jahrhunderts,* Bern/Stuttgart/ Wien.

Krätke, M. R. 1997. *Globalisierung und Standortkonkurrenz.* In Leviathan 2.

Kremer, U. and R. Löckener 1995. "Regionalisierte Strukturpolitik in Nordrhein-Westfalen — Konzeption Umsetzung und Perspektiven der Weiterentwicklung". In A. Ziegler, H. Gabriel and R. Hoffmann eds. *Regionalisierung der Strukturpolitik,* Marburg.

Krumbein, W. 1990. "Industriepolitik — Ordnungspolitische Kontroversen um ein neues steuerungstheoretisch interessantes Politikfeld". In BDWI (Hrsg.) *Studienheft 'Forschungs- und Technologiepolitik',* Marburg.

Krumbein, W., C. Friese, F. Hellmer and H. Kollros 1994. "Industrial Districts und 'Normalregionen' — Überlegungen zu den Ausgangspunkten einer zeitgemäßen Wirtschaftsförderpolitik". In W. Krumbein ed. *Ökonomische und politische Netzwerke in der Region*. Beiträge aus der internationalen Diskussion, (Schriftenreihe Politik und Ökonomie, Vol. 1), Münster/Hamburg.

Kruse, H. 1990. *Reform durch Regonalisierung. Eine politische Antwort auf die Umstrukturierungen der Wirtschaft*, Frankfurt an Main/New York.

Leborgne, D. and A. Lipietz 1994. "Nach dem Fordismus—Falsche Vorstellungen und offene Fragen". In P. Nolle, W. Prigge and K. Ronneberger eds. *Stadt-Welt. Über die Globalisierung städtischer Milieu*,. Frankfurt an Main/New York.

Lompe, K., A. Blöcker, B. Lux and O. Syring 1996. *Regionalisierung als Innovationsstrategie — Die VW-Region auf dem Weg von der Automobil — zur Verkehrskompetenzregion*, Berlin.

Ludwig, U. 1994. "Konjunkturprognosen für Ostdeutschland—ein Rückblick". In Institut für Wirtschaftsforschung Halle eds. *Wirtschaft im Systemschock. Die schwierige Realität der ostdeutschen Transformation*, Halle.

Luhmann, K. 1984. *Soziale Systeme — Grundriß einer allgemeinen Theorie*, Frankfurt.

Luhmann, K. 1989. "Steuerbarkeit — Streitgespräch mit F.W. Scharpf". In H.H. Hartwich ed. *Macht und Ohnmacht politischer Institutionen*, Opladen.

Luttwak, E. 1994. *Weltwirtschaftskrieg, Export als Waffe — aus Partnern werden Gegner*, Reinbek bei Hamburg.

Mayntz, R. 1993. "Policy Netzwerke und die Logik von Verhandlungssystemen". In A. Héritier ed. *Policy-Analyse. Kritik und Neuorientierung* (PVS-Sonderheft 24), Opladen.

Nägele, F. 1994. "Strukturpolitik wider Willen? — Die regionalpolitischen Dimensionen der Treuhandpoliti". In *Aus Politik und Zeitgeschichte B43-44*, Bonn.

Narr, W. D. and A. Schubert 1994. *Weltökonomie*, Frankfurt an Main.

Neumann, G. 1996. "Regionales Change-Management. Das Nürnberg-Programm. Ein exemplarischer Ansatz zur Verknüpfung von Regional-, Wirtschafts- und Arbeitsmarktpolitik". In *WSI-Mitteilungen* Vol. 12., Düsseldorf.

Nolte D. and A. Ziegler 1994. "Neue Wege einer regional- und sektoralorientierten Strukturpolitik in Ostdeutschland" — Zur Diskussion um den 'Erhalt industrieller Kerne'. In *Informationen zur Raumentwicklung*, Vol. 3.

Ohmae, K. 1994. *Die neue Logik der Weltwirtschaft*, Hamburg.

————— 1995. "Putting Global Logic Fierst". In *Harvard Business Review*, January/February.

Pohlmann, M. 1994. "Vom Mythos des Netzwerkes. Branchentypische Figurationen an der Schnittstelle von Beschaffung und Zulieferung". In E. Lange ed. *Der Wandel der Wirtschaft — Soziologische Perspektiven*, Berlin.

Priewe, J. and R. Hickel 1992. *Der Preis der Einheit — Bilanz und Perspektiven der deutschen Vereinigung*, Frankfurt.

Pyke, F., G. Becattini and W. Sengenberger 1990. *Industrial Districts and Inter-Firm Cooperation in Italy*, Genf.

Rehfeld, D.J. *Betriebliche Innovationen und Regionale Technologiepolitik*. Institut Arbeit und Technik. Materialien IAT-IE 02.

Reich, R. B. 1993. *Die neue Weltwirtschaft*, Frankfurt an Main.

Sabel, C. F. 1989. "Flexible Specialisation and the Re-emergence of Regional Economies". In P. Hirst and J. Zeitlin (Hrsg.), *Reversing Industrial Decline? Industrial Structure and Policies in Britain and her Competitors*, Berg/Oxford.

Scharpf, F.W. 1991. "Die Handlungsfähigkeit des Staates am Ende des zwanzigsten Jahrhunderts". In *Politische Vierteljahresschriften*, 32.

Schumann, M. and D. Gerst 1997. "Produktionsarbeit — Bleiben die Entwicklungstrends stabil?" In IfS—Frankfurt and Main; NIFES — Stadtbergen; ISF — München; SOFI — Göttingen eds. *Jahrbuch Sozialwissenschaftliche Technikberichterstattung 1996 — Schwerpunkt Reorganisation*, Berlin.

Soskice, D. 1996. "German Technology Policy, Innovation, and National Institutional Frameworks". In *Discussion Paper — For-*

schungsschwerpunkt Wirtschaftswandel und Beschäftigung, WZB. Berlin.

Storper, M. and A. J. Scott 1990. "Geographische Grundlagen und gesellschaftliche Regulation flexibler Produktionskomplexe". In R. Borst, S. Krätke, M. Mayer, R. Roth and F. Schmoll eds. *Das neue Gesicht der Städte — Theoretische Ansätze und empirische Befunde aus der internationalen Debatte* (Stadtforschung aktuell), Vol. 29., Basel/Boston/ Berlin.

Sturm, R. 1991. *Die Industriepolitik der Bundesländer und die europäische Integration — Unternehmen und Verwaltungen im erweiterten Binnenmarkt,* Baden-Baden.

Sydow, J. and A. Windeler eds. 1994. *Management interorganizationaler Beziehungen — Vertrauen, Kontrolle und Informationstechnik,* Opladen.

Thurow, L. 1996. *Die Zukunft des Kapitalismus,* Düsseldorf.

Voelzkow, H. 1996. "Der Zug in die Regionen — Politische Regionalisierung als Antwort auf die Globalisierung der Ökonomie". In *Berliner Debatte INITIAL,* 5.

Voskamp, U., K. Blum and V. Wittke 1993. "Industriepolitik als Experiment. Erfahrungen aus der großchemischen Industrie in Sachsen-Anhalt". In *WSI-Mitteilungen,* Vol. 10.

Wade, R. 1996. "Globalization and its Limits: Reports of the Death of the National Economy are Greatly Exaggerated". In S. Berger and R. Dore eds. *National Diversity and Global Capitalism,* Ithaca, London.

Wilke, H. 1992. *Die Ironie des Staates,* Frankfurt.

Wirtschaft and Markt 5/1997. *Zukunftsvisionen an der Elbe.*

Womack, J.P., D.T. Jones and D. Roos 1991. *Die zweite Revolution in der Autoindustrie. Konsequenzen aus der weltweiten Studie des Massachussetts Institute of Technology,* Frankfurt an Main/New York.

14 AN INDUSTRIAL POLICY AGENDA 2000 AND BEYOND — EXPERIENCE, THEORY AND POLICY

Wolfram Elsner

Introduction

The new technical and infrastructural opportunities of tele-information and telecommunication, new global transport (combined with low relative prices for the use of natural goods), new forms of production and management of value-added chains and—last not least—the global trend of withdrawal of the national governments from their responsibilities to balance economy, society and natural environment, have changed the world dramatically since the eighties.

Social scientists, politicians, managers, unionists, social and environmental activists and even the man in the street have become used to discussing related phenomena under the headlines of globalization/glocalization, the dominance of technological innovation, a new competitive environment, post-Fordism and ubiquitous cooperation and networking—each single issue defining a vast area of discussion.

What really is going on in the global, continental, national and regional economies and whether people are using adequate concepts or

mere symbols, metaphors, or ideologies in their discussions and policies
(see Champlin, Olson, 1994) has to be reconsidered at the end of the
nineties in order to develop sustainable foundations for economic
policies for the first decade(s) of the 21st century and to design structural
policies for reality—not for wishful thinking (see ibid.).

The purpose of this concluding chapter, therefore, is to reconsider
recent experience and discussion, new empirical evidence, theoretical
conceptualizing and policy recommendations—broadly presented and
discussed in the present volume—in order to redesign industrial policies
for the year 2000 and beyond—independent, for the time being, of the
leading policy conceptions of "more competition", "acceleration of
innovation", "privatization", "flexibilization", "decentralization" etc.

The prevailing conceptions and ideologies, all in all, do not seem to
have given adequate answers to the new challenges of the nineties, or to
have contributed considerably to the solving of the problem, but have
rather worsened the problems of environmental deterioration, growing
social costs of economic restructuring, regional divergence, growing
poverty, power concentration, dominance and dependency, decreasing
cultural diversity, nationalist and racist conflicts and violence, and
decreasing abilities of the public to control these complex socio-
economic and political processes. Hardly any major socio-economic
issue seems to have improved during the eighties and nineties under the
dominant conceptions of what is (falsely) called neo-liberalism (which
seems to be neither new (neo) nor all in all liberal)—except some areas
of technological dynamics and related mobilization of resources.

This chapter will, therefore, proceed to reconsider central issues like
glocalization, market failure, power and dominance, cooperation and
networking etc., using the material and the arguments that have been
brought forward in this volume, and to design the outlines of an
industrial policy that could hold into the beginning of the 21st century
and that could enable a sustainable socio-economic development.

1. The Ubiquity of "Glocalization"

The common message from the vast amount of literature about
globalization from the eighties onwards is that the links of the value-
added chains are becoming increasingly disconnected (vertical

disintegration) and globally optimized in new locations (regional clustering and integration of specific corporate functions). We are used to assuming an increased competitive pressure, a related acceleration of production and innovation processes and an increased efficiency stemming from the global restructuring of corporate functions and their locations. Doubtlessly, the systems of division of labor have become organized on a global scale, and usually these processes are traced to the improved telecommunication and transportation technologies and infrastructures world-wide, to new and more competitive forms of production with lower costs, improved technology, accelerated turnover of capital and the dominance of financial markets.

However, the world is being divided, in this way, into a global level where mobile capital can control the processes and a regional/local level where the processes take place physically. If the world has become an entity consisting of regional locations, then the global-regional-nexus becomes a crucial issue of the functioning of the world's economy and the wealth of nations (for recent empirical examples see, for instance, Hanson, 1998). Firms whose structures are dissolving under the regime of flexible specialization into network forms of production are becoming dependent upon networks "forming a bridge between local and global economies", as Bianchi puts it in his chapter in this book. Figure 14.1 illustrates this conventional wisdom about globalization and regionalization which needs not to be discussed here in more detail.

Specialized regional networks are supposed then to strengthen regional economies through their effective competitive climate, their supplier structures, including services, and the specific infrastructures available to them and, in this way, seem to promise the best way to global economic efficiency.

Clusters, networks and cross-sectors

Some specification of terms seems appropriate at this early point. We define (regional) clusters as (regionally concentrated) groups of firms which are functionally interconnected (vertically as well as horizontally), including manufacturing and services, plus related ("hard" or "soft") infrastructures and public, semi-public, and social agents financing and/or running them. The crucial point here is the functional relationships which are determined through the market either as vertical

Figure 14.1 Globalization—Regonalization— "Glocalization".
A schematic depiction

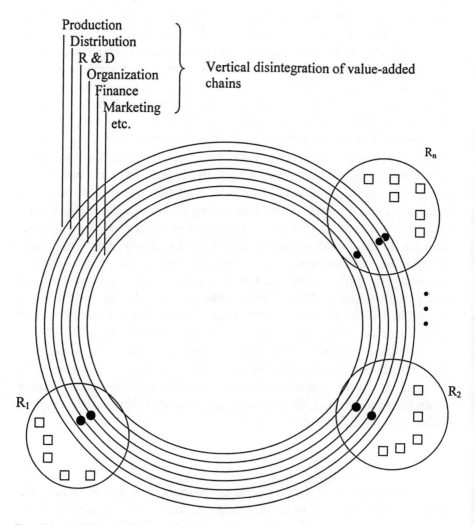

Production
Distribution
R & D
Organization
Finance
Marketing
etc.
} Vertical disintegration of value-added chains

R_n

R_1

R_2

$R_1 ... R_n$ = Individual regions
● = Regional nodes of global value-added chains (e.g. regional establisments of globally active companies, "relays")
□ = Regional companies (e.g. regional supplier firms).

supplier relationships or, in the horizontal case, as specific substitutional or complementary relations among the products of participating firms (including, in this way, what is often called technological "network externalities").

The network, in contrast, shall be understood as strategic, as distinct from "functional". Thus, a network normally is based on a cluster. The functional interdependence in clusters may result in the strategic interaction in networks. We define (regional) networks, therefore, as (regional) clusters which develop an intensive, lasting and comprehensive multilateral cooperation, which utilize specific infrastructures and which, therefore, cooperate with relevant public, semi-public, and social agents.

The notion of cross-sectors, finally, focuses on official statistics. Clusters and networks will normally consist of firms belonging to several branches as defined by official statistics. Modern cluster-oriented industrial policies may, therefore, require clustered and networking industries to be statistically defined and measured adequately. This would imply regrouping statistically defined branches as cross-sectors. Where tertiary functions within the manufacturing sector have to be analyzed in combination with conventionally defined service industries—logistics may serve as an example here—functional (occupational) statistics may be combined with conventional branches statistics (see, for instance, Elsner, Kirchhoff, 1997).

Socio-politico-economic dimensions of globalization

If we look upon globalization from a socio-economic and political-economic point of view, it becomes obvious that it is a politically-made system, which creates a publicly provided (global) space, or level, for more or less exclusive utilization by private capital, i.e. by those firms which are able to use the globe as their strategic field for acquisition of natural resources, labor, finance, R&D-services, transportation services and, last not least, regional government support.

This space has become more or less free from the "society" and the "state". The leading national governments have carefully paid attention to creating a space for unrestricted capital movements, which should be free from the traditional social and public agents, i.e. an exclusive liberalized level for large companies with drastically changed relations between these and the other agents who have usually been present at the national level. The leading national governments have taken care, for the last twenty years, not to provide social groups, except capital interests, with the "normal" institutional conditions on the international/global level.

This system of exclusion and more or less unrestricted capital restructuring is, of course, also a system of global regrouping of markets and, in this way, of increased competitive pressure for companies, for the nation states and for the regions as well. In this way, it is also a system of aspired accelerated capital turnover, of speeded up innovation and of an international oligopolistic restructuring "race" (see, for instance, Ruigrok, van Tulder, 1995, 60 ff.).

The governments of the leading nations, or triad centers, have, in this way, also been careful to withdraw from the responsibility to fulfil their normal socio-economic duties and to create, on the international level, public and social structures which could match the legal frameworks, infrastructures and technologies they supported to facilitate international capital restructuring. They carefully refrain, under the postulates of "neoliberal" ideologies, from binding the global economic process to the society and the state in any considerable respect. Consequently, there is no socio-economic framing and shaping, nor an internationally coordinated industrial policy. On the global level, the market seems to be on its way to "perfection".

There is no doubt, however, that this construction has its repercussions upon the traditional power, wealth and income structures that have been usually existent in the developed industrialized countries since World War II.

... and its regional outcomes

No wonder that there is no even spatial development taking place in any respect. Even the whole conception of globalization could be questioned against the background of regional divergence (for instance, see ibid., 119 ff., see also Markusen, 1996a).

Globalization, suggesting a more uniform spatial development, has turned out to be a triadization instead (see Ruigrok, van Tulder, 1995, 148ff.). Considering all continents, countries and regions, there is no witness of global integration in the sense of equilibrium, equalization, or convergence of regional per capita incomes (for instance, see Unger, 1997, 99 ff.). Even when average measurements of income distribution may not indicate regional divergence, or indicate even slight convergence during some growth periods, this is consistent with the group of the richest regions as well as the group of the poorest ones diverging from the general average, thus leaving the average unchanged.

Anyway, the overall view reveals global uneven development between unequal partners (for instance, see Nayyar 1997; Adams, Gupta 1997). Dependencies seem to be more than ever ubiquitous in the international economic system (see Ruigrok, van Tulder, 1995, passim).

Political outcomes

The globalization of this disintegrated, exclusive and socially, politically and ecologically non-embedded type also entails "a national reaction, a revival of nationalism" (Svetlicic, Singer, 1996, p. 16). Globalization thus even may stimulate political disintegration. What may, at first glance, look as a clever strategy of some powerful multinational enterprises—i. e. global freedom for the powerful on the one hand, nationalism, regionalism, racism and authoritarianism for the common people, namely the poor and underdogs, on the other hand—may turn out to be the Achilles' heel of the whole process of economic internationalization in the future. While the national welfare state emerged to tame the destructive side of capitalist market economies, "changes in the international economy have undermined the ability of the democratic welfare state to do this job" (Wilber, 1998, p. 465).

Thorstein Veblen, at his time, discussed at length that national societies have their enabling myths to keep common people nationally restricted, to stress racial, cultural and political differences, to divide them and to make invidious distinctions between "us" and "them" pervasive (see, for instance, Veblen, 1919). With globalizing capital activities and, specifically, with a global leveling of continental, national and regional consumer markets and consumer behavior through the supply strategies of global players, any invidious distinctions on a regional, national or racial basis contrast more than ever with reality and with reasonable patterns of behavior. Today, this "false consciousness" —like Veblen has analyzed at his time—leads the common man (not only in less developed countries with their regional conflicts, but also in the highly developed western countries) again to support military adventurism and interventionism of—as it stands today—a plutocratic group of leading powers, which decides who is "good" and who is "bad" (normally accompanied by "news" campaigns of the mass media which always show us the "good" suffering and dying so that the military machines "cannot avoid" helping them for "humanitarian reasons", as we all honestly believe and wish to believe).

Against the background of a non-embedded, exclusive, uneven, power-led, potentially violent and military-interventionist mode of globalization, B. McClintock has recently concluded in a Veblenian approach to the international economic (dis)order:

> The peoples of the world are faced with either establishing governance of the global economic process that focuses on improving the lot of the common (wo)men, a truly new international order, or sliding into a high-tech barbarism or disorder fit for the twenty-first century (McClintock, 1997, 10).

The strategic dilemma of trade policy and the "race to the bottom"

Those "dichotomized states" outlined above have liberalized conditions for specific agents, while keeping the others restricted in their national and regional cages. Parallel to this, they also unevenly distribute deregulation and interventionism, subject to the interests of those playing on the international markets. As Svetlicic/Singer put it:

> While in the international arena industrial countries are advocating deregulation they are resorting to interventionism within national economies in order to strengthen the competitive position of their producers (Svetlicic, Singer, 1996, p. 15).

This seems also to be the issue of the literature on strategic trade policy. Its overall message boils down to a modernized beggar-my-neighbor approach in which all countries are supporting their global players in order to reach the position of "taking it all", and in this way getting rewarded with more than the initial subsidies they gave to their domestic champions. It is obvious that nation states, in a world of more or less decreasing economic policy options (see below for a more detailed discussion) and ubiquitous retaliation are trapped in simple but nevertheless powerful prisoners' dilemmas (PD) as Markl and Meißner discuss in this volume. Strategic trade policy thus involves the same strategic dilemma of traditional trade policy, although endowed with some more sophisticated technological policy instruments and some more sophisticated analyses of their background structures.

It seems, therefore, that the developed countries have themselves become victims of their leading ideology of "neo-liberalism". The international integration process, dominated by that (politically organized) non-embedded, non-integrated mechanism which we are used to calling deregulated markets or competition, seems to require to cut off essential historically grown national and regional institutions. In such a non-embedded global economy, every agent, companies as well as national governments, seems to become more and more caught in PD-situations, as is extensively demonstrated in the field of global environmental policies.

To a certain degree, namely in the field where they provide for deregulated conditions for global capital movement, national governments try to solve problems by cooperation. However, by and large they refuse, or are unable, to embed the global economy, and they will continue to participate in a competitive race, using their financial and non-financial subsidies in favor of their home champions. These and other costs of international non-coordination are paid by those with less power, the common taxpayer, those dependent on welfare aid (being cut), by the populations of the less developed and less powerful countries, and, last not least, the great non-human source of inputs called the natural environment.

A race to the bottom of social and environmental conditions indeed seems to take place in favor of globally mobile factors—at the expense of all more or less immobile factors (see for the "race to the bottom discussion", for instance, Markusen et al., 1995; Oates, Schwab, 1988; Wilson, 1996; Sinn, 1997). Among these are entire spatial units at all levels (nations, regions, local communities), but also more or less immobile labor, with their institutions and cultures which have historically grown in, and are bound to, time and space. Their "price elasticities" of supply of locational conditions are invariably low. There is a strong theoretical case and empirical evidence for the expectation that international competition of national (regional etc.) governments may be fiscally ruinous for all and end up in a race for lowering environmental and social quality standards (for instance, see Sinn, 1997; Lindlar, Trabold, 1998).

The ubiquitous inherent diseases of the market can only be healed within well balanced, internationally and intra-nationally negotiated institutional frameworks which comprise fine-tuned mixtures of allocative mechanisms able to embed markets. But the leading market purist ("neoliberal") ideologies, that have been more or less adapted by all leading governments in the world (whether conservative or social-democratic) and that have helped to spread enormous expectations about innovation, modernization and welfare, have led governments to exercise market rhetorics while, at the same time, subsidizing and intervening into the domestic socio-economy even more and in an even more intransparent (but nevertheless socially systematic) way. The dark side of "neoliberal" market theology thus turns out to be uncontrolled proliferating dirigism, since "neo-liberalism" stands brightly in the ideological sphere but is not fit for a complex reality. If the market were a "perfect" mechanism, market-driven globalization would not multiply the structural problems we already have at home, but help to solve them. However, it is not.

2. The Ubiquity of Market Failure

Dropping out of the paradise of perfection, efficiency and welfare growth

The long-lasting discussions about what the market really is, about its optimality and its failure, about market structures, conduct and performance, about market concentration, firm size and profitability, market contestability and entry, competitive pressure and innovative dynamics, and other questions of competition theory and industrial economics have become ramified to such a degree that they cannot even be roughly discussed here with any claim to comprehensiveness. An overall evaluation must end up stating that the intellectual and political welfare paradise, which mainstream economics used to promise, can only be explained and justified by that wonderful neoclassical (Walrasian, Jevonsian or Debreuian) invention of general perfect competition. As soon as we come to conclude that we have to modify even the slightest of its assumptions we drop out of its paradise (into worlds of "second best"), as is well known, and are not able anymore to prove that everybody will be best off through the working of markets.

Not even the most sophisticated contestable markets enthusiast of the Chicago brand, nor any new industrial economist, is able to prove, that any non-perfect, i.e. non-polypolistic, non-perfectly informative, non-homogeneous etc. etc. form of market—even when exhibiting the most fierce competition—is beneficial to the consumer, or common man, or the common employee. We have learned to take refuge in flight from this fundamental problem to the pervasive effects of "dynamics", "innovation", "growth" etc. But there is no doubt: We are beyond the paradise of welfare maximization and optimal welfare distribution. With huge firms' sizes and corporate structures (hierarchies), the common consumer and the common employee simply cannot be the winner of the market system in an allocative welfare sense, as was elaborated already by generations of institutionalist economists (for instance, see Means, 1962). New industrial economics, and even the efficient competition and contestable markets paradigm, thus, reveal a lasting and indissoluble intermingling between size, market structure, concentration degree, profitability, innovative speed and market (and related socio-political) power (for instance, see Waterson, 1985). Not even the wildest market fundamentalist should dare, therefore, to claim that the common man is the winner, in a welfare sense, in a market system other than the "perfect" one. No market reveals any mechanism to fairly distribute proportional gains of (possibly) increased efficiency (who should ever know about this?) of oligopolistic, dynamic and innovative competition into the hands of the consumer or common man. Adam Smith's vision of the "natural" superiority of the competitive market system (subjected by him to a strong institutional framework) has long faded away in history with the fading of the dominance of the small self-employed polypolistic entrepreneur.

Today, economists cannot even tell what a market, let alone an efficient market, really is. Has the Chicago-advocated destruction of state-socialist formal institutions in the former Soviet Union released a "market" economy in any reasonable sense? Are those great state-free areas and areas free of any reasonable social institutions, mostly turning into areas with the fiercest Mafia competition, what the Chicago school intended? These are decentralized allocation mechanisms, i.e. markets, doubtlessly, though maybe oligopolistic ones, but because they are, what do "markets" really mean (see for a detailed discussion of the "transformation" issue, for instance, Petr, 1996; Lichtenstein, 1996; Intriligator,1996, for a discussion of the different institutional embeddings of different market economies, see, for instance, Groenewegen, 1997)?

Even the pure model, which is the only one in which the consumer (logically) is proved to be best off, has been largely questioned because of its inherent inconsistencies, for instance due to the fact that all participants accept given prices and thus price changes cannot be logically explained (see, for instance, Arrow, 1959, see also Gschwendtner, 1993). An equivalent of Arrow's "logical gap" is to say that Walrasian GE theory has considerable implicit institutional presuppositions such as an auctioneer (who is the authority responsible for changing prices). From this starting point, institutional economics of all brands have, at length, elaborated that the market comprises and, at least implicitly, presupposes a whole bundle of institutions, i.e. settled patterns or paradigms of perception, belief, sense-making, valuation and behavior, and thus requires, implicitly, additional modes of coordination (for instance, see Friedland, Robertson (eds.) 1990; Sawyer, 1993; Lutz, 1996), such as contracts, hierarchies and lasting cooperation/ network forms of interaction (see also, for instance, Neale, 1994; Choudhury, 1996).

From "anomalies" to evolution

Market failure is discussed at length in the present volume (for instance, see Sawyer, Michie, Schenk, Elsner). The major critical assumptions of the old "paradise" model and the features of more realistic market models have come under reconsideration there. Among these are—beyond "imperfect" market structures like oligopolies—also the mainstream textbooks' "anomalies" such as

- scale economies/increasing returns,
- factor indivisibilities,
- sunk costs/asset specificity,
- barriers to entry,
- external effects,
- innovation-benefits-inappropriability,

- collective goods,
- endogenous technology,
- transaction costs,
- institutions and routinized decision-making,
- bounded rationality/(over-)complexity/strong uncertainty,
- informational asymmetries,
- direct interdependency, possibly with dilemma structures,
- recurrent interaction with undefined end,
- learning
  etc.

We are far from being able to construct models or schemes of logical relationships among these critical factors. Each one of them could be taken as an instance to entail market failure in one or another form.

Many of the more recent developments in market theory and industrial economics nowadays come, surprisingly or not, close to approaches institutionalist and evolutionary economists have developed for a long time.

If we only assume

- direct interdependencies among agents (which is equivalent with social, i.e. multi-personal situations, and with external effects),
- recurrency, i.e. infinitely or unspecified finitely repeated ("strategic") interactions,
- dilemma structures (namely of the PD-type, which is equivalent to collective good-type problems) and
- sequential decision-making, which induces imperfect information and strong uncertainty about the others' actions and, thus, about the future, and entails the necessity of signaling and learning,

then we are dealing with considerably realistic problem settings (for instance, see Sawyer and Elsner in this volume). Resulting evolutionary PDs seem to be rather basic aspects of day-to-day situations in spontaneous decentralized (i.e. "market") economies, as for instance the coordination failure debate has shown for different well-known macroeconomic and industrial/sectoral problems (for instance, see Cooper, John 1988; Ball, Romer, 1991).

The solutions to such dilemma-prone problems, that have been developed, in a formal way, mainly in the framework of game theory have helped to pave the way to a basically process-oriented, sequential and, to be more specific, evolutionary approach, through which conceptions of systems' dynamics have been further specified as conceptions of path-dependence, irreversibility, autopoiesis, homeostasis, equifinality and related characteristics of complex socio-economic systems which, specifically, have been analyzed as characteristics of systems that are able to solve repeated social dilemma situations (see Schotter, 1981; Axelrod, 1984 as some of the classics of this line of argument, and Lesourne, 1991; Lindgren, 1997 and Chattoe, 1998 as instances from the vast more recent literature; see also the discussion in the contribution of Elsner to this volume). This is of course not to say that any coordination and behavior institutionalization under any circumstances is productive in the sense of social problem solving. Institutionalists are well aware of the Janus-faced character of institutions opening up a trade-off between certainty and flexibility (for the coordination failure line of argument, see, for instance, Mischel, 1998). We will return to the discussion of the evolution of solutions to social dilemmas below.

Innovation, uncertainty and market failure

Despite the apparent enormous dynamics of "market" driven economies, markets typically can fail with respect to the central and dominant symbol and motivator of economic dynamics and modernization, i.e. innovation. As is well known, and has been largely discussed, only few basic conditions which are ubiquitous in reality, such as sunk costs, oligopolistic market structure, positive external effects and strong uncertainty may be sufficient to create technological lock-ins, i.e. innovation failure (with non-innovation or low innovative speed) (see David, 1985 as a classical instance, see also Nelson and Winter, 1982; Hakansson, Lundgren, 1997). Generally spoken, the more basic the innovation is, the stronger will be uncertainty and the collective good dimension, or the positive external effects, of innovation, and the more probable will market failure be. Innovative market failure may even be consistent with any dynamics taking place "in the market" for any other reasons.

Under conditions of basic innovations and strong uncertainty, the market-related conception of efficiency loses its meaning since the very requirement agents have to fulfil in dealing with innovation, futurity and uncertainty, is not so much efficiency, but future-oriented flexibility and learning, i.e. the ability to adapt to unanticipated events (for the revived discussion on strong uncertainty, for instance, see Lawson,1985, 1994; Davidson, 1989; Minsky, 1996; Dequech, 1997). The "market" per se is not only unable to help agents dealing with a truly uncertain future but may even be distortuous:

> The problem posed by the efficiency/flexibility trade-off lies not so much in some mistaken pursuit of efficiency, but in the very structure of the market system in which a firm operates ... Whatever combination of strategies a firm may choose, markets by themselves provide no mechanism to successfully resolve the trade off between efficiency and flexibility. If anything, competitive pressures may distort the choice made" (Freedman 1996, 226, 236).

Institutions and trust

The systemic, or societal, remedy of market failure with respect to (basic) innovation and (strong) uncertainty is institutionalization of behavior. The individualistic, Shacklenian (see, for instance, Shackle, 1958) remedy may be pure   creativity, completely individual adaptability, or adventurism, but the societal solution is institutions, routines, i.e. settled patterns of behavior, established in billions of multipersonal interactions, especially in specified social groups or sub-populations, including mutual expectations of behavior and a sanction mechanism. Institutions can also be depicted as informational mechanisms reducing uncertainty to a level where people are enabled to act and to create the minimum level of trust necessary to be encouraged to become innovative (for instance, see Elsner, 1987, 1989; Neale, 1994; for an illustration of the basic relations among group size, innovation, institutions and trust, see Figure 14.2). We will return to the structure of this social problem solving below.

Institutions, emerging from frequent social interaction in social groups, help to reduce complexity and (mainly informational) transaction costs and in this way also may facilitate and stabilize innovation   processes.   In   particular,   sophisticated   forms   of

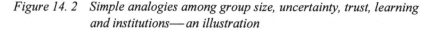

Figure 14. 2   Simple analogies among group size, uncertainty, trust, learning and institutions— an illustration

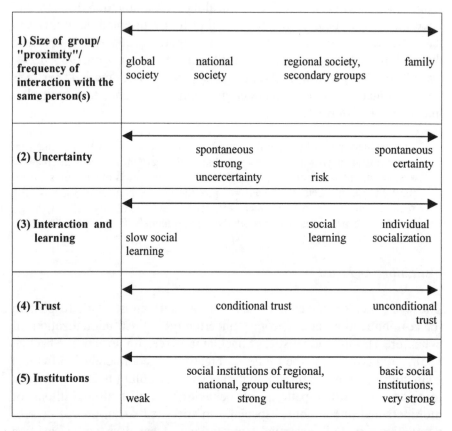

1) Size of group/ "proximity"/ frequency of interaction with the same person(s)	global society	national society	regional society, secondary groups	family
(2) Uncertainty		spontaneous strong uncercertainty	risk	spontaneous certainty
(3) Interaction and learning	slow social learning		social learning	individual socialization
(4) Trust		conditional trust		unconditional trust
(5) Institutions	weak	social institutions of regional, national, group cultures; strong		basic social institutions; very strong

institutionalized cooperation, such as networks, may solve specific problems in the context of innovation processes (for a general discussion, see, for instance, Deakin et al., 1997).

This is also one of the main issues also of this volume, and is discussed at length in several chapters. It has been reported from many regional studies that institutionalized network forms of multi-agents interaction are apt to create a competitive advantage mainly by facilitating and speeding up innovation processes (for instance, see Saxenian, 1994; Coombs et al. (eds.) 1996, Hanson, 1998). Against this background, one of the neo-classical issues of innovation policy, i.e. optimizing patent law in order to internalize positive external effects, also largely loses its basis. The time to innovate and to market can be considerably reduced by adequate, culturally adapted and embedded forms of networking making patenting redundant.

As, for instance, Saxenian (1994) reports, patents may lose their values as instruments of corporate innovation strategies and public innovation policies. Not only has reverse engineering largely undermined the protection provided by patents, but the Silicon Valley highly innovative microelectronics networks participants normally automatically agree to cross-license patents for mutual exploitation by the network members. The crucial point here is that specific forms of networks—being "neither market nor hierarchy"—enable the partners to speed up the innovation processes in such a way that patents as well as reverse engineering drastically lose their edge. It has been reported, that even competitors specialized in "imitating and improving" through reverse engineering get overwhelmed by the innovative speed of network based innovation, it has been reported.

In this way, non-market mechanisms have to provide a framework for the market to get things working, to make more basic innovations feasible in shorter time periods and thus to ensure a cooperative advantage to their participants.

There is, of course, no guarantee that institutions of cooperation and networking are seminal in this way under any condition. They also have their life cycles and may run into the pitfalls of mere routine and inflexibility. Adaptability and anticipative institutional design are, therefore, a continuing challenge to institutional theory and institutionally-based industrial policy. We will return to this issue later when discussing regional networks.

The "evolution of cooperation"

The great promise, in this respect, of evolutionary game theory from the early eighties on was that institutionalized cooperation—the alternative, or complement at least, to a non-embedded "market", that would help to overcome the blockages of innovation and other problems of market failure and to get innovative dynamics off the ground—would emerge on the basis of the same decentralized individualistic process which is inherent in the market. While we generally have to conceive economic problem situations different from the "market"—model, with direct social interdependence, social dilemmas and recurrent social interaction (see above), it seems striking that the opposite to the "market"—i.e. institutionalized basic social cooperation - can be proved to emerge out of a more or less individualistic setting. In what respect institutionalized cooperation and networking is really feasible from a neo-classically inspired spontaneous process, is discussed in this volume in more detail (see Elsner). While it is questionable that pure neo-classical agents are sufficient to explain an evolutionary process of institutionalization of cooperation (see below), it can also be doubted that a decentralized evolutionary process alone leads to the "solution" of typical social dilemma situations within a reasonable time span and with a reasonable degree of certainty.

Simulations and experiments have recorded of hundreds and thousands of interaction rounds, or generations, necessary to gain evolutionary stability of institutions-based solutions (and even then they remain fragile). Practical industrial policy cannot wait for so long to initiate and stabilize the necessary socio-economic processes. No doubt, evolutionary game theory has increased the awareness for the practical relevance of social dilemmas and their paralyzing power pervasive in many social processes (for instance, see also Liebrand, Messick, (eds.) 1996). It has also helped to examine the logical structures of many problems first developed and discussed in socio-economics and (neo-) institutionalism, such as social interaction, selection processes among strategies/cultures, adaptation and learning etc., and has turned—from a partially neo-classical starting point—to real-world social problems such as bounded and asymmetric information, learning, beliefs, signaling, reputation, the "history" of interactions, the role of verbal communication, group size, frequency of contacts, mobility, expectations and institutions (for instance, see Bicchieri, 1993; Axelrod, 1997; Offerman, Sonnemans, 1998; Dawid, 1998; Fudenberg, Levine, 1998). Many authors, in this process, have frankly changed camps, ending up straightforwardly in socio-economics/neo-institutionalism where they have found deeper understanding of the complexities of individualistic conflicts and social dilemmas, institutionalization and evolutionary change within a broader cultural process.

By and large, evolutionary game theory provides no firm grounds for the expectations of those who might wish to stay firmly on neo-classical (or "neo-liberal") grounds, i.e. that solving the problems of market failure by institutionalized cooperation, routinization etc. will emerge from individualistic and decentralized processes. First, individual learning to cooperate, one of the crucial issues of cultural evolution (see Elsner in this volume), is more than detecting the contrahent's strategy and adapting one's own accordingly to "win the battle" (see, for the state-of-the-art of learning in game theory, again Fudenberg, Levine, 1998). The required, seemingly neo-classical, individual turns out to be an individual who has to be able to fantasize a future different from free riding, to find a way to realize it by offering cooperation, taking into account to be inevitably worse off compared to his less cooperative counterpart. Second, the whole conception is undetermined, as has been argued above, with respect to whether institutionalized cooperation will emerge at all in repeated social dilemmas and whether it will emerge in real-life time spans.

The argument boils down to the fact that decentralized processes in individualist societies are not stable and self-sufficient; they need an embedding provided by different, deliberately designed and genuinely collective mechanisms. We will resume this point under the headline of meritorics.

The inefficiency of size

As is well known, the market as a decentralized allocative mechanism has an inherent tendency to eliminate itself by the process of concentration. The merger mania waves that have pushed concentration in the triad countries since the eighties is only the tip of the iceberg. Despite general trends towards self-employment, outsourcing and small and medium-sized enterprises, centralization and concentration, including the differential growth of size of corporations, remain the dominating aspects of industrial development, being pushed more and more by stock-market-manias. Mergers and acquisitions are largely justified by mainstream economics on the ground of efficiency. This is also widely discussed in this book.

Schenk reports on an overwhelming empirical evidence which does not justify the assumption that mergers and acquisitions have positive effects on firms' performances. He explains their dark side, i.e. the neglect of investment and of the development of internal strengths. He also discusses social costs in terms of slowing down of innovations through private regulation within a power-dominated corporate system (for earlier arguments in this line, see Munkirs, 1985; Prasch, 1992, for a critical profit rates differentials analysis, see, for instance, Schohl, 1992). Michie also reports about corporate lock-ins resulting from straining after short run gains. And Dietrich and Burns illustrate strategic intra-firm lock-ins with the example of institutionalized ceremonial accounting systems' dominance over other (instrumental) firms functions—aggravated today by the stock-markets' claims for pure, short-run shareholder values and by overvalued external financial reporting. Their case study shows that even a publicly awarded R&D result was scotched because it did not seem rewarding in the view of an accounting system based on institutionalized contribution routines:

> Rather than resulting from a random walk, the choice of technology can therefore ... be more appropriately understood as the path dependent response of dominant ideologies in leading organizations within particular settings (Dietrich and Burns, in this volume).

Hayden and Bolduc, finally, with their highly innovative social fabric matrix analysis, demonstrate in their case study about a "normal" contractual network that network constructions dominated by powerful large firms turn out to be wealth and power redistributing mechanisms, even in the case of big public utilities—at the expense of the public:

> Those who have the power may enforce a system that is quite inconsistent with general social beliefs. Therefore, policy scientists cannot avoid the issue of power and social conflict when evaluating for efficiency (Hayden and Bolduc, in this volume).

The ubiquity of power, dominance and dependency in institutions, clusters and innovative networks

Thus, finally, we have to address the perhaps most pervasive issue of market failure: power. Hayden and Bolduc's analysis suggests that cluster and network relationships analysis, with relations being contractualized or informal, should have to be the starting point of any industrial economics discussion. Michie, in his chapter in this book, refers to the older national dependency approach of Friedrich List, (1841) who had argued against power-dominated "free" trade and suggested his infant industry/endogenous development approach mainly to equalize power conditions.

Power, dominance and dependence are ubiquitous in industrial clusters and networks as they are in the socio-economy in general. Spatial economic structures, therefore, will sooner or later adapt to these power conditions, regardless of their subnational (i.e. regional), national or global extension. Corporate dominance/dependence structures and power relations in spatial clusters shape spatial networks and characterize related types of regions (for instance, see Lasuén, 1996).

The dependency relations in industrial complexes (clusters) and networks can be grouped into several categories dependent on the relative influence of the core firm and the partner firms (see Ruigrok/van Tulder, 1995, 18 ff.). Different types of power-dominant relations can then be characterized as "structural control", "direct control", "coalition" and "compliance", exhibiting decreasing influence of the core firm and increasing influence of the partner firms in this sequence. Pure competition and pure cooperation would be ideal opposing powerless poles of this range. These cluster types have also inherent links to certain spatial orientations, or strategies of companies (see id., 272 ff.), although there certainly is no deterministic scheme of sectoral-spatial interaction in clustering or networking.

As the eighties and nineties have been a phase of deregulated international/global expansion and dis-embedding of markets, there is, consequently, also a global expansion and growth of the main disease of dis-embedded markets, uncontrolled power. While capital and finance are restructuring globally, overwhelming the encultured relationships between economic and social agents both intra- and inter-nationally, this very process, and its politically made (regulated and deregulated) preconditions, not only represent a considerable redistribution of power in itself but also give rise to subsequent continuing dynamics of private power accumulation.

These processes have been widely discussed. While, as P. Baker has asserted, these "restructuring strategies .. are in essence socially repressive" and "capital is attempting to reassert its power over labor in the developed world" (Baker, 1996, p. 275), the spatial outcomes of these processes may be disastrous to a "normal" region. While the most powerful globally operating corporations weave networks, as Komninos (1997) has argued, over large geographical scales and get themselves rid of specific spatial constraints, the "normal" region, being immobile like all regions are, by its very nature, stands with its back to the wall. Hellmer in this volume, generally draws the somewhat disappointing picture of low networking and innovation levels in more or less dependent "normal" regions.

Industrial districts and regional industrial clusters might be confronted with corporate "diffused strategies for innovation and technology transfer" (Komninos, 1997, p. 181) and might lose their attractiveness in favor of "post-technopolitan command centers" (id., 193 f.). Even new industrial districts, innovative clusters and networks, therefore, may well be viewed not as regional solutions to global restructuring but also as symptoms of crisis (Baker, 1996) because they also are dominated by power relations controlled from very few spatial power centers.

A. Pratt (1997) has analyzed the interaction of technology and power in networks and cites Clegg and Wilson (1991) saying that "technology conceals power, and hence protects capital's interests" (Pratt, 1997, p. 129).

To free technology from its domination by narrow interests, being pushed forward through ceremonially warranted institutionalized values, beliefs, objectives and procedures, and to make innovation more sustainable, innovation networks would have to be re-constructed under careful consideration of power relations:

> This "power/institution" argument counters the idea of institution as "context" ... it also resists the representation of networks as neutral ... What is important is the analysis of the processes by which stabilization of objects and agents happens and what power effects they have ... (Pratt, 1997, 133f.).

The conception of institutions used in this argument corresponds neatly with the institutional dichotomy of Veblenian institutionalism (see for an overview, Neale, 1994). In this view, there is neither an unspoiled direct relationship between the problem ("to innovate") and the social and organizational devices for its solution ("to institutionalize one's behavior", "to cooperate", "to form networks in order to let trust come to work" etc.), nor is power simply a crude disturbing or intervening factor from the "external" world. It is the societal device itself for solving social dilemmas, i.e. the institutions, which may enable and stabilize problem solving and, at the same time, may contain and promote power relations, already existent in the social interactions basic to the institutionalization process. This is included in the ceremonial dimension of institutions. Power is a distortion of social problem solving, already existent in the ceremonial dimension of the main device of problem solving and, thus, also connected with society's technological processes. For a simple illustration of this conception see Figure 14.3.

The dynamics of socio-economic problem solving, institution building and technological change may well be dominated by the ceremonial dimension of social institutions which is based on values of status and invidious distinction. The ceremonial dimension of institutions tends to dominate the behavioral patterns of the society and, thus, to distort the technological process. Neoinstitutionalists have considered these dynamics, within a theory of institutional change, under the heading of ceremonial encapsulation (see Bush, 1987, 1994). It provides also a case for market failure.

The regional and cluster dimension of power: hub&spoke, satellite platforms and the like

The regional dimension of power dominated industrial clusters and networks has been discussed under the headings of hub-and-spoke-districts, satellite platform districts etc. A. Markusen (1996b), in agreement with earlier arguments (for instance, see Storper, Harrison, 1991), has rejected the new industrial districts conception as the dominant configuration which suggests that regions are intra- and inter-actively responding to global challenges. The tacit assumption connected with this conception, she argued, is that the interactions take place on a power-free, equal basis. However, there is no cluster or network structure conceivable in empirical studies that could be viewed as being power-free. This would hold even more in an era of unrestricted proliferation, at the international level, of non-embedded mechanisms called "markets" (see discussion above).

Despite the general power argument discussed above, Markusen contends that new industrial districts with their alleged more or less SME-dominated structures are a rare exemption. She has found power dominated configurations to be more prominent in reality. Both hub&spoke and satellite platform types of inter-corporate regional structures subject regions to power dominated structures and processes.

Figure 14.3   The relations between innovation, institutions and power —
            a simple illustration

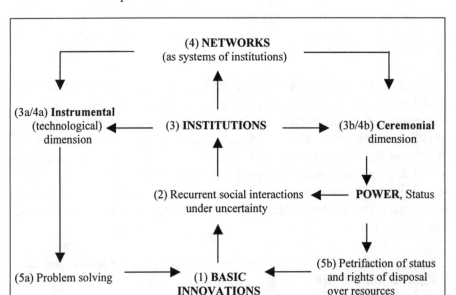

Hub&spoke districts are organized around one or more dominant firms
having their headquarters located within the region, but being largely
externally (globally) oriented. They often provide an exclusive channel
between regional suppliers and global networks. This allows them to
organize and dominate the regional SMEs. Satellite platform regions are
dominated by branch plants which are dependent, in turn, on external
links with their parent companies. They are also able to organize
relevant parts of regional SME incumbents and often also provide the
only external links for them.

Since power dominated regional clusters and networks can be a major
source of distortion of the technological and the general socio-economic
development, both hub&spoke, and satellite, regions may seriously
suffer from the petrifaction of structures. The Route 128 case in A.
Saxenian's pervasive comparison of the divergent developments of
Silicon Valley and Route 128 with regard to the microcomputer
revolution since the late seventies may serve as a major instance here
(see Saxenian, 1994). Markusen has argued that also mixtures of
hub&spoke, satellite and state-anchored districts (the latter focussed on

public-sector procurement, public R&D orders, subsidies, military spending and the like) remain "sticky" places.

The often disappointing pictures of real industrial districts (US-American in the above mentioned cases, see Hellmer in his volume for the analysis of German districts) are of course not the last word to be said on new industrial districts. This is why we have to return to the districts and regional networks issue later in order to consider conditions of sustainably innovative regional networks. While power may dominate the majority of regional cluster configurations, the new industrial districts of the Third-Italy variant may still serve as a target to guide network construction and network governance and corresponding policy recommendations. The most prominent "innovative milieu" case, Silicon Valley, seems to have proved, according to Saxenian, that even large firms like Hewlett Packard, Sun Microsystems, Intel and others are able (or can be motivated) to collaborate with their smaller innovative partners on an (more or less) equal basis, provided instrumental problem solving, time to innovate and to market and cooperative advantage have become a common interest dominant over power execution. This also requires that participating SMEs are rarely dependent on their large partners by more than 20 or 25 percent of their sales, as Saxenian has also reported. We will return to this point, discussing views about a possibly positive function of dominating firms in globally oriented regions and about the great expectations connected with Italianate new industrial districts.

3. The Ubiquity of Meritorics

If power is ubiquitous in clusters, regions, institutions and networks, also the whole conception of (stable, given, so-called exogenous) preferences may well be questioned. In reality, people's preferences may permanently be changed endogenously in an economy that is driven by power-based supply side dynamics, in favor of powerful vested interests. Generally, the changeability and evolution of preferences has long ceased to be a rare anomaly in economics. Preferences (which mostly have been used to keep the neo-classical camp unified in abstaining from interventionist temptations) normally change and evolve in the economic process, whether through massive powerful psychological and emotional advertising, forced change of behavior, mass hysteria, or value-sensitive education and corresponding slow cultural value change. The emphasis mainstream economics used to lay on the notion of "wrong" preferences (being an "anomaly") as the basis for merit goods and allocative economic policy intervention has, therefore, lost its ground (for instance, see Norton et al. 1998), although it was the basis originally provided by R.A. Musgrave at the beginning of meritorics.

In the present framework, it is the deficient institutional arrangements that provide the basis for meritorization and pave the way for policies that care for adequate institutional arrangements. This is consistent with the more recent argument of Musgrave himself, when he brings emerging "community preferences" to the fore (see Musgrave, 1987; see also Ver Eecke, 1998).

In the framework of a socio-economic, i.e. cultural and evolutionary, policy conception, as a positive basis for pro-active democratic state intervention in the sense of a negotiated economy broadly founded by John R. Commons in the twenties and thirties (see Commons, 1934, for a more recent conception, see for instance Nielsen, Pedersen, 1988; Ramstad, 1991), market failure, instead of "wrong preferences", would provide the basis of an active industrial policy approach.

Goods analysis would rather be the starting point of this approach, instead of "preferences". If the processes of interactions of individual agents are non-optimal or defective, because they are dilemma-prone, if agents have to struggle with basic innovations and corresponding true uncertainty, with uncertain futurity in general and with direct interdependencies and recurrent social interactions, then the macro- and meso-economic outcomes have to be reconsidered and evaluated through complementary institutional arrangements, i.e. by public agencies, and possibly to be altered and improved through this different allocative mechanism expressive of democratic collective decision-making.

Our argument is in line with the conclusions of a contribution to the earlier merit goods/merit wants-debate, that the merit goods concept is crucial to any case for government intervention and that the preference evaluation issue can be transformed into the issue of comparative allocative mechanisms evaluation, i.e. of an evaluation of market institutions by their working and outcomes (see Brennan, and Lomasky, 1982). And we agree with the same authors when they argue that

> the merit goods debate ... is much more important than the profession so far has appreciated (id., 206).

Elsner discusses the issue in his chapter in this book. Hayden and Bolduc explain, in their chapter, how technical progress normally is induced by meritorization of goods through technical standards set by state legislation. Innovation, in this way, is widely a function of social and political regulatory pressure, i.e. of the meritorization of those outcomes of the market processes that are viewed as not being socially reasonable. Most authors in the present volume advocate a strengthened role of a democratic state "in order to stimulate market forces" (Bianchi).

Both the choice of the mixture of allocative mechanisms (processes) a society   wishes   to   adopt   and   utilize   and   the   degree   of publicity/collectivity of goods (outcomes) are applications of meritorics. Elsner focuses, on the background of unreasonable empirical industrial and regional outcomes of the market processes, on certain collective and private goods to be the objects of meritorization. If we follow Musgrave at least in his explanation that merit goods basically are private goods, then we have to show, and, in an evolutionary game-theoretic setting, we are also able to show, that collective goods may become private ones in an evolutionary process. Individuals may by themselves solve the problem   of   social   dilemmas   in   a   decentralized   system   by institutionalization of cooperation. (This is, however, not proved by a single-shot PD-supergame, as has been argued, nor by Axelrod's selection process of cultures alone; Schotter seems to come nearest to the requirement to exhibit the cultural process, or complete sequence, of this transformation including learning; for a recent more comprehensive evolutionary model see, for instance, Franke, 1998.) However, the security of provision and the time requirements of the evolutionary emergence of cooperation, as has been mentioned above, are such that a societal meritorization has to be integrated into the processes in order to improve and speed up this social production process, and sometimes even initiate it.

The sequence of the argument, in the framework of a cooperative industrial development and industrial policy approach, is illustrated in

Figure14.4. It suggests that a public process of socio-political decision-making, meritorization and application of specific cooperative industrial policy instruments comes into being in the case of "insufficient" outcomes of the "private" decentralized processes. This would either deblock the cooperative decentralized process (if necessary) or accelerate and stabilize such a process. In the (purely theoretical) case of a congruence between public goals and "private outcomes", the decentralized process could be assumed to be of such a quality that an evolutionary cooperative process would stabilize itself and no policy intervention would be necessary.

Meritorization policies also ubiquitous even in the world of market driven economies and even under "neo-liberal" governments. This holds even more if we consider that the reality of market economies does not really fit with "neo-liberal" conceptions. Thus, the dark side of "neo-liberal" policies has always been massive meritorization, as has been argued above with respect to "neo-liberal" dirigism, although "neo-liberal" ideologies force governments to do so in the way of an even more disordered, proliferating and non-transparent interventionism (into labor relations, sectoral conditions etc.). World-wide subsidies races speak for themselves.

And even the "pure" capitalist firm, as a set of institutions, has always been politicized, despite the great capitalist restoration of the last two decades, by their managers, industrial associations' representatives and politicians, to fulfil diverse social and political purposes. This intensive, and growing, intermingling of private firms and political purposes, the "politicization of private sector firms" (Donald, Hutton, 1998) has always been a specific type of meritorization of processes and outcomes of the socio-economic process. Socio-economic policy reform to create a transparent and democratic negotiated economy would not mean a complete revolution in this respect, but simply introduce control of the power and information structures involved. The capitalist power center called "firm" would be transformed into a social institution where stakeholder interests would also be represented (for recent case studies of public purposes of private firms, see id.).

It is even more necessary to develop conceptions, strategies and governance arrangements for a proactively interventionist, transparent, cooperative, and democratic industrial policy. This has been dealt with in the chapters of the present volume in many aspects and ways. We

Figure 14.4 A sequence of the cooperative production of meritorized goods and of cooperative industrial policy

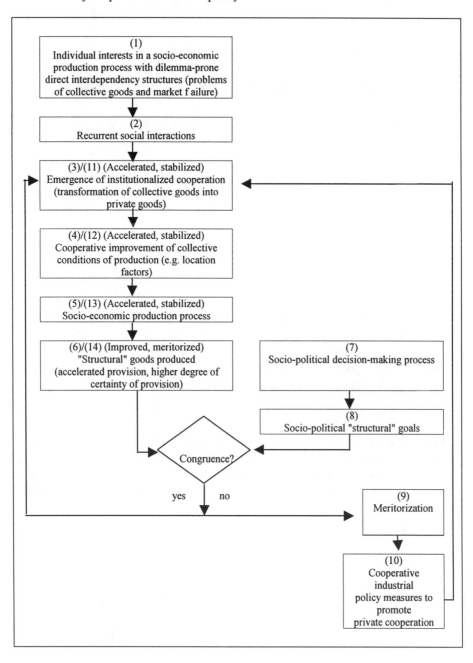

will discuss the synergetic consequences for industrial policies in the following.

4. What's it All About: Meso-Economics

"Real" economics vs. money-ism, industrialists vs. shareholders

Industrial policy conceptions that could be sustainable in the next decade(s) need adequate theoretical foundations. These seem to be provided at best by reorganizing economics around meso-level economics with its inherent focus on "real", as opposed to pure monetarian, financial and fiscal, economic phenomena. Meso-economics tends to focus on real relationships between individual agents as embedded in socially evolved and settled patterns of behavior, beliefs, values, norms, organizational forms etc., including cooperations and networks. Furthermore, it focuses on "real" structures between branches, sectors, clusters and spatial units of economic activity.

Dominant ceremonially warranted values in the capitalist market economies of the late twentieth century, on the other hand, are focusing the interests of many people, including the hard core capitalist, the wealthy rentier, even many a poor man on the street, and, last not least, the mainstreams of economists, on issues of money, currency, international finance, interests and stock market quotations (for a discussion of more general aspects of those drifts in the common belief system, see Toruno, 1997). While the public responsibility has been more and more withdrawn from controlling mesoeconomic structures, while economic structures have been completely devolved to the monetary policies of the central banks and while this has been supported by the mainstreams of economics (mainly neoclassically inspired microeconomics), the market economies have developed more or less into shareholder economies. Consequently, the whole common belief system and related social values have been reshaped to focus on money, finance and shareholding.

The increasing neglect of real structures and processes of the economy in public policies, corporate management, mass media, academic economics and the social value and belief structure, and the focus on money, have all in all not helped to solve any of the fundamental and pervasive problems of decentralized "market" economies, but have made the national economic and social systems and the global economic, social and ecological structures more vulnerable, as is increasingly expressed from within and without economics (see, for instance, Kuttner, 1997; Forrester, 1996). For a growing number of contemporary writers this represents the alternative "survival or destruction", more equality or social anarchy, regaining social control over the economy or barbarism (see, for instance, Slabbert, 1996; Briggs, 1998).

But it is the common pattern of thinking, also that of the "common" economist, that lends, unwarrantedly, dominance to pure financial interests and mechanisms, which are not able, and not interested, to create sustainably developing socio-economic structures. The current situation, for instance, allows the CEO of the German Mercedes Benz corporation, by merging with Chrysler, to increase his annual income from about three million marks to about twenty million marks, i.e. by several hundred percent. And the mass media are justifying such global player mergers for pure pecuniary reasons like those discussed above. As long as this is the case, our future socio-economic alternatives seem to be still "social control vs. social anarchy" (see again Briggs, 1998).

Why has the interest in the development of the real structures of the economy and in the promotion of the sustainability of structures decreased so much in the last two decades? In an interesting debate on industrial policies vs. financial and monetary macroeconomic policy, W. Alonso has argued that macroeconomic policy issues "move faster" and therefore command more attention (see Alonso, 1996). Macropolicies indeed seem to have a bias to short-terminism. In this respect, see G. Sweeney's discussion on innovation strategies:

> The failure to perceive the significance of local/regional systems of innovation is due ... to the absorption of politicians, administrators and their advisors in short term cycles and actions. They fail to observe that the development of society occurs in complex cycles (Sweeney, 1995, p. 37).

Socio-economic restructuring and change could be better governed at the meso-economic level, but only with adequate time spans and cycles. A. Markusen, in a rejoinder to Alonso, has pointed out, that it is also the political condition and the power distribution in the socio-economy which count:

> Macroeconomic policy is paramount for financial interests, which are well organized and dominant in central government institutions like the Treasury and Federal Reserve. Industrial policy matters more to industrialists and organized labor, which are less well organized and often opposed by Wall Street ... In the past decade, globalization has accelerated the ascendancy of financial interests, while industrial .. policy (has) continued to lose both forceful advocates and ground (Markusen, 1996c, p. 83).

While macroeconomic policies, at the same time, have considerably lost momentum during the eighties and nineties (the reasons will not be discussed here), there are effectively new scales and scopes for meso-economic, i.e. industrial and regional policies, to overcome macroeconomic stagnation and macro-policy numbness by mobilizing, reviving and improving structures, innovation processes and socio-economic interactions from bottom to top. Amable and Petit (1996) have discussed these and also analyzed revitalizing macroeconomic effects of coordinated industrial policies which will, however, not be discussed here.

We seem to need a new focus, and belief system, in economics in order to bring industrial policy issues to the fore. Similarly, we need a new type of industrialist at the tops of the corporations who is again interested in, and encouraged by, profits from real production, labor and technology, instead of stock market quotations and shareholders values. Only with a new thinking in the economy and the society, and in economics, will we be able to bring real meso issues, namely industrial policy issues, back to the center of the political agenda.

The subjects of meso-economics

As has been mentioned earlier, meso-economics deal with (1) institutions, cooperations and networks, (2) branches, sectors and clusters and (3) spatial units and the spatial dimension of the economy, namely regions. In other words, it focuses on the social, sectoral and spatial structures of the socio-economy. For the sectoral level, we have already introduced, with respect to clusters and networks, the distinction between the functional and the strategic dimension of related meso-economic phenomena. This refers to the type of process by which those phenomena are created and sustained. Functional processes, it is assumed, are spontaneous, not deliberately controlled and directed (i.e. evolutionary processes, including decentralized "market" processes), while cooperations and networks are seen as results of strategic processes basing on deliberate action. No doubt, the borders between the two types are blurred, but the distinction seems useful in order to categorize the relevant set of crucial phenomena in those three dimensions of meso-economics. For a schematic representation, see Figure 14.5.

Figure 14.5   A classification of major meso-economic phenomena

Type of process Meso-economic dimension	Functional	Strategic
Social	Institutions	Cooperations, Networks
Sectoral	Sectoral clusters	Sectoral networks
Spatial	Agglomerations, functional regions	Regional networks

With respect to institutions, at least, some explanation about this characterization as meso-economic seems due. Institutions, indeed, are existent at the micro-, meso- and macro-levels at the same time. Furthermore, since an individual can be characterized by the set of institutions that shape his behavior, institutions can be viewed also as being a sub-individual, i.e. a micro-micro phenomenon. While we acknowledge institutions, accordingly, as being a sub-micro-level phenomenon, their social existence classifies them also as a meso- and macro-phenomenon. Since they normally display a limited "cultural" validity with respect to time and space, however, they seem most appropriately assigned to meso-economics. As has been discussed by Elsner in this book, the conditions of their emergence refer to social groups, or sub-populations, equivalent to sectoral and spatial (regional) phenomena. They have, therefore, a (theoretical) affinity to meso-economics. For a simple illustration of the assigned socio-economic dimensions of institutions, see Figure 14.6. Figure 14.6 suggests that a certain social institution B1 (the "genotype") finds its specific expression (its "phenotype") in a specific individual. An individual is defined, then, not only by the specific combination of institutions inherent in this individual but also by the specific shape a single institution assumes with this individual. For instance, an institution of cooperation may take its specific form as an individual style of cooperation of a certain individual. In a similar way, certain (sub-) cultures could be identified by the specific shape a social institution assumes with this group of individuals (as their specific "style").

From micro to meso: remedying micro deficits at the meso level

Industrial policies presuppose, in theoretical terms, deficits of the "market" process, or, to be more general, of decentralized social interaction processes. None of the contributors to this book contend that "the market"

Figure 14.6 The sub-micro and meso-levels of institutions—an illustration

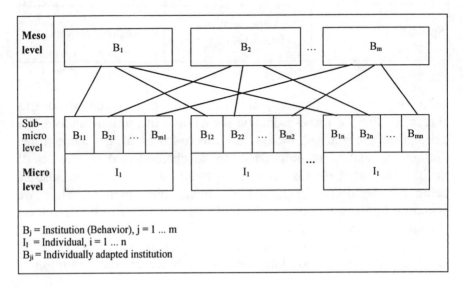

B_j = Institution (Behavior), j = 1 ... m
I_i = Individual, i = 1 ... n
B_{ji} = Individually adapted institution

does it all, most of them, however, contend that the results of the market process need to be reconsidered, evaluated, controlled, corrected or improved. If markets are established in a world of direct interdependencies, recurrent interactions, or even social dilemma structures, their functioning will normally be deficient, instead of efficient, as has been discussed by several authors in this book. Markets, then, are subjected to blockades or produce insufficient outcomes. Many writers, nevertheless, hesitate to refer too much to the market failure paradigm, as it involves the presumption, and value judgement, that the market is a primary end in itself, which defines the scope of policies. No doubt, there are theoretical foundations for public policies prior to the market failure argument.

Nevertheless, institutions of cooperation, network forms of allocation and the like are the remedies which socio-economies normally create to overcome social dilemmas, lock-ins etc. in markets, and to embed markets into countervailing allocation mechanisms. These include collective action through structural policy.

This does not mean that impacts of deficient micro processes may not be effected also at the macro level. Macro-policies have also to be launched, of course, to reshape "wrong" structures between the macro-economic aggregates (see below). However, it is the meso-level, where the socio-economy, by creating institutions, cooperations and networks which are promoted, in turn, by meso-policies, creates its main remedies to unblock processes and to stabilize them. Why then should public policies not take the chance to reshape meso-structures, to coordinate themselves with existing cooperations and networks, and to redesign existing institutions or create new ones (as has been schematically depicted in Figure 14.4 above)? Macro-policies indeed seem to be too far removed from the socio-economy in order to perform this.

From macro to meso: framing meso policies at the macro-level

Generally, there can be no reasonable and sustainable meso-economic structures without reasonable macro-economic structures. This is not to say, however, that meso-economic structures can be determined by macro policy alone. Macro policy exhibits degrees of freedom with respect to sectoral and spatial structures, which implies a high possibility that the meso structures effected by macro policies are not reasonable or sustainable and are unintentionally disturbed by the side effects of macro policies.

The meso-macro-interrelatedness behind industrial policies is also widely discussed in this book. Bianchi and Lagendijk for instance, discuss the changing national and international context of industrial policies, where national governments have devolved responsibilities to regional levels. Bianchi also discusses the two (national and regional) levels of structural policies with a clear role also for macro policies. The role of the national state, he argues, needs to be strengthened in order to stimulate the market and to establish a regulatory framework in which sectoral and regional agents can act. National governments, therefore, may not withdraw from responsibilities for specific international and national collective goods, even in a globalizing economy (for this line of argument see also, for instance, Amin, 1998). Despite the macro-policy deficiencies mentioned above, there may be, in other words, a strong framing role for macro policies in an industrial policy conception.

As Lane has argued earlier, regulatory functions of the national governments have remained very important. While national governments have changed their roles from selective and defensive industrial policies to "orchestrating" economic consensus, she says, they have not lost their economic role (see Lane, 1995, chapter 9, see also Jessop, 1994; Fransman, 1995).

So the task remaining for national governments seems to be to develop a more cooperative, pro-active and participating role for national and supra-national macro-policy agencies in order to improve the conditions of interaction among meso-economic actors, e.g. to reduce competitive pressure for the regions and to care for an even regional development. It is indeed widely felt—and theoretically as well as empirically confirmed—that the worldwide deregulation processes have entailed a degree of competition among regional industrial policy agents that is highly dysfunctional and counterproductive. The idea that competition is a question of a workable degree, instead of yes or no, is increasingly acknowledged in modern market theories. Schreyer, in this volume, has elaborated this fact with simulations in a SME-market-context. Macro policy, therefore, has to frame industrial policies through institutional design, creating considerable degrees of competition among regional industrial policy agents.

Macro-institutional policy, furthermore, has to be combined with demand side policies in order to take into consideration workable degrees of competition among regions and their industrial policy agents. Michie, in his chapter in this book, argues that there cannot be an efficient industrial policy which is also not in sync with demand side policies—a fact that is ignored, for instance, by the type of industrial policy that is advocated by the new trade theory, which deals with trade policy as a variant of industrial policy, ignoring the macroeconomic impacts of its recommendations, he argues.

What has been said for the macro policies is true for the national as well as the international, supranational or global level. As has been mentioned earlier, in a market-driven, deregulated globalizing process there are increasingly collective goods that need to be controlled and managed at the international level. This is discussed in several chapters of this book and we will return to the point discussing uneven regional development.

5. Clusters + Regions + Policies = Networks; Approaching a Core Area of Industrial Policy

Networking as social problem solving

Regional networks is probably the most discussed conception in the industrial economics and industrial policy literature of the last decade, whether they are seen as an objective, or addressee, of industrial policy measures (to initiate, stabilize or improve networks), or as an instrument of industrial policies (to use networks to achieve defined industrial policy goals). Comprehensive networks normally will be based upon sectoral clusters in specific regions.

Figure 14.4 and related considerations (see above) suggest that networks generally are the deliberately established social solutions to problems that a market dominated economy leaves unsolved (or creates).

Being a social solution to problems of the market economy conforms, by the way, with the Marxian view that the proceeding factual socialization of the means of production, under capitalist property conditions, requires answers and reactions, such as capital concentration and centralization and the increasing intersection and combination of private and public resources (see also the discussion on meritorization and the public purposes of private firms above). In this view, networks could easily be seen as an (capitalist) answer to the growing objective socialization of the means of production. The Marxian view, thus, would generally support the characterization of network forms of institutionalized cooperation as sophisticated social solutions (Marxians probably would refuse the conception of a "solution") to specific problems of market economies that cannot be dealt with adequately on a pure individual and decentralized basis.

Global networks and regional networks

Like clusters and regions, networks are also not restricted to neatly separated regional areas, but can exhibit very different spatial ranges, from global, to national and regional (sub-national), and may form very complex webs of interconnected and overlapping parts.

The increasing role of global forms of decision-making, whether they be hierarchical, like multinational firms, or cooperative and networked, has raised the question for the potential of regional resources to be developed through networking (see above). Regions facing globalization have to strive for the mobilization of their resources under any conceivable choice of developmental paths they want to go, even if they would strive for complete self-sufficiency. As is known from the literature, there are specific conditions in which the regional potential for networking is weakened as well as conditions in which it is strengthened, under the regime of globalization. Some conditions, for instance, of making the agglomeration a successful and self-reinforcing process have been discussed under the heading of the new economic geography (see, for instance, Martin, Sunley, 1996; Ottaviano, Puga, 1997). We will discuss some of these points below under the heading of the "high road" to regional economic restructuring.

Whatever the concrete spatial range of a network may be, its working principle is that it provides proximity in the sense of "dense", i.e. frequent interaction, be it promoted by certain spatial or sectoral (professional) conditions.

A simple regional economic logic of networking

If networks fulfil their alleged purposes, they entail a simple logical regional economic effect which has seldom been considered explicitly, although the supposed regional economic effects of networking can be easily put in line with the traditional regional economic export base argument. If we assume a most simplified regional multiplier equation

$$\Delta Y = [1/ (1-c+m)] \, \Delta X$$

(with c = consumption ratio, m = import ratio, Y = regional income, X = regional exports), then regional clustering and networking obviously aim at (1) increasing regional exports by improving the interregional competitiveness of the participants, or the region as a whole, through a whole set of conceivable measures taken, and at (2) substituting regional imports through (a) increased competitiveness of participants (gained through the same set of measures) and/or (b) increased information about regional suppliers/demanders and increased linking together of regional suppliers and demanders. While (1) increases regional exports, (2) reduces the regional import ratio. Networking thus has a twofold effect in a simple (and admittedly, partial) regional economic income equation: an increase in export demand and an increase of the multiplier as such. The combined result normally should be a considerable increase of the regional GNP in the long run:

$$\Delta Y \uparrow\uparrow = [1/ (1-c+m\downarrow)] \, \Delta X \uparrow.$$

The twofold potential of networks

While we can only roughly refer here to the general new industrial district and network literature, the overall message that networks are able to accelerate innovation and development and increase the competitiveness of participants and of the whole region, seems to be in no doubt (see, for overviews: OECD 1991; Powell, Smith-Doerr, 1994; Harrison et al. 1996; Larédo, Mustar, 1996).

The reverse side of this is, however, the potential of networks, under specific internal and external conditions, to grow old through their very success, before being eliminated by some evolutionary selection mechanism, to become restrictive, petrified, sclerotic, and locked-in (see, for instance, Grabher, 1993). The costs of cooperation and networking, then, may exceed their normal transaction costs, and their social benefits, by far.

The discussion of this potential of regional networks is also a crucial issue in the contributions to this book. Especially Markl and Meißner discuss the costs and benefits of network cooperation and the resulting optimal size, intensity, and industrial policy promotion of cooperations at length.

The Janus-faced character of networks, being synergetic or restrictive under different internal and external conditions, leads us to the question of "optimal" network governance.

Network governance

The rapidly growing literature on different allocation arrangements, of which network forms seem to be the most interesting ones, cannot be reviewed here. Some very few conclusions from this literature must be sufficient.

First, being "beyond market and hierarchy", networks basically seem to be the answer to the growing complexity of the global environment wherein socio-economic action takes place (see, for instance, Amin, Hausner, 1997). Networks seem to deliver the interactive governance required for dealing with complexity. This is why Amin and Hausner conclude to recommend (to those agents whom it may concern, including those who are responsible for industrial policy) that interactive powers should be created in order to overcome typical problems of growing complexity, related uncertainty and lock-ins of agents in the market, i.e. to consider openness and adaptability in the same way as for cooperation, institutionalization of behavior and related reduced uncertainty.

Furthermore, interactive capabilities building seems to be equivalent to reshaping the socio-economy in the transparent, uncertainty reducing, participative way that the conception of the negotiated economy developed by J.R. Commons suggests (we have mentioned this earlier, see Commons 1934; Nielsen, Pedersen, 1988; see also de Bruijn, ten Heuvelhof, 1995; 173ff., Jessop, 1997).

Network building and building the powers for optimal network governance is strongly advocated by, and can be easily based upon, the (neo-)institutionalist research and policy agenda dealing with comparative institutions and institutional change, and leading to a focus on the governance of processes by specific institutional design (see, for instance, Elsner, 1987; Weimer, 1995).

Networks exhibit a whole range of characteristics that qualify them as solutions to problems of complexity, uncertainty, repeated direct interdependence, pluriformity and instability in decentralized processes (see again de Bruijn, ten Heuvelhof, 1995, 163 ff.). They are multipersonal (multilateral) arrangements, moderately informal agreements, moderately lasting structures, they provide access to a collective good, entail institutionalizations of behaviors, a common socialization, group loyalty, a sense of community, trust etc. (see, for instance, Lindberg et al., 1991, 28ff.).

These elements, however, are far from being integrated into a causal model connecting environmental conditions, required structural features and resulting effects of networks. We will try to sort some of those factors below. Two issues out of a long list of interconnected network issues shall be mentioned: first, networks cannot be governed as pure multilateral structures, due to the simple fact that the number of direct relations (r) in a network increases with the number of agents (a) participating according to the equation $r = a \bullet (a - 1)/2$ which would already result in near "chaos" with medium-sized networks (compared to pure hierarchy where the number of relations changes according to $r = n - 1$). The basic social solution to the "chaos" problem of a pure democratic (i.e. anarchic) network is institutionalization: institutionalized behavior and institutionalized relationships form patterns in the ideal anarchic structure, which give weight and sense to the relations, thus in fact reducing them to numbers that agents can deal with. Networks, thus, need institutions.

The second issue of networks is their life cycle, already mentioned in the foregoing section, involving possibly the petrifaction of network structures under certain conditions. A socio-politico-economic theory of networks would connect their life cycles to an ideal life cycle of their region, as is illustrated in Figure 14.7.

As a solution to the danger of petrifaction, it is suggested in the literature to conceptualize, organize and govern networks with a focus

*Figure 14.7 A socio-economic model of regional development and of the
development of regional networks—an illustration*

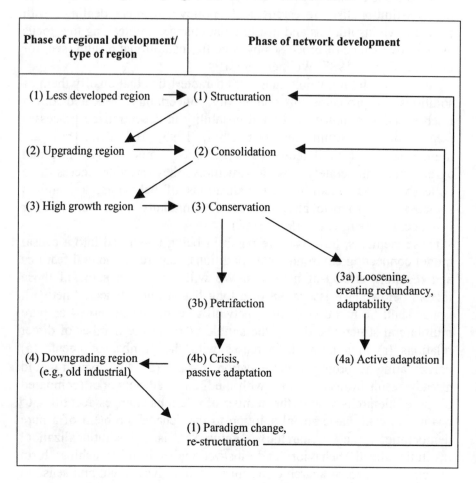

on entry, loose coupling, redundancy creation, flexibility ensuring and permanent informational input. This has been widely discussed in the literature and needs no further comment here (see again, for instance, Grabher, 1993; de Bruijn, ten Heuvelhof, 1995, see also Figure 14.7).

Some authors have utilized results from the neural model and computer science to conceptualize optimal network governance, viewed as economic neural networks, in an evolutionary framework (see, for instance, Maggioni, 1997) and have reached considerable insights on this basis.

All in all, this has resulted in a set of network features that shall be tentatively (and not at all in a clear cut manner) classified into conditional, structural and resulting features, which denote the initial, or framework, conditions of networks, the characteristics of their working principles, and the structures of their outcomes, resp.:

Conditional features:
- Multipersonal situations, direct "strategic" interdependence, externalities;
- sequential recurrent interaction, frequency of interaction, "proximity";
- possibly dilemma-prone decision space;
- complexity, bounded rationality, uncertainty.

Structural features:
- Reciprocity, distributional equality, control of free riders;
- multicentered structure, pluriformity;
- non-hierarchy, open technology;
- control (removal) of power and dependence, self-organization;
- open access, interaction with the environment;
- new information and innovation through guaranteed entry and voice, control of inertia; making the common future count high;
- redundancy, parallel processes.

Resulting features:
- Joint learning, institutionalization of behavior;
- common language, common world view;
- external economies, synergies, collective goods;
- trust;
- extended competence;
- reduced transaction (information) costs, increased efficiency;
- increased stability.

All of these features, can be, under certain circumstances, interpreted, shaped and used as factors of good governance. What can be assumed as favorable conditions, what can be shaped as structural elements of networks and what can be seen as an outcome of both, largely depends on specific conditions. Good network governance is a permanent task.

6. Global Orientation? Decentralization? Commercialization?
—The Lean Road and the High Road to Economic Restructuring

Pure regionalization? The dark side of new regionalism

The withdrawal of national governments worldwide, under the command of "neo-liberal" ideologies, from their traditional responsibilities for national (and international) collective goods, such as industrial and regional structures, reasonable income distribution or reasonable levels of social security, a withdrawal not confined to traditional "conservative" parties and governments, has entailed a trend towards the devolution of responsibilities for structural change to the regions. We have argued earlier that pure decentralization/ regionalization cannot be the final word in the "glocalization" debate because an increasing number of pressing international and global collective goods of an industrial, regional, social and environmental character have become left untreated. The force and speed of international decision-making and action in the military sector, i.e. violent intervention in all kinds of internal conflicts of third countries, seems to be the core policy area where international coordination really seems to work. Instead, such an international capacity to act seems much more required in (peaceful, non-interventionist) international tackling of unsolved industrial, social and environmental problems.

The trend towards the devolution of responsibilities to the regions as a background of the glocalization debate, all in all, seems to have resulted in a bias of our general conceptions of regionalization/decentralization, assigning too high an importance to "pure" regionalization while neglecting the inter-regional collective goods, such as inter-regional equality or inter-regional balancing (see, for instance, Cheshire, Gordon, 1998).

In their chapter of this book, Hellmer et al. discuss, on the basis of their empirical evidence from Germany, the overestimation of the potential of regionalization. The dark side of the new regionalism seems to be a dysfunctionally high degree of inter-regional competition (see also, for instance, Jensen-Butler, et al. (eds.) 1997; Elsner, 1998).

J. Lovering, in a recent paper, argues that this New Regionalism seems to be theory led by policy and discusses the inadequacies of an overemphasized regionalist thinking (see Lovering, 1998; for the related question, whether the scientific paradigm of New Regionalism can survive, see Lagendijk, 1998). Lovering refers to the innovation process which cannot be tackled on the regional level alone but needs a macroeconomic framework (see our discussion above). He also contends the absence, on a broad scale, of efficient private financial capital on the regional level, and he refers to the labor market which is more and more utilized, he argues, as a simple service instrument for the requirements of global players luring and threatening with inward investment: the region as a labor market with no sociology. All in all he contends:

> As a general factual claim, the idea of an economic resurgence of regions in the contemporary world *in general* is simply false ... As a rather vague framework within which to speculate on some possible relationships between hypothetical agents at a vaguely specified level of abstraction it has some limited utility. As an ideologically-loaded discourse which is proving to be extremely useful for existing organizations, corporations and a new regionally constituted service class it is fabulously successful (Lovering 1998, p. 21).

Lovering develops roughly the alternative of globalization-regionalization as a politico-economic-cultural restructuring, which seems to fit rather well into the institutionalist-evolutionary framework we have tried to depict as a conceptual basis for industrial policy here and which we will try to operationalize further in the following.

Pure global orientation? Pure commercialization?

Critical investigations of regional "politico-economic-cultural restructuring" discussed earlier have mainly focussed on power and on regional industrial spaces as symptoms of crisis rather than a solution (see again Baker, 1996, Pratt, 1997). A power focussed analysis of regionalization strategies of national governments and large firms has recently argued, for the case of France, that large firms have taken the chance of regionalization to become more competitive, not so much by their own efforts but rather by rent seeking from regionalization. Specifically, they take advantage of the side-effects of new regionalized technology policies which involve higher subsidies being offered to them by the regions that are now fiercely competing against each other (see Hancké 1997).

The entrepreneurial model of regional restructuring and industrial policy and the global region conception, that focus on a dominant global orientation of regions, on the priority of attracting foreign investment from large companies and on a related reshaping of the whole regional socio-economy is widely advocated in the literature (see, for instance, Huggins, 1997). In the present volume, Lagendijk, in particular, discusses this model. It abandons the older "developmental" and redistributive conception, that aimed at a high degree of societal integration in the region, in favor of competitive races and bidding, imitation of the successful regions, a certain sort of events, spectacles and related infrastructure investments (conference centers, theme parks, musical theaters etc.) and the like (see Lagendijk in this book). Unions become marginalized while business associations and chambers of commerce are shifted even more into the centers of the regional power structures, which more or less informally decide on the direction regional development should take. This all results in a "Macchiavellian" (or plutocratic) regional culture. Traditional, established regional socio-economic structures become turned upside down.

Crucial to this model is the role foreign investors play in reconfiguring the regional institutional structure. They execute the alleged requirements of the global markets and create a hub&spoke region of the exogeneously determined type, where the centers of regional networks are large firms, mostly not incumbents, however, but foreign subsidiaries. Regional industrial clusters are shaped into core-ring-systems where powerful large firms can control access to networks and to international markets. Advocators of such hub&spoke-type regions (exogeneously determined) regard them as superior to other forms of industrial districts because of their most effective adjustment of the region to the global economy requirements (see Lagendijk, in this volume, for a more detailed discussion). Some regions and even complete countries (Ireland serves as an example here) have been rather successful with this orientation.

The entrepreneurial model: power, redistribution, negative redundancy

The criticism of this conception might refer to the criteria of sustainable networks discussed above. The strongly power-based hub&spoke, or core-ring-systems indeed seem to be in contrast to what optimal network governance theory suggests, namely control of power asymmetries, open access, open technology, voice and entry. Power-dominated networks, in contrast, become devices of manipulation and control of competition instead of coordinating independent agents and in this way creating new capabilities (see Lagendijk).

While it is said that "entrepreneurial" regional strategies haven taken their leaves from traditional redistributional conceptions, their major feature indeed seems to be redistribution of income and power (see, for instance, Elsner, 1998). And there is good reason not to rely too much on the general strategies of large firms that seem to be more determined by power and shareholder considerations than by effectiveness and productive or technological considerations, which is widely supported by evidence given by Schenk in this volume. Bianchi, also in this volume, argues, that there is the danger of a dual economy and a broken society dividing those with strong international relations and those depending purely on local conditions.

Empirical evidence also shows that, in an "entrepreneurial" model, resources are redistributed in a way that intermediary economic promotional organizations, being public, semi-public or private, are proliferating and doubling, financed or at least financially supported by the regional government, so that they even start competing to find customers. Intransparency in the market of intermediary organizations grows, and support for companies often becomes fragmented (see Lagendijk, in this book, see also Huggins, 1997, 119f.). This seems to be also a symptom of regional resources redistribution, creating affluence and inefficiency in subsidizing companies, and a symptom of a reversal of social structures, that might deteriorate the whole regional culture. Viewed under the aspect of efficient regional network governance (see above), this duplicity of economic promotional services seems not to be what could be recommended as creative redundancy, since all of these agencies pursue the same policy agendas to meet the alleged requirements of the global market.

The risk involved in power-led regional clustering and networking seems to be that they get petrified and lose innovative impetus—and, last not least, create regional dependency and interregional divergence. Hellmer et al., in this volume, argue that, at least in what they call a normal region, networking in the sense of new industrial districts does not exist to any considerable degree. Their results are based upon evidence from the new German "Laender", that have been shaped mainly through power-led, "imperialist" taking-over strategies of established large western German firms after 1989. The "entrepreneurial" global region conception, in general, seems to be facing such dangers of non-sustainability.

Uneven development and divergence—versus creating diversity

Another implication of mainly global-oriented and power-dominated regionalization seems to be inter-regional divergence. The bench-marking, or imitate the best strategies seem, at first sight, to release a race to the top, i.e. a quality competition with individual as well as overall systemic efficiency effects where the fittest survive in the global behavioral "genes" pool. However, the conditions to run such races are so different that the great majority of "normal" regions will hardly ever have the chance to gain much from an imitation race, or from unifying "perfect" competition. So they start running the opposite race to the bottom and play the cards of low wage, low taxes and low social and environmental standards.

Evidence shows that, even in the EU where active regional policies are pursued, there is no sustained, uniform regional convergence. Instead, the top regions as well as the bottom regions seem to deviate from the overall average, at least in phases of slow growth. Interregional divergence of per capita incomes, instead of what is suggested by market-centered economic theories, seems to be the main feature of interregional development worldwide, despite (or because) of the market-driven, deregulated international economic development. We have discussed this earlier.

Theories of uneven development (in the line of Gunnar Myrdal or Stephen Hymer) have explained the phenomena of regional divergence also by focussing on the corporate level. If the firm is seen as the center of strategic decision-making in the international economic arena and if considerable strategic failure of (overloaded) corporate hierarchies is pervasive, then tendencies of poverty as well as wealth and underdevelopment together with fast growth are no surprise at all in a world dominated by (dis embedded) transnational corporations,

> because the structure of the world's economies, the distribution of wealth and the pattern of development would reflect the hierarchical structure of transnational corporations (Sugden, 1996, 15).

Uneven development and tendencies of racing to the bottom among the non-privileged, "normal" regions seem to be quite consistent, perhaps surprisingly, with findings stating that there is no tendency of regional policy conformity. It is frequently argued, that the conduct of transnational enterprises as powerful (and strategically failing) hierarchies under globally competitive conditions reduces the number of regional and industrial policy options for the (national or regional) governments, since they compete for the same foreign direct investments. Reduced policy options seem to be quite common and consistent with accelerated competitive races among regions. Some writers have argued, however, that there is no general trend towards convergent policies. Despite the notion of "market failure in systems competition", they contend that industrial policies would rather diverge, since the regions are subjected to an increasing international specialization (see, for instance, Bellak, 1995). Uneven development, interregional divergence, and competitive races, are completely consistent with a growing interregional division of labor and specialization and, thus, also with different, and diverging, regional industrial policy strategies. This is simply because the objective conditions of the regions to meet the requirements of an increasing competitive pressure are different, and divergent, on a global scale.

All these multifarious effects of glocalization, viewed in an evolutionary, cultural perspective, boil down to the question of the motives and mechanisms of inter-regional divergence, since a global inter-regional competitive unification and conformity (of the "fittest") would not be desirable, even if it were the dominant trend. Instead of divergence and specialization, both dominated and conducted by the same, globally mobile, powerful and hierarchical forces, inter-regional cultural diversity should come to the focus. Diversity, as is well known from evolutionary economics, is a crucial feature of all evolving systems, decisive for their systemic effectiveness, problem solving capacity, resilience, and sustainability (see, for instance, Delorme, Dopfer (eds.) 1994, Hong, Page, 1998). Ensuring, creating and improving diversity, therefore, is also crucial to the global interregional system (see, for instance, Unger, van Waarden (eds.) 1995, Keyman 1997, chapter. 2, Giampietro, Mayumi ,1998). As Grabher and Stark have put it recently:

> ... although all-encompassing privatization and marketization might foster adaptation in the short run, the consequent loss of organizational diversity will impede adaptability in the long run (Grabher, Stark, 1997, 533).

The criterion for the causes and effects, motives and objectives of regional development changes, in this perspective, together with a change of the dimension, by which regions, networks and industrial policy agents compare themselves and evaluate their strategies. In a cultural, evolutionary perspective, they would also compare their contemporary position and strategies with their historical paths and would develop their future path from their identity resulting from this history, instead of exclusively making global cross-regional short-run comparisons in order to imitate the "best". In this way, they could gain much energy from creatively interpreting the path dependence of their developments.

Figure 14.8 illustrates this point. It is meant to suggest that different cultural entities (such as nations, regions, organizations, social interaction systems etc.), which have covered a certain path in the past, may end up at different points in the present "cultural space" (which is a complex, aggregated dimension in itself) in a way that a simple imitation of cultures, i.e. an "import" of culture A by culture B, would not be in the range (or funnel) of future opportunities which is open to culture B at its specific location in the present cultural space. Figure 14.8 should, however, not be misunderstood to mean a strict dichotomy of views. The existing one-sidedness of views and strategies in regional development, rather, should be mitigated. This should be considered as the argument of the evolutionary approach.

This view is quite consistent with an inter-regional procedural competitive interaction, but not with cross-culturally imitating or imposing the models of the "fittest". Diversity includes the conception of workable, reasonable degrees of competitive interaction among

Figure 14.8 Changing perspectives between inter-regional market competition and inter-cultural diversity

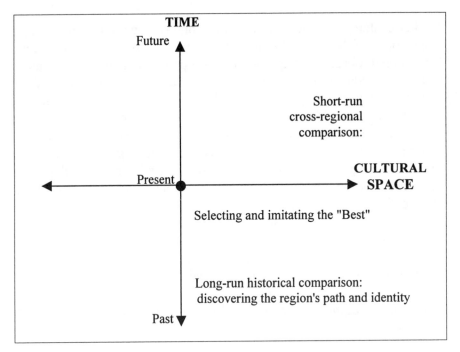

```
                           TIME
                     Future ▲
                            │
                            │
                            │        Short-run
                            │        cross-regional
                            │        comparison:
                            │
                            │                        CULTURAL
                    Present │                   ──►  SPACE
        ◄───────────────────●──────────────────────►
                            │    Selecting and imitating the "Best"
                            │
                            │
                            │    Long-run historical comparison:
                            │      discovering the region's path and identity
                            │
                      Past ▼
```

regions. Compared to the dysfunctionally high degree of competition in deregulated global markets, this means that the degree of competition among regions and nations as industrial policy agents has to be considerably reduced by national and international macro institutional policies (see above).

If this approach could be operationalized and transmitted into regional strategies, regional agents entering the international sphere and entering international networks would "do so evolving out of and growing from the histories, traditions and cultures of their own localities", as R. Sugden has put it in a recent paper (Sugden, 1996, 32):

> This means that the notion of horizontal industrial strategies ... i.e. strategies which apply uniformly across ... all localities, is (a) contradiction in terms. Strategies must take account of particular histories, etc. In fact more than this; it is not even sufficient simply to be rooted in local histories,

multinational webs can only be borne out of, and be grown from, such histories (id., 28).

Market-centered world views, in contrast, paired with vague conceptions of dynamics, innovation, efficiency, growth and modernity, have forced a basic strategic orientation upon nation states and regions that have reduced their *views* to short-run, invidious, competitive comparisons with others, largely neglecting their own history, features, competences, conditions, inclinations, objectives etc. A sustainable industrial policy after 2000, however, requires that the industrial localities of the world and their industrial policy agents change their views to integrate their history and characteristics and develop their interaction on the basis of sustaining "coopetitive" diversity. Their abilities to do so require that the leading national governments cooperatively change those conditions of interaction, i.e. reduce competitive pressure to a degree that leaves a considerable scope for specific industrial policy strategies of the regions. The governments have to perform this by global institutional design.

What kind of regional networks for the high road to economic restructuring?

Returning from the more basic perspective to concrete industrial policy strategies of jurisdictions, we refer here again to the issue of "good" regions and networks governance. We have mentioned already phases of regional and network development together with corresponding types of regions and have discussed different regional cluster and network structures. Combining the two dimensions provides a rough scheme (1) to synthesize the two strands of discussion, (2) to classifiy specific regions, as examples, and (3) to supply a another starting point for the following discussion of the high road to regional economic restructuring, which will refer to the most widely discussed example (being not at all out of fashion) of the Third Italy. Figure 14.9 gives a scheme to classify regional examples of types of economic restructuring. It tentatively classifies some few examples known from the international literature.

Figure 14.9 Types of Marshallian industrial districts, according to regional
development phase and to network power structure (with some
regional examples)

Type of cluster or network power structure \ Phase of regional development/ type of region	(1) Less developed region	(2) Upgrading (climber) region	(3) High growth region	(4) Down-grading region (old industrial)
Satellite platform (Exogenously determined)			Technopoles	
Hub&Spoke, exogenously			Techno-metropolitan areas	
Hub&Spoke, endogenously			Silicon Valley, Baden-Württemberg	Ruhr Area (in the eighties)
Italianate (Endogenously determined)		Third Italy		

A high road to economic restructuring. What remains of the third Italy?

The new industrial districts literature has widely discussed the example of the Third Italy, which has emerged since the mid-seventies. In the early nineties, F. Pyke and W. Sengenberger, for instance, generalized the model as the high road of economic restructuring (see Pyke, Sengenberger (eds.) 1992, see also Benko, Dunford (eds.) 1991). During the nineties, however, it has also been contended that the new industrial districts of the Third Italy have lost their dynamics, have partly failed to develop further and, therefore, have lost their role as a model for new industrial districts (see Bianchi, 1998), while others hold that the Italian districts are neither a myth nor an interlude (see, for instance, Trigilia, 1992). G. Bianchi (1998), in his "Requiem for the Third Italy", has argued that the Third Italy has dissolved as a unified set of spatial and social districts during the late eighties and early nineties. Lagendijk, in the present book, has discussed the Italian variant of industrial districts as the "Romantic view" of the revival of regional economies and contrasts it with the "realistic" view of the "entrepreneurial global region" already discussed above. Thus, the question remains open what the example of the unique success of the Third Italy, at least during the seventies and the eighties, can tell us today and which of its elements can be elaborated as crucial success factors to be integrated into a conception of sustainable industrial policies after 2000.

Even the most widely accepted symbol of a new industrial space, with its high speed innovative dynamics, entrepreneurial culture and global integration, the Silicon Valley has been called into question and has been proved to have its specific myths and romanticisms (see, for instance Florida, Kenney, 1990). Critics have identified a Hobbesian anarchy with industrial fragmentation and even notorious innovation dilemmas, being deficient in coordination, exhibiting a missing connection with the broad consumer markets and few extra-regional spread effects, while start-up mania and quick-shooting venture capital were only parts of its supporting myths (see ibid.). Experts of informatics may not be surprised about all that, since many of them have their own opinion about the quality of some of the best-known and best-selling software and hardware products from Silicon Valley. They have known for long that high innovative speed and good global sales do not guarantee a high quality product in terms of the consumers' (users) utility when good sales is determined by quasi-monopolistic market power. Earlier studies of the case of Silicon Valley have contended a deterioration of environmental conditions and social relations and ended up to speak of a "new technology in an old society" (see, for instance, Ruegemer, 1985).

A. Saxenian (1994), to whom we have referred earlier, has told a different story about the regional advantage of Silicon Valley. Her comparative study of Silicon Valley and Route 128 is optimistic enough to enable us to figure out some possible success factors from this case. Compared to social standards, Silicon Valley may perform badly in terms of societal disintegration, ecological deterioriation or missing broader links and coordinating instances, but compared to its big US high-tech counterpart, Route 128, the Silicon Valley network system, nevertheless, has performed excellently in terms of innovation, developmental speed and sales. The basic success factors, Saxenian has elaborated, seem to be a culture of organized interaction between the players (vs. strict corporate independence and high vertical integration in Route 128 companies), furthermore, a sense of community, in spite of competition, instead of a hierarchical culture in Route 128, the enormous experiment of interfirm openness ("blurring 'firms' boundaries"), i.e. open technology to network participants, open patent information (cross-licensing), communicated mid-term corporate plans within networks, fast proliferation of new technological ideas, organizational experimentation and the like. Large companies like HP seem to interact with small, specialized high-tech suppliers on an equal basis, even commonly ensuring mutual independence in terms of sales ratios and ownership. This culture may be related only to a small sector of the regional economy (and, doubtlessly, there are those "dual" parts of low wage, low-tech sub-sub-suppliers and mechanical assemblers), but this sector exhibits a sense of agents' diversity in the networks and in this way seems to succeed to perform a fast change ("Protean places" as Saxenian has named it).

In contrast to Silicon Valley's Protean places (if this characterization is right), A. Markusen (1996b) has analysed sticky places such as hub&spoke regions and satellite platforms (see above). In her paper, she also has tried to figure out the key elements (to which we have referred earlier) of Italianate industrial districts. In this way, some key elements seem to have been elaborated in the literature, from empirical regional case studies and network analyses, that make up an ideal Italianate variant of future industrial districts as a high road to continuing effective restructuring, continuously high adaptability, learning systems and, as a result, inter-regional competitiveness and, high socio-economic performance. And if the districts of the Third Italy will succeed in remaining learning regions, the Third Italy itself might remain an example other regions could learn from in the future.

First, the power structure of clusters and related networks has to be controlled. Uneven, or unequal, power structures might provide for (short-run) high dynamics, but may also immobilize the agents. An even power structure, in contrast, seems to best ensure sustainable effectiveness. Industrial policy agents and entire industrial districts should not gather around a single power center so that individual corporate strategic failure cannot impede the region's path of industrial restructuring (see Sugden 1996).

Second, "high road" districts are dominated by small and medium-sized enterprises. These are normally regionally owned so that the process of continuous restructuring, learning and adaptation will be an endogenous one in character. This also implies that key investment decisions be made regionally and that there will exist a relatively great portion of sales performed as intra-district trade so that easily identifiable clusters and a high degree of equal-based cooperation among competitors will come into existence. Bianchi and Schreyer discuss at length policies for a substantial role of SMEs in industrial restructuring in the present book. The dominance of (publicly supported) SMEs also implies that single-centered power-structures will not become a considerable factor.

Third, the whole development is heavily based on a workers' culture, i.e. organized labor (in the Third Italy cases paired by a long tradition of left wing regional governments with their specific proactive policy strategies), a highly participative employee orientation, workers motivated and mobilized by relatively high wage levels. Furthermore, it is based on a commitment on the part of employees to the district, resulting in a highly mobile labor force and a flexible labor market in total, where personnel is easily exchanged between customers, suppliers and competitors, and, finally, on workers participating in technological innovation, design etc. (see, for instance, Markusen, 1996b, 297 ff.). While in Silicon Valley this participative mobilization of human resources is confined to highly qualified white collar employees, the Italianate variant seems to exhibit a social participation on a broader scale.

In this sense, the Italianate industrial restructuring process is that of a drawing heavily upon the role and development of human capital (see, for instance, Simmie (ed.) 1997, Conclusions, 233 ff., Asheim 1996). In this way, the "high road" to industrial development gives also a concrete meaning to what we call a socio-economy or what has been dealt with in the literature as an integral, or socially inclusive, economic approach fusing private capital interests and social interests (see, for instance, Sugden, 1996, pp. 25—27; Amin, 1998, 16ff.). If social integration and *social embeddedness* of firms' activities and inter-firm clusters and networks are high, power is less likely to come to function as the dominating mechanism of resources allocation, as C. Lane and R. Bachmann (1997) have argued. In this way, also the allocative mechanism of voice (instead of exit and shirking) may better come into functioning. The crucial role of social cohesion has been stressed by G. Sweeney in the general proposition that

> (in) an individualist cultural environment, technical change is resulting in unemployment, in a socially cohesive environment it results in employment creation. Unfortunately, the socially cohesive environments are under considerable pressure from the currently dominant individualist culture and the decline of economies characterized by such a culture (Sweeney, 1995, p. 36).

Fourth, as has already been suggested above, a strong, proactive role of local and regional governments is called for on the high road. Bringing social and public interests into the game (and into networks), and utilizing their potential initiating, coordinating and mediating roles, means that corporate or industry networks are broadened and further developed into truly regional networks. Regional governments, however, must have developed proactive industrial policy approaches and an interactive, networked policy conception in order to put coordination, mediation and communication between firms, trade associations, chambers of commerce, unions and social agents at the core of their policies, and before they can really do this. Forrant and Flynn, for instance, in a recent regional study on industrial revitalization in Greater Springfield, Massachusetts, have shown how "industrial policy came to western Massachusetts" to develop another "successful case of the 'bootstrapping' approach to local economic development" with a new proactive approach and new institutions and forms of collaboration (see Forrant, Flynn, 1998).

Fifth, specialized sources of finance available to the region and to locally owned firms is called for. In the Third Italy case, it was reported of the existence of patient capital (eventually taking the form of direct crediting among suppliers), with creditors who would be willing to commit themselves to the regional development, possibly at the expense of lower interest yields, thus considerably decreasing capital costs (see, for instance, Ottati, 1994). A regionally embedded and committed financial sector will face reduced risks, at the same time, if it plays a role as a partner in a regional development cooperatively pursued by all major agents. This would serve as a basis for reducing interest rates for cooperative regional projects. Schenk has developed a model of regionally based stock-markets in his chapter of this volume, to serve as regionalized, SME-oriented patient venture capital. Bianchi also discusses problems of the financial sector, in this book, to be solved in order to promote new entrepreneurship.

Markusen (1996b) has discussed positive results of the Italianate high road in terms of reducing complexity, reducing and sharing uncertainty, stabilizing expectations, sharing innovation and the like, which have been generally discussed above. Trust, as we have argued, is a central outcome to unblock, or unlock, dilemma-prone multi-personal situations. Lane and Bachmann (1997) have argued that trust is more reliably produced when industry associations, legal regulations and other social institutions and organizations are strong and consistent and when business is embedded into this institutional environment (for the role of trust and on trust vs. formal contracting see, for instance, Sabel 1992, Deakin, Michie (eds.) 1997, 19 ff., and Lyons, Mehta, 1997, 50 ff.).

The agents may become aware, then, of the procedural and socio-economic character of the economic restructuring process and they may adopt a long-run, process-oriented, developmental approach. Thus a high cultural identity may "evolve" in the regional clusters. Regional development may combine with the unlocking of processes, with motivation, mobilization, innovation and increased inter-regional competitiveness and socio-economic performance. Networked economic restructuring may turn the localities, where it takes place, into upgrading and climbing regions. The surprising success of the "historical" case of the Third Italy in reverting processes of decline, that seemed to be an iron low in other European regions, in developing solutions alternative to the decline of "old" craft-based industries and in bringing less developed regions to the top of the national income scale has proven that a high road to industrial development is possible, given a creative combination of the major socio-economic factors discussed. If there are open, human-capital based, learning and interacting districts, working on an equal power basis within their clusters and networks, their success might become continuous, while they do not secure their future at the expense of other regions or future generations.

7. For Sustaining Industrial Policies After 2000

Against the background of the preceding discussion and of the general literature on industrial policy (see for overviews, for instance: Amable, Petit, 1996, Elsner, Huffschmid, 1994, Sawyer 1995, see also Antonelli, Marchionatti, 1998), we are able to group, or regroup, the policy areas normally connected to the management of industrial restructuring. Among these are infrastructure policy, training policy, investment promotion policy, competition and SME policies, innovation policy and finance sector policy, namely venture capital supply promotion.

In addition, as we have discussed above, macro framework policies like international policy coordination, institutional design and demand side policy have to be considered.

Finally, we have to consider, in the conception to be summarized in the following, the crucial feature of sustainable industrial policies in the future: networks and institutions, and the role of productive redundancy, active adaptability and learning for a sustainable management of interactive structures.

We have also argued above that the meso-level of the economy is not only the level inherently addressed to in industrial policy, but it is the level from which the whole process of economic restructuring should be refocussed if it is to be sustainable. G. Sweeney has concluded from his analysis of innovation policy:

> There are a few areas where it might be claimed that the science or the product system is so big that it can be managed only from the national level, through national policies, programmes and funding ... Only at the local level can national policies and programmes be integrated into a dynamic entrepreneurial innovation system (Sweeney, 1995, 35 f.).

From our preceding discussing we can further develop a conception of the different policy areas mentioned, which can shape an industrial policy in a wider sense. We will group them by policy areas and by the micro-, meso- and macro-levels of the economy. Figure 14.10 gives a rough overview of the policy areas of a more comprehensive industrial policy at these economic levels, classifying some groups of measures, that have been discussed. Being far from completing and discussing the entire matrix cell-wise, we will pick and discuss a few examples of groups of measures. They all are discussed in more detail in the

Figure 14.10   *Groups of industrial policy measures, by policy area and level of the economy (examples)*

Policy area / Aggregative Level of the Economy	(1) Policy coordination, institutional design	(2) Demand side management, procurement policies	(3) Infrastructure policy	(4) Human capital mobilization and participation policy, training policy	(5) Real capital investment promotion
(III) Macro (national, international)	Setting standards in an international industry policy agenda; cooperation to overcome lock-ins and stagnation; managing regional convergence; macro institutional design to optimize degrees of competition.	Improving the environment of industrial policy; promoting a workable degree of competition.	National and international infrastructure policy.	National and international training/re-training and participation support.	National innovative private investment support.
(II) Meso (industrial, regional, institutional, network-oriented)	Inter-regional policy coordination; managing regions networks.	...	Creating cluster-oriented and regionally specific infrastructures	Cluster- and region-specific training measures and related infrastructures; managing social embeddedness and cohesion.	Regional cluster specific innovative investment support; industrial rejuvenation support.
(I) Micro	...	...	...	Supporting regional and cluster-related training markets: training suppliers, households, intra-company training.	Company technological and organizational investment

Figure 14.10   Groups of industrial policy measures, by policy area and level of the economy (examples) (continued)

Policy area / Aggregative Level of the Economy	(6) Power control, SME-policy, competition policy	(7) Innovation policy	(8) Finance, venture capital, patient capital	(9) Industrial cluster policy, networks policy, social cohesion promotion, institutional design	(10) Creating productive redundancy
(III) Macro (national, international)	⋮	Ensuring non-commercial basic and applied research	Supporting credit supply-structures on an inter-regional basis	Supporting cluster-specific regional interactive and learning structures; creating multi-regional web	⋮
(II) Meso (industrial, regional, institutional, network-oriented)	Supporting regional SME-clusters and -networks; controlling for optimal degrees of turbulence and manageable degrees of competition	Supporting rejuvenation of "old" clusters	Managing region-specific "patient capital" supply	Initiating and managing regional networks and innovative milieus; improving network governance; controlling for interdependence structures: social fabric matrix analysis	Managing overlapping regional networks
(I) Micro	No merger support	⋮	Managing inter-company mutual trust- and flexible credit-relations	Unfreezing intra-company lock-ins; organizational change: managing open, learning organizations and inter-firm cooperation	⋮

chapters of this book. The final discussion shall give an impression, on a concrete and operational level, of what a sustainably effective industrial policy could be after 2000.

If e turn, for instance, to cell I 6 in Figure 14.10, in the policy area normally thought of as competition policy, here considered as power control, at the micro-level, we can refer again to the discussion on the power, efficiency and social cost impacts of mergers and to the advocacy of Schenk (and also of Dietrich and Burns) to control mergers and to carefully refrain from merger support as an industrial policy measure. We can also refer to Sawyer's discussion of privatization policies followed by mergers of privatized units and his question whether any competition is beneficial under such circumstances.

Turning to cell II 6, we can refer to Schreyer's insightful empirical and theoretical analysis of the turbulence in the environment of firms. The degree of turbulence is decisive if we want to answer the question for beneficient or maleficient effects of competition. Against the background of Schreyer's analysis, no simple, or unspecific, SME-support can be justified. Schreyer shows that there exists a degree of competitive pressure which is dysfunctional and obstructive.

A workable degree of competitive pressure, consequently, is a major task of institutional design as a dimension of industrial policies. Specifically, the degree of turbulence existent in markets today, and the corresponding degree of uncertainty SMEs are subjected to, should be reduced through networking. Certain degrees of turbulence and flexibility can be counter-productive and Schreyer's orientation of SME-oriented industrial policies to the optimal degree of turbulence in the market calls for a major reorientation of industrial policies, which he suggests in a very operational and specific manner.

With regard to innovation policy, a policy area largely integrated in, or overlapping with, regional networking in the approaches developed in this book, we can refer, in cell III 7, to Bianchi's advocacy of ensuring a considerable non-commercial R&D-sector, public research and higher education infrastructure in order to guarantee society's ability to keep a long term perspective.

The venture capital/patient regional capital issue (see cell II 8) is specifically elaborated as a group of industrial policy measures by Schenk and Bianchi in their respective chapters. Regional capital markets will be of a major importance in future industrial policies if the regional, SME-based interactive context becomes the core arena of economic restructuring.

Finally, we will turn to the cross-policy-area, located at the core of future industrial policies, the management of interactive meso-economic structures. On the international macro-level (see cell III 9), R. Sugden has advocated multinational webs:

> ... we can search for ways in which more and more of the people affected by (corporate - W.E.) strategic decisions can be involved in the process of making those decisions ... The search need not mean that policy initiatives should be explored in a narrow national or intra-national context. Whilst this is an option, I am also suggesting research into the possibility of creating multinational webs. Economies where such webs are prominent would be economies where people in many countries work together ... they would not be economies where transnational corporations have absolute reign (Sugden 1996, 32).

The idea refers to the general idea of overlapping networks either on a spatial basis (regional, national, multinational) or on a socio-economic basis (sectoral, professional and social networks).

Turning to cell I 9, we refer to the advocacies of Schenk, Michie and Dietrich and Burns, in this book, to control intra-company decision inefficiencies. Dietrich and Burns have developed a conception to provide for the unfreezing of intra-company strategic lock-ins as a specific sub-area of network policies.

One of the core cells of a future industrial policy seems to be cell II 9 where the contributors to this book unanimously advocate the initiation, creation, mediation and continuous change and improvement of regional networks, innovative milieus and new districts (see, for instance, Sawyer, Bianchi, Michie, Schenk, Lagendijk, and Markl and Meissner). It will not be attempted to summarize the whole issue here. Central is here, as has been discussed, the issue of power control, since uncontrolled power in clusters and networks can lead to regional stagnation and innovative slackness (see also Hellmer et al., in their chapter, on those "normal regions").

Lagendijk has concluded his empirical case studies with the advocacy for monitoring and democratic control of inter-active structures. In this regard, Hayden and Balduc introduce a most revealing socio-economic research and management instrument for networked structures, with their social fabric matrix analysis. Good network governance can be supported with a pervasive operational control system through this approach.

Good network governance has been largely discussed in the entire book. Industrial policy measures can be taken in this respect to provide for

- multicentricity, pluriformity and diversity;
- frequent and continuous interaction;
- making the common future of agents important;
- power-control and "voice";
- open access, entry and open technology;
- broad stakeholder participation;
- interaction with the environment, external links;
- self-organization and long-term procedural and evolutionary perspective;
- productive redundancy and parallel processing;
- regional relevance and (regional) vision;
- public mediation;
- funding and support infrastructure;
  etc.

If we take, for instance, a cooperative industrial policy approach (see Elsner in this book), familiar industrial policy instruments (e.g. networking and R&D subsidies) as well as some more unknown and innovative ones (such as agreed-upon mid-term company restructuring plans) can be grouped into, and re-interpreted within, two main categories developed on the basis of this interactive conception. These categories are the pay-offs to agents and the degree by which their common future can be made important to them. Figure 14.11 gives examples of some industrial policy measures advocated on this theoretical basis.

To sum up, all contributions to this book, starting from their different subject fields, displaying a range of theoretical, methodological and policy approaches and providing a great amount of empirical and case study material, come to advocate a modern proactive industrial policy strategy, going to the heart of future economic change and economic policies. They develop a systemic, but at the same time specific and selective, and what Dietrich and Burns have called strategic and

*Figure 14.11   Industrial policy instruments, by theoretical category and
level of the economy*

Theoretical category / Aggregative level of the economy	Changing in the pay-offs	Increasing the importance of the common future
MESO **Entire region**	...	Support of specific regional and cluster-oriented infrastructures; mid-term fiscal planning for support of cluster restructuring; networking: creating regional councils and specific committees; providing mediation etc.
Regional stakeholder organizations	Supply of improved information and contacts; support of public appreciation etc.	Support of participation in regional councils and specific committees.
MICRO **Regionally located companies**	R&D subsidies; supply of improved information and contacts: support of public appreciation etc.	Jointly developing mid-term company restructuring plans; cooperation and joint projects etc.; intra-company restructuring councils.

institutional approach to industrial policy. This requires a public agent which Sawyer calls a strong developmental state. The type of politics involved is not interventionist or dirigistic in a conventional sense, it is pro-active and institutional in the sense of "rewriting the rules that correlate behavior", as M. Tool has generally defined institutionalist politics (see Tool, 1994, 156).

No doubt that this would involve a huge long-term reform program even if pro-active regional and national governments proliferated, as has been the case at the end of the nineties in Western Europe. The inheritance of the "neo-liberal" decades of the seventies, eighties and nineties, in terms of poor economic performance, social polarization and regional divergence provide enough reason to take up this challenge, develop a new conceptional basis and gather more practical experience in interactive industrial policies, as outlined in this book, on the way into the twenty-first century. We shall have to endeavor on this path, if mankind is to survive the coming century in reasonable socio-economic conditions.

References

Adams, F. and S.D. Gupta 1997. *The Political Economy of Globalization: An Introduction.* In: S.D. Gupta ed. 1—12.

Alonso, W. 1996. "On the Tension between Regional and Industrial Policies", *International Regional Science Review,* Vol. 19, 79—83.

Amable, B. and P. Petit 1996. "New Scale and Scope for Industrial Policies in the 1990s", *International Review of Applied Economics,* Vol. 10, 23—41.

Amin, A. 1998. "An Institutionalist Perspective on Regional Economic Development", paper presented at the Economic Geography Research Group Seminar, London, July 3, Durham: University of Durham, to Appear, *International Journal of Urban and Regional Research,* 1999.

Amin, A. and J. Hausner 1997. *Interactive Governance and Social Complexity.* In id., eds. 1—31.

————— eds. 1997. *Beyond Market and Hierarchy. Interactive Governance and Social Complexity,* Cheltenham, UK, Lyme, US: Edward Elgar.

Antonelli, C. and R. Marchionatti 1998. "Technological and Organizational Change in a Process of Industrial Rejuvenation: The Case of the Italian Cotton Textile Industry", *Cambridge Journal of Economics,* Vol. 22, 1—18.

Arrow, K.J. 1959. "Towards a Theory of Price Adjustment". In *The Allocation of Economic Resources,* M. Abramowitz ed., Stanford (CA): Stanford University Press.

Asheim, B.T. 1996 "Industrial Districts as "Learning Regions": a Condition for Prosperity". In *European Planning Studies,* Vol. 4, 379—400.

Axelrod, R. 1984. *The Evolution of Cooperation,* New York: Basic Books.

———— 1997. *The Complexity of Cooperation. Agent-Based Models of Competition and Collaboration*, Princeton (N.J.): Princeton University Press.

Baker, P. 1996. "Spatial Outcomes of Capital Restructuring: 'New Industrial Spaces' as a Symptom of Crisis, not Solution", *Review of Political Economy*, Vol. 8, 263—278.

Ball, L. and D. Romer 1991. "Sticky Prices as Coordination Failure", *American Economic Review*, 81/3: 539—552.

Bellak, C. 1995. *International Trade, Multinational Enterprise, and Industrial Policy Choice*. In B. Unger and F. van Waarden eds. 80—107.

Benko, G. and M. Dunford eds. 1991. *Industrial Change and Regional Development: the Transformation of New Industrial Spaces*, London/ New York: Belhaven Press.

Bianchi, G. 1998. "Requiem for the Third Italy? Rise and Fall of a too Successful Concept", *Entrepreneurship & Regional Development*, Vol. 10, 93—116.

Bicchieri, C. 1993. *Rationality and Coordination*, Cambridge (Mass.): Cambridge University Press.

Brennan, G. and L. Lomasky 1982. *Institutional Aspects of "Merit Goods" Analysis: Finanzarchiv, N.F.* 41, 183—206.

Briggs, V.M. 1998. "American-Style Capitalism and Income Disparity: The Challenge of Social Anarchy", *Journal of Economic Issues*, Vol. XXXII, 473—480.

Bush, P.D. 1987. "The Theory of Institutional Change", *Journal of Economic Issues*, XXI: 1075—1116.

———— 1994. *Art. Theory of Social Change*. In G.M. Hodgson, W.J. Samuels and M.R. Tool eds. 291—296.

Campbell, J.L., J.R. Hollingsworth and L.N. Lindberg, eds. 1991. *Governance of the American Economy*, Cambridge et al.: Cambridge University Press.

Champlin, D. and P. Olson 1994. "Post-Industrial Metaphors: Understanding Corporate Restructuring and the Economic Environment of the 1990s", *Journal of Economic Issues*, Vol. XXVIII, 449—459.

Chattoe, E. 1998. "Just How (Un)realistic are Evolutionary Algorithms as Representations of Social Processes?", *Journal of Artificial Societies and Social Simulation*, 1, 3.

Cheshire, P.G. and I.R. Gordon 1998. "Territorial Competition: Some Lessons for Policy", *The Annals of Regional Science*, Vol. 32, 321—346.

Choudhury, M.A. 1996. "Markets as a System of Social Contracts", *International Journal of Social Economics*, Vol. 23, 17—36.

Clegg, S., F. Wilson 1991. *Power, Technology and Flexibility in Organisations.* In J. Law ed.

Commons, J.R. 1934. *Institutional Economics*, 2 Vols., New York: Macmillan, repr. New Brunswick (NJ) 1990: Transaction Publishers

Coombs, R., A. Richards, P.P. Saviotti and V. Walsh eds. 1996. *Technological Collaboration. The Dynamics of Cooperation in Industrial Innovation*, Cheltenham, UK, Brookfield (VT), US: Edward Elgar.

Cooper, R. and A. John 1988. "Coordinating Coordination Failures in Keynesian Models", *Quarterly Journal of Economics*, 103: 441—463.

David, P.A. 1985. "Clio and the Economics of QWERTY", *American Economic Review, Papers and Proceedings*, Vol. 75, 332—337.

Davidson, P. 1989. "The Economics of Ignorance or Ignorance of Economics", *Critical Review*, Vol. 3, 467—487.

Dawid, H. 1998. *On the Stability of Monotone Discrete Selection Dynamics with Inertia*, July.

de Bruijn, J.A. and E.F. ten Heuvelhof 1995. *Policy Networks and Governance.* In D.L. Weimer ed. 161—179.

Deakin, S. and J. Michie eds. 1997. *Contracts, Cooperation, and Competition*, Oxford: Oxford University Press.

Deakin, S., C. Lane and F. Wilkinson 1997. *Contract Law, Trust Relations, and Incentives for Cooperation: A Comparative Study.* In Deakin, S., and J. Michie eds.

Delorme, R. and K. Dopfer eds. 1994. *The Political Economy of Diversity. Evolutionary Perspectives on Economic Order and Disorder*, Aldershot, UK, Brookfield, US: Edward Elgar.

Dequech, D. 1997. "Uncertainty in a Strong Sense: Meaning and Sources", *Economic Issues*, Vol. 2/2, 21—43.

Donald, D. and A. Hutton, Alan 1998. "Public Purpose and Private Ownership: Some Implications of the "Great Capitalist Restoration" for the Politicization of Private Sector Firms in Britain", *Journal of Economic Issues*, Vol. XXXII, 457—464.

Elsner, W. 1987. "Institutionen und ökonomische Institutionentheorie", *Wirtschaftswissenschaftliches Studium (WiSt)*, Vol. 16, 5—14.

———— 1989. "Adam Smith's Model of the Origins and Emergence of Institutions: The Modern Findings of the Classical Approach", *Journal of Economic Issues*, Vol. XXIII, 189—213.

———— 1998. "Die Zukunft unserer Städte und Regionen: Städte und Regionen im Konkurrenzkampf und die Kehrseiten des Neuen Regionalismus", *WSI-Mitteilungen*, Vol. 51, No. 11.

Elsner, W. and J. Huffschmid 1994. *Art. Industrial Policy*. In: G.M. Hodgson, W.J. Samuels and M.R. Tool eds. 343—351.

Elsner, W. and P. Kirchhoff 1997. "Logistik-Sektor und Region", *IKSF discussion paper* No. 13, Bremen: University of Bremen, Dept. of Economics.

Florida, R. and M. Kenney 1990. "Silicon Valley and Route 128 Won't Save US", *California Management Review*, 68—88.

Forrant, R. and E. Flynn 1998. "Seizing Agglomeration's Potential: The Greater Springfield Massachusetts Metalworking Sector in Transition, 1986—1996" *Regional Studies*, Vol. 32.3, 209—222.

Forrester, V. 1996. *L'Horreur Économique*, Paris: Librairie Arthème Fayard.

Franke, R. 1998. "Coevolution and Stable Adjustments in the Cobweb Model", *Journal of Evolutionary Economics*, 8/4: 383—406.

Fransman, M. 1995. "Is National Technology Policy Obsolete in a Globalized World? The Japanese Response" *Cambridge Journal of Economics*, Vol. 19, 95—119.

Freedman, C. 1996. "Citizen Murdoch — A Case Study in the Paradox of Economic Efficiency", *Journal of Economic Issues*, Vol. XXX, 223—241.

Friedland, R. and A.F. Robertson eds. 1990. *Beyond the Marketplace. Rethinking Economy and Society*, New York: A. de Gruyter.

Fudenberg, D. and D.K. Levine 1998. *The Theory of Learning in Games*, Cambridge (Mass.), London: The MIT Press.

Giampietro, M. and K. Mayumi 1998. "Another View of Development, Ecological Degradation, and North-South Trade", *Review of Social Economy*, Vol. LVI, 20—36.

Grabher, G. 1993. "The Weakness of Strong Ties. The Lock-in of Regional Development in the Ruhr Area." In: *The Embedded Firm.*

On the Socioeconomics of Industrial Networks, id. ed. London/New York: Routledge, 255—277.

Grabher, G. and D. Stark 1997. "Organizing Diversity: Evolutionary Theory, Network Analysis and Postsocialism", *Regional Studies*, Vol. 31, 5, 533—544.

Groenewegen, J. 1997. "Institutions of Capitalisms: American, European, and Japanese Systems Compared", *Journal of Economic Issues*, Vol. XXXI, 333—347.

Gschwendtner, H. 1993. "A Reconsideration of the Perfect-Competition Model". In *Jahrbücher für Nationalökonomie und Statistik*, Vol. 212, 451—462.

Gupta, S.D. ed. 1997. *The Political Economy of Globalization*, Boston/ Dordrecht/London: Kluwer Academic Publishers.

Håkansson, H. and A. Lundgren 1997. *Paths in Time and Space — Path Dependence in Industrial Networks*. In L. Magnusson and J. Ottosson, eds.

Hancké, B. 1997. "Modernisation Without Flexible Specialisation. How Large Firm Restructuring and Government Regional Policies became the Step-parents of Autarchic Regional Production Systems in France", Berlin: Science Center Berlin for Social Research, *discussion paper* FS I 97—304.

Hansen, N., K.J. Button, and P. Nijkamp eds. 1996. *Regional Policy and Regional Integration*, Cheltenham, UK, Brookfield, US: Edward Elgar.

Hanson, G.H. 1998. "Regional Adjustment to Trade Liberalization". In *Regional Science and Urban Economics*, Vol. 28, 419—444.

Harrison, B., M.R. Kelley and J. Gant 1996. "Innovative Firm Behaviour and Local Milieu: Exploring the Intersection of Agglomeration, Firm Effects, and Technological Change". In *Economic Geography*, Vol. 72, 233—258.

Hodgson, G.M., W.J. Samuels and M.R. Tool eds. 1994. *The Elgar Companion to Institutional and Evolutionary Economics*, Aldershot, UK, Brookfield (VT), US: Edward Elgar.

Hong, L. and S.E. Page 1998. *Diversity and Optimality*.

Huggins, R. 1997. *Competitiveness and the Global Region. The Role of Networking*. In J.M. Simmie ed. 101—123.

Intriligator, M.D. 1996. "Reform of the Russian Economy: the Role of Institutions". In *International Journal of Social Economics*, Vol. 23, 58—71.

Jensen-Butler, C., A. Shachar and J. van Weesep eds. 1997. "European Cities in Competition", Aldershot, UK, Brookfield, US, et al.: Avebury.

Jessop, B. 1994. *Changing Forms and Functions of the State in an Era of Globalization and Regionalization.* In R. Delorme and K. Dopfer, eds. 102—125.

——————— 1997. *The Governance of Complexity and the Complexity of Governance: Preliminary Remarks on Some Problems and Limits of Economic Guidance.* In A. Amin and J. Hausner eds. 95—128.

Keyman, E.F. 1997. *Globalization, State, Identity/Difference. Toward a Critical Social Theory of International Relations*, New Jersey: Humanities Press.

Komninos, N. 1997. *After Technopoles. Diffused Strategies for Innovation and Technology Transfer.* In J. Simmie ed., 181—195.

Kuttner, R. 1997. *Everything for Sale. The Virtues and Limits of Markets*, New York: Alfred A. Knopf.

Lagendijk, A. 1998. "Will New Regionalism Survive? Tracing Dominant Concepts in Economic Geography", *draft paper*, Centre for Urban and Regional Development Studies, University of Newcastle upon Tyne.

Lane, C. 1995. *Industry and Society in Europe. Stability and Change in Britain, Germany and France*, Aldershot, UK, Brookfield, US: Edward Elgar.

Lane, C. and R. Bachmann 1997. "Cooperation in Inter-firm Relations in Britain and Germany: the Role of Social Institutions" *British Journal of Sociology*, Vol. 48, 226—254.

Larédo, P. and P. Mustar 1996. "The Technoeconomic Network: A Socioeconomic Approach to State Intervention in Innovation". In R. Coombs, R. et al., eds. 143—164.

Lasuén, J.R. 1996. "Urbanisation and Development — the Temporal Interaction between Geographical and Sectoral Clusters". In N. Hansen, et al. eds. 43—68.

Law, J. ed. 1991. *A Sociology of Monsters: Essays on Power, Technology and Domination*, London: Routledge.

Lawson, T. 1985. "Uncertainty and Economic Analysis", *The Economic Journal*, Vol. 95, 909—927.

——————1994. *Art. Uncertainty.* In G.M. Hodgson, W.J. Samuels and M.R. Tool eds.

Lesourne, J. 1991. "From Market Dynamics to Evolutionary Economics", *Journal of Evolutionary Economics*, Vol. 1, 23—27.

Lichtenstein, P.M. 1996. "A New-Institutionalist Story about the Transformation of Former Socialist Economies: A Recounting and an Assessment", *Journal of Economic Issues,* Vol. XXX, 243—265.

Liebrand, W.B.G. and D.M. Messick eds. 1996. "Frontiers in Social Dilemmas Research", Berlin et al.: Springer.

Lindberg, L.N., J.L. Campbell and J.R. Hollingsworth 1991. "Economic Governance and the Analysis of Structural Change in the American Economy". In J.L. Campbell et al., eds. 3—34.

Lindgren, K. 1997. "Evolutionary Dynamics in Game-Theoretic Models". In *The Economy as an Evolving Complex System II*, W.B. Arthur, S.N. Durlauf and D.A. Lane, eds. Reading (Mass.): Addison-Wesley, 337—367.

Lindlar, L. and H. Trabold 1998. "Globalisation, Unemployment and Social Inequality: A Farewell to Welfare?", *Konjunkturpolitik*, Vol. 44, 1—30.

Lovering, J. 1998. "Theory Led by Policy? The Inadequacies of The New Regionalism in Economic Geography Illustrated From the Case of Wales", *paper* presented at the Economic Geography Research Group Seminar, London, July 3, to appear in *International Journal of Urban and Regional Research,* 1999.

Lutz, M.A. 1996. "Doubts About Competition". In *Social Economics: Promises, Findings, and Policies*, E.J. O'Boyle ed., London: Routledge, 109—124.

Lyons, B. and J. Mehta 1997. *Private Sector Business Contracts: The Text between the Lines,* S. Deakin and J. Michie eds., 43—66.

Maggioni, M.A. 1997. "Firms, Uncertainty and Innovation Policy. Some Spatial Considerations in an Evolutionary Framework". In *Economics of Structural and Technological Change*, G. Antonelli and N. De Liso ed., London/New York: Routledge, 230—257.

Magnusson, L. and J. Ottosson eds. 1997. *Evolutionary Economics and Path Dependence*, Cheltenham, UK, Brookfield, US: Edward Elgar.

Markusen, A. 1996a. "Interaction between Regional and Industrial Policies: Evidence from Four Countries", *International Regional Science Review*, Vol. 19, 49—77.

——— 1996b. "Sticky Places in Slippery Space: A Typology of Industrial Districts", *Economic Geography,* Vol. 72, 293—313.

——— 1996c. "Response to William Alonso", *International Regional Science Review*, Vol. 19, 83.

Markusen, J.R., E.R. Morey and N.D. Olewiler 1995. "Competition in Regional Environmental Policies when Plant Locations are Endogenous", *Journal of Public Economics*, Vol. 56, 55—77.

Martin, R. and P. Sunley 1996. "Paul Krugman's Geographical Economics and Its Implications for Regional Development Theory: A Critical Assessment", *Economic Geography*, Vol. 72, 259—292.

McClintock, B. 1997. "A Veblenian Approach to the Evolving International Economic (Dis)Order", *paper* presented to the annual meeting of the Association for Evolutionary Economics, New Orleans 1997.

Means, G.C. 1962. *The Corporate Revolution in America*, New York: Crowell-Collier Press.

Minsky, H.P. 1996. "Uncertainty and the Institutionalist Structure of Capitalist Economies", *Journal of Economic Issues*, Vol. XXX, 357—368.

Mischel, K. 1998. "Sticky Prices as a Coordination Success", *Atlantic Economic Journal*, Vol. 26, 162—171.

Munkirs, J.R. 1985. *The Transformation of American Capitalism. From Competitive Market Structures to Centralized Private Sector Planning*, Armonk et al.: M.E. Sharpe.

Musgrave, R.A. 1987. "Art. Merit Goods", *The New Palgrave*, London, Basingstoke, 452—453.

Nayyar, D. 1997. "Globalisation: The Game, the Players and the Rules". In *Gupta,* D. Satya ed. 13—40.

Neale, W.C. 1994. *Art. Institutions.* In G.M. Hodgson, W.J. Samuels, and M.R. Tool eds.

Nelson, R.R. and S.G. Winter 1982. *An Evolutionary Theory of Economic Change*, Cambridge (Mass.), London: Belknap Press of Harvard University Press.

Nielsen, K. and O.K. Pedersen 1988. "The Ngotiated Eonomy: Ideal and History, *Scandinavian Political Studies*, 2, 79—101.

Norton, B., R. Costanca and R.C. Bishop 1998. "The Evolution Of Preferences. Why "Sovereign" Preferences May Not Lead To Sustainable Policies And What To Do About It", *Ecological Economics*, 24: 193—211.

Oates, W.E. and R.M. Schwab 1988. "Economic Competition Among Jurisdictions: Efficiency Enhancing or Distortion Inducing?", *Journal of Public Economics*, Vol. 35, 333—354.

OECD 1991. "Techno-Economic Networks and Science and Technology Policy", *Science, Technology, Industry Review*, No. 14, Paris: OECD, 59—117.

Offerman, T. and J. Sonnemans 1998. "Learning by Experience and Learning by Imitating Successful Others", *Journal of Economic Behavior & Organization*, 34: 559—575.

Ottati, G.D. 1994. "Trust, Interlinking Transactions and Credit in the Industrial District", *Cambridge Journal of Economics*, Vol. 18, 529—546.

Ottaviano, G.P. and D. Puga 1997. "Agglomeration in the Global Economy: A Survey of the New Economic Geography", London: London School of Economics and Political Science, Centre for Economic Performance, *Discussion Paper* No. 356.

Petr, J.L. 1996. "Discontinuities in Economic Evolution: Lessons from the Eastern Front", *paper* presented at the annual meetings of the Association for Evolutionary Economics, San Francisco, unpublished.

Powell, W.W. and L. Smith-Doerr 1994, "Networks and Economic Life", *The Handbook of Economic Sociology*, Princeton, New York, 368—402.

Prasch, R.E. 1992. "Economics and Merger Mania: A Critique of Efficient Markets Theory", *Journal of Economic Issues*, Vol. XXVI, 635—643.

Pratt, A. 1997. *The Emerging Shape and Form of Innovation Networks and Institutions*. In J. Simmie ed., 124—136.

Pyke, F. and W. Sengenberger eds. 1992. *Industrial Districts and Local Economic Regeneration*, Geneva: ILO.

Ramstad, Y. 1991. "From Desideratum to Historical Achievement: John R. Commons's Reasonable Value and the "Negotiated Economy" of Denmark", *Journal of Economic Issues*, Vol. XXV, 431—439.

Ruegemer, W. 1985. *Neue Technik — Alte Gesellschaft. Silicon Valley*, Cologne (Germany): Pahl-Rugenstein.

Ruigrok, W. and R. van Tulder 1995. *The Logic of International Restructuring*, London/New York: Routledge.

Sabel, Ch.F. 1992. *Studied Trust: Building New Forms of Cooperation in a Volatile Economy*. In F. Pyke and W. Sengenberger eds. 215—250.

Sawyer, M.C. 1993. "The Nature and Role of the Market". In *Transaction Costs, Markets and Hierarchies*, C. Pitelis ed. Oxford, 20—40.

——————— 1995. "Industry: Performance and Policies". In: D. Coates, ed., *Economic and Industrial Performance in Europe*, Aldershot, UK, Brookfield, US: Edward Elgar, 93—124.

Saxenian, A. 1994. *Regional Advantage. Culture and Competition in Silicon Valley and Route 128*, Cambridge (Mass.), London: Harvard University Press

Schohl, F. 1992. *Renditeunterschiede und Schumpetersche Entwicklung*, Berlin: Duncker&Humblot.

Schotter, A. 1981. *The Economic Theory of Social Institutions*, Cambridge: Cambridge University Press.

Shackle, G.L.S. 1958. *Time in Economics*, Amsterdam: North-Holland.

Simmie, J.M. ed. 1997. *Innovation, Networks and Learning Regions?*, London, Bristol (PA): Jessica Kingsley Publishers.

Sinn, H.-W. 1997. "The Selection Principle and Market Failure in Systems Competition, *Journal of Public Economics*, Vol. 66, 247—274.

Slabbert, A. 1996. "Capitalism at the Crossroads" *International Journal of Social Economics*, Vol. 23, 41—50.

Storper, M. and B. Harrison 1991. "Flexibility, Hierarchy and Regional Development: The Changing Structure of Industrial Production SysTems and Their Forms of Governance in the 1980s", *Research Policy*, Vol. 20, 407—422.

Sugden, R. 1996. "Multinational Economies and the Law of Uneven Development", *Occasional Papers in Industrial Strategy*, No. 37, Research Center for Industrial Strategy, The University of Birmingham.

Svetlicic, M. and H.W. Singer 1996. World Economy: Challenges of Globalisation and Regionalisation". In M. Svetlicic and H.W. Singer eds. 15—37.

————eds. 199. *The World Economy. Challenges of Globalization and Regionalization*, Houndmills, London: Macmillan.

Sweeney, G. 1995. "National Innovation Policy or a Regional Innovation Culture", *EUNIP Working Papers* in European Industrial Policy, No. 1, Birmingham: The University of Birmingham, Research Centre for Industrial Strategy.

Tool, M.R. 1994. *John Art. Dewey.* In G.M. Hodgson, W.J. Samuels and M.R. Tool eds. 152—157.

Toruno, M.C. 1997. "Blind Drift and the Rightist State", *Journal of Economic Issues*, Vol. XXXI, 585—593.

Trigilia, C. 1992. "Italian Industrial Districts: Neither Myth nor Interlude". In F. Pyke and W. Sengenberger eds. 33—47.

Unger, B. 1997. "Limits of Convergence and Globalisation" In *Gupta*, D. Satya ed. 99—127.

Unger, B. and F. van Waarden eds. 1995. "Convergence or Diversity?" *Internationalization and Economic Policy Response*, Aldershot, UK, Brookfield, US: Avebury.

Veblen, Th.B. 1919. *The Vested Interests and the Common Man*, repr. New York: Capricorn, 1969.

Ver Eecke, W. 1998. "The Concept of a "Merit Good". The Ethical Dimension in Economic Theory and the History of Economic Thought or the Transformation of Economics Into Socio-Economics", *Journal of Socio-Economics*, 27: 133—153.

Waterson, M. 1985. "Lessons for Competition Policy from Industrial Economic Theory". In *Fiscal Studies*, Vol. 6, 49—58.

Weimer, D.L. 1995. "Institutional Design: Overview". In *id.* ed., 1—16.

———— (ed.) 1995. *Institutional Design*, Boston/Dordrecht/London: Kluwer Academic Publishers.

Wilber, Ch.K. 1998. "Globalization and Democracy", *Journal of Economic Issues*, Vol. XXXII, 465—471.

Wilson, J.D. 1996. "Capital Mobility and Environmental Standards: Is there a Theoretical Basis for a Race to the Bottom?" In J. Bhagwati, R.E. Hudec, eds. *Fair Trade and Harmonization: Prerequisites for Free Trade?*, Cambridge (MA), 393—427.

List of Contributors

Patrizio Bianchi, University of Ferrara, Italy
Steven Bolduc, University of Nebraska-Lincoln, USA
Waltraud Bruch-Krumbein, Institut für Regionalforschung e.V. an der
Ernst-August-Universität Göttingen, Göttingen, Germany
John Burns, University of Manchester, United Kingdom
Michael Dietrich, University of Sheffield, United Kingdom
Wolfram Elsner, University of Bremen, Germany
John Groenewegen, Erasmus University Rotterdam, the Netherlands
Gregory Hayden, University of Nebraska-Lincoln, USA
Friedhelm Hellmer, Institut für Regionalforschung e.V. an der Ernst-
August-Universität Göttingen, Göttingen, Germany
Wolfgang Krumbein, Institut für Regionalforschung e.V. an der Ernst-
August-Universität Göttingen, Göttingen, Germany
Arnoud Lagendijk, University of Nijmegen, the Netherlands
Rainer Markl, Johann Wolfgang Goethe University, Frankfurt
Werner Meissner, Johann Wolfgang Goethe University, Frankfurt
Jonathan Michie, Cambridge University, United Kingdom
Pascal Petit, CEPREMAP, Paris, France
Malcolm Sawyer, University of Leeds, United Kingdom
Hans Schenk, Erasmus University Rotterdam, the Netherlands
Paul Schreyer, OECD, Paris, France
Mark Setterfield, Trinity College, Hartford, USA

List of Tables and Figures

490

Index

492